ELGAR FINANCIAL LAW AND PRACTICE

Series Editor: Roger McCormick, *London School of Economics and Political Science, UK*

The Elgar Financial Law and Practice series is a library of works by leading practitioners and scholars covering discrete areas of law in the field of banking and finance. Titles in the series are both analytical and descriptive in approach, highlighting and unpicking the legal issues that are most critical and relevant to practice. Designed to be detailed, focused reference works, the books in this series offer an authoritative statement on the law and practice in key topics within the field, from Financial Collateral to Private Equity, from Secured Transactions to Financial Crime, and from Financial Derivatives and Hedge Funds to Bank Resolution and Bank Capital.

THE LAW ON CORPORATE GOVERNANCE IN BANKS

IRIS H-Y CHIU

Reader in Laws, University College London, UK

Consulting Editor
MICHAEL MCKEE

Partner, DLA Piper, UK

With contributions from

Anna P Donovan
Rod Edmunds
Andreas Kokkinis
John Lowry
Marc T Moore
Arad Reisberg
Georgina Tsagas
Edward Walker-Arnott

ELGAR FINANCIAL LAW AND PRACTICE

PUBLISHING

Cheltenham, UK • Northampton, MA, USA

Published by
Edward Elgar Publishing Limited
The Lypiatts
15 Lansdown Road
Cheltenham
Glos GL50 2JA
UK

Edward Elgar Publishing, Inc.
William Pratt House
9 Dewey Court
Northampton
Massachusetts 01060
USA

A catalogue record for this book
is available from the British Library

Library of Congress Control Number: 2014950969

This book is available electronically in the **Elgar**online
Law subject collection
DOI 10.4337/9781782548867

ISBN 978 1 78254 885 0 (cased)
ISBN 978 1 78254 886 7 (eBook)

Typeset by Columns Design XML Ltd, Reading
Printed and bound in Great Britain by T.J. International Ltd, Padstow

CONTENTS

EXTENDED TABLE OF CONTENTS

6. CORPORATE GOVERNANCE AND RISK MANAGEMENT IN BANKS AND FINANCIAL INSTITUTIONS

Iris H-Y Chiu

7. CORPORATE REPORTING AND THE ACCOUNTABILITY OF BANKS AND FINANCIAL INSTITUTIONS

Iris H-Y Chiu

8. SYSTEMS AND CONTROLS IN ANTI-BRIBERY AND CORRUPTION

Anna P Donovan

9. THE MARKET FOR CORPORATE CONTROL IN THE BANKING INDUSTRY

Georgina Tsagas

ABOUT THE AUTHORS

EDITORS

Iris H-Y Chiu (Editor)

Iris is a Reader in Law at University College London, and her research expertise lies in financial regulation and corporate governance. She has published extensively on corporate governance, as well as regulatory theories and governance in the financial sector, in over 20 peer-reviewed journals in the UK and US. She has published a number of books including *Regulatory Convergence in EU Securities Regulation* (Wolters Kluwer 2008) which deals with EU securities regulation and a systemic analysis of harmonisation in the law in books as well as the law in action; *The Foundations and Anatomy of Shareholder Activism* (Hart Publishing 2010) which deals with the legitimacy issues surrounding various forms of shareholder activism in the UK and EU; and *The Foundations and Future of Financial Regulation* (Routledge, 2014, co-authored with Mads Andenas). Her books have been well received (see positive reviews of the *Shareholder Activism* title, Katelouzou, *JCLS* 2012, and Masouros, *JBL* 2011). She is executive editor of the European Business Law Review and co-series editor of the Palgrave Macmillan Corporate and Financial Law Series. She was a Visiting Professor of Law at Singapore Management University (2014).

Michael McKee (Consulting editor)

Michael McKee is a partner and Head of Financial Services Regulation at DLA Piper UK LLP. Michael has many years of advising clients and working with financial institutions and regulators in the UK, in Europe and internationally. He is an Executive Board member of the UK's International Regulatory Strategy Group which develops financial services strategy for the UK's financial services industry. He has been appointed to a number of European Union bodies and groups in the past working on EU financial services legislative issues and has given evidence to both the European Parliament and the House of Lords on such issues.

CONTRIBUTORS

Anna P Donovan

Anna is a Lecturer at UCL Laws and an advisory board member of the Faculty's Centre for Ethics and Law. Anna's research expertise lies in corporate governance and regulation, with a specific focus on corporate compliance strategies and anti-corruption measures. Prior to UCL, Anna was a senior corporate solicitor in London, specialising in corporate restructuring and governance where she advised boards extensively on their corporate governance obligations. During her time in practice Anna a was a principal author of both editions of *A Practical Guide to the Companies Act 2006 – A Guide for Busy Directors and Company Secretaries* (2nd edn, CCH 2010). Anna is also a qualified attorney, admitted to the New York bar.

Rod Edmunds

Rod joined Queen Mary University of London as a Senior Lecturer in 2003. He previously held academic appointments at Sussex University and the University of Nottingham, and also held the post of Director of Education at D J Freeman & Co in London.

Andreas Kokkinis

Andreas is a Teaching Fellow at the University of Warwick and teaches both at the undergraduate and postgraduate degrees. Prior to that Andreas taught at UCL Laws, Kent Law School and the University of Buckingham School of Business. He holds a PhD from UCL (2014), an LLM (Distinction) from LSE (2009) and an LLB (Distinction) from the National University of Athens (2008). He has undertaken professional legal training in Greece and is a qualified advocate, member of the Athens Bar Association since 2011. Andreas' doctoral research was on the corporate governance of banks in the UK and focused on whether banks present unique governance problems that have to be addressed by bank-specific corporate governance rules, with a view to ensuring the sustainable development of the banking industry. Andreas has been honoured by several academic awards including a PhD scholarship from the Greek State Scholarships Foundations, the 1 Essex Court LLM Prize for the best performance in Corporate Law during the 2008–09 academic year in LSE and Achilles Balis Foundation prize in 2008 for his overall performance during his LLB in Athens' Law School. Andreas' publications include: 'The reformed "fit and proper" test: A call for a broader rethink of bank corporate governance?' (2012) 9(1) *International Corporate Rescue* and 'Rethinking banking prudential regulation: Why corporate governance rules matter?' (2012) 7 *Journal of Business Law* 611.

John Lowry

John is Chair of Commercial Law at Hong Kong University, and Emeritus Professor of Commercial Law at UCL. He has taught law in the USA and practised in Canada specialising in corporate litigation. He has written widely in domestic and international journals on directors' fiduciary obligations, shareholder remedies and insurance law. He is co-author of a number of books including, *Limitation of Actions* (LLP, 1998); *Company Law* (OUP 2012); *Pettet's Company Law* (Pearson 2014); *Insurance Law: Doctrines and Principles* (Hart 2011); and *Insurance Law: Cases and Materials* (Hart 2004). He is also a contributing editor to *Gore-Browne on Companies* (Jordans) and *Annotated Companies Legislation* (OUP). He is a member of a number of editorial boards, including the *Journal of Business Law, Company Lawyer* and *International Corporate Rescue*. In 2001 he was a Visiting Fellow at the University of Connecticut and he was made an Honorary Fellow of Monash University in 2009. In 2010 he was elected Distinguished Global Jurist Visiting Professor at the Chinese University of Hong Kong.

Marc T Moore

Marc is Reader in Corporate Law and Director of the Centre for Corporate and Commercial Law (3CL) in the Faculty of Law, University of Cambridge. He is also a Fellow of Murray Edwards College, Cambridge; an Honorary Reader in the Faculty of Laws, University College London; and Deputy Chief Examiner for Company Law on the University of London's external LLM programme. Marc has previously held teaching positions at University College London, the University of Bristol, and Seattle University. Marc's principal area of expertise is Anglo-American corporate law and governance. He has authored and co-authored a number of articles and papers in this field within leading international publications. In 2013 his book, *Corporate Governance in the Shadow of the State* (Hart Publishing 2013), was shortlisted for the SLS Peter Birks Prize for Outstanding Legal Scholarship. In 2012, Marc was awarded a Philip Leverhulme prize in recognition of outstanding research achievement to date. Marc is a commissioning editor of a new Palgrave-Macmillan text series on corporate and financial law, and in 2010 he was UK national reporter on corporate governance for the XVIIIth Congress of the International Academy of Comparative Law at Washington DC.

Arad Reisberg

Arad is currently a Reader in Corporate and Financial Law and Director, UCL Centre for Commercial Law. He acted as Vice Dean (Research) at UCL Faculty of Laws between 2009–12. He has been teaching at the Faculty since September 2003, and joined it full time in September 2006. He was formerly a Senior Arts Scholar (2001–03) and a Tutor at Pembroke College Oxford, where he taught law at six colleges at Oxford University between 2001–05. He has also been a Visiting Lecturer at Oxford University (2005) and more recently, a Visiting Professor of Law at Brooklyn Law School (Fall Term 2012), and a Visiting Professor of Law at NUS (2014). He is the recipient of numerous academic scholarships and awards and has written widely on shareholder remedies and directors' duties. Arad is the author of *Derivative Actions and Corporate Governance* (OUP 2007), the first book to provide a detailed and theoretical explanation of the law governing derivative actions. He is also an Academic Member of ECGI (European Corporate Governance Institute), a co-editor of *Pettet's Company Law*, sits on the editorial boards of the *International Corporate Rescue* and the *Journal of Corporate Ownership and Control*, and is a contributing author to *Annotated Companies Legislation* (OUP).

Georgina Tsagas

Georgina is a Lecturer in Law at the University of Bristol Law School and her research expertise lies in takeover regulation and corporate governance. She has formerly held posts at University College London, Faculty of Laws, as a Postdoctoral Research Associate (2013–14) (and at Queen Mary University of London, School of Law, as a Teaching Fellow (2010–2012). Georgina holds a PhD from Queen Mary University of London sponsored by a Full Scholarship (2009–12) award from QMUL School of Law. She has written on the prospective reform of the EU Takeover Directive and the changes to the UK City Code on Takeovers and Mergers following the reform prompted by the Kraft–Cadbury deal in 2011. Georgina is a qualified Solicitor of England and Wales and an attorney-at-law in Greece. She has lectured on the LLM and LLB programmes at UCL, Centre for Commercial Law Studies, QMUL and BPP Law School respectively and has acted as a guest academic tutor at LSE Summer School. Her recent publications include: 'A long-term vision for UK Firms? Reconsidering target director's advisory role post the takeover of Cadbury's plc' (2014) 14(1) *Journal of Corporate Law Studies* 241 and 'The revision of the EU Takeover Directive in light of the 2011 UK takeover law reform' (2013) 10(1) *International and Comparative Company Law Journal* 21.

Edward Walker-Arnott

Edward is a Visiting Professor at UCL's Faculty of Laws. He has been with Herbert Smith Freehills throughout his professional career and was senior partner between 1992–2000. He sat on the Departmental Committee (the Cork Committee) inquiring into insolvency law between 1977–82. The report resulted in the enactment of the Insolvency Act 1986. At the beginning of 1983, Edward was appointed one of the first three nominated members of the Council of Lloyd's, sitting on the Council for six years. He chaired the Investigations Committee at Lloyd's, which conducted the investigations of the many Lloyd's scandals of the late 1970s and early 1980s and prosecuted the subsequent disciplinary proceedings. He is well known in the City having been involved in many high-profile cases including a number of celebrated take-over battles.

Edward has also served as Governor of the South Bank Centre between 1999–2009; he was on the Board of the Royal National Theatre from 2000–08 and served as Governor of the Wellcome Trust from 2000–10. Edward is currently a non-executive director of a private company with significant commercial and property interests in the UK and in Europe and of a biotech start-up company backed by both the Wellcome Trust and the Gates Foundation. He is a member of the Takeover Appeal Board and was made a QC (Hon) in 2013.

PREFACE: THE LAW OF THE CORPORATE GOVERNANCE OF BANKS AND FINANCIAL INSTITUTIONS

The corporate governance of banks and financial institutions came under the spotlight in the wake of the global financial crisis 2008–09, the subsequent conduct scandals such as the manipulation of the London Inter-Bank Offered Rate by several UK and international banks, and other miss-selling, corruption and financial crime scandals. Although misjudgements in risk and sub-optimal corporate behaviour are not uncommon in the corporate sector, the utility and systemic risk profiles of the banking sector, in particular, are important attributes that warrant public concern with any failings in the internal governance of banks that could culminate in excessive risk-taking or sub-optimal corporate behaviour.

In this volume, we address key themes in the internal governance of banks and financial institutions that we believe are of topical interest. The law and Corporate Governance Code discussed in this volume are stated as at March 2014. In Chapter 1, Andreas Kokkinis discusses the governance structure of most widely held banks and financial institutions, and the incentives that may result in excessive risk-taking. He reveals that conventional agency-based corporate governance frameworks may be unsuitable for banks and financial institutions as they arguably do not address the governance challenges in banks and financial institutions and may indeed entail counter-productive incentives exacerbating governance problems.

In Chapter 2, Edward Walker-Arnott discusses the importance of the board as collectively managing and making key decisions in banks and financial institutions, and argues that neither company law nor financial regulation address the issue of collective responsibility and how that can be boosted to improve board stewardship. This thought-provoking chapter takes stock of recent policy discussions and proposals for legislative reforms but critically asks if new law and new provisions in governance codes are really on the right track.

In Chapter 3, John Lowry and Rod Edmunds shift the focus from collective directorial responsibility by asking whether individual directorial responsibility for banks and financial institutions could be enhanced via the application of the directors' disqualification regime. They highlight that to date it has not been applied notwithstanding some clear political pronouncements (including those of UK's Business Secretary, Dr Vince Cable) that it should be harnessed to prevent certain named directors in the UK's failed banks (RBS and HBOS in particular) from holding directorships in the immediate future. As the chapter indicates, the reasons why disqualification proceedings have not been initiated is all the more intriguing in the light of both the recent proposals for reforming the regime and also the introduction of the new offence of 'reckless misconduct in the management of a bank' contained in the Financial Services (Banking Reform) Act 2013.

Chapter 4 turns the attention to shareholders of banks and financial institutions and the excessive short-termism that prevails in the securities markets that characterise the nature of such shareholding. Short-termist shareholding entails behaviour such as preference for exit over voice and disengagement from monitoring, issues that have been flagged up in the Walker Report of 2009, relating to weaknesses in bank and financial institution corporate governance. Arad Reisberg critically discusses the development of short-termism as a prevalent notion in the UK securities markets and argues that although a slate of tax and corporate governance reforms (which are re-surfacing in recent reforms) may seek to change short-termist behaviour, answers to behavioural changes are far from easy and would take time to bed down.

Chapters 5–8 then address specific issues of internal governance in banks and financial institutions. In Chapter 5, Marc Moore discusses the legal and Corporate Governance Code framework for setting remuneration, and the specific controls provided in financial regulation to control excessive remuneration in the banking sector. This is an area that has seen many recent reforms at the UK and EU levels but it may be queried as to whether appropriate remuneration design can be micro-managed by legal frameworks and institutions.

Chapter 6 deals with the issue of risk management in banks and financial institutions, identified as a key problem in the global financial crisis of 2008–09. Iris Chiu discusses the failures of risk management culminating in excessive risk-taking by banks and financial institutions and how reforming the corporate governance frameworks at the highest management levels may address risk management sub-optimalities.

In Chapter 7, Iris Chiu addresses the issue of reliable and timely corporate reporting by banks and financial institutions and the role that such corporate reporting may play in incentivising market discipline. The weaknesses of corporate reporting frameworks are discussed and recent reforms are also critically examined to inquire into the objectives of corporate reporting and how that may serve as a mechanism to enhance internal governance of banks and financial institutions and external scrutiny by markets.

Chapter 8 deals with a particular issue of systems and controls in banks and financial institutions, that of instituting anti-bribery and corruption controls. Anna Donovan examines the interpretation and impact of the Bribery Act 2010 on the corporate sector and highlights particular challenges and issues faced by banks and financial institutions.

Finally, in Chapter 9 Georgina Tsagas addresses the efficacy of the UK/EU legal framework regulating the market for corporate control in the banking industry. With reference to a series of case studies, including the RBS takeover of ABN-AMRO prior to the global financial crisis, the chapter specifically examines whether the market for corporate control in the banking industry functions perversely, how this function affects and is affected by prudential concerns and whether the parties involved in an offer effectively discharge their roles respectively. The chapter highlights the consequences that may flow from a failed change in the corporate control of a bank and ultimately questions the shareholder primacy norm followed in the case of banks proposing regulatory reforms in the interests of prudence.

This volume takes on both academic and critical perspectives in some highly topical issues in the corporate governance of banks and financial institutions. Many of its insights are also drawn from and applicable to the general corporate sector. Not only does a financial crisis give rise to reforms pertaining to the financial sector, but the mood for critical scrutiny generally of the corporate sector also paves the way for more broad-based reform at the UK and EU levels. The contributions in this volume reflect this broader context and interest.

Iris H-Y Chiu

TABLE OF CASES

UK CASES

EUROPEAN CASES

INTERNATIONAL CASES

TABLE OF LEGISLATION

UNITED STATES OF AMERICA

EUROPEAN UNION

Regulations

Directives

INTERNATIONAL CONVENTIONS

A PRIMER ON CORPORATE GOVERNANCE IN BANKS AND FINANCIAL INSTITUTIONS: ARE BANKS SPECIAL?

Andreas Kokkinis

1. INTRODUCTION

1.01 This chapter serves as an introductory chapter to the present volume on bank corporate governance. As such, it seeks to capture some of the specific corporate governance problems banks face, and to provide a useful background for the discussion of more detailed aspects of the topic in the forthcoming chapters. Of course, the views expressed herein are the author's own and other contributors to the volume may not agree with them. The analysis mainly focuses on UK banks that are listed on the London Stock Exchange, in other words, on large systemic banks.[1]

1.02 The corporate governance of banks is an area under continuous development which has changed dramatically in recent years both nationally and internationally. As all listed companies, UK banks are expected to comply with the UK Corporate Governance Code.[2] In addition, the 2009 Walker Review introduced a series of governance recommendations specific to banks and other financial institutions.[3] Many of these have since then been implemented by the PRA[4] and now form part of the PRA Handbook.[5] More recently, the report of the Parliamentary Commission on Banking Standards urged for broader changes to bank corporate governance including the approved persons' regime and directors' duties.[6] In parallel, the fourth Capital Requirements Directive (CRD IV), impacts on bank corporate governance with regard to executive remuneration.[7] Many of these issues will be explored in depth in the following chapters of this volume.

1.03 The principal aim of this chapter is to illustrate that the private ordering model of bank corporate governance is prone to lead to high negative externalities by undermining financial stability. Profit maximisation necessarily entails taking substantial risks that, even if desirable from the point of view of bank shareholders, may still be excessive from the society's perspective, due to the systemic consequences of crises in any major bank. This problem is not unique to the banking sector, but is far more severe in banks than in other large companies due to the crucial economic functions performed by banks and the special risks

---

1 As of 1 January 2014, the following FTSE 100 companies can be classified as banks: Barclays plc, HSBC Group plc, Lloyds Banking Group plc, the Royal Bank of Scotland Group plc and Standard Chartered plc. The discussion in this chapter also bears some relevance to other financial institutions, such as insurance companies.

2 The UK Corporate Governance Code (2012) available at: http://www.frc.org.uk/Our-Work/Codes-Standards/Corporate-governance/UK-Corporate-Governance-Code.aspx, accessed 1 January 2014.

3 See D Walker, 'A review of corporate governance in UK banks and other financial industry entities: Final Recommendations' (2009), available at: https://www.icaew.com/en/library/subject-gateways/corporate-governance/codes-and-reports/walker-report, accessed 1 January 2014.

4 Since 2013 the FSA has been succeeded by the Prudential Regulation Authority (PRA), which is a subsidiary of the Bank of England and the Financial Conduct Authority (FCA). An analysis of the Financial Services Act 2012 can be found in A Kokkinis, 'The Financial Services Act 2012: The recent overhaul of the United Kingdom's financial regulatory structure' (2013) 24(9) *ICCLR* 325. See also P Rawlings, 'Bank reform in the UK: Part II – Return to the Dark Ages?' (2011) 8 *ICR* 55.

5 See in particular PRA Handbook, SYSC 19A.3.12–3.49.

6 See Parliamentary Commission on Banking Standards, *Changing Banking for Good* (2013–14, HL 27-II, HC 175-II) Chs 6–7.

7 See Directive 2013/36/EU of the European Parliament and of the Council of 26 June 2013 on access to the activity of credit institutions and the prudential supervision of credit institutions and investment firms, amending Directive 2002/87/EC and repealing Directives 2006/48/EC and 2006/49/EC [2013] OJ L176/338, art 94. See also Commission, 'Corporate governance in financial institutions and remuneration policies' COM (2010) 284 final.

banks face, most notably, systemic risk. In addition, it will be illustrated that this problem is materially exacerbated by the limited ability of shareholder and creditor governance to curb excessive risk-taking by banks.

The chapter is structured as follows. Section 2 provides a background discussion **1.04** of agency theory with a particular focus on the mechanisms that purport to align the interests of senior managers with the interests of shareholders in large widely held public companies. Section 3 explores the public market failure of the conventional corporate governance regime, that is, the negative consequences of risk-taking on the financial system and society as a whole. Then, Section 4 proceeds to demonstrate the private market failures[8] of shareholder and creditor governance in the case of banks, taking each main type of creditors separately, and explains how this additional feature of the banking sector exacerbates the aforementioned problem. Section 5 builds on the previous argument by proposing a regulatory approach to bank corporate governance and ascertaining the existing regulatory intervention in the area. Section 6 summarises the discussion and concludes.

A. Agency theory: Aligning the interests of managers and shareholders

i. A brief overview of agency theory

A principal-agent relationship is a concept frequently used in economics and **1.05** political science to describe a situation in which one person appoints another person to act on his behalf and in his best interests, occasionally in exchange for remuneration.[9] In this sense, the relationship between voters and members of Parliament, patients and doctors, and shareholders and managers in a company are all examples of principal-agent relationships. It is worth noting that this concept of agency is broader than the legal notion of agency[10] and encompasses all fiduciary relationships as well as other relationships. Frequently an agency relationship gives rise to a principal-agent problem. This happens when the agent does not have the same interests as the principal, and there is information asymmetry between the two. In other words, the agent is in possession of relevant information which is not available to – or cannot be properly understood by – the principal. In such cases the principal cannot prima facie ensure that the agent will use his powers in the principal's best interests. Assuming that

---

8 I am indebted to Dr Marc Moore for the useful distinction between public and private market failures. See M T Moore, *Corporate Governance in the Shadow of the State* (Hart Publishing 2013) 23842.

9 See J E Stiglitz, 'Principal and agent' in *The New Palgrave: A Dictionary of Economics* (vol 3, New Palgrave 1987) 966–71.

10 In law, an agent is a person who is given the power (the authority) to alter the legal position of another person (the principal), especially by entering into contracts on behalf of the principal. An agent's authority can be actual, which is conferred by agreement between the principal and the agent, or apparent.

the agent is a rational actor who seeks to maximise his own utility, it can be expected that the agent will shirk his duties and may even transfer wealth from the principal to himself.[11]

1.06 In companies it is the separation of ownership and control, first empirically observed by Berle and Means,[12] which gives rise to an agency relationship between the shareholders, who are the principals, and the directors and senior managers,[13] who are their agents. The separation of ownership and control occurs when the ownership of shares is so dispersed that no shareholder – or small group of shareholders – holds a majority of shares, or even a minority interest that guarantees effective control of the company. This means that no individual shareholder (or small group) acting alone can usually determine the outcome of a shareholder vote.[14] On these conditions the costs faced by shareholders who wish to attempt to influence corporate decision-making are significant, especially with regard to analysing relevant information and putting together a shareholder coalition. At the same time, the potential benefit from activism is relatively small and any benefits are equally spread among all shareholders. As a result, each shareholder is tempted to remain passive and wait for someone else to engage, a phenomenon described as the rational apathy of the shareholders.[15] The outcome of this is that the recommendations of the board are nearly invariably approved by the shareholders. This includes the election of directors, and thus in normal times boards are indeed self-perpetuating organs.[16]

1.07 This phenomenon, which since the late 1960s is prevalent in the UK nearly as much as in the US, gives rise to agency costs, which are imposed by senior managers to shareholders. These costs are of two types: i) lack of optimal effort and diligence by senior managers in discharging their duties; and ii) the risk that

---

11   A conflict of interest between the principal and the agent occurs when the personal interests of the agent clash with the interests of the principal.

12   In the early 1930s, Berle and Means' empirical work confirmed that 44 per cent of the 200 largest US corporations were managerially controlled, i.e. no single shareholder owned more than 5 per cent of shares. See A A Berle and G C Means, *The Modern Corporation and Private Property* (rev. edn, Harcourt, Brace & World 1967) 108–9.

13   Although the terms are often used interchangeably in economic literature, is should be kept in mind that in law only members of the board of directors are subject to directors' duties.

14   See B S Black, 'Agents watching agents: The promise of institutional investor voice' (1991–1992) 39 *UCLA L Rev* 811, 821–2.

15   For a modern explanation of the dynamics of shareholder voting and the rational apathy of the shareholders from a US perspective, see C Gulinello, 'The retail investor vote: Mobilizing rationally apathetic shareholders to preserve or challenge the board's presumption of authority' (2010) 3 *Utah Law Review* 547, 573–6.

16   The first scholars who observed the collective action problems faced by dispersed shareholders were Berle and Means. See above n 12, 76–82 and 129–31.

senior managers may pursue objectives other than the maximisation of share-holder wealth, such as the advancement of their own financial interests. This can be achieved (inter alia) by self-dealing, exploiting corporate opportunities, misappropriating corporate assets and receiving excessive remuneration. Additionally or alternatively, managers may pursue non-value-maximising objectives to serve their non-financial interests. An example of that is corporate 'empire-building' i.e. the creation of inefficiently large corporate groups with a view to enhance senior managers' personal power, prestige and security of office.[17]

In order to reduce primary agency costs, shareholders have to engage in monitoring managers by keeping themselves informed on the performance of companies and getting involved when necessary. In parallel, senior managers also wish to signal to potential investors that agency costs will be held in tight control in order to encourage investment in the company's shares. To do so, senior managers put in place majority independent boards which have the power to monitor their performance and replace them. Of course, monitoring by shareholders and using bonding devices by managers are costly activities in their own right, so they can be seen as types of agency costs themselves. This explains why Jensen and Meckling classify agency costs into three categories, namely monitoring costs, bonding costs and residual agency costs.[18] **1.08**

In major UK banks the phenomenon of separation of ownership from control is as prevalent as in other large public companies.[19] Of course, the recent partial nationalisation of RBS and Lloyds has led to the government being a substantial block holder in both these major banks.[20] However, the analysis in this chapter disregards the temporary effect of the government's large investments in these banks, as the government has resolved to manage its holdings in a purely commercial manner and with a view to the quickest possible sale of its investments.[21] **1.09**

---

17 Large corporations that own diverse businesses and operate in various markets are generally less susceptible to insolvency and hostile takeovers.

18 See M C Jensen and W H Meckling, 'Theory of the firm: Managerial behavior, agency costs and ownership structure' (1976) 3 *Journal of Financial Economics* 305, 308–10.

19 Still, on a global basis, concentrated ownership is the norm in the banking sector, as 75 per cent of banks have a block holder controlling at least 10 per cent of voting rights. See G Jr Caprio, L Laeven, and R Levine, 'Governance and Bank Valuation' (2003) World Bank Working Paper No. 3202, available at: http://papers.ssrn.com/sol3/papers.cfm?abstract_id=463240, accessed 1 January 2014.

20 The UKFI holds 82 per cent of the equity capital (66 per cent of voting rights) in RBS and 32.7 per cent of the ordinary share capital of Lloyds. In September 2013 the UKFI sold 6 per cent of Lloyds' shares, while Northern Rock was sold to Virgin Money on 1 January 2012. The Government intends to dispose of its shares in RBS in the near future, available at: http://www.ukfi.co.uk/about-us/market-investments/, accessed 1 January 2014.

21 The Government's commercial approach was challenged unsuccessfully by People and Planet, an environmental protection NGO. In *R (on the application of People and Planet) v HM Treasury* [2009] EWHC 3020

ii. Agency costs and risk-taking by companies

1.10 One particular aspect of the misalignment of interest between managers and shareholders is the different attitude to risk that these two groups have. The reason why we focus on risk is that, as will be demonstrated below, one of the key specific characteristics of banking is the unique risks banks face and the consequences of risk-taking by a large bank on other banks and the economy as a whole.

1.11 It is trite to say that in order for businesses to make profits they need to take risks, as business activity necessarily entails making decisions with limited information. Evidently, investors require a risk premium (i.e. a higher expected return) to invest in more risky securities. For instance, generally, corporate bonds that carry the risk that the issuing company may go insolvent bear a higher interest rate than government bonds, which are presumed to be risk-free as the government is extremely unlikely to default on its debt.[22] Shares are even more risky investments as there is no specified return and share capital is the first to be lost if a company goes insolvent. As such shareholders are described as the residual risk bearers.[23]

1.12 Nevertheless, shareholders do not seem to be risk averse, but rather they are generally risk neutral. This is due to the practice of portfolio diversification which is followed by the vast majority of investors. According to portfolio management theory,[24] investors spread their funds to different types of assets (e.g. shares, corporate bonds, government bonds, derivatives) and different issuers. Thus, only a fraction of an investor's capital will be invested in shares and this amount will be spread amongst a large number of public companies, possibly in more than one markets. As a result, the investment of any shareholder in any company is only a very small fraction of their total funds. The effect of portfolio diversification on shareholders' risk appetite is that shareholders are very close to being risk neutral. Since diversified shareholders are partly insulated from the low actual return or failure of one of their investments, as their total income is evened out by other investments, they have no reason to

---

(Admin) esp [34], Sales J refused the application and observed that if the government imposed its policy on climate change and human rights on the board of RBS it would be contrary to their duty to promote the success of RBS for the benefit of its shareholders as a whole. See also S F Copp, 'Section 172 of the Companies Act 2006 fails People and Planet' (2010) 31 *Comp Law* 406.

22   At least this is accurate for UK Government bonds. However, the recent Eurozone sovereign debt crisis demonstrates that Eurozone Government bonds are not necessarily zero risk.

23   Contractarian theory claims that the shareholders bear the residual risk. See F H Easterbrook, and D R Fischel, *The Economic Structure of Corporate Law* (Harvard University Press 1991) esp. 14–16.

24   See e.g. E J Elton and others, *Modern Portfolio Theory and Investment Analysis* (8th edn, John Wiley & Sons Inc. 2010).

avoid risk as such. It follows that diversified shareholders are happy for companies to take any risk which they estimate to have a positive net expected value, irrespective of the gravity of the consequences of risk taking in the worst-case scenario.[25]

Of course, senior managers have no immediate reason to satisfy the risk appetite of the shareholders, as in widely held companies they enjoy in practice a very wide discretion to manage companies as they think fit.[26] Indeed, taking into account that managers are full-time employees who have invested their personal capital in the company, it becomes clear that they are, in general, risk averse compared to the shareholders. Human capital is not diversifiable and the potential failure of a company normally has a huge reputational cost for a senior manager and is likely to reduce his chance to obtain an equivalent position in the future. It follows that in a widely held company senior managers can be expected to be less prone to take risks than shareholders, as only the latters' investment is fully diversified.

1.13

This apparent misalignment of risk appetite between senior managers and shareholders has been the target of academic criticism by contractarian scholars since the 1980s. Two major mechanisms have been used to align the risk appetite of the two groups: hostile takeovers and variable executive remuneration. A hostile takeover occurs when the majority of the shares – and hence the control – of a company are bought by another company without the approval of the target company's board. A hostile takeover results in the target company becoming a subsidiary of the acquirer[27] and in the directors and senior managers of the target being replaced. It follows that the market for corporate control[28] ensures that companies' managers face a powerful incentive to do their best to maximise shareholder value, which includes adopting a neutral approach to risk-taking.

1.14

Granted, it is well established that in the banking sector hostile takeovers are uncommon both internationally[29] and in the UK.[30] However, major UK banks

1.15

---

25   The crucial significance of this point with regard to financial stability will be analysed below in Section 3.

26   On the general limitations of shareholders as decision makers and the desirability to trust the board with all business decisions, see S M Bainbridge, 'Director primacy and shareholder disempowerment' (2006) 119 *Harv L Rev* 1735.

27   At least this is the practice followed in the UK. In the US it is more common for the two companies to merge.

28   US lawyer Henry Manne was the first to introduce the concept of a market for corporate control. See H G Manne, 'Mergers and the market for corporate control' (1965) 73 *The Journal of Political Economy* 110.

29   See e.g. S D Prowse, 'The corporate governance system in banking: What do we know?'(1997) (March) *Banca del Lavoro Quarterly Review* 11.

30   The only hostile takeover of a major UK bank in recent years was that of National Westminster Bank by the Royal Bank of Scotland in 2000, subsequent to a failed friendly merger of the former with Legal & General and

are sometimes engaged in hostile takeovers of foreign banks,[31] and do frequently resort to friendly mergers,[32] which are generally facilitated by the implicit threat of a possible hostile takeover. Therefore, although the pressures from the market for corporate control are somewhat limited in the special case of banks, there is still an incentive for bank senior managers to maintain the share price of the bank so as to minimise the likelihood of a hostile takeover offer arising.

1.16 The second mechanism used to achieve risk appetite alignment is variable executive remuneration. Until the 1980s, executive remuneration in large US and UK companies was generally insensitive to performance. The influential work of Jensen and Murphy in 1990 demonstrated that the remuneration of US CEOs was not strongly linked to performance, and that the overall level of CEO pay in the 1980s was in real terms lower than in the 1930s.[33] They attributed this phenomenon to the political influence of trade unions, the media and certain shareholders. Jensen and Murphy urged for an increase in variable remuneration, as better-aligned incentives would leave shareholders much better off despite the increase in overall levels of remuneration. Indeed, the 1990s brought an explosive rise of variable remuneration (especially in the form of stock options) and of overall levels of pay both in the US[34] and the UK.

1.17 However, it is not clear whether variable remuneration achieves its intended goals or it is used as a device for managers to extract rents from shareholders. The influential work of Bebchuk and Fried asserts that managerial power shapes executive remuneration.[35] They argue that all market forces that are supposed to restrain managerial rent-seeking, according to the optimal contacting theory, are not strong enough to bring about this outcome. In parallel, formally independent remuneration committees are frequently loyal to CEOs and depend on them for relevant information. US shareholders also have very limited direct powers to intervene in remuneration decisions.[36] Hence, Bebchuk and Fried argue that managers have significant influence in deciding their

---

a failed hostile takeover bid by the Bank of Scotland. The takeover was central to the rise of RBS to one of the Big Four clearing banks and made it one of the largest companies in the world.

31 An obvious recent example is the takeover of ABN AMRO by a consortium led by RBS.

32 Recent examples include the merger between Lloyds TSB and HBOS in 2009, the acquisition of Abbey National by Santander in 2004, the merger of Halifax and Bank of Scotland in 2001, and the acquisition of the Midland Bank by HSBC in 1992.

33 See M C Jensen, and K J Murphy, 'CEO incentives – It's not how much you pay, but how' (1990) (May–June) *Harvard Business Review* 138.

34 In the US the favourable tax treatment of variable remuneration since 1993 further facilitated the shift towards performance-based pay.

35 See L A Bebchuk, J M Fried, and D I Walker, 'Managerial power and rent extraction in the design of executive compensation' (2002) 69 *U Chi L Rev* 751, esp. 789–94.

36 In the UK shareholders are given broader approval powers by the Companies Act 2006, ss 439–439A.

own remuneration. In addition, various forms of performance-based remuneration have been criticised as depending on luck and rewarding executives for merely increasing the volatility of their company's share price rather than its profitability. Executive pay can therefore be a source of agency costs, rather than a tool to minimise them.[37]

2. THE FAILURE OF CONVENTIONAL CORPORATE GOVERNANCE IN THE CASE OF BANKS: PROFIT MAXIMISATION V THE PUBLIC INTEREST

A. The public interest in financial stability

The previous section offered a brief overview of agency theory and conventional **1.18** corporate governance techniques with a special emphasis on the ways in which corporate governance fosters risk-taking by the senior managers of large companies within the broader framework of shareholder value maximisation. In this section I explain why running major banks with a view to profit maximisation potentially undermines financial stability. The misalignment between the private interests of bank shareholders and the public interest is arguably the major distinct characteristic of the banking sector which warrants a radically different approach to bank corporate governance which would not be necessarily appropriate for non-financial companies.[38] As a preliminary point, this part identifies the specific economic characteristics of the banking sector that render financial stability a public good and justify its crucial importance for the economy as a whole.[39]

A detailed doctrinal analysis of financial stability as the statutory objective of **1.19** relevant UK regulatory authorities falls outside the scope of the chapter. It is sufficient to note here the recent legislative emphasis on financial stability, as a response to the financial crisis. Indeed, the Banking Act 2009 added section 2A to the Bank of England Act 1998 and thus added to the Bank's statutory

---

37 Jensen and Murphy (in spite of their original contribution to the optimal contracting theory) have criticised prevailing executive remuneration practices during the 1990s, and admitted in 2004 that executive pay was excessive and still not truly aligned with corporate performance. See M C Jensen, K J Murphy and E G Wruck, 'Remuneration: Where we've been, how we got to here, what are the problems, and how to fix them' (2004) Harvard Business School NOM Research Paper No. 04–28, 98, available at: http://ssrn.com/abstract=561305, accessed 1 January 2014.

38 See e.g. P Ciancanelli and J A Reyes-Gonzalez, 'Corporate governance in banking: A conceptual framework' (European Financial Management Association conference, Athens, June 2000), available at: http://ssrn.com/abstract=253714, accessed 1 January 2014.

39 A public good is a good that is both indivisible and one that no person can be excluded from its use, such as national defence. It is a case of market failure, as markets cannot produce public goods at the socially desirable level.

objectives a financial stability objective.[40] The latter was further strengthened by the Financial Services Act 2012 which amended the financial stability objective by asserting that the Bank ought to protect and enhance the stability of the financial system of the UK rather than merely to contribute to protecting and enhancing stability, as the previous wording of the section was.[41] In addition, the 2012 Act introduced the Financial Policy Committee of the Bank of England which is charged with contributing to the achievement of the Bank's financial stability objective.[42] Finally, the broader restructuring of the banking regulatory landscape can be said to prioritise macro-prudential issues over micro-prudential ones, and separates prudential regulation from conduct of business regulation thus allowing for greater focus on financial stability than under the previous structure.[43]

i. The economic significance of banks

1.20   First, I shall briefly explain the vital importance of the financial sector and of banks in particular for any modern economy. As financial intermediaries banks efficiently transfer liquidity from depositors and bondholders to individual, corporate and sovereign borrowers, allowing for economic growth and expansion. In fact they generate liquidity, as they fund illiquid assets (loans) using the money deposited in them.[44] Indeed, by accepting deposits and relending most of them and then reaccepting the money back (as after certain transactions it goes back to the bank) and relending it, and so on, circulating money is multiplied several times. This is the so-called money multiplying effect, which explains the need to supervise overall lending by the authority charged with monetary policy.[45]

1.21   In addition, banks operate a complex payment services system which facilitates the transactions of their private and corporate clients, inter alia, via cheques, credit cards, debit cards, cash cards, electronic purses, money transfers, and

---

40   Banking Act 2009, s 238 (1).
41   Financial Services Act 2012, s 2 (2).
42   See Bank of England Act 1998, s 9C (inserted by the Financial Services Act 2012, s 4).
43   On that, see Kokkinis, see above n 4.
44   Of course, financial intermediation is not the only activity of banks in recent years. It has been illustrated that the financial intermediation role of banks is nowadays less important than in the past, as their main source of income is fees and trading activities rather than the margin between interest rates paid by borrowers and interest rates paid to depositors. See e.g. F Allen, and A M Santomero, 'What do financial intermediaries do?' (2001) 25 *Journal of Banking & Finance* 271.
45   In the UK monetary policy is independently administered by the Bank of England (and its Monetary Policy Committee) within the inflation target set by the Treasury. See Bank of England Act 1998, s 10 which abolishes the power of the Treasury to give direction to the Bank with regard to monetary policy; and s 11 which lexically prioritises the Bank's objective to maintain price stability above its duty to support the Government's economic policy.

standing orders. In this way banks can be said to resemble utility companies providing an intangible network of essential importance for society as a whole. Banks are also large employers, especially in countries like the UK where the financial sector accounts for nearly 10 per cent of the GDP. Last but not least, banks significantly influence the corporate governance of other companies through debenture covenants and informal monitoring of financed companies.

Furthermore, the occurrence of a bank crisis has detrimental consequences for **1.22** the real economy. First, bank lending is curtailed as ailing banks seek to reduce their loan portfolios. The resulting credit crunch undermines the ability of firms to raise debt and expand, and can thus cause the economy as a whole to enter into a recession[46] and unemployment to rise.[47] To make matters worse, Government spending to prevent the failure of large banks (and thus the collapse of the financial system), and the overall economic recession leads to the inescapable consequence of increasing the public debt with potentially serious long-term consequences for the economy.[48] It seems that whatever policy is followed to manage a banking crisis, serious negative externalities are generated when a large bank fails, and the losses are borne not only by other banks but also by the real economy and taxpayers. Indeed, the consequences of bank crises are so severe that it is highly unlikely that any benefits accruing from increased risk taking during the period leading up to a crisis (e.g. in the form of lower unemployment and faster growth) will outweigh the cost of a financial crisis (although formal economic evidence on this is difficult to find).[49]

ii. The unique business risks faced by banks

Due to the maturity mismatch between: on the one hand, deposits, that are **1.23** typically payable on demand, and, on the other, loans, that are to be repaid after a fixed period, it follows that no bank can meet a significant fraction of its liabilities at any given time. Banks cannot even do so relatively quickly, as their

---

46 For instance, in 2009 UK GDP declined by 4 per cent as a result of the 2008 financial crisis.

47 The unemployment rate rose from around 5.3 per cent in 2007 to 8 per cent in 2011 and is predicted to be at 7.3 per cent in 2015. See European Economic Forecast Autumn 2009 (2009), available at: http://ec.europa.eu/economy_finance/publications/publication_summary16053_en.htm, accessed 1 January 2014, 156; and European Economic Forecast Autumn 2013 (2013), available at: http://ec.europa.eu/economy_finance/eu/forecasts/2013_autumn_forecast_en.htm, accessed 1 January 2014, 101.

48 The UK national debt to GDP ratio increased from 43.30 per cent at the end of the 2007–08 fiscal year to 88.10 per cent at the end of 2012–13. It is predicted to rise to 97.80 per cent by the end of the 2015–16 year. Ibid.

49 The UK Government's support to the banking sector peaked at £1,162bn in 2009 and currently stands at £141bn. The exact final cost to UK taxpayers is difficult to calculate as it will ultimately depend on the price at which the Treasury's shares in rescued banks are sold. Taking into account the share prices of RBS and Lloyds at 31 March 2013, the loss to the Treasury stood at £28bn. Another £3bn was the cost of resolving Northern Rock and Bradford & Bingley. The additional interest paid by the Treasury to fund its investments in the banking sector amounts to £20bn in four years. Overall, the cost of the recent crisis to the Treasury can be estimated at £51bn. See HM Treasury, *Annual Report and Accounts 2012–13* (2013–14, HC 34).

assets are illiquid and cannot therefore be sold en masse at short notice, other than at very low prices. If a large number of depositors are persuaded that their bank is in a precarious position and rush to draw their funds, they will cause the collapse of the bank, no matter how healthy it is. In other words, the inability of rational depositors to coordinate their actions[50] can lead to a creditors' run, if the reputation of a bank is damaged. A run reduces depositors' aggregate wealth in a classic collective action problem situation. Therefore, any retail bank is constantly dependent on the confidence of its depositors and can at any time be diminished to cash flow insolvency merely as a result of a crisis of confidence.[51] This is a feature of banks that distinguishes them from ordinary companies whose assets are usually more easily realisable and whose liabilities such as term loans and bonds mature over a relatively long and predictable period of time.

1.24 Furthermore, investment banking activities such as trading in securities, on behalf of clients or on banks' own behalf, exposes banks to the volatility of the financial markets. It follows that investment banks, which in the UK are integrated parts of banking groups, are susceptible to sharp changes in their risk profile due to their sensitivity to the conditions of financial markets. It is often argued that the combination of retail and investment banking activities further increases the risks faced by banks, and that this accounts for the number of banking crises that have happened internationally since the integration of retail and investment banking in the 1980s and 1990s.[52]

iii. Systemic risk

1.25 The major feature of the banking industry which renders financial stability a public good is systemic risk. So far it has been explained why individual banks face specific risks that are not faced (at the same extent) by other companies. However, if the failure of one bank left its competitors strengthened and the system intact, as is the case in most other industries, the problem of safeguarding financial stability would not arise. On the contrary, the failure of a relatively large bank has spill-over effects on the entire system. Other major banks suffer and a series of failures may be triggered. Problems in one bank can thus infect

---

50 See M C Ungureanu, 'Banks: Regulation and corporate governance framework' (2008) 5 *Journal of Corporate Ownership and Control* 449, 450–51.

51 Deposit insurance reduces the risk of creditors' runs and thus protects financial stability.

52 In the UK the Vickers Report recommended a mild form of separation of retail banking from investment banking known as ring fencing of the domestic retail activities of banking groups, which are to be taken by a separate subsidiary with stronger capital. See Independent Commission on Banking, *Final Report: Recommendations* (2011), available at: http://webarchive.nationalarchives.gov.uk/+/bankingcommission.independent. gov.uk, accessed 1 January 2014, esp. para 9.2. Recently, Policy Exchange, a major think tank published a report which criticises ring fencing as likely to bring more costs than benefits. See Policy Exchange, *Ring fencing UK Banks: More of a problem than a solution* (J Barty (ed.), Heron, Dawson and Sawyer 2013).

the whole of the financial system and lead to a serious banking crisis, as happened in the UK in 2007–09.[53]

This phenomenon is due to the very high interconnection and interdependence of banks, which conduct a major part of their business with other banks.[54] Banks, for instance, rely on the inter-bank lending market to ensure that they have adequate liquidity to meet their liabilities. They borrow large sums for short periods of time from other banks to respond to frequent shortages of liquidity due to various reasons such as an increase in the withdrawals of deposits. Another component of systemic risk is the reputational one. The failure of an important bank may cause a crisis of confidence in the system as a whole and depositors' runs may affect other banks, or at least an increase in deposit withdrawals may occur. Finally, the opacity of the sector, which will be explored in detail in Section 3 of the chapter, is a cause of systemic risk.[55] The inability of other banks to value the assets of an ailing bank precipitates the collapse of the latter. In parallel, the inability of financial markets to distinguish between sound and unsound banks in times of crisis can paralyse inter-bank lending, and makes it more difficult for banks to raise additional equity capital in times of crisis. Similarly, the general inability of depositors to distinguish between sound and unsound banks, precipitates a widespread crisis of confidence once a major bank collapses.[56]

1.26

iv. The peculiar capital structure of banks

To appreciate the magnitude of the threat that systemic risk poses to financial stability it is necessary to refer to another peculiar characteristic of banks, namely their heavy reliance on debt finance. In banks, as in all limited liability companies, insolvency risk increases the more highly leveraged the company is. Indeed, if a company's activities are mostly funded by equity, then there is a large buffer to absorb losses and hence insolvency is unlikely. Conversely, if a

1.27

---

53 For a succinct discussion of the main banking failures in the UK, see E Walker-Arnott, 'Company law, corporate governance and the banking crisis' (2010) 7 *ICR* 19, 19 and 24–26.

54 See P Mulbert, 'Corporate governance of banks after the financial crisis – Theory, evidence, reforms' (2010) ECGI Working Paper No. 151/2010, 11–12, available at: http://papers.ssrn.com/sol3/papers.cfm?abstract_id= 1448118, accessed 1 January 2014.

55 A recent empirical study on the banking industry found evidence that suggests that opacity causes contagion by exacerbating the cycles of bubbles and crashes. In other words, more opaque banks benefit in times of euphoria and then suffer in times of crisis. See J S Jones, W Y Lee, T J Yeager, 'Opaque banks, price discovery, and financial instability' (2012) 21 *Journal of Financial Intermediation* 383.

56 It has been empirically confirmed that financial crises have a long-term negative effect on investor confidence. Immigrants to the US who have experienced a bank crisis in their country of origin are less likely to open a bank account. See U O Osili and A Paulson, 'Bank crises and investor confidence: An empirical investigation' (2008) Federal Reserve Bank of Chicago Working Paper No. 2008–17, available at: http://www.chicagofed.org/webpages/publications/policy_discussion_papers/2009/pdp_9.cfm, accessed 1 January 2014

company relies primarily on debt capital, it runs a higher risk of insolvency if for any reason its income is reduced, the value of its assets decreases or it fails to roll-over its debt.[57] Unlike most other large companies, banks rely heavily on debt capital. A typical bank is approximately 95 per cent debt financed[58] (deposits and bonds) and only 5 per cent equity financed. Indeed, the equity to assets ratios[59] of major UK banks are currently in the area of 5 per cent (and hence their gearing ratio is in the area of 1:19), and have consistently been at approximately that level in recent years, as can be seen in Table 1.1.

Table 1.1   FTSE 100 UK banks' equity to assets ratio 2000–12

	31/12/2000	31/12/2006	31/12/2012
Barclays	4.17%	2.83%	4.22%
HSBC	6.49%	5.97%	6.20%
HBOS	4.10%	3.58%	NA
Lloyds	4.57%	3.35%	4.83%
RBS	7.22%	4.60%	5.19%
Standard Chart.	5.74%	5.22%	7.24%

Note: For 2012, the table measures Tier 1 equity rather than Core Tier 1 equity (introduced after the recent crisis) to achieve comparability with 2000 and 2006 data.

Source: All data is taken from the Annual Reports and Accounts of the relevant banks, which can be found online.

1.28   The reason why banks are far more highly leveraged than other companies is that their profitability rises as their equity to assets ratio falls.[60] Unlike generic companies, banks do not incur debt in order to do business, but rather their core business activity is to incur debt by accepting deposits and lending the funds out to borrowers. Hence, if we apply the balance sheet test of insolvency on banks, they will always be near-insolvent, as their liabilities are nearly equal to their assets. Therefore, even when banks are perfectly healthy, their capital structure resembles that of a near-insolvent, non-bank firm. The outcome of this is that bank shareholders have stronger economic incentives to support a high level of risk taking than the shareholders of generic companies. As banks are very highly leveraged, shareholders have the incentive to push managers to adopt

---

57   If markets were perfect the capital structure of a company would not matter with regard to profitability, as posited by the Modigliani-Miller theorem.

58   See J R Macey and M O'Hara, 'The corporate governance of banks' (2003) 9 *Federal Reserve Bank of New York Economic Policy Review* 91.

59   Equity includes called-up share capital, preference shares, the share premium account, the profit and loss account, other reserves, and minority interests.

60   An economic explanation of the reason why banks are so highly leveraged can be found in H DeAngelo and R M Stulz, 'Why high leverage is optimal for banks' (2013) Fisher College of Business Working Paper, available at: 2013–03–08 http://papers.ssrn.com/sol3/papers.cfm?abstract_id=2254998, accessed 1 January 2014.

very risky strategies as they risk only their relatively small investment and reap the benefits from 'betting' the whole of a bank's balance sheet, which is mostly funded by debt.

B. The misalignment between the interests of bank shareholders and the public interest

Having examined the idiosyncratic economic characteristics of banks which **1.29** render financial stability a public good, in this part I argue that there is a fundamental misalignment between, on the one hand, the private interests of dispersed shareholders, and on the other, the general public interest in financial stability. The main problem is that the level of risk, which is optimal from the point of view of bank shareholders, will tend to be excessive from the point of view of society.

Generally, rational dispersed shareholders prefer the corporate strategy with the **1.30** highest risk-adjusted return, even if it engenders a risk to the company's survival, since they are risk-neutral and seek to maximise the economic returns on their investment. It follows that rational dispersed shareholders would be happy to support a corporate strategy with high net expected returns even if this strategy involves a low probability risk that the bank will face serious troubles or fail.

Table 1.2 provides an illustration of the point that in some cases it is value- **1.31** maximising for rational shareholders of a bank to prefer a business strategy with a high net risk-adjusted value which may lead to the failure of the bank. All figures are hypothetical. They show the expected value of a bank, after two alternative strategic options (a conservative and an aggressive one) have been implemented at point B in time. The initial value of the bank is 100 (at point A in time). In both cases there is a good scenario (99 per cent probability of happening) and a bad scenario (1 per cent probability of happening). The expected value of the bank at point B is the weighted average of values in the good and bad scenario.[61] As can be seen in the table, taking the risky option which entails a 1 per cent risk of the bank going insolvent leads to a higher expected profit than taking the safe option which does not jeopardise the bank's survival.

---

61   For strategy A, this is 99% x 102 + 1% x 101, which equals to 100.98 + 1.01= 101.99. Therefore the expected profit is 101.99 − 100 = 1.99. For Strategy B, this is 99% × 104 + 1% × 0, which equals to 102.96 + 0 = 102.96. Therefore the expected profit is 102.96 − 100 = 2.96.

Table 1.2   Rational shareholders' attitude to risk

| | Bank value at point A | Bank value at point B | | | **Expected profit** (exp. value at B– value at A) |
		Good scenario (99%)	Bad scenario (1%)	Expected value at B	
Strategy 1	100	102	101	101.99	1.99
Strategy 2	100	104	0	102.96	2.96

1.32 In other industries, this phenomenon is unproblematic as company failures are not perceived as a problem but rather as a manifestation of the operation of market forces that ensure the efficient allocation of capital and hence the development of the economy. Indeed, limited liability itself and the relatively low standard of care imposed on company directors[62] are legal institutions designed to encourage risk-taking. However, in the banking sector the failure of a major bank can have systemic consequences and foster a crisis, which then has catastrophic consequences on the economy as a whole.

1.33 Systemic risk does not reduce the incentives of the shareholders of individual banks to encourage the aforementioned level of risk taking. Indeed, if rational shareholders of hypothetical major bank *A* expect that all other systemic banks will engage in high risk-taking to maximise their profits, it still makes sense from their point of view to do the same, despite the potential negative consequences of this behaviour to the financial system as a whole. If all the shareholders of all systemic banks could collectively agree on a level of risk taking, they would take into account systemic risk and would refrain from taking the level of risk that seemingly maximises profits at the level of each bank. However, given the inability of bank shareholders to co-ordinate at an industry-wide level,[63] the shareholders of each bank face a rational incentive to support a profit maximisation policy, as they will in any case suffer the consequences of risk taking by other banks, if the latter leads to a systemic crisis.

1.34 This is an example of a prisoner's dilemma situation, where the inability of 'players' to co-ordinate leads to an outcome that reduces the aggregate wealth of the players. It follows that the current bank corporate governance regime does

---

62   On bank directors' duties, see Chapter 3 of this volume.
63   Collective action by dispersed shareholders is difficult even at the level of individual companies. On the limited cooperation between institutional shareholders of UK companies, see B S Black, and J C Jr Coffee, 'Hail Britannia? Institutional investor behavior under limited regulation' (1993–94) 92 *Mich L Rev* 1997. On a sector wide basis, co-ordination would be even more difficult to achieve especially given the increasing fragmentation and internationalisation of share ownership in recent years, On this, see B R Cheffins, 'The Stewardship's Code Achilles Heel' (2010) 73 *MLR* 1004, esp. 1017–23.

not necessarily maximise the aggregate wealth of the shareholders of all systemic banks, as the run of each bank to maximise its profits decreases the overall expected value of the system. This is not to say that any strategy that would be optimal for the shareholders of all systemic banks would necessarily be compatible with the public interest, as the problem of negative externalities caused by bank failures would persist. Rather, it means that financial stability is a public good both for society as a whole, and for the shareholders of systemic banks as a whole. Still, systemic bank shareholders, if capable of co-ordinating, would favour taking more risk than is in the society's interest, but less risk than they tend to accept absent co-ordination.

Therefore, where risk-taking is concerned, banking regulators (representing the **1.35** public interest) and bank shareholders are markedly different. A shareholder-oriented corporate governance system is thus likely to lead to constant pressures on banks' senior management to take on excessive risks. This is not merely a theoretical assertion. Evidence given by major UK banks in Parliament demonstrates that in the years up to the 2007 crisis most active bank shareholders enthusiastically supported further increases in leverage and balance sheet restructurings with a view to increase short-term profits.[64] In addition, performance-based remuneration incentivised bank managers to take very high risks and may thus have contributed to the making of catastrophic strategic decisions that led to the recent financial crisis.[65]

As a result, the prevalent managerial norm of shareholder value maximisation, **1.36** embedded in section 172 (1) of the Companies Act 2006, and practically enforced via performance-based remuneration, the market for corporate control and institutional shareholder activism, leads to banks adopting a risk profile that may seem to be optimal for their shareholders but is detrimental to

---

64 Parliamentary Commission on Banking Standards, *Changing Banking for Good*, see above n 6, paras 326–327. There is also strong empirical evidence that internationally these banks that have more institutional shareholders took higher risks before the crisis and suffered more during the crisis. See D H Erkens, M Hung and P Matos, 'Corporate governance in the 2007–2008 financial crisis: Evidence from financial institutions worldwide' (2012) 18 *Journal of Corporate Finance* 389. Given that institutional shareholders are the main type of shareholder who are risk neutral (unlike block holders who are not diversified) and capable of influencing banks' behaviour (unlike small individual shareholders), this evidence suggests that shareholder pressures have contributed to excessive risk taking.

65 There is empirical evidence that the financial benefits that accrued to the senior managers of failed US banks during the years leading up to the crisis exceed the losses the managers suffered as a result of the collapse of their institutions. See L A Bebchuk, A Cohen and H Spamann, 'The wages of failure: Executive compensation at Bear Sterns and Lehman 2000–2008' (2010) 27 *Yale Journal of Regulation* 257. See also R DeYoung, E Y Peng and M Yan, 'Executive compensation and business policy choices at U.S. Commercial Banks' (2013) 48 *Journal of Financial and Quantitative Analysis* 165.

financial stability.[66] This finding justifies the regulation of risk taking by banks and provides prima facie support to a regulatory approach in dealing with major bank corporate governance problems[67] such as board composition, and executive remuneration.[68]

3. THE LIMITED POTENTIAL OF SHAREHOLDERS AND CREDITORS TO MONITOR RISK TAKING BY BANKS

1.37   Corporate governance structures, such as performance-based remuneration and the market for corporate control, provide senior managers with powerful incentives to take substantial risks in line with the risk appetite of fully diversified shareholders. However, the inadequate design of remuneration packages and the short-term investment horizons of many shareholders can lead to a situation where it is in the personal interest of senior managers to take more risk than fully informed shareholders with a long-term commitment to the company would accept.[69] In theory, the incorporation of long-term prospects into the market price of shares[70] and enhanced monitoring of corporate performance by – at least some of – the institutional shareholders[71] should prevent such a problem from arising at all. In parallel, monitoring by the main providers of debt capital to companies such as bondholders and major creditors also operates as a check on excessive risk-taking especially given the legal position of creditors. In perfect market conditions, monitoring by shareholders and creditors precludes the assumption of a level of risk that is not in the private interests of these groups, as the level of risk taken is fully reflected in the value of companies' shares and bonds and on the interest rates paid by companies to their creditors.[72]

---

66   In that sense, it has been argued that it was not the failure but the *success* of (conventional) corporate governance that led to the recent crisis See N C Howson, 'When "Good" corporate governance makes "Bad" (financial) firms: The global crisis and the limits of private law' (2009) 108 *Mich L Rev* (First Impressions) 44, 49–50.

67   On the importance of the corporate governance framework from the perspective of prudential regulation, see A Kokkinis, 'Rethinking banking prudential regulation: Why corporate governance rules matter?' (2012) 7 *JBL* 612.

68   On these aspects of bank corporate governance see below Chapters 2, 3, 4 and 5 of this volume.

69   This problem has given rise to a much greater emphasis on risk management at board level in recent years. On this, see M T Moore, 'The evolving contours of the board's risk management function in UK corporate governance' (2010) 10 *J Corp L Stud* 279.

70   According to the efficient markets hypothesis, all publicly available information is reflected on the prices of shares. On this, see E Fama, 'Efficient capital markets: A review of theory and empirical work' (1970) 25 *The Journal of Finance* 383.

71   Here I refer to institutional investors who manage their portfolio actively, rather than to passive index funds which invest across the market.

72   In addition, in a perfect market all corporate constituencies would protect themselves against risk-taking by a company. For instance, employees would bargain for a higher salary to compensate themselves for the increased risk of the company failing and them being dismissed.

This section argues that risk-monitoring by market players is unlikely to be **1.38** effective in the case of banks, whose business, assets, capital structure, and regulatory framework is different than that of generic companies. By saying so, I do not purport to imply that in non-financial public companies markets work perfectly efficiently and the level of risk taken is aligned with the interests of all their private constituencies. There is a widespread concern that UK equity markets are permeated by short-termism and investor myopia. This phenomena arguably lead to under-investment in sound long-term projects and to an excessive emphasis on corporate restructurings and portfolio management and possibly perverse incentives to follow excessively risky business or financing strategies.[73] My argument is that banks face essentially the same problems in this regard as all major public companies, but that due to the special nature of the banking sector, these problems are generally more severe in banking than in generic companies. I proceed by first explaining the limits of risk monitoring by bank shareholders, then by bondholders and finally by depositors, who provide the greatest part of bank capital.

A. The limits of shareholder governance of risk taking by banks

To appreciate the limitations of shareholder monitoring of risk-taking by banks **1.39** it is necessary to provide some background on the specific nature of banks' business and assets, namely the so-called opacity of banks' assets. There is some confusion in this area due to the way that the efficient market hypothesis is often misinterpreted.[74] The efficient market hypothesis is a model that purports to provide a generally plausible abstraction of reality and (in its semi-strong version) claims that the prices of shares and other securities reflect publicly available information.[75] It does not claim that market prices reflect the fundamental or inherent value of securities. As there is no way to observe the intrinsic value of a security, we can only conclude ex post facto that at some point in time a security was overvalued. An example of this is the shares of a

---

73   These concerns prompted a BIS consultation and the publication of the influential Kay Review which acknowledges the need to focus on relationships of trust between market players rather than on a trading culture. See BIS, available at: 'A long-term focus for corporate Britain – A call for evidence' (2010), available at: https://www.gov.uk/government/consultations/a-long-term-focus-for-corporate-britain-a-call-for-evidence, accessed 1 January 2014; J Kay, 'The Kay Review of UK equity markets and long-term decision making: Interim Report' (2012), available at: https://www.gov.uk/government/news/kay-review-of-equity-markets-publishes-interim-report, accessed 1 January 2014; and 'The Kay Review of UK equity markets and long-term decision making: Final Report' (2012), available at: https://www.gov.uk/government/news/kay-review-publishes-report-on-uk-financial-sector, accessed 1 January 2014.

74   On the frequent misinterpretation of the hypothesis, see the insightful analysis of R Ball, 'The global financial crisis and the efficient markets hypothesis: What have we learned?' (2009) 21 *Journal of Applied Corporate Finance* 8.

75   For a critical discussion of the hypothesis, see L A Stout, 'The mechanisms of market inefficiency' (2003) 28 *Journal of Corporation Law* 635.

company that engages in fraudulent accounting practices (e.g. Enron[76]) until the fraud is disclosed. Furthermore, there is nothing in the efficient markets hypothesis that implies that past returns on a security will be repeated in the future. The unprecedented movements in share prices during the recent financial crisis do not therefore undermine the validity of the efficient markets hypothesis, but rather suggest that risk in financial markets is non-stationary.[77] Therefore, the extent to which the market price of securities reflects their fundamental value depends on the quality of available information and on the costs investors face to acquire and process information.

i The opacity of banks' assets

1.40 The argument here is that in the case of banks relevant information is more difficult to process than in other companies both by banks themselves in preparing their financial disclosures to the market, and by investors and analysts when they adjust their behaviour subsequent to a disclosure. If this is the case, we may infer that the shares of banks will be more volatile than other shares for a considerable period after a financial crisis,[78] and that there will be scope for banks' senior managers to influence the share prices of banks in normal economic conditions – until the true state of affairs becomes apparent to the market. In the following paragraphs I seek to explain why processing information on banks' financial performance is particularly difficult.

1.41 There is a considerable body of financial literature that focuses on banks and questions whether banks are specific in their market behaviour and governance problems.[79] More recent research highlights the specificity of banks, especially with regard to the opacity (or opaqueness) of their assets and the regulatory

---

76 An academic analysis of the Enron scandal focusing on the limited independence of auditors can be found in D Kershaw, 'Waiting for Enron: The unstable equilibrium of auditor independence regulation' (2006) 33 *Journal of Law and Society* 388.

77 A non-stationary process is a stochastic process whose joint probability distribution is not constant when shifted in time. There is a rich body of relevant mathematical literature, but its examination fall outside the scope of this volume.

78 Indeed, the volatility of bank shares increased sharply since 2008 and has remained at high levels compared to the shares of non-financial companies since then. See e.g. A Atkeson and W E Simon Jr, 'The rising fear in bank stock prices' *The Wall Street Journal* (28 November 2011), available at: http://online.wsj.com/news/articles/SB10001424052970204531404577052493270860130, accessed 1 January 2014.

79 Early American literature on the subject generally viewed banks as not posing any special governance problems. See e.g. A Saunders, E Strock, and N G Travlos, 'Ownership structure, deregulation and bank risk-taking' (1990) 45 *The Journal of Finance* 643; L Allen, and S A Cebenoyan, 'Bank acquisitions and ownership structure: Theory and evidence' (1991) 15 *Journal of Banking and Finance* 425; SD Prowse, 'Alternative methods of corporate control in commercial banks' (1995) *Federal Reserve Bank of Dallas Economic and Financial Policy Review* 3, 24; A J Crawford, J R Ezzell, and J A Miles, 'Bank CEO pay-performance regulations and the effects of deregulation' (1995) 68 *Journal of Business* 231.

framework within which they operate.[80] The reason that banks are more opaque than other companies[81] is that their assets consist primarily of claims against borrowers, and financial instruments. A loan portfolio is far more difficult to value than most other assets, such as manufacturing plants and machinery. Of course, some loans are secured by mortgages or charges so that the bank's claim can be satisfied by selling the collateral in the case of a borrower's default. Still, security does not eliminate the risky nature of loans, since the value of the collateral may not be sufficient to cover the whole claim, especially if there are sharp changes in the relevant market[82] or if accrued interest and penalties have significantly increased the amount of the claim. Furthermore, it is very challenging for an external investor to assess the quality of loans and to predict the rate of defaults, as this depends on the creditworthiness of individual personal and corporate borrowers.

Securitisation of loans and investment banking activities such as proprietary **1.42** trading in various securities[83] on behalf of banks further exacerbates asset opacity. The process of securitisation which became extremely popular until the recent crisis involves a bank selling a number of loans to a special purpose vehicle (a separate company) which then issues debt instruments to investors on the collateral of the income stream from the loans. For instance, asset-backed securities (ABSs) are debt instruments serviced by the cash flows of a discrete pool of fixed or revolving assets (e.g. mortgages, credit cards, student loans, etc). Collateralised debt obligations (CDOs) are structured ABSs, divided into different risk tranches. Senior tranches are to be serviced first so they are in theory safe even if the underlying loans are given to borrowers with low creditworthiness. The complex nature of the securitisation process arising out of packaging together loans of different nature and risk, and the uncertainty with regard to the continuing liability of the originating bank in case of default of the special purpose vehicle (SPV), exacerbate asset opacity as investors are likely to disagree about the value of such instruments. Indeed, Cheng et al found in 2008 that US banks which engaged in securitisation were more opaque

---

80 See e.g. R Levine, 'The corporate governance of banks: A concise discussion of concepts and evidence' (2004) World Bank Policy Research Working Paper 3404, available at: http://elibrary.worldbank.org/doi/book/ 10.1596/1813–9450–3404, accessed 1 January 2014; A Polo, 'The corporate governance of banks: The current state of the debate' (2007), available at: http://ssrn.com/abstract=958796, accessed 1 January 2014; Macy and O'Hara, see above n 58; Ungureanu, see above n 50; D Heremans, 'Corporate governance issues for banks. A financial stability perspective' (2007) University of Leuven Working Paper, available at: http://ssrn.com/ abstract=1024693, accessed 1 January 2014; Mulbert, see above n 54.

81 See Levine, see above n 80, 7–9.

82 The collapse of the US real estate market undermined the value of the collateral banks possessed. This caused a sharp fall in the prices of mortgage-backed securities, which came to be known as toxic assets.

83 These include several types of securities such as derivatives and options. Credit default swaps for instance are contracts whereby the protection buyer makes a series of payments to the protection seller in exchange for a pay-off in the event that the underlying credit instrument, bond or loan, defaults.

than those that did not, and that opacity increased in tandem with the size of securitised assets.[84]

1.43 Given that bank assets are difficult to value, we should expect that in times of financial turmoil, when a substantial number of borrowers default, banks' opacity would deteriorate as banks face a strong incentive to conceal their losses by preserving or refinancing troubled loans rather than calling off the facilities and reporting them as non-serviced loans. Given that banks with troubled assets will not disclose the extent of their losses, the market will – in all likelihood – be unable to distinguish between 'good' and 'bad' banks, and thus it is likely that market confidence in the whole sector will suffer.[85] The hypothesis that bank opacity increases sharply in times of crisis as banks avoid disclosing relevant information on their assets, has found strong empirical support in a recent study by Flannery et al. The study examined bank opacity over a 20-year period and confirmed that during the recent financial crisis the opacity of bank assets increased to a level that is unique to the banking sector.[86] This evidence provides formal support for the widespread view that the distrust among banks about the quality of their assets during the crisis indicates that 'even banks themselves find it difficult to assess the riskiness of other banks accurately'.[87]

1.44 Although it is uncontroversial to say that banks are generally much more opaque than generic companies in times of crisis, whether banks are always particularly opaque is an empirical question that has yet to be settled. A number of studies have failed to find any significant difference between banks and other companies in normal economic conditions.[88] However, several other studies confirm that bank opacity is a pervasive feature of the sector at all times and not only in times of crisis.[89] Each study uses a different methodology to measure

---

84 The study covers the period before the onset of the crisis. See M Cheng, D Dhaliwal and M Neamtiu, 'Banks' Asset securitisation and information opacity' (2008) University of Southern California Working Paper, available at: http://www.usc.edu/schools/business/FBE/seminars/papers/ARF_5–2-08_NEAMTIU.pdf, accessed 1 January 2014.

85 This is a type of market failure conventionally described as a 'market for lemons' whereby products of the lower quality prevail because of the inability of customers to distinguish between high- and low-quality products.

86 See M J Flannery, S H Kwan, and M Nimalendran, 'The 2007–09 financial crisis and bank opaqueness' (2010) Federal Reserve Bank of San Francisco Working Paper 2010–27, available at: http://www.frbsf.org/economic-research/files/wp10–27bk.pdf, accessed 1 January 2014.

87 See Mulbert, above note 54, 11.

88 See e.g. M J Flannery, S H Kwan, and M Nimalendran, 'Market evidence on the opaqueness of banking firms' assets' (2004) 71 *Journal of Financial Economics* 419; 'The 2007–09 financial crisis and bank opaqueness' see above n 86.

89 Morgan found that credit rating agencies were more likely to disagree on the rating of bonds issued by banks than by other companies between 1983 and 1993. See D P Morgan, 'Rating banks: Risk and uncertainty in an opaque industry' (2002) 92 *American Economic Review* 874. The same was found with respect to European banks in the period 1993–2003 by Iannota. See G O Iannotta, 'Testing for opaqueness in the European banking industry: Evidence from bond credit ratings' (2006) 30 *Journal of Financial Services Research* 287. In addition,

asset opacity (which cannot be observed directly) such as the disagreement amongst credit rating agencies on the rating of bonds issued by banks,[90] and the likelihood of analysts' forecasts errors. On balance, the opacity of banks' assets is generally accepted by the relevant literature[91] as one of the main components of bank specificity. From the perspective of the argument here, it is sufficient that available evidence supports the proposition that banks' assets are intrinsically opaque. It may be true that in normal economic conditions market confidence reduces the degree of disagreement between market players about the value of bank assets, and hence reduces observable opacity,[92] but the sharp increase of observable opacity in times of crisis shows that bank assets are intrinsically difficult to value.

ii.   The effect of asset opacity on risk-monitoring by bank shareholders

The opacity of banks' assets severely limits the effectiveness of market discipline **1.45** of risk-taking by banks for the following reason. Since equity investors are not capable of assessing the real value of the assets in banks' balance sheets based on available information, the prices at which banks' shares trade does not reflect this, but rather mostly reflect the profits made by banks and the dividends paid. Indeed, there is evidence that in the years leading up to the recent financial crisis investors did not appreciate that the increased returns on bank equities were achieved by increasing leverage and taking on more risk.[93] It follows that banks were not punished by a higher cost of capital as a result of increased risk-taking. In other words, increasing leverage and engaging in risky activities were virtually costless for banks. It is evident that in such conditions, the senior managers of large banks faced a powerful incentive to follow risky strategies in

---

Iannota and Navone found that between 1990 and 2000 US banks were more likely to suffer abrupt negative changes in their share prices (crashes) than other companies. See G Iannota and M A Navone, 'Crashes and bank opaqueness' (2009) Universita Luigi Bocconi CAREFIN Research Paper No. 20/09, available at: http://papers.ssrn.com/sol3/papers.cfm?abstract_id=1600190, accessed 1 January 2014. Consistent with the hypothesis that banks are more opaque than other companies are the findings of Haggard and Howe that the shares of banks incorporate less firm-specific information than other companies of similar characteristics. See K S Haggard and J S Howe, 'Are banks opaque?' (2007) University of Southern Mississippi Working Paper, available at: http://www.scribd.com/doc/156507098/Haggard-Stephen-K-John-S-Howe-2007-Are-Banks-Opaque-Jan-11-41-Pp, accessed 1 January 2014.

90   The use of split credit ratings as a proxy for asset opacity has been criticised by Hauck and Neyer. See A Hauck and U Neyer, 'Are rating splits a useful indicator for the opacity of an industry?' (2008) Heinrich-Heine-University of Düsseldorf Economics Finance, and Taxation Discussion Paper No. 3/2008, available at: http://papers.ssrn.com/sol3/papers.cfm?abstract_id=2103169, accessed 1 January 2014.

91   See above n 80.

92   Before the recent crisis market confidence in banks was also supported by the implied government support that large systemic institutions enjoyed.

93   From 2002 to 2007 large global banks raised their dividends on average by 15 per cent per annum. At the same time investors did not price correctly the greater risks taken by banks until the crisis began. On this, see M R King, 'The cost of equity for global banks: a CAPM perspective from 1990 to 2009' (2009) (September) *BIS Quarterly Review* 56, 70–71.

order to earn the highest possible performance-based remuneration. Thus, far from acting as a constraint on risk-taking, the capital market facilitated a level of risk,[94] which fully informed investors would not have sanctioned without demanding an appropriate risk premium.[95]

1.46 A connected problem is that, since the assets of banks cannot be accurately valued by the investors, senior managers can easily manipulate banks' financial results and hence manage their share prices. This enables them to reach targets set by their remuneration contracts and entrench themselves in their positions. At this point it is essential to clarify that the argument here does not suggest that senior managers of UK banks have been engaging in unlawful market abuse, which carries criminal and civil penalties.[96] Rather, the point is that, given the asset opacity explored above, it can be expected that bank managers will tend to engage in borderline practices of managing financial announcements and strategically forming corporate policy in order to influence a bank's share price. Indeed, there is considerable empirical evidence that in the years leading up to the crisis banks (and other companies) resorted to securitisation at carefully selected points in time, when their earnings were low, to prevent a fall in their share prices.[97] There is also strong evidence that banks can manage the

---

94 One additional way in which banks can take excessive risk is by expanding their assets via irresponsible lending. This was particularly easy in the early- to mid-2000s in part due to the favourable general market conditions and low interest rates.

95 Jones et al observed a feedback effect in the share prices of banks between 2000 and 2006. This means that risky banks were rewarded with higher equity values and hence other banks were encouraged to invest in risky and more opaque assets. See J S Jones, W W Lee and T J Yeager, 'Valuation and systemic risk consequences of bank opacity' (2013) 37 *Journal of Banking & Finance* 693.

96 The modern UK regime is based on EU law. Sections 52 and 53 of the Criminal Justice Act 1993 implemented the Insider Dealing Directive. See Council Directive 89/592/EEC of 13 November 1989 coordinating regulations on insider dealing [1989] OJ L334/30. Further amendments to the UK regulatory framework were introduced in compliance with the Market Abuse Directive (MAD), including new section 118 of the Financial Services and Market Act (FSMA) 2000, which identifies seven types of prohibited behaviour. See Directive 2003/6/EC of the European Parliament and of the Council of 28 January 2003 on insider dealing and market manipulation (market abuse) [2003] OJ L96/16. There are several English and European cases clarifying the test to be used, see e.g. *Winterflood Securities Ltd v The Financial Services Authority* [2010] EWCA Civ 423; Case C-45/08 *Spector Photo Group NV and Chris Van Raemdonck v Commissie voor het Bank,-Financie-en Assurantiewezen (CBFA)* [2010] OJ C-51/6. On the effect of MAD see J L Hansen, 'Insider dealing after the market abuse directive' in D Prentice and A Reisberg (eds) *Corporate Finance in the UK and EU* (OUP 2011).

97 See P M Dechow and C Shakespeare, 'Do managers time securitization transactions to obtain accounting benefits?' (2006), available at: http://papers.ssrn.com/sol3/papers.cfm?abstract_id=928741, accessed 1 January 2014. In addition, the same authors found that CEO pay sensitivity to securitizations is high thus allowing for a perverse incentive to manage the timing of the transactions. See P M Dechow, L A Myers and C Shakespeare, 'Fair value accounting and gains from asset securitizations: A convenient earnings management tool with compensation side-benefits' (2010) 49 *Journal of Accounting and Economics* 2.

information content of their periodic financial disclosures and hence influence the price of their shares without being noticed by investors and analysts.[98]

Overall, the preceding discussion establishes that equity market discipline on risk-taking by banks is severely limited as potential equity investors cannot accurately value banks' assets and assess the risks taken by banks. This phenomenon enables bank senior managers to take excessive risks and manage the share price by appropriately tailoring financial disclosures and balance sheet restructurings. I therefore argue that in banks shareholder agency costs are higher than in non-financial companies. Taking into account the opacity of banks' assets discussed above, it is evident that it is more difficult for bank shareholders to monitor senior management and protect themselves against excessive risk taking. **1.47**

B. The limits of bondholder monitoring of risk taking by banks

Generally, creditor governance is a substantial check on risk-taking by companies, as creditors demand higher interest rates to advance credit to companies that take higher risks. Covenants in loan facilities also serve a governance function in generic companies with regard to their business activities and risk profile.[99] In the context of banks, it is necessary to distinguish between two main types of creditors, namely depositors and bondholders. Bonds are debt securities issued by banks that are traded on a regulated market. For regulatory purposes, it is common practice for bonds to be subordinated to the ordinary creditors of banks (depositors) so that they can serve as loss absorbing capital. Reference to bonds will thus imply subordinated bonds that rank after the claims of depositors. Depositors are the beneficiaries of bank accounts and their potential monitoring role will be explored in the following part. **1.48**

Bondholders have a rational incentive to monitor risk-taking by banks and to demand higher interest rates to compensate for increased risk-taking. Indeed, bondholders' attitudes to risk is markedly different than that of the shareholders, as creditors risk losing their investment in the event of failure, but have nothing to gain if a bank does exceptionally well. Faith in bondholder governance is reinforced by the fact that investors in bonds are usually professional **1.49**

---

98 In particular, a US study found that quarterly disclosure of impaired loans was only meaningful in quarters that banks were examined by regulators. See A Ashcraft and H Bleakley, 'On the market discipline of informationally opaque firms: Evidence from bank borrowers in the federal funds market' (2006) Federal Reserve Bank of New York Staff Report 257, available at: http://www.newyorkfed.org/research/staff_reports/sr257.html, accessed 1 January 2014.

99 In term loans to commercial companies banks typically include covenants that restrict the freedom of the borrower to change its business or enter into substantial transactions without the approval of the bank.

funds with a reasonable level of expertise and a substantial investment size that allows for monitoring expenditure. Indeed, in recent years banks have been encouraged to use subordinated debt (bonds) as an additional tier of capital and it has been contemplated that market discipline would complement supervision by public authorities.[100] In particular, if risk-taking by banks was accurately reflected in the interest rates they paid on bonds (and on the prices at which bonds trade on the secondary market), banks would be discouraged from taking excessive risks, and a clear signal would be given to regulators at once that a bank was perceived by the market as highly risky.[101]

1.50 However, the opacity of banks' assets limits the potential of the capital market to price accurately the bonds issued by banks and thus exposes bondholders to the same risk of managerial opportunism. The preceding analysis on bank opacity and the evidence examined in the previous section is also relevant from the perspective of bondholders. If the market cannot distinguish between more and less risky banks, then both shareholders and bondholders are unable to assess the riskiness of their investment and the return they demand will not reflect the level of risk taken by the issuing bank. In particular, as noted above, empirical studies on bank opacity confirm that in the case of bonds issued by banks credit rating agencies are more likely to disagree on their ratings than in bond issues by other companies.[102]

1.51 To be sure, I do not purport to claim that bond market discipline is obsolete in the case of banks. The bond market provides a degree of discipline and reflects available information on banks' riskiness.[103] However, as explained in the previous section, information on the quality of bank assets is more difficult to process and verify, and banks tend to withhold relevant information in times of crisis. Bank opacity thus diminishes the disciplinary effect of the bond market especially with regard to bond issues where credit ratings agencies produce split ratings.[104]

---

100 The emphasis on market discipline until the crisis was reflected in Basel II. Currently, subordinated debt can qualify as Tier 2 capital. See Basel Committee on Banking Supervision, 'Basel III: A global regulatory framework for more resilient banks and banking systems' (Rev edn, 2011) para 58.

101 This is an example of enrolling private parties to perform regulatory functions as part of modern reflexive regulatory techniques. On this, see J Black, 'Paradoxes and failures: New governance techniques and the financial crisis' (2012) 75 *MLR* 1037.

102 See above paras 1.40–1.44. See also Morgan, above n 89.

103 See N Esho and others, 'Market discipline and subordinated debt of Australian banks' (2005) Australian Prudential Regulation Authority Working Paper, available at: http://www.apra.gov.au/AboutAPRA/Research/Documents/Market-Discipline-and-Subordinated-Debt-of-Australian-Banks-October-2005.pdf, accessed 1 January 2014.

104 See D P Morgan and K J Stiroh, 'Bond market discipline of banks: Is the market tough enough?' (1999) Federal Reserve Bank of New York Staff Report 95/1999, 13–14, available at: http://www.newyorkfed.org/research/staff_reports/sr95.html, accessed 1 January 2014.

Furthermore, risk-monitoring by bondholders is weakened as a result of the **1.52** perception of an implied government guarantee in the case of bonds issued by large banks.[105] Although bonds are not protected by deposit insurance schemes, the market may perceive very big banks as being 'too-big-to-fail' and thus expect that they will be rescued by the government if they face financial difficulties. Indeed, in the UK the government recapitalised and rescued the Royal Bank of Scotland and Lloyds Banking Group at a very high cost to UK taxpayers of approximately £51bn,[106] but – unlike shareholders – bondholders did not lose their investments.

Of course, forthcoming regulatory reforms at the EU level aim to restore **1.53** market discipline on banks by ensuring that the private creditors of banks, especially bondholders, stand to lose their investment if a bank fails. In the UK, the Financial Services Act 2010, which amended the Financial Services and Markets Act 2000, has already introduced a requirement for regulated institutions to draft recovery and resolution plans, also known as living wills.[107] Recovery plans aim to facilitate the rescue of the business of a troubled financial company as a going concern to avoid systemic contagion which may be triggered by a failure. Resolution plans aim to ensure an orderly winding-up in the event of failure in order to minimise systemic disruption.[108] Recovery and resolution plans are to be evaluated by the PRA and, if found inadequate, the institution must take any appropriate steps to amend them. In parallel, a fourth stabilisation option, namely bail-in stabilisation, will shortly be added in the Banking Act 2009 framework as a result of the Financial Services (Banking Reform) Act 2013.[109]

The forthcoming Recovery and Resolution Directive (RRD)[110] will emphasise **1.54** the use of debt capital as a means to absorb bank losses in advance of using public funds, thus implementing relevant international standards.[111] It is

---

105   Ibid., 14–15.

106   On the cost of the recent crisis to the UK Government, see above para 1.22 and n 49.

107   Section 7 of the Financial Services Act 2010 introduces ss 139B–139F into FSMA 2000.

108   A discussion of the complex issues arising out of the resolution of systemic banks can be found in S Claessens, R J Herring and D Schoenmaker, 'A safer world financial system: Improving the resolution of systemic institutions' (Centre for Economic Policy Research, 2010).

109   Section 2 of Sch 2 to the Act will insert ss 12A and 12B into the Banking Act 2009 when it comes into force.

110   In December 2013 representatives of the European Parliament and Council reached prima facie agreement on a Recovery and Resolution Directive. The EU authorities intend the Directive to come into force on 1 January 2015 and the bail-in system to apply from 1 January 2016. See European Parliament News, 'Deal reached on bank bail-in directive' (12/12/2013), available at: http://www.europarl.europa.eu/news/en/news-room/content/20131212IPR30702/html/Deal-reached-on-bank-%E2%80%9Cbail-in-directive%E2%80%9D, accessed 1 January 2014.

111   International resolution standards were drafted by the FSB and endorsed by G-20 leaders in 2011. See Financial Stability Board, 'Key attributes of effective resolution regimes for financial institutions' (2011), available at: https://www.financialstabilityboard.org/publications/r_111104cc.htm, accessed 1 April 2014.

envisaged that at the stage of recovery any contingent convertible bonds banks have issued will be turned into equity. Then, at the resolution stage the bail-in procedure seeks to limit the extent of the use of public funds.[112] The shareholders and bondholders will be the first to lose their investment before any public money is used to rescue the ailing bank, at least until 8 per cent of the bank's assets are lost. Conversely, depositors with funds in excess of £85,000 would be affected only after the use of the money available at the bank-funded resolution fund, which is expected to reach 1 per cent of covered deposits until 2025. These forthcoming reforms have already undermined the perception of an implied government guarantee on bonds issued by banks, and may in the future effectively tackle this aspect of the problem,[113] but will still not affect the fundamental problem of bank asset opacity identified above.

1.55 To sum up, the preceding analysis shows why bondholders are not fully capable of monitoring risk-taking by banks, and are not in the same position as bank managers to access and process relevant information due to bank opacity. The wealth of bondholders, therefore, depends on bank managers, since bondholders cannot adequately protect themselves by contract. It can be argued thus that the interest rates paid by the banks on their bonds do not adequately reflect their risk profile.[114] A principal-agent relationship between bondholders and bank managers can therefore be established.[115]

C. The very limited risk-monitoring by depositors

1.56 The depositors of UK banks cannot be relied on to perform an effective risk-monitoring function because of the combined effect of three factors. First, depositors lack the necessary expertise to process relevant information on the level of risk taken by banks. Retail depositors, especially, are in a very weak

---

112   On the future implementation of bail-ins in the UK, see the speech given by the director of the Special Resolution Unit of the Bank of England: A Gracie, 'A practical process for implementing a bail-in resolution power' (British Bankers' Association, London, 17 September 2012), available at: http://www.bankof england.co.uk/publications/Documents/speeches/2012/speech600.pdf, accessed 1 April 2014.

113   A critical discussion of special resolution regimes can be found in C Hadjiemmanuil, 'Special resolution regimes for banking institutions: Objectives and limitations' in W-G Ringe and P M Huber (eds), *Legal Challenges in the Global Financial Crisis* (Hart Publishing 2014). Hadjiemmanuil highlights the inconsistency between: on the one hand the policy objective of reducing moral hazard by ensuring that shareholders and debtholders suffer losses; and, on the other, the objective of reducing contagion when a crisis occurs, which militates against imposing losses to debtholders as doing so undermines investor confidence in other banks within the same financial system.

114   Bank creditors can thus be said to have incomplete contract, like shareholders. The concept of incomplete contracts was introduced by Williamson. See O E Williamson, *Markets and Hierarchies: Analysis and Antitrust Implications: A Study in the Economics of Internal Organization* (Collier Macmillan 1975).

115   On the role of bondholders, see also K J Hopt, 'Corporate governance of banks after the financial crisis' in E Wymeersch, K J Hopt and G Ferranini (eds), *Financial Regulation and Supervision: A post-crisis analysis* (OUP 2012).

position to process relevant information as they are unsophisticated individuals who lack an adequate understanding of the banking sector and of financial reporting.[116] Large companies are in a slightly better position than individuals and small businesses, but still evaluating the creditworthiness of a bank falls outside the ability of most corporate officers. In addition, companies seek to raise loans from banks, and hence the willingness of banks to advance credit is the major determinant of their choice of the main bank of a company, rather than the assessment of the bank's soundness.

Second, depositors are in a relatively weak bargaining position vis-à-vis banks **1.57** and therefore it is difficult for them to demand a higher interest rate if they think that a bank is more risky. The retail banking market in the UK is oligopolistic and despite fierce competition to attract depositors the practical difficulties of moving one's accounts from one bank to another, combined with the feeling of loyalty that many depositors have for their banks raises an additional obstacle to the operation of market discipline.[117] Creditor self-help measures such as adjusting the interest rates, demanding security, drafting appropriate covenants and monitoring debtors work well for banks as the major creditors of businesses and individuals, but are not available to depositors who are unsecured, inexpert and relatively badly resourced.

The third and most decisive factor that neutralises depositor monitoring is **1.58** deposit insurance by the UK Financial Services Compensation Scheme.[118] Given the immunity of most depositors from bank failures, it follows that their incentives to monitor banks are very weak, especially if it is taken into account that processing the relevant information is costly and time consuming. Even depositors who hold large deposits can still structure their portfolio so as to be fully covered, as the maximum limit of £85,000 applies to accounts held with each separately licensed banking group. In addition, given that depositors need

---

116 A review of the literature on the inability of depositors to monitor banks and its implications can be found in J A C Santos, 'Bank capital regulation in contemporary banking theory: A review of the literature' (2001) 10 *Financial Markets, Institutions & Instruments* 41, 46–52.

117 On this, see Treasury Committee, 'Competition and choice in retail banking' (HC 2010–11, 612-I). The report finds that the retail banking market is particularly concentrated as more than 90 per cent of current accounts are held with the five largest banks (para 47). Although market concentration does not necessarily indicate limited competition, the committee considered that – on the balance of evidence – competition in the retail banking market is limited (paras 49–50).

118 Since 31 December 2010, the coverage limit has been raised to the equivalent in pounds of €100,000 i.e. £85,000 in compliance with EU law. See Directive 2009/14/EC of the European Parliament and of the Council of 11 March 2009 amending Directive 94/19/EC on deposit-guarantee schemes as regards the coverage level and the pay-out delay, Article 1. The amount is payable in full for each account (or set of accounts) or other eligible non-equity investment in a separately licensed bank to natural persons and small companies. Until December 2010 the coverage limit was £50,000 and until October 2008 it was £35,000. It is interesting to note that until October 2007 depositors could only claim 90 per cent of the sum between £2,000 and £35,000 so the maximum payoff could reach £31,700.

not worry about the creditworthiness of banks, they face a perverse incentive to place their funds with riskier banks which can pay higher interest rates (as they are more profitable), rather than with prudent banks. It follows that far from acting as a constraint on risk taking, market pressures in this context actually encourage increased risk taking as a means to attract depositors.

1.59 The inability of depositors to monitor risk-taking by banks would seem to support the finding that they are susceptible to suffering managerial agency costs, similarly to bondholders. However, deposit protection and government intervention insulates (most) depositors from managerial agency costs and transfers these costs to the public. It follows that while bondholders stand to bear the costs of managerial opportunism directly, depositors are protected from bank failures and, instead, it is the taxpayers who stand to suffer from excessive risk-taking in the banking sector.

4. THE EFFECT OF BANK OPACITY ON THE CORE PROBLEM OF THE MISALIGNMENT BETWEEN THE PUBLIC INTEREST AND CONVENTIONAL CORPORATE GOVERNANCE

1.60 Bringing together the findings of Section 3 on the externalities caused by running banks with a view to profit maximisation and of the present section, it must be emphasised that the argument advanced in that section does not depend on the finding here that banks are more opaque than other companies. One may therefore inquire what does the previous evidence on the limited ability of bank shareholders and creditors to monitor risk-taking add to the chapter. I will seek to explain that bank opacity and the absence of effective risk monitoring is relevant from the perspective of the problem of externalities in a number of ways.

1.61 First, bank opacity serves to explain the persistence of systemic risk that affects the banking industry.[119] One of the main reasons that the failure of one major institution is likely to undermine the soundness of other institutions is that since banks are opaque, both equity and debt investors cannot distinguish between sound and problematic banks. As a result, at times of crisis they lose their confidence in the banking system as a whole thus prompting depositors' runs, liquidity shortages and making it difficult for banks to raise additional share capital during a crisis.

---

119   On this, see above paras 1.25–1.26

Second, the finding that risk-monitoring by bank shareholders and creditors is **1.62** ineffective demonstrates that the misalignment identified in Section 3 is a very serious one. Even if market discipline ensured that equity and debt providers were fully compensated for the risk taken by banks, systemic risk[120] would still lead to bank failures causing negative externalities on the shareholders and creditors of other banks. However, the limited ability of bank shareholders and creditors to restrain risk-taking by bank managers, combined with the incentives the latter face to take excessive risks, means that banks take more risk than fully informed investors would accept. It follows that the profit maximisation norm leads to the assumption of a level of risk that is excessive even from the perspective of banks' shareholders and creditors and is far higher than the level of risk that is socially desirable. Indeed, as shown in the following section, the bank failures that caused the recent financial crisis can be partly attributed to excessive risk-taking encouraged by the urge to maximise short-term profitability. In this sense, bank opacity strengthens the finding of Section 3 that the current corporate governance regime undermines financial stability.[121]

Third, the deep-rooted causes of bank opacity that go beyond the availability of **1.63** information and include the inability of investors to process relevant information suggest that the misalignment between the current corporate governance paradigm and financial stability cannot be effectively tackled by reinforcing market discipline. The previous analysis shows that the introduction of further regulatory requirements to disclose more information[122] would be unlikely to materially increase the risk monitoring potential of bank shareholders and bondholders.[123] It follows that reliance on market discipline to alleviate the financial stability consequences of risk-taking and profit-seeking by banks is misguided and unlikely to achieve its purpose. This finding supports the need for a direct regulatory approach to tackle this problem.[124]

---

120 It should be kept in mind that opacity is not the only cause of systemic risk and hence it would exist even if banks were no more opaque than other companies.

121 Even authors who argue that market-based corporate governance mechanisms operated well during the recent crisis, accept that in the case of banks there have been corporate governance failures. See e.g. B R Cheffins, 'Did corporate governance "fail" during the 2008 Stock Market meltdown? The case of the S&P 500' (2009) ECGI Law Working Paper No. 124/2009, available at: http://papers.ssrn.com/sol3/papers.cfm?abstract_id= 1396126, accessed 1 January 2014.

122 Existing requirements are set out in Regulation (EU) No 575/2013 of the European Parliament and of the Council of 26 June 2013 on prudential requirements for credit institutions and investment firms and amending Regulation (EU) No 648/2012 [2013] OJ L176/1, arts 431–455.

123 On this see E Avgouleas, 'The global financial crisis and the disclosure paradigm in European financial regulation: The case for reform' (2009) 6 *European Company and Financial Law Review* 440.

124 Another complication is caused by the fact that increased transparency of bank assets, even if feasible, can potentially undermine financial stability if a number of large banks have suffered losses. In this sense, it is arguable that bank opacity is a threat to financial stability because of its ex ante effects on market discipline, but simultaneously transparency can threaten financial stability ex post when a crisis is on the verge of erupting.

1.64 Fourth, the finding that the current regime, although apparently focused on shareholder value maximisation, does not actually lead to this outcome, as it allows a level of risk-taking that is excessive for bank shareholders and creditors, further supports the case for regulating risk-taking by banks, as it defeats the potential objection that regulation is value decreasing for bank shareholders. Regulating risk-taking by banks would benefit shareholders by preventing senior managers from taking risks that are excessive from the shareholders' point of view, but would come at the cost of leading to a level of risk that is lower than the one preferred by perfectly informed and co-ordinating shareholders.

5. TOWARDS A REGULATORY APPROACH TO BANK CORPORATE GOVERNANCE

1.65 The preceding analysis suggests that a regulatory approach to bank corporate governance, as a complement to tougher capital standards and better crisis management tools, is the best available option to reform the area. Indeed, the vital importance of bank corporate governance reforms has become widely accepted in policy-making and regulatory circles in recent years and a number of reform initiatives in the UK and EU have already radically changed the landscape of bank corporate governance, as will be illustrated in the following paragraphs. Still, these reforms fall short of fundamentally changing the existing shareholder-centric and facilitative nature of bank corporate governance and therefore further reform is necessary.

A. The recent regulatory interventions to bank corporate governance

1.66 An integral part of the international regulatory response to the recent financial crisis was a series of reforms in bank corporate governance beginning with the publication of the Principles for Enhancing Corporate Governance in late 2010.[125] Although significant in achieving a degree of international convergence in the area, the recommendations did not add much to the UK bank corporate governance regime, as most of these requirements were already in place here, subsequent to the Walker Review Recommendations and the latest revision of the UK Corporate Governance Code. The Principles focus on effective boards, sound risk management, executive remuneration, the simplification of group structures and transparency. They are modelled on the OECD

---

125 See Working Group on Corporate Governance of the Basel Committee, *Principles for Enhancing Corporate Governance* (Nouy Daniele et al, Bank of International Settlements 2010).

Principles of Corporate Governance[126] which apply generally to listed companies. Indeed, apart from their emphasis on risk management evinced in the requirements for a board risk committee, a Chief Risk Officer and the scrutiny of new products and mergers, the Basel Principles do not differentiate bank corporate governance from the governance of ordinary non-financial companies.

From the point of view of this chapter, the most notable contribution of the **1.67** Principles is that they illustrate the attitude of major regulators worldwide on bank corporate governance. First, it is acknowledged that corporate governance is 'of great relevance'[127] both at the micro-level of individual banks and at the macro-level of the stability of financial systems, since it can provide proper incentives to bank controllers, facilitate supervision and foster market confidence. Secondly, the recent crisis is seen as partly due to governance failures, since poor governance is liable to lead both to individual banks' failures and to wider problems, due to the loss of confidence in the financial markets.[128] Thirdly, great emphasis is placed on the role of supervisors[129] who are expected to evaluate the corporate governance structures of individual banks, including the expertise and integrity of prospective directors and senior managers, and to have formal powers to take remedial action, should the governance of a bank be judged to be defective.

Perhaps the most striking example of the incipient regulatory encroachment of **1.68** bank corporate governance is the regulation of the structure of senior executive remuneration under the CRD IV framework.[130] Broadly speaking, variable pay cannot exceed 100 per cent of fixed remuneration,[131] unless the shareholders of a bank approve a higher rate, which cannot exceed 200 per cent of fixed remuneration.[132] In parallel, the Directive allows Member States to allow banks

---

126 The Principles were last revised in April 2004 and are at the time of writing under review. See Organisation for Economic Co-operation and Development, 'OECD Principles of Corporate Governance' (2004), available at: http://www.oecd.org/corporate/oecdprinciplesofcorporategovernance.htm, accessed 1 April 2014.

127 See Principles for enhancing corporate governance, see above n 125, 1–2.

128 Ibid., 5.

129 Ibid., 30–32.

130 A critical evaluation of the impact of CRD IV on bank corporate governance can be found in J Winter, 'The financial crisis: Does good corporate governance matter and how to achieve it?' in Wymeersch, Hopt and Ferranini (eds), *Financial Regulation and Supervision*, see above n 115, especially paras 12.19–12.33.

131 See CRD IV, art 94(1)(g)(i) and PRA Handbook SYSC 19A.3.44.

132 See CRD IV, art 94(1)(g)(ii) and PRA Handbook SYSC 19A.3.44A-C. The procedure to be followed for shareholders to approve a higher variable component (up to 200 per cent of fixed pay) is the following: all shareholders must be given a reasonable notice period in advance of the relevant meeting and must be provided with a detailed statement by the institution on the impact of the proposed increase of variable pay on the bank's ability to maintain a sound capital base. In addition, the resolution approving the increase must be passed by at least 66 per cent of the share capital provided that at least 50 per cent of the shares are represented at the

to apply a discount rate to up to 25 per cent of total variable remuneration[133] provided that it is paid in instruments that are deferred for at least five years in accordance with guidelines to be published by the EBA. The draft guidelines published by the EBA take into account four factors to calculate the discount rate, namely the national inflation rate, the average interest rate paid on EU sovereign bonds, the length of the deferral period and any additional retention period requirement.[134]

1.69 In addition, CRD IV introduced several mandatory rules regulating the structure of bank boards. The Directive's approach to the functioning of bank boards is based on the uncontroversial acceptance of five general principles, namely: sufficient collective knowledge; time commitment; adequate resources; diversity; and honesty.[135] Crucially, CRD IV precludes banks from combining the positions of CEO and chairman of the board without the consent of the regulator,[136] and requires nomination committees to consist exclusively of non-executive directors.[137] Although these requirements coincide with the existing recommendations of the Corporate Governance Code[138] and – to a large extent – with the actual practice of UK banks,[139] the juridification of the relevant rules from comply-or-explain soft law (enforceable via market pressure) to regulatory standards is noticeable. Furthermore, CRD IV imposes a cap on parallel board appointments to the effect that the same person cannot hold more than: either one executive and two non-executive appointments; or four non-executive appointments.[140] Appointments at non-for-profit organisations and charities are excluded from the cap,[141] and competent regulators are given the discretion to allow bank directors to hold one additional non-executive position.[142]

1.70 In parallel, the recent Financial Services (Banking Reform) Act 2013 will – as soon as fully implemented – overhaul the approved persons' regime for bank

---

meeting, or by 75 per cent of the share capital. Any shareholders who are affected by the decision (e.g. directors or managers of the bank) are disqualified from voting.

133   CRD IV, article 94 (1) (g) (iii) and PRA Handbook SYSC 19A.3.44D.
134   See EBA, 'Draft Guidelines on the applicable notional discount rate for variable remuneration under Article 94(1)(g)(iii) of Directive 2013/36/EU' (2013) EBA/CP/2013/40.
135   See CRD IV, art 91(1), (2) and (7)–(9).
136   CRD IV, art 88(1)(e).
137   CRD IV, art 88(2).
138   See UK Corporate Governance Code, paras A.2.1 and B.2.1 respectively.
139   All major UK banks operate fully independent nominations committees, and have a separate board chairman and CEO, although board chairmen are not always independent, the most notable example being the case of HSBC.
140   The cap will be effective on 1 July 2014. See CRD IV, art 91(3).
141   CRD IV, art 91(5).
142   CRD IV, art 91(6).

directors.[143] Traditionally, UK regulatory authorities took a light-hand approach towards the 'fit and proper' test for bank directors and senior managers and generally relied on banks' judgement for the suitability of key persons, and only focused on the honesty and integrity of proposed candidates. This approach started to change subsequent to the recent crisis, when regulators adopted a more inquisitive and pro-active stance emphasising the competence of proposed bank directors as much as their honesty.[144] The recent legislative change will further reinforce the substantial role of regulators in ensuring that bank boards are appropriately structured and composed thus marking the departure from the orthodox market-based approach to corporate governance.

B. A broader reconceptualisation of bank corporate governance

Despite these reforms, the shareholder-centric character of bank corporate governance persists through the substantial remaining components of variable remuneration, the pressures from the market for corporate control and institutional shareholders, and the application of directors' duties on banks in the same manner as in generic companies. In the same vein, most scholars still perceive bank corporate governance as synonymous to an exercise of aligning the interests of senior managers to the interests of dispersed shareholders,[145] thus obfuscating the potential complementarity between a regulatory approach to corporate governance and other aspects of prudential regulation. **1.71**

The argument here is that it is necessary to revisit the theoretical understanding of bank corporate governance under the prism of a regulatory approach as a necessary prerequisite to the successful implementation of existing bank corporate governance reforms and to the future development of the area. Indeed, a regulatory model of bank corporate governance would serve as a clear theoretical basis and practical guide for regulators to discharge their new functions on executive remuneration and the approved persons' regime. Furthermore, it would serve as the basis for a radical reform of banks' corporate objective and directors' duties to reflect the change of focus from profit maximisation to entity preservation. **1.72**

---

143   Part 4 of the Act will amend the FSMA 2000 (ss 18–35) and introduce a new criminal offence for bank senior managers (ss 36–38).

144   A detailed discussion of the evolution of the fit and proper test until early 2012 can be found in A Kokkinis, 'The reformed "fit and proper" test: A call for a broader rethink of bank corporate governance?' (2012) 9 *ICR* 5.

145   For instance, White reviews the interplay between corporate governance and financial regulation and assumes that corporate governance necessarily aims to protect the interest of the shareholders. He thus concludes the achievement of regulatory objectives requires a worsening of bank corporate governance. See L J White, 'Corporate governance and prudential regulation of banks: is there any connection?' in J R Barth, C Lin and C Wihlborg (eds), *Research Handbook on International Banking and Governance* (Edward Elgar 2012).

1.73 The main characteristics of a regulatory approach to bank corporate governance would be the change of focus from serving the private interests of shareholders to protecting the public interest in financial stability, and the abandonment of reliance on shareholders and market discipline in favour of regulatory supervision of governance structures. Since the unqualified pursuit of profit is incompatible with safeguarding financial stability, it follows that a regulatory approach would have to lexically prioritise the preservation of financial stability in the public interest over the maximisation of profits for the benefit of banks' shareholders.

6. CONCLUSION

1.74 This chapter sought to provide an overview of the corporate governance problems faced by banks. In doing so, the discussion focused on several widely accepted economic characteristics of banks, which are unique to the sector, especially the extremely high leverage, systemic risk, and the crucial importance of the sector to the economy as a whole, and the opacity of banks' assets.

1.75 The main finding is that running banks with a view to profit maximisation under the current private ordering corporate governance paradigm creates negative externalities in the form of undermining financial stability. In parallel, the opacity of banks limits the ability of bank shareholders and bondholders to monitor risk taking by banks and thus exacerbates the above problem and suggests that reliance on market discipline cannot effectively respond to it. It follows that shareholder empowerment, which is a conventional remedy to corporate governance problems, can actually have negative consequences on the resilience of the financial system.

1.76 Therefore, the analysis here supports a radical change of approach to bank corporate governance from the current facilitative market-based approach, which focuses on shareholder value maximisation, to a regulatory approach which would focus on safeguarding financial stability. Indeed, a series of recent bank corporate governance reforms, both at the UK and EU levels, manifest the increased regulatory intervention in bank corporate governance subsequent to the recent financial crisis. Still, a broader reconceptualisation of bank corporate governance including their corporate objective and directors' duties is necessary as the basis for the future development of the regulation of bank corporate governance.

SELECTED BIBLIOGRAPHY

Allen, F and A M Santomero, 'What do financial intermediaries do?' (2001) 25 *Journal of Banking and Finance* 271.

Allen, L and S A Cebenoyan, 'Bank acquisitions and ownership structure: Theory and evidence' (1991) 15 *Journal of Banking and Finance* 425.

Ashcraft, A and H Bleakley, 'On the market discipline of informationally opaque firms: Evidence from bank borrowers in the federal funds market' (2006) Federal Reserve Bank of New York Staff Report 257, available at: http://www.newyorkfed.org/research/staff_reports/sr257.html, accessed 1 April 2014.

Atkeson, A and W E Simon Jr, 'The rising fear in bank stock prices', *The Wall Street Journal* (28 November 2011), available at: http://online.wsj.com/news/articles/SB10001424052970 2045314045770524932708601 30, accessed 1 January 2014.

Avgouleas, E, 'The global financial crisis and the disclosure paradigm in European financial regulation: The case for reform' (2009) 6 *European Company and Financial Law Review* 440.

Bainbridge, S M, 'Director primacy and shareholder disempowerment' (2006) 119 *Harv L Rev* 1735.

Ball, R, 'The global financial crisis and the efficient markets hypothesis: What have we learned?' (2009) 21 *Journal of Applied Corporate Finance* 8.

Basel Committee on Banking Supervision, 'Basel III: A global regulatory framework for more resilient banks and banking systems' (Rev edn, 2011).

Bebchuk, L A, Fried, M Jesse, and D Walker, 'Managerial power and rent extraction in the design of executive compensation' (2002) 69 *U Chi L Rev* 751.

Bebchuk, L A, A Cohen and H Spamann, 'The wages of failure: Executive compensation at Bear Sterns and Lehman 2000–2008' (2010) 27 *Yale Journal of Regulation* 257.

Berle, A A and G C Means, *The Modern Corporation and Private Property* (rev. edn, Harcourt, Brace & World 1967).

BIS, 'A long-term focus for corporate Britain: A call for evidence' (2010), available at: https://www.gov.uk/government/consultations/a-long-term-focus-for-corporate-britain-a-call-for-evidence, accessed 1 January 2014.

Black, B S, 'Agents watching agents: The promise of institutional investor Voice', (1991–1992) 39 *UCLA L Rev* 811.

Black, B S, and J C Coffee Jr, 'Hail Britannia? Institutional investor behavior under limited regulation' (1993–1994) 92 *Mich L Rev* 1997.

Black, J, 'Paradoxes and failures: New governance techniques and the financial Crisis' (2012) 75 *MLR* 1037.

Caprio, G Jr., L Laeven and R Levine, 'Governance and bank valuation' (2003) World Bank Working Paper No. 3202, available at: http://papers.ssrn.com/sol3/papers.cfm?abstract_id= 463240, accessed 1 January 2014.

Castanias, R, 'Bankruptcy risk and optimal capital structure' (1983) 38 *The Journal of Finance* 1617.

Cheffins, B R, 'Did corporate governance "fail" during the 2008 Stock Market meltdown? The case of the S&P 500' (2009) ECGI Working Paper No. 124/2009, available at: http://papers.ssrn.com/sol3/papers.cfm?abstract_id=1396126, accessed 1 January 2014.

Cheffins, B R, 'The Stewardship's Code Achilles Heel' (2010) 73 *MLR* 1004.

Cheng, M, D Dhaliwal and M Neamtiu, 'Banks' asset securitisation and information opacity' (2008) University of Southern California Working Paper, available at: http://www.usc.edu/schools/business/FBE/seminars/papers/ARF_5-2-08_NEAMTIU.pdf, accessed 1 January 2014.

Ciancanelli, P, and J A Reyes-Gonzalez, 'Corporate governance in banking: A conceptual framework' (European Financial Management Association conference, Athens, June 2000), available at: http://ssrn.com/abstract=253714, accessed 1 January 2014.

Claessens, S, R J Herring and D Schoenmaker, 'A safer world financial system: Improving the resolution of systemic institutions' (Centre for Economic Policy Research, 2010).

Copp, S F, 'Section 172 of the Companies Act 2006 fails People and Planet' (2010) 31 *Comp Law* 406.

Crawford A J, J R Ezzell and J A Miles, 'Bank CEO pay-performance regulations and the effects of deregulation' (1995) 68 *Journal of Business* 231.

DeAngelo, H, and R M Stulz, 'Why high leverage is optimal for banks' (2013) Fisher College of Business Working Paper 2013–03–08, available at: http://papers.ssrn.com/sol3/papers.cfm?abstract_id=2254998, accessed 1 January 2014.

Dechow, P M, and C Shakespeare, 'Do managers time securitization transactions to obtain accounting benefits?' (2006), available at: http://papers.ssrn.com/sol3/papers.cfm?abstract_id=928741, accessed 1 January 2014.

Dechow, P M, L A Myers and C Shakespeare, 'Fair value accounting and gains from asset securitizations: A convenient earnings management tool with compensation side-benefits' (2010) 49 *Journal of Accounting and Economics* 2.

DeYoung, R, E Y Pen, and M Yan, 'Executive compensation and business policy choices at U.S. commercial banks' (2013) 48 *Journal of Financial and Quantitative Analysis* 165.

Easterbrook, F H, and D R Fischel, *The Economic Structure of Corporate Law* (Harvard University Press 1991).

Elton, E J et al., *Modern Portfolio Theory and Investment Analysis* (8th edn, John Wiley & Sons Inc. 2010).

Erkens, D H, M Hun, and P Matos 'Corporate governance in the 2007–2008 financial crisis: Evidence from financial institutions worldwide' (2012) 18 *Journal of Corporate Finance* 389.

Esho, N and others, 'Market discipline and subordinated debt of Australian Banks' (2005) Australian Prudential Regulation Authority (APRA) Working Paper, available at: http://www.apra.gov.au/AboutAPRA/Research/Documents/Market-Discipline-and-Subordinated-Debt-of-Australian-Banks-October-2005.pdf, accessed 1 January 2014.

European Commission, Green Paper, 'Corporate governance in financial institutions and remuneration policies' COM (2010) 284 final.

European Parliament News, 'Deal reached on bank bail-in directive' (12/12/2013), available at: http://www.europarl.europa.eu/news/en/news-room/content/20131212IPR30702/html/Deal-reached-on-bank-%E2%80%9Cbail-in-directive%E2%80%9D, accessed 1 January 2014.

Fama, E, 'Efficient capital markets: A review of theory and empirical work' (1970) 25 *The Journal of Finance* 383.

Financial Stability Board, 'Key attributes of effective resolution regimes for Financial institutions' (2011), available at: https://www.financialstabilityboard.org/publications/r_111104cc.htm, accessed 1 April 2014.

Flannery, M J, S H Kwan, and M Nimalendran, 'Market evidence on the opaqueness of banking firms' assets' (2004) 71 *Journal of Financial Economics* 419.

Flannery, M J, S H Kwan and M Nimalendran, 'The 2007–09 financial crisis and bank opaqueness' (2010) Federal Reserve Bank of San Francisco Working Paper 2010–27, available at: http://www.frbsf.org/economic-research/files/wp10–27bk.pdf, accessed 1 January 2014.

Gulinello, C, 'The retail investor vote: Mobilizing rationally apathetic Shareholders to preserve or challenge the board's presumption of authority' (2010) 3 *Utah Law Review* 547.

Hadjiemmanuil, C, 'Special resolution regimes for banking institutions: Objectives and limitations' in W-G Ringe and P M Huber (eds), *Legal Challenges in the Global Financial Crisis* (Hart Publishing 2014).

Haggard, K S and J S Howe, 'Are banks opaque?' (2007) University of Southern Mississippi Working Paper, available at: http://www.scribd.com/doc/156507098/Haggard-Stephen-K-John-S-Howe-2007-Are-Banks-Opaque-Jan-11–41-Pp, accessed 1 January 2014.

Hansen, J L, 'Insider dealing after the market abuse directive' in D Prentice and A Reisberg (eds) *Corporate Finance in the UK and EU* (OUP 2011).

Hauck, A and U Neyer, 'Are rating splits a useful indicator for the opacity of an industry?' (2008) Heinrich-Heine-University of Düsseldorf Economics Finance, and Taxation Discussion Paper No. 3/2008, available at: http://papers.ssrn.com/sol3/papers.cfm?abstract_id=2103169, accessed 1 January 2014.

Heremans, D, 'Corporate governance issues for banks. A financial stability perspective' (2007) University of Leuven Working Paper, available at: http://ssrn.com/abstract=1024693, accessed 1 January 2014.

Hopt, K J, 'Corporate governance of banks after the financial crisis' in E Wymeersch, K J Hopt and G Ferranini (eds), *Financial Regulation and Supervision: A post-crisis analysis* (OUP 2012).

Howson, N C, 'When "good" corporate governance makes "bad" (financial) firms: The global crisis and the limits of private law' (2009) 108 *Mich L Rev* (First Impressions) 44.

Iannota, G and M A Navone, 'Crashes and bank opaqueness' (2009) University Luigi Bocconi CAREFIN Research Paper No. 20/09, available at: http://papers.ssrn.com/sol3/papers.cfm?abstract_id=1600190, accessed 1 January 2014.

Iannotta, G O, 'Testing for opaqueness in the European banking industry: Evidence from bond credit ratings' (2006) 30 *Journal of Financial Services Research* 287.

Independent Commission on Banking, 'Final Report: Recommendations' (2011), available at: http://webarchive.nationalarchives.gov.uk/+/bankingcommission.independent.gov.uk, accessed 1 January 2014.

Jensen, M C and K J Murphy, 'CEO incentives – It's not how much you pay, but how' (1990) (May–June) *Harvard Business Review* 138.

Jensen, M C, and W H Meckling, 'Theory of the firm: Managerial behavior, agency costs and ownership structure' (1976) 3 *Journal of Financial Economics* 305.

Jensen, M C, K J Murphy and E G Wruck, 'Remuneration: Where we've been, how we got to here, what are the problems, and how to fix them' (2004) Harvard Business School Research Paper No. 04–28, available at: http://ssrn.com/abstract=561305, accessed 1 January 2014.

Jones, J S, W Y Lee and T J Yeager, 'Valuation and systemic risk consequences of bank opacity' (2013) 37 *Journal of Banking and Finance* 693.

Jones, J S, W Y Lee, T J Yeager, 'Opaque banks, price discovery, and financial instability' (2012) 21 *Journal of Financial Intermediation* 383.

Kay, J, 'The Kay Review of UK equity markets and long-term decision making – Final Report' (2012), available at: https://www.gov.uk/government/news/kay-review-publishes-report-on-uk-financial-sector, accessed 1 January 2014.

Kershaw, D, 'Waiting for Enron: The unstable equilibrium of auditor independence regulation' (2006) 33 *Journal of Law and Society* 388.

King, M R, 'The cost of equity for global banks: a CAPM perspective from 1990 to 2009' (2009) (September) *BIS Quarterly Review* 56.

Kokkinis, A, 'The Financial Services Act 2012: The recent overhaul of the United Kingdom's financial regulatory structure' (2013) 24(9) *ICCLR* 325.

Kokkinis, A, 'The reformed "fit and proper" test: A call for a broader rethink of bank corporate governance?' (2012) 9 *ICR* 5.

Kokkinis, Andreas, 'Rethinking banking prudential regulation: Why corporate governance rules matter?' (2012) 7 *JBL* 612.

Levine, R, 'The corporate governance of banks: A concise discussion of concepts and evidence' (2004) World Bank Policy Research Working Paper 3404, available at: http://elibrary.worldbank.org/doi/book/10.1596/1813–9450–3404, accessed 1 January 2014.

Macey, J R, and M O'Hara, 'The corporate governance of banks' (2003) 9 Federal Reserve *Bank of New York Economic Policy Review* 91.

Manne, H G, 'Mergers and the market for corporate control' (1965) 73 *The Journal of Political Economy* 110.

Moore, M T, 'The evolving contours of the board's risk management function in UK corporate governance' (2010) 10 *J Corp L Stud* 279.

Moore, M T, *Corporate Governance in the Shadow of the State* (Hart Publishing 2013).

Morgan, D P, 'Rating banks: Risk and uncertainty in an opaque industry' (2002) 92 *American Economic Review* 874.

Morgan, D P, and K J Stiroh, 'Bond market discipline of banks: Is the market tough enough?' (1999) Federal Reserve Bank of New York Staff Report 95/1999, 13–14, available at: http://www.newyorkfed.org/research/staff_reports/sr95.html, accessed 1 January 2014.

Morgan, D P, and K J Stiroh, 'Bond market discipline of banks: The asset test' (2001) 20 *Journal of Financial Services Research* 195.

Mulbert, P, 'Corporate governance of banks after the financial crisis: Theory, evidence, reforms' (2010) ECGI Working Paper No. 151/2010, available at: http://papers.ssrn.com/sol3/papers.cfm?abstract_id=1448118, accessed 1 January 2014.

Organisation for Economic Co-operation and Development, 'OECD Principles of Corporate Governance' (2004), available at: http://www.oecd.org/corporate/oecdprinciplesofcorporate governance.htm, accessed 1 April 2014.

Osili, U O, and A Paulson, 'Bank crises and investor confidence: An Empirical investigation' (2008) Federal Reserve Bank of Chicago Working Paper No. 2008–17, available at: http://www.chicagofed.org/webpages/publications/policy_discussion_papers/2009/pdp_9.cfm, accessed 1 January 2014.

Parliamentary Commission on Banking Standards, *Changing banking for good* (2013–14, HL 27-II, HC 175-II).

Policy Exchange, *Ring fencing UK Banks: More of a problem than a solution* (James Barty ed, Heron, Dawson and Sawyer 2013).

Polo, A, 'The corporate governance of banks: The current state of the debate' (2007) http://ssrn.com/abstract=958796 accessed 1 January 2014.

Prowse, S D, 'Alternative methods of corporate control in commercial banks' (1995) *Federal Reserve Bank of Dallas Economic and Financial Policy Review* 3.

Prowse, S D, 'The corporate governance system in banking: What do we know?'(1997) (March) *Banca del Lavoro Quarterly Review* 11.

Rawlings, Philip, 'Bank Reform in the UK: Part II – Return to the Dark Ages?' (2011) 8 *ICR* 55.

Santos, J A C, 'Bank capital regulation in contemporary banking theory: A review of the literature' (2001) 10 *Financial Markets, Institutions and Instruments* 41.

Saunders, A, E Strock and N G Travlos, 'Ownership structure, deregulation and bank risk taking' (1990) 45 *The Journal of Finance* 643.

Stiglitz, J E, 'Principal and agent' in *The New Palgrave: A Dictionary of Economics* (vol 3, New Palgrave 1987).

Stout, L A, 'The mechanisms of market inefficiency' (2003) 28 *Journal of Corporation Law* 635.

Treasury Committee, *Competition and choice in retail banking* (HC 2010–11, 612-I).

Ungureanu, M C, 'Banks: Regulation and corporate governance framework' (2008) 5 *Journal of Corporate Ownership and Control* 449.

Walker-Arnott, 'Company law, corporate governance and the banking crisis' (2010) 7 *ICR* 19.

Walker, D, 'A review of corporate governance in UK banks and other financial industry entities: Final Recommendations' (2009), available at: https://www.icaew.com/en/library/subject-gateways/corporate-governance/codes-and-reports/walker-report, accessed 1 January 2014.

White, L J, 'Corporate governance and prudential regulation of banks: Is there any connection?' in J R Barth, C Lin and C Wihlborg (eds), *Research Handbook on International Banking and Governance* (Edward Elgar 2012).

Williamson, O E, *Markets and Hierarchies: Analysis and Antitrust Implications: A Study in the Economics of Internal Organization* (Collier Macmillan 1975).

Winter, J, 'The financial crisis: Does good corporate governance matter and how to achieve it?' in E Wymeersch, K J Hopt and G Ferranini (eds), *Financial Regulation and Supervision: A post-crisis analysis* (OUP, 2012).

Working Group on Corporate Governance of the Basel Committee, *Principles for Enhancing Corporate Governance* (Nouy Daniele et al, Bank of International Settlements 2010).

2

CORPORATE GOVERNANCE AND BANKS: THE ROLE AND COMPOSITION OF THE BOARD

Edward Walker-Arnott

1. COMPANY LAW AND THE BOARD

2.01 English company law has always proceeded on the basis that its fundamental provisions apply to all companies alike, whatever their size or nature. A distinction is drawn for certain limited purposes between public and private companies, and the accounting and auditing requirements make exceptions for small and dormant companies. But the essentials – the nature and consequences of incorporation, limited liability and the protection of share capital for the benefit of creditors, public filings, annual accounts, the duties of directors, winding-up and the division of power and authority between members and directors – all apply to the generality of companies. It is the fact that this last essential concept – the two organs of power, the shareholders in general meeting and the board – applies to all companies alike that explains the remarkable brevity of company law's provision for the role of boards and how that role should be executed. What is fit for a husband and wife company offering consulting services is not fit for a substantial bank. The approach to issues such as how many directors should there be, what sort of expertise should they have, how often should they meet, what should they delegate and what not, must necessarily be completely different.

Virtually all articles of association follow The Companies (Model Articles) **2.02**
Regulations 2008[1] in these three crucial respects:

1. subject to the articles (and, by necessary implication, to statute) the
    directors are responsible for the management of the business and may
    exercise all the powers of the company;
2. the directors may delegate their powers to anyone and in any way, as they
    think fit; and
3. the directors make their own rules of procedure.

It is, consequently, for each board of directors, in the light of the particular
circumstances of its company's business, to determine how the business is
managed, what is dealt with by the board and what is delegated to others and
how the board should operate.

It is not only statute that is terse in its treatment of the role of a board and the **2.03**
exercise of its power. There is little case law. The role of the board is to manage
the business. The courts have long treated business decisions as, in the main,
non-justiciable. 'There is no appeal on merits from management decisions to
courts of law: nor will courts of law assume to act as a kind of supervisory board
over decisions within the powers of management honestly arrived at.'[2] And
governance issues, as well as issues concerning the procedures by which a board
exercises its powers, seldom reach the courts because of a fundamental principle
of agency law, ratification: what has been done without authority and hence
invalidly, because some internal rule has not been observed, can be subsequently
rendered valid by decision of the body with authority acting in due compliance
with all relevant rules.

The law of meetings (notice, quorum, adjournments, participation of those **2.04**
attending, voting and so on) applies as much to board meetings as it does to
shareholders' meetings. So, in theory, one director wrongly denied by his
chairman an opportunity to contribute to debate and discussion of the issue in a
single-topic board meeting could apply to the court to strike down the
resolution passed (with his vote alone against) as invalid. But in practice this
would be pointless: the majority could always prevail by appropriate retrospective ratification at a second meeting, properly conducted. Mistakes in the
proper conduct of board meetings can almost always be remedied at the will of
the majority.

---

1 SI 2008/3229.
2 Lord Wilberforce: *Howard Smith Ltd v Ampol Petroleum* [1974] 2 WLR 689 at 694F.

2.05 There is nothing in statute law about collective responsibility. Yet the heading to Article 7 in the Model Articles reads: 'Directors to take decisions collectively'[3] and it follows necessarily from the directors being enabled to 'exercise all the powers of the company' that their decision-making must be collective and their responsibility likewise.[4] The Court of Appeal has said 'the collegiate or collective responsibility of the board of directors of the company is of fundamental importance to corporate governance under English company law'.[5] The duties of directors, now codified in statute, are expressed to apply individually: 'A director of a company must … '[6] and the court's power to relieve necessarily turns on the facts of the individual case.[7] And so suit against directors, even when all the directors are sued, always proceeds on a one-by-one basis.[8] Enforcement of collective responsibility as such is impossible: a claimant cannot sue a group.

2.06 Again statute has little to say in relation to delegation. There is no list of matters reserved for decision-making by the board. The approval of the accounts, the directors' report, the directors' remuneration report and the directors' remuneration policy must all be 'by the board of directors'.[9] But, otherwise, statute contemplates unlimited powers of delegation. Case law again provides the corrective. 'A proper degree of delegation and division of responsibility is of course permissible, and often necessary, but total abrogation of responsibility is not.'[10] What the irreducible minimum for the board should be has to be determined company by company. With the larger listed companies there is a tension and hence a balance to be struck between, on the one hand, a full-time executive team's desire for unconstrained authority and, on the other, a board's undue interference.

2.07 There is little in the law about the composition of boards. There is a minimum number but no maximum.[11] Corporate directors are permissible[12] but there must be one natural person.[13] Directors must be at least 16 years of age.[14] There

---

3   SI 2008/3229, Sch 3.
4   Hence the prescription of matters reserved to the board: see 2.12 below.
5   *Re Westmid Packing Services Ltd* [1998] 2BCLC 646 per Lord Woolf MR at 653a.
6   See, e.g. Companies Act 2006 (CA 2006), s 172(1).
7   Ibid., s 1157.
8   *City Equitable Fire Insurance Co Ltd.* [1925] Ch 407; and see *Equitable Life Assurance Society v Bowley* [2004] 1BCLC 180.
9   CA 2006, ss 393, 394, 414, 419, 422 and 422(A).
10 Per Lord Woolf MR *Westmid Packing Services Ltd* at 653b. And see *Australian Securities and Investments Commission v Healey* [2011] CA 717.
11 CA 2006, s 154.
12 See *HMRC v Holland* [2010] 1WLR 2793.
13 CA 2006, s 155(1).
14 Ibid., s 157(1).

is no prescription about executive and non-executive representation. Boards, in law, can be wholly non-executive[15] wholly executive[16] or any combination of the two.

There is a similar absence of particularity about the procedures of a board. **2.08** Statute contains a single provision: that minutes of meetings of directors are to be kept.[17] The Model Articles provide that, subject to the few express rules in the Articles, 'the directors may make any rule which they may think fit about how they take decisions'.[18] These express rules supplement the principle that directors' decisions should be taken collectively by enabling written resolutions signed by all the directors entitled to vote[19] and, for a meeting, any form of participation provided each director can communicate to the others, wherever they all may be.[20] The rules also cover the power to call meetings, notice, quorum, conflicts (and exclusion from participation of voting);[21] they also contain two fundamental provisions, first, that 'a decision is taken at a directors' meeting by a majority of votes of the participating directors'[22] and, secondly, that 'the directors may appoint a director to chair their meetings'.[23] The rules are silent as to what should precede the taking of a decision and as to what are the responsibilities of a chairman.

The rules as regards notice, quorum and conflicts have no practical significance to outsiders by virtue of section 40 of the Companies Act 2006[24] and seldom concern insiders because of the scope of ratification as well as the chairman's power to make final and binding decisions on issues of participation for quorum and voting purposes.[25]

In sum it is clear that the law has very little to say that bears on the effectiveness **2.09** of a board. An intelligent bystander would rightly observe that the quality of collective decision-making by a group of individuals depends, first, on who makes up the group and what skills and understanding each member brings to the deliberations, secondly, on what issues are addressed by the group and what not and thirdly, on how the group goes about its work; and as regards this last

---

15 As were, in the late nineteenth century and the first half of the twentieth century, the boards of major banks and insurance companies: and as are, now, the boards of charitable companies.
16 As with a small quasi-partnership.
17 CA 2006, s 248.
18 SI 2008/3229, Sch 3, art 19.
19 Ibid., art 18.
20 Ibid., art 9.
21 Ibid., arts 8, 10, 16.
22 Ibid., art 13(1).
23 Ibid., art 12.
24 Provided the outsider is 'dealing…[with the company] … in good faith'.
25 SI 2008//3229, Sch 3, art 16(5).

consideration, the bystander would immediately mention the number of meetings a year, the length of meetings, the time given to different items of business, the clarity and comprehensibility of the papers made available to the group and the chairman's control of the debate within it. But all of this the law treats as a matter of practice and for what is good practice rather than bad it is necessary to turn to the UK Code of Corporate Governance (the Code).[26]

2. THE CORPORATE GOVERNANCE CODE

2.10 The Code applies to all companies with a premium listing of equity shares regardless of the place of incorporation. Unlike English company law, it attempts to define the role of the board of directors in the context of a perennial practical issue: what issues are for the whole board, composing both full-time executives and part-time non-executives, and what are for the executive team?

2.11 The Code proceeds on the basis of Main Principles, Supporting Principles and Code Provisions in each of the areas it addresses. (References to the Code below follow the Code's lettering and numbering.)

2.12 The Main Principle on role (A.1) is that 'every company should be headed by an effective board which is collectively responsible for the long-term success of the company'. The Supporting Principles (A.1) state that the board:

> should provide entrepreneurial leadership of the company within a framework of prudent and effective controls which enables risk to be assessed and managed. The board should set the company's strategic aims, ensure that the necessary financial and human resources are in place for the company to meet its objectives and review management performance. The board should set the company's values and standards …

As regards risk, the Walker Report[27] recommended that the boards of FTSE 100 listed banks should establish a board risk committee separate from the audit committee.[28]

The board's role in relation to risk generally is addressed in Chapter 6.

---

26 Published by the Financial Reporting Council (FRC) September 2012.
27 A review of corporate governance in UK banks and other financial industry entities. Final Recommendations in the Second Report 26 November 2009.
28 The Salz Report (see 2.51 below) observed that Barclays had had a separate board risk committee many years before the Walker recommendation. And the Final Report of the Parliamentary Commission in 2013 (see 2.55 below) at para 729 of Vol 2 endorsed the requirement of a separate committee.

The Code Provisions cover the number of meetings ('The board should meet sufficiently regularly to discharge its duties effectively') and the reservation of matters to the board ('There should be a formal schedule of matters specifically reserved for its decision') (A.1.1.).

The accountancy profession was involved in the formulation of the Code from the outset and it is the Financial Reporting Council that oversees its regular review and its effectiveness. So it is not surprising that the Code has many provisions relating to disclosures in the annual report and accounts. One such is the requirement for a ' high level statement of which types of decisions are to be taken by the board and which are to be delegated to management' (A.1.1.).   **2.13**

That there must be a division of responsibilities between board and executive is obvious. FTSE 350 companies must have boards at least half of which (excluding the chairman) comprise independent non-executive directors (NEDs) (B.1.2.). The non-executives are not simply part-time but significantly part-time. They cannot begin to master the detail involved in the operation of large complex businesses (often, in the case of major banks, wholly different in nature from one another). Judgement and self-discipline are required for a NED to assess that 'this is something which concerns me and that is something which does not'. The Code states as a Main Principle (A.4) 'non-executive directors should constructively challenge and help develop proposals on strategy'. And in Supporting Principles (A.4) that they should 'scrutinise the performance of management in meeting agreed goals and objectives and monitor the reporting of performance'.   **2.14**

There is however great difficulty in moving from generality (and the Code is necessarily expressed in terms of generality) to participation in the collective operation of a board in practice. What is strategy? What can, sensibly, be the subject matter of challenge? When does 'scrutinising performance' become unwarranted interference and a trespassing by non-executives beyond their proper domain?

The effectiveness of any group of individuals which has decisions to make turns essentially on the internal human dynamics of the group – the relationships and the chemistry among the individuals. In this hard world of reality, away from the admirable concepts and exhortations of the Code, experience has shown that there are three key considerations –   **2.15**

1. the number and quality of the people sitting round the board room table, their expertise, their commitment and the time they give;

2.   their knowledge and understanding of the businesses for which they are responsible; and

3.   the effectiveness of their operation as a collective and this principally turns on the leadership of their chairman.

2.16   It is striking that neither the law nor the Code specifies a maximum number of directors, especially as the Code could do so by way of guidance. The Code simply counsels that the board 'should not be so large as to be unwieldy' (B.1). A gathering of 24 people for discussion, debate and decision is entirely different in character from a gathering of 12. With the larger number there tend to be formal presentations to an audience with less scope for sustained challenge from an individual director: with a smaller, the opportunity for deeper probing and analysis, with more continuous interchange in argument, is greater.

2.17   The significance of relevant expertise and experience among the NEDs and of their commitment (in terms of energy and hard work) and the time devoted by them (especially in periods of crisis) hardly require elaboration. They are clearly dealt with in the Code. (B.2.2., B.6, B.3).

There is law on the proposition that directors should know and understand the business which they are responsible for managing. In a leading disqualification case concerning a failed bank, Barings,[29] Jonathan Parker J said:[30]

> It is a truism that if a manager does not properly understand the business which he is seeking to manage, he will be unable to take informed management decisions in relation to it.

After a careful review of the authorities he summarised the relevant duties of directors in this way[31]

> (i) directors have, both collectively and individually, a continuing duty to require and maintain a sufficient knowledge and understanding of the company's business to enable them properly to discharge their duties as directors.

> (ii) whilst directors are entitled (subject to the articles of association of the company) to delegate particular functions to those below them in the management chain and to trust their competence and integrity to a reasonable extent, the exercise of the power of delegation does not absolve a director from the duty to supervise the discharge of delegated functions.

---

29   The issue in a disqualification case is whether or not a person is 'unfit to be concerned in the management of a company'. Company Directors Disqualification Act 1986. s 6.

30   *Re Barings plc* [1999] 1BCLC 433, at 528.

31   Ibid., at 489 (approved by the Court of Appeal [2000] 1BCLC 523, at 535).

(iii) no role of universal application can be formulated as to the duty referred to in (ii) above. The extent of this duty, and the question whether it has been discharged, must depend on the facts of each particular case, including the director's role in the management of the company.

And in the same case the judge drew a distinction between breach of duty on the one hand and unfitness founded on incompetence on the other, in these terms:[32]

It is, I think, possible to envisage a case where a respondent has shown himself so completely lacking in judgement as to justify a finding of unfitness, notwithstanding that he has not been guilty of misfeasance or breach of duty.

International Financial Reporting Standards have introduced great complexity **2.18** into the presentation of the annual accounts, particularly of banks and financial institutions. Every director has a responsibility in relation to the annual accounts[33] and as Middleton J made clear in the *Australian Centro* case:[34]

The case law indicates that there is a core, irreducible requirement of directors to be involved in the management of the company and to take all reasonable steps to be in a position to guide and monitor. There is a responsibility to read, understand and focus upon the contents of those reports which the law imposes a responsibility upon each director to approve or adopt.

Of course a pre-condition to understanding the accounts is understanding the business.

Some companies' businesses – particularly those of large international banks – are of bewildering range and complexity and the task, particularly for NEDs, to understand, and, by virtue of understanding, monitor may seem impracticable. Nevertheless, although there can be reliance on executive directors, all directors must master the basic essentials that, substantially, impact on the company's success or failure.

The discharge of the role of the board is all about the operation of a group of **2.19** individuals acting collectively.[35] This makes the leadership of the chairman of

---

32   Ibid., at 486.
33   CA 2006, ss 393, 394 and 414.
34   *Australian Securities Investment Commission v Healey* [2011] FCA 717.
35   The critical distinction between individual and collective responsibility is often obscured in practice and lawyers advising boards are not free from blame. Draft minutes prepared by external solicitors for bank boards often contain references to the duties of directors codified in ss 170–177 of the Companies Act 2006. All of these apply to 'a director'. Similarly the high level Statement of Principles issued by the PRA/FCA as regards the conduct of approved persons (see APER2.1A.3 of the PRA/FCA Handbook) all apply to 'an approved person'.

paramount importance. And this is why the UK Code – contrary to the practice in some other jurisdictions – prescribes a division of function at the top of companies; a chairman to lead the board and a chief executive to run the business (A.2). There must be two individuals, not an Executive Chairman, combining both roles.

2.20 The logic of this can be seen if there is imagined a major acquisition proposal on which the chief executive has set his heart and devoted much energy and attention in supervising the preparation of the papers for the board so as to gain its approval. It is difficult, if he is also chairman, for him to ensure a clear indication of the risks involved and of the argument against: and yet more difficult to run the meeting so that challenging NEDs get a fair hearing. Successful chief executives achieve seniority by being decisive, backing their own judgement and 'selling' propositions. This is not what a chairman does in a well-run board meeting.

As the UK Code makes clear (A.3) the chairman sets the agenda, must ensure adequate time for discussion and promote openness in debate, facilitating the contributions of the NEDs. And it is his responsibility to monitor the information sent to them to ensure it is clear, of the right length, raising the relevant issues and sent in good time before the meeting (A.3).

2.21 Although the Companies Act 2006 (s 168) gives shareholders of companies the right to remove a director and fill the vacancy created, in practice, where, as is usual, although not universal, in the listed sector, shareholdings are diffused and control of the board does not lie with any one shareholder or group of shareholders, the composition of the board, that is the succession of retirements and appointments, is determined by the board itself. Similarly the appointment and removal of the chairman, the chief executive officer, and each of the other executive directors is determined by the board.

2.22 It is a central tenet of corporate governance that the body best equipped to decide on the composition of the board is the board itself. The board is responsible for the management of the business. It knows the nature of the business, the plans for the future, the type of experience and expertise needed within the board to enhance deliberations and decision-making and the skills

---

Governance (see the definition introduced into the Financial Services and Markets Act 2000 by the Companies Act 2006) is about 'the organs of the issuer' and 'the manner in which organs of the issuer conduct themselves'. Of course the duties and responsibilities of individual directors cannot be ignored. Nevertheless the essence of governance concerns the discharge of the collective responsibilities.

and experience needed for each of the executive posts. No outsider can have the equivalent knowledge and bring to bear the same informed judgement.

Regulatory oversight of the membership of bank boards is dealt with in section 3 of this chapter. But it is important to recall that it is oversight only. The body with the resources and the skills and, at law, the responsibility to take effective care with board appointments is the board itself. The difficulties in the way of the regulator in discharging its oversight responsibilities are considerable.[36]

Of course there is a danger that boards pick individuals with whom, as a matter of background and culture, they feel comfortable: and so characteristics can be perpetuated and invigorating refreshment postponed. And similarly there can be a danger that a chairman prevents appointments of challenging, radically minded individuals so as to avoid difficulties within the boardroom and damage to the team ethos.

2.23 But the good sense of any system should never be judged only on the basis of particular instances of its going wrong. It is fundamental to good governance that the ultimate collective responsibility for the management of the business lies with individuals who together constitute the board and that the board, collectively, decides who those individuals are, unless and until the shareholders exercise their rights to intervene.

2.24 The chairman who, under the Code is, 'responsible for leadership of the board and ensuring its effectiveness on all aspects of its roles' (A.3) has a special interest in appointments since they affect the overall character of the board, its collegiality and its operation as a team. But it is an abrogation of the board's overall responsibility for the chairman to have, individually, the right to nominate or the right to veto. The views of the chairman, nevertheless, carry especial weight.

---

36   These were highlighted in the House of Commons Treasury Select Committee examination of Mr Clive Adamson on 7 January 2014. He was, then, director of Supervision at the FCA having previously held a senior position in the FSA. In that FSA role he had interviewed Mr Paul Flowers prior to his appointment as the Chairman of the Co-operative Bank. The bank got into serious difficulties in 2012/2013 and following media revelations of drug use, Mr Flowers, who was a Methodist minister without any banking experience, resigned from the board. It became clear that prior to his appointment as Chairman he had had two criminal convictions (one for indecent assault and the other for drunken driving). Understandably, the thrust of the examination of Mr Adamson was: 'How could the Regulator have approved the appointment?' Mr Adamson was unrepentant as regards the decision made at the time it was made. The examination revealed these issues, among others, for the Regulator – (i) the seniority and experience of the persons conducting the interview; (ii) the length of the interview; (iii) the material available for the Regulator prior to the interview; (iv) the due diligence conducted, independently, by the Regulator prior to the interview. (For a full transcript of the examination visit www.parliament.uk).

2.25   On composition, the Code's Main Principle (B.1) is that:

> The board and its committees should have the appropriate balance of skills, experience, independence and knowledge of the company to enable them to discharge their respective duties and responsibilities effectively.

On size, the Supporting Principles state (B.1):

> The board should be of sufficient size that the requirements of the business can be met and that changes to the board's composition and that of its committees can be managed without undue disruption, and should not be so large as to be unwieldy.

2.26   The Code's requirement that (except for companies outside the FTSE 350) half the board excluding the chairman should comprise independent NEDs (B.1.2.) involves a determination of 'Independence'. This is a matter for the judgement of the board as regards the 'character and judgement' of the individual concerned having regard to the relevant circumstances, particularly actual or historic relationships with the company. Certain relationships are highlighted in the Code Provisions (B.1.1) as tending to compromise independence (e.g. employment with the company within the last five years, material business relationships in the last three years, significant shareholding, etc.)

2.27   As regards appointment, B.2 of the Code states the Main Principle as:

> There should be a formal, rigorous and transparent procedure for the appointment of new directors to the board.

Under the Code Provisions (B.2.1) there must be a nomination committee which takes the lead and makes recommendations to the board. (In this respect the nomination committee is to be contrasted with the remuneration committee which has delegated responsibility for setting the remuneration of all the executive directors and the chairman.) A majority of the nomination committee must be independent NEDs. (B.2.1.)

The nomination committee (B.2.2) proceeds by evaluating 'the balance of skills, experience, independence and knowledge on the board' and in the light of this it must then 'prepare a description of the role and capabilities required for a particular appointment'.

2.28   The Supporting Principles (B.2) make specific reference to 'merit', 'objective criteria' and 'the benefits of diversity on the board, including gender'.

The transparency requirements involve disclosure of a nomination committee's terms of reference and a section in the annual report describing the process of board appointments including an explanation, if neither an external search consultancy nor open advertising have been used, as regards the appointment of a chairman or any non-executive director.

As regards re-appointments Code Provisions B.7.1 and B.7.2 make clear that all directors of FTSE 350 companies should be subject to annual re-election by shareholders and that, as regards a NED, the board should explain 'why they believe an individual should be elected' and the chairman should confirm that, 'following formal performance evaluation, the individual's performance continues to be effective and to demonstrate commitment to the role'.

The Code treats 'relations with shareholders' (E) as part of the role of the board. **2.29** NEDs are encouraged to 'develop an understanding of the views of major shareholders … for example through direct face-to-face contact …' (E.1.2.) and the 'board as a whole has responsibility for ensuring that a satisfactory dialogue with shareholders takes place' (E.1 Main Principle). This part of the Code links with the UK Stewardship Code and is dealt with in Chapter 4 of this volume.

The Code contains important provisions relating to the role of the board as **2.30** regards remuneration and accounts and audit: and it mandates two committees, additional to the nominations committee, the remuneration committee and the audit committee. These aspects of the role are deal with in Chapters 5 and 7 of this volume.

3. THE APPROVED PERSONS REGIME

Fit and proper person tests are commonplace in licensing regimes and have a **2.31** long history. And so when the Financial Services and Markets Act 2000 (FSMA) introduced a comprehensive licensing regime for all financial services activities, with the Financial Services Authority (FSA) as the regulator, issuing permissions and monitoring conduct, it was inevitable that the test was adopted for persons holding, or intending to hold, prescribed positions within a business seeking a permission or already authorised. The relevant positions were characterised as 'controlled functions'[37] and persons fulfilling these roles ('Approved Persons') had to pass a fit and proper test.[38] Controlled functions were

---

37   FSMA 2000, s 59.
38   FSMA 2000, s 61.

principally 'significant influence functions' (SIF) or 'customer-dealing functions'; and the three SIFs relevant to this chapter were 'director function', 'non-executive director function' and 'chief executive function'. By virtue of the Financial Services Act 2012 the FSA has now been replaced by the Financial Conduct Authority (FCA) and the Prudential Regulation Authority (PRA) but the essential framework governing the suitability of those seeking to take up or retain positions on the boards of banks remains as it was.[39] The exception is the regulatory change described in 2.62 of this chapter which will, in due course, impact on the appointment and responsibility of bank executive directors.

2.32 In a case concerning an on-licence application (the sale of intoxicating liquor for consumption on the premises) Lord Bingham said this:

> ... some consideration must be given to the expression 'fit and proper' persons. This is a portmanteau expression, widely used in many contexts. It does not lend itself to semantic exegesis or paraphrase and takes it colour from the context in which it is used. It is an expression directed to ensuring that an applicant for permission to do something has the personal qualities and professional qualifications reasonably required of a person doing whatever it is that the applicant seeks permission to do.[40]

2.33 The changes in the UK regulation of banks came into force on 1 April 2013. The PRA, a subsidiary of the Bank of England, is responsible for prudential supervision while the FCA has responsibility for consumer protection, market integrity and building competitive financial markets. Both the PRA and the FCA have a regulatory interest in Approved Persons but it is the PRA that has oversight of the application of the fit and proper test to members of a bank board.

2.34 Section 1 explained that in its treatment of the role and composition of boards company law makes no distinction between big and small companies or between banks and other companies. Section 2 showed that the Code applies to

---

39 Originally specified by FSA and now adopted by both FCA and PRA. The framework was set out in the FSA Handbook and explained in FSA Policy Statements. See, for example, Policy Statement 10/15 'Effective Corporate Governance – Significant influence controlled functions and the Walker Review' published in September 2010 which sets out the FSA approach to such matters as interviews, due diligence and time commitment from proposed directors.

40 *R v Crown Court Warrington ex parte RBNB* [2002] 1 WLR 1954. That Lord Bingham was not using the term 'professional' in any narrow sense involving the gaining of a qualification is clear from para 17 at p 1964B where he says:

> a simple and specific question which, before the justices and the Crown Court, had to be asked and answered: was Mr Kehoe a fit and proper person to be the licensee of the Weavers Hotel? The factual findings already recited already make it plain that he was, personally and professionally, a fit and proper person.

all companies with a premium listing. (But large non-listed companies invariably follow its basic, applicable principles.) The regulatory regime of the FSMA 2000 necessarily extends to all banks, regardless of size or ownership. Large unlisted banks, private banks, mutuals, subsidiaries of banks within and without the European Union and overseas banks operating through branches all fall within what is now the PRA/FCA regulatory supervision. It will be obvious that the considerations brought to bear by the PRA as regards the fit and proper test will vary considerably in relation to the size and character of the bank concerned.

The application of the fit and proper test by the regulator and the Parliamentary **2.35** Commission's criticism of the regulator's approach and its response to the financial crisis are relevant to any consideration of the composition of the boards of banks. They are dealt with in section 4 below, as are the changes introduced by the Financial Services (Banking Reform) Act 2013.

4. BANKS AND FINANCIAL INSTITUTIONS

In the first two decades of the twenty-first century banks and financial **2.36** institutions have assumed a special position as regards corporate governance and, in particular, those principles which affect the role and composition of boards. There are two principal reasons for this.

First, banks have a central role in society. They enable the movement of money, they hold money, they lend money, they provide a range of financial services, all for the general public in both private and business capacities. In aggregate, the banks bulk large in the national economy, generating a significant proportion of Gross Domestic Product and of the national tax revenue. Individually each of the UK's biggest banks has systemic importance both to the national and to the global economies.

Secondly, in late 2007 and 2008 five UK banks failed and had to be saved by HM Government. The assets of these banks, in aggregate, well exceeded the UK's Gross Domestic Product. The support for the Royal Bank of Scotland (RBS) for example (in 2008 the largest bank in the world by assets and the fifth largest by market capitalisation) involved the state injecting £45.5 billion of equity capital and committing £282 billion to the asset protection scheme. The early general reports into the banking failures were unanimous in their suggestion that boards of directors were at fault. Sir David Walker was commissioned by the Government to conduct a review of corporate governance in UK banks and other financial industry entities.[41] In paragraph 1.16 of his second report he stated:

> In the light of the scale and scope of the financial crisis, the key questions from a corporate governance perspective must be: could boards of failed entities have done more to prevent the collapse and, if so, what stood in their way? … [I]t is critically important to know how the boards of the entities that best survived the storm were different or 'better' than the boards of entities that were effectively taken over by the State or lost their identity through forced merger.

2.37 There have been two detailed investigations by the FSA (into the failures of RBS and Halifax Bank of Scotland (HBOS)); in addition there has been sustained activity within Parliament both from the Treasury Committee of the House of Commons and the Parliamentary Commission on Banking Standards (the former as regards RBS and the second as regards HBOS). Further, a bank that did not fail (Barclays) became subject during 2010–12 to increasing reputational criticism (concerning among other things allegations of aggressive accounting and tax schemes, unco-operative interaction with the regulator exhibiting technical cleverness but a disregard for the obvious spirit of the rules, mis-selling of payment protection insurance and interest swaps to small- and medium-sized enterprises and, finally, the LIBOR-rigging scandal). The last led in the summer of 2012 to the departure of the Chairman and the Chief Executive and the appointment of Sir Anthony Salz to conduct an independent review of Barclays' values, principles and standards of operations.

2.38 In the governance context, the spotlight has been on banks, and much has been written; and there have been many recommendations for improvement. Especially relevant to the composition and role of boards, in addition to the Walker Report, are the FSA investigation into the collapse of RBS, the Parliamentary Commission's analysis of the failure of HBOS and the Salz Report on Barclays.

A. Royal Bank of Scotland

2.39 In May 2009 the FSA launched a supervisory investigation into RBS. The issues addressed were first, whether or not any regulatory rules had been broken and, secondly, what, if any, action was appropriate. In December 2010 the FSA announced that it had completed the investigation and that the conclusion was that although 'RBS had made a series of bad decisions', these were not 'the result of a lack of integrity by any individual' and that the FSA had not

---

41 A Review of Corporate Governance in UK Banks and Other Financial Industry Entities: first report for consultation published July 2009; second report with final recommendations published November 2009.

identified either 'any instances of fraud or dishonest activity by RBS senior individuals or a failure of governance on the part of the Board'.[42]

It was clear from the outset of the financial crisis that the role of the boards of **2.40** the failed banks required examination. In March 2009 the Turner Review (A Regulatory Response to the Global Banking Crisis) issued by the FSA[43] had stated:

> While some of the problems could not be identified at firm specific level, and while some well-run banks were affected by systemic developments over which they had no influence, there were also many cases where internal risk management was ineffective and where boards failed adequately to identify and constrain excessive risk-taking.

And Sir David Walker's second report stated:[44]

> But serious deficiencies in prudential oversight and financial regulation in the period before the crisis were accompanied by major governance failures within banks.

Of course, as regards RBS, the FSA was embarking on an enforcement **2.41** procedure. It was necessarily constrained by its own statutory functions and purposes. Just as third parties cannot sue boards as a group, so regulators have no enforcement sanctions against boards as a group: the rule of law requires any disciplinary action to proceed on a one-by-one basis. This made the FSA, from the outset, an inappropriate body to investigate failures of board governance. And there were other reasons why an FSA investigation was unlikely to be illuminatory as regards the discharge of the board's collective responsibility. First, the conduct of the regulator itself was in issue: had it failed? Secondly, the exchanges between the bank and the regulator were highly relevant to any consideration of the conduct of the directors. What was the understanding within the boardroom of the attitude of the regulator and of the nuances of the regulator's approach to the different businesses within the bank? What was the board's reliance on reports produced by the regulator? What was the direct contact between individual members of the board and the regulator? And what did those individual directors tell the other members of the board about that contact? In addition, a full report could not be published because the information gathered from RBS remained confidential under the FSMA.[45]

---

42   FSA Press Statement, 2 December 2010.
43   At p 36.
44   See above n 41.
45   FSMA, s 348.

2.42   The terseness of the FSA announcement in December 2010 and the absence of any detailed explanation of why RBS had failed caused both a public and a parliamentary outcry. Following correspondence between the Chairman of the House of Commons Treasury Committee and the Chairman of the FSA it was agreed that the FSA would prepare a report for publication and would accept an independent external review of that report by special advisers to the Committee.

On 12 December 2011 the FSA published its report.[46] It set out what the FSA considered to be the primary causes of RBS's failure and also examined deficiencies in the FSA's regulation and supervision of the firm. The FSA would have needed the co-operation of RBS to circumvent the restrictions on publication of confidential information contained in the 2000 Act and so the December 2011 report can be assumed to have involved some negotiation with RBS. RBS was controlled by the Government which looked, in due course, to sell it back to the private sector and it stood in jeopardy of litigation proceedings from outsiders. In the event, the corrections in the 2011 Report to the assertion in the 2010 Statement that the FSA had not identified 'a failure of governance on the part of the board' were very limited.

2.43   There was only one definitive conclusion and that concerned the decision of the board to approve the acquisition of ABN-Amro. At paragraph 443 the report stated:

> The RBS Board's decision to make a bid of this scale on the basis of inadequate due diligence entailed a degree of risk-taking that can reasonably be criticised as a gamble.

At paragraph 600 the report stated the conclusion that:

> the judgment of the RBS Board in respect of the ABN-Amro acquisition was not characterised by the degree of moderation and sensitivity to strategic risk appropriate to a bank. With so much at stake there was a critical need for more fundamental probing, questioning and challenge by the Board.

In paragraph 601 the report indicated that the deficiencies were not sufficient to justify enforcement action and went on: 'However, this fact does not justify a view that governance at RBS was effective during the review period in relation to the ABN-Amro acquisition. In the opinion of the review team, it was not.'

---

46   The failure of the Royal Bank of Scotland: Financial Services Authority Board Report.

Apart from this one clear conclusion, notwithstanding the further work **2.44**
between December 2010 and December 2011 and the oversight from the
independent reviewers appointed by the Treasury Committee, there were, as
regards board governance, only questions raised rather than conclusions
reached. In paragraph 26 the report stated that:

> the review team's analysis prompts the following questions in addition to the conclusion
> … about the ABN-Amro bid:
> - Whether the board's mode of operation, including challenge to the Executive, was
>   as effective as its composition and formal processes would suggest.
> - Whether the CEO's management style discouraged robust and effective challenge.
> - Whether RBS was overly focused on revenue profit and earnings per share rather
>   than on capital liquidity and asset quality and whether the board designed a CEO
>   remuneration package which made it rational to focus on the former.
> - Whether RBS's board received adequate information to consider the risks associ-
>   ated with strategy proposals, and whether it was sufficiently disciplined in question-
>   ing and challenging what was presented to it.
> - Whether risk management information enabled the board adequately to monitor
>   and mitigate the aggregation of risk across the group, and whether it was sufficiently
>   forward looking to give early warning of emerging risk.

B. Halifax Bank of Scotland

HBOS was created in 2001 from the merger of the Bank of Scotland and **2.45**
Halifax which had been the UK's largest building society. In September 2008,
in circumstances of extreme financial difficulty, the board of HBOS recommended a takeover by Lloyds TSB. This was not completed until January 2009.
HBOS turned to the Bank of England for Emergency Assistance on 1 October
2008 and HM Government provided in total £20.5 billion to support HBOS
while Lloyds Banking Group (the new merged company) itself provided a
further £7.5 billion.

On 9 March 2012 the FSA published a Final Notice of Censure of Bank of **2.46**
Scotland (BOS). It had:

> … failed to take reasonable care to organise and control its affairs responsibly and
> effectively, with adequate risk management systems, in that the Firm did not:
>
> (1) have adequate risk management systems for the high risk business and lending
>   strategy which it pursued;
> (2) have adequate risk management systems for the aggressive growth strategy pursued;
>   and
> (3) therefore take reasonable care to organise and control its affairs responsibly and
>   effectively in its pursuit of the high risk business and lending strategy and the
>   aggressive growth strategy.

The FSA stated that the breaches were:

> particularly serious in the light of the following:
>
> (1) it was clear that the aggressive growth strategy that Corporate[47] pursued would necessarily entail a significant increase in the already high level of risk and exposure to the economic cycle in the portfolio, at a time when … [BOS]… recognised that the economic cycle was at or near its peak;
> (2) rather than identify that a more prudent approach was vital as market conditions continued to worsen, [BOS] continued to pursue a strategy of aggressive growth;
> (3) [BOS] disregarded warnings from the divisional risk function and HBOS's auditors that the level of provisioning was optimistic rather than prudent.

2.47 The FSA stated: 'A financial penalty proportionate to the misconduct identified in this notice would be both merited and very substantial.' However no financial penalty was imposed given that HM Government by virtue of its support had acquired 43.4 per cent of the ordinary share capital of Lloyds Banking Group.

2.48 On 12 September 2012 Peter Cummings, who had been on the board of HBOS and was the Chief Executive of the Corporate Division was fined £500,000 by the FSA and given a life-time ban from the financial industry.

2.49 The Parliamentary Commission on Banking Standards established a panel to consider the failure of HBOS.[48] It heard evidence in October–December 2012. On 4 April 2013 the Commission published a report 'An accident waiting to happen: The failure of HBOS.'

The conclusions as regards corporate governance were hard-hitting.

At paragraph 91 the report states:

> The corporate governance of HBOS at board level serves as a model for the future, but not in the way in which Lord Stevenson and other former Board members appear to see it. It represents a model of self-delusion, of the triumph of process over purpose.

At paragraph 92 the report states:

> The Board in its own words had abrogated and remitted to the executive management the formulation of strategy a matter for which the Board should properly have been responsible.

47　The Bank's Corporate Banking Division.
48　See, for the establishment of the Commission itself, 2.55 below.

At paragraph 93 the report states:

> There was insufficient banking expertise among HBOS's top management. In consequence they were incapable of even understanding the risks that some elements of the business were running, let alone managing them.

At paragraph 94 the report states:

> The non-executives on the Board lacked the experience or expertise to identify many of the core risks that the bank was running. In Sir James Crosby's revealing phrase, it was not composed in the manner that would be appropriate for 'a business concentrating entirely on banking'. The board was composed in a manner which appeared suitable for a retail-oriented financial services company but that board lacked the necessary banking experience among its non-executives, particularly in relation to high-risk activities, for a bank whose strategy and business model was posited on asset-led growth led by non-retail divisions of the bank

At paragraph 95 the report states:

> Judging by the comments of some former board members, membership of the Board of HBOS appears to have been a positive experience for many participants. We are shocked and surprised that, even after the ship has run aground, so many of those who were on the bridge still seem so keen to congratulate themselves on their collective navigational skills.

The report found (para 116) that 'the HBOS failure was fundamentally one of solvency'. And that (para 124) 'The problems of solvency were a direct consequence of the strategy set by the Board and the failure of controls on the practices that were fostered by its commitment to an asset-led, high-risk approach to growth.'

2.50 The Commission was ready to be severely critical of individuals, picking out two Chief Executives (Sir James Crosby and Andy Hornby) and the Chairman (Lord Stevenson) (para 135):

> In the view of this Commission, it is right and proper that the primary responsibility for the downfall of HBOS should rest with Sir James Crosby, architect of the strategy that set the course for disaster, with Andy Hornby, who proved unable or unwilling to change course, and Lord Stevenson who presided over the Bank's board from its birth to its death.

C. Barclays plc

2.51 Barclays did not fail during the financial crisis and so avoided rescue by HM Government. It is the second largest UK bank with assets of £1.5 trillion, 140,000 employees and 60 million customers and clients worldwide. At the end of June 2012 the FSA fined Barclays for significant failings in relation to London Interbank Offered Rate (LIBOR) submissions. This led to the resignations of the Chairman and the Chief Executive and the commissioning in July 2012 of the Salz Review, 'An Independent Review of Barclays' Business Practices', essentially an independent assessment of 'Barclays' values, principles and standards of operation'. The report was published in April 2013.

2.52 Given that the Code states (A.1): 'The board should set the company's values and standards … ' and that the Salz Report was, essentially, into the culture prevailing at Barclays during the financial crisis and up to the Autumn of 2012, it is not surprising that there is a considerable volume of material in the report relating to the role of the board and its composition. Salz lays considerable emphasis on the 'complexity of the business': 'Barclays became complex to manage, tending to develop silos with different values and cultures' (2.13); 'the complexity of Barclays' businesses makes … [for] … a particular challenge for its leaders' (2.20); 'we also believe the Board found it difficult at times to penetrate into what was a large complex organisation' (2.22).

Salz made a number of recommendations[49] relevant to the role and composition of the board.

> 2: Setting high standards
>
> The Board and senior leadership, as custodians of Barclays' reputation should promote and safeguard the trust in which it is held. They should state clearly Barclays' purpose and report regularly on how it is fulfilling that purpose. They should promote standards and support Barclays' ambition to be seen as leader in business practices among its peer institutions …
>
> 7: Board experience
>
> Barclays should include among its Non-Executive Directors a sufficient number with directly relevant banking expertise … it is essential that the board includes appropriate diversity of experience, without causing it to be excessively large
>
> 8: Non-Executive Directors
>
> Barclays should maintain and put into action a plan for Non-Executive Directors over a period of time to engage with each major business and geography …

---

49   At 2.40.

11: Group Chief Executive succession

The Board should agree periodically the criteria and personal characteristics required for the role of Group Chief Executive as part of its succession planning. The framework for succession planning should include the long term development of future leaders, Board exposure to potential internal candidates thorough consideration of external candidates and assessment of alignment with Barclays' culture and values.

14: Board effectiveness

The Board must be actively engaged in the process of improving its own effectiveness, including through regular and rigorous evaluations.

Consistently with the Code Salz said (at 8.52):   **2.53**

'A board has an important role to play in protecting the culture of its institution by overseeing how effectively management promotes and embeds its stated values.'

The Salz analysis (at 8.53) was that 'the Barclays' Board did not spend much time discussing the culture, values and business practices developing in the group …'. Salz found that in 'the absence of a common purpose, shared culture and a set of values reinforced from the top …' the various divisions devised their own 'values framework' and that in March 2012 the Barclays Brand and Marketing team identified a number of different values and behaviours spread across the group and its business. These included 'winning together', 'best people', 'loving success' and 'energy'. The five values, which the new regime will seek to embed throughout the bank, are significantly different, being:

1. Respect
2. Integrity
3. Service
4. Excellence
5. Stewardship

Salz proposes (at 8.65) that, 'The board should consider establishing a programme of assurance to enable it to access the extent to which the organisation is living up to its values.'

Salz devotes a chapter (9) to Board governance. It makes the important point **2.54** (at 9.5 and 9.7) that a consequence of all the reviews and the parliamentary and media attention is that 'the level of expectation placed on bank boards, particularly in terms of what can be accomplished by non-executive directors, is extremely high – perhaps unrealistically so'. 'It will be unhelpful if the ever-increasing expectations of bank board governance – driven by reviews, regulators, parliamentary enquiries and the media – deter those with the competencies and experience from offering to join bank boards.'

The recommendations on governance are set out above but Chapter 9 contains a significant paragraph (9.17) about the role of the board in providing '"Challenge" to the actions of management'.

> Sir David Walker explained this to the Parliamentary Commission on Banking Standards as the combination of the quality of individuals and their interaction: 'The test is not only the quality of the individuals but the board dynamic – what happens in the board room – and if you don't have the right dynamic, however good the people are, you won't have the right challenge'. In addition to the quality of people and as contributors to the board dynamic, we would add the overall composition of the board and their understanding as a group of the bank's businesses, the time non executives have to give, the openness of the executive directors and the information available to the board.

Salz quotes (9.19), with obvious approval, a seminal section of the second Walker Report dealing with the effectiveness of boards in practice. The quotation is from 4.3 and 4.4 of the report and is as follows:

> The pressure for conformity on Boards can be strong, generating corresponding difficulty for an individual board member who wishes to challenge group thinking. Such challenge on substantive policy issues can be seen as disruptive, non-collegial and even as disloyal. Yet, without it, there can be an illusion of unanimity in a board, with silence assumed to be acquiescence. The potential tensions here are likely to be greater the larger the board size, so that an individual who wishes to question or challenge is at greater risk of feeling and indeed of being isolated.

> Critically relevant to success of the challenge process in any well-functioning board will be the demeanour and capability of the CEO, who is unlikely to be in the role without having displayed qualities of competence and toughness which are not dependably tolerant of challenge. Even a strong and established CEO may have a degree of concern, if not resentment, that challenge from the NEDs is unproductively time-consuming, adding little or no value, and might intrude on or constrain the ability of the executive team to implement the agreed strategy. Equally, however, the greater the entrenchment of the CEO, perhaps partly on the basis of excellent past performance and longevity in the role, the greater is likely to be the risk of CEO hubris or arrogance and, in consequence, the greater the importance (and quite likely difficulties) of NED challenge. Achieving an appropriate balance among potentially conflicting concerns is frequently the most difficult part of the overall functioning of the board.

Salz then proceeds (9.20): 'Responsibility clearly rests with the Chairman for sorting this out, including the engagement with the Chief Executive ... The culture and style of the board is a core continuing responsibility of the Chairman ... .'

D. Parliamentary Commission on Banking Standards

2.55 The fining of Barclays for its involvement in the manipulation of LIBOR in late June 2012 led to both Houses of Parliament establishing, in mid-July 2012, the Commission to 'consider and report on ... professional standards and culture of the UK banking sector'. The Commission set up a number of panels including one on HBOS. The report of the Commission following this panel's work has been considered above. The final report of the Commission 'Changing banking for good' was published in June 2013.

The Commission was able to give expression to public opinion. For example in paragraph 86 of volume 1 of the report it is stated:

'The public are rightly appalled by the small number of cases in which highly paid senior bankers have been disciplined for the costly mistakes that they have allowed to occur on their watch.'

And again at paragraph 234 of volume 1:

> Faced with the most widespread and damaging failure of the banking industry in the UK's modern history, the regulatory authorities seemed almost powerless to bring sanctions against those who presided over massive failures within banks. Public concern about this apparent powerlessness is both understandable and justified, but the need for a more effective enforcement regime does and should not arise from a public demand for retribution.

2.56 In making, both in the HBOS report and the final report, forthright, pungently expressed criticisms both of directors of banks and of regulators, the Commission had two significant advantages deriving from Article 9 of the Bill of Rights 1689. (This prohibits the impeachment or questioning of the freedom of speech and debates in proceedings in Parliament in any court out of Parliament, a prohibition applying to Parliamentary Committees.)[50] In the first place, absolute privilege was available as regards any defamation. And in the second place, the obligation to act fairly in accordance with the principles of natural justice (which act as a constraint on inspectors in Companies Act investigations under

---

50   *R v Chaytor* [2010] 3 WLR 1707.

section 431 of the Companies Act 1985)[51] did not apply. Thus, for example, there was no need to put matters which could form the basis of a criticism of an individual to that individual, prior to publication of the report, so that he or she had an opportunity to rebut or explain. These two advantages are very significant as regards the speed and complexity of any investigation and the scope for the author of any report.

The Commission's final report contains material that is relevant to the composition and role of boards of banks. It deals with regulatory oversight and also has a number of relevant observations and suggestions.

i. Regulatory oversight of boards

2.57 The second Walker Report contained recommendations as to the FSA's oversight of the composition of boards. In particular the Report proposed that 'the FSA supervisory process should give close attention to the overall balance and capability of the board in relation to the risk strategy of the business' and that where a proposed NED:

> does not bring relevant recent financial industry experience, an interview process should become the norm and should involve questioning and assessment by one or more seniors with relevant past industry experience at or close to board level of a similarly large and complex entity who might be engaged by the FSA for the purpose, possibly on a part-time panel basis.[52]

2.58 In paragraphs 540–566 of its report the Commission tells the remarkable story of how, since the financial crisis and the recommendations of the Walker Report, virtually no change has been made to the Approved Person regime as regards bank directors. With the demise of the FSA and the succession of the PRA and the FCA, no change is likely for some time, the PRA having announced an intention to undertake a fundamental review of the regime.

2.59 The FSA issued a consultation paper in January 2010 identifying nine possible new SIF roles such as chairman, chairman of specific board committees, and executives in charge of finance, risk and internal audit. As regards interviewing, the Commission was told, in the evidence given to it, that many SIFs are no longer interviewed:

> … we have pulled back from the number of what we call significant influence function interviews – SIF interviews – and we do not do as many now as we were doing. We

---

51   *Pergamon Press Ltd* [1971] Ch 388 and *Maxwell v DTI* [1974] QB 523.
52   See Chapter 3 – 3.25 (i) and (ii) of the Report.

would still do them for the roles that are absolutely critical – obviously, the chief executive and finance director of [sic] important jobs in important institutions – we do not do them for other [sic] non-executive posts or for other roles that we think are not quite so critical.[53]

In September 2010 the FSA confirmed a policy commitment to bring these new roles within the Approved Person Regime with a timetable for implementation by July 2011. In March 2011 the FSA announced a deferral 'until further notice'. Then in April 2013 the FCA stated that the changes 'had to be deferred for operational reasons' and that the plans were being considered 'in the light of the new regulatory framework'. The PRA would deal with the director, NED and chief executive functions at banks but there would be consultation and review.

In paragraph 565 of volume 2 of its final report the Commission said: **2.60**

> Faced with the weaknesses of the Approved Person's Regime laid bare by the failure of individuals in recent years, the FSA responded to the need for the reform with dilatoriness, seemingly paralysed by the operational deficiencies of the existing system and unwilling to contemplate moving away from the familiarity it represents. Changes first mooted in January 2010 and agreed in September of that year have gone back to the drawing board and have been made subject to a further consultation, preceded by a pilot review and then a full review.

And, after the publication of the Commission's final report in June 2013, the enactment, in December of that year, of the Financial Services (Banking Reform) Act 2013 meant that consultation by the PRA and the FCA during 2014 needed to have regard to the provisions concerning senior management functions. These are addressed in 2.62 of this chapter.

ii. Comments and suggestions

(i)   The final report has a section[54] addressing the contention that many of the **2.61**
large international banks are too big and too complex to manage. The conclusion in paragraph 86 was 'many banks remain too big and too complex to manage effectively'. In paragraph 79 Sir Mervyn King, Governor of the Bank of England throughout the financial crisis and retiring in 2013, is quoted as referring to 'evidence that these institutions were simply too big and complex for anyone genuinely to know exactly what was going on'. And evidence was given on behalf of HSBC that:

---

53   The Commission's final report, vol 2, para 552.
54   Ibid, paras 75–86.

At the end of 2010 HSBC was doing auto insurance in Argentina, sub-prime credit cards in the United States and corporate banking in Hong Kong. There is nothing in those activities that is remotely similar. There are no economies of scale from the systems that you can achieve and there is no common risk platform that you can achieve.

As we have seen Salz also referred to the complexity of the Barclays business.

(ii)   The Commission was troubled at the rarity of enforcement action against individuals. Exceptions, the Commission thought, proved the rule. At paragraph 1136 of volume 2 there is a reference to Peter Cummings the former head of Bank of Scotland's corporate division being fined £500,000 and given a life-time ban from the industry and the same paragraph states:

> The FSA intended to pursue an industry ban on Johnny Cameron,[55] but ended their investigation in 2010 when he voluntarily agreed not to work in the industry again. In neither case did enforcement action intrude into the worlds of those at the very top of these failed banks. The chairman and successive chief executives of HBOS have so far escaped any public enforcement action. The same can be said in the context of the chairman and chief executive of RBS. Nor has the most significant conduct failure of recent years with the largest impact on bank customers – the systematic mis-selling of PPI over a long period – led to any enforcement action against senior individuals in banks …

(It is to be noted that Sir Fred Goodwin (the chief executive of RBS) was stripped of his knighthood and that Sir James Crosby voluntarily relinquished his knighthood.) At paragraph 1165 of volume 2 the Commission lamented: 'Faced with the most widespread and damaging failure of the banking industry in the UK's modern history, the regulatory authorities seemed almost powerless to bring sanctions against those who presided over massive failures within banks.'

The Commission felt that fixing individuals with responsibility was made difficult because of the concept of a collective responsibility of boards. 'Top bankers dodged accountability for failings on their watch by claiming ignorance or hiding behind collective decision-making.' (Summary, vol 1, p 8 of the report.)

'Regulators have rarely been able to penetrate an accountability firewall of collective responsibility in firms that prevents actions against individuals' (Summary, vol 1, p 10 of the report). At paragraph 538 of volume 2 of the report the Commission asserts, '… collective nature of official decision-making has also served to insulate individuals from a sense of personal responsibility'.

---

55   Former head of RBS's investment bank.

(iii) The Commission stated (vol 2, para 675 of its report) that 'UK corporate governance has improved in recent years. But when in the case of banks it was tested, it was found wanting. Board failures in the banking sector have been widespread and are not restricted to those banks which required tax payers support or failed during the banking crisis.' And the Commission cited the argument of 'many experts' (vol 2, para 685) 'that improving the effectiveness of boards is the key to addressing many of the problems in the banking sector'. Nevertheless the Commission stated its caution (vol 2, para 676) 'about making a great many recommendations in this field which may do little more than create yet more lucrative work for corporate governance professionals'!

(iv) Nevertheless the Commission did address corporate governance. First, it expressed itself as unhappy with the operation of the nominations committee system prescribed by the Code. The FRC was asked to address 'the widespread perception that some 'natural challengers' are sifted out by the nomination process. The nomination process greatly influences the behaviour of non-executive directors and their board careers. Fundamental reform may be needed'. In particular the FRC was invited to examine 'whether a nomination committee should be chaired by the chairman of a bank … '. At paragraph 123 of volume 1 of the final report it is stated 'there is a danger that the non-executive directors of banks are self-selecting and self-perpetuating'. Regulators were invited to consider, for the largest banks, public advertisement.

Secondly it made the specific recommendation (see vol 1, p 45, para 126 of the final report) that ' a full-time chairman should be the norm'.

(v) As regards the regulatory overlay, the Commission felt that 'the Approved Persons Regime has created a largely illusory impression of regulatory control over individuals, while meaningful responsibilities were not in practice attributed to anyone'. (Summary, vol 1, p 8). Its principal recommendation, accordingly, related to the regulator assigning specific responsibilities to named individuals: 'all key responsibilities within a bank must be assigned to a specific, senior individual';[56] 'the attribution of individual responsibility will, for the first time, provide for full use of the range of civil powers that regulators already have to sanction individuals'.

(vi) In addition the Commission had some recommendations as regards the law.

1. there should be 'personal responsibility for each individual director for the safety and soundness of the firm …' with 'a Government

---

56   The Senior Person Regime, intended to replace the Significant Influence Function of the Approved Persons Regime.

consultation on amending the Companies Act to prioritise financial safety over shareholder interests in the case of banks'.

2. there should be 'direct personal responsibility on the chairman to ensure the effective operation of the board ...'

3. there should be 'individual responsibility for a named non-executive director, usually the chairman, to oversee fair and effective whistle-blowing procedures'.

The Commission argues (see vol 1, para 124 of its report) that 'the obligations of directors to shareholders in accordance with the provisions of the Companies Act 2006 create a particular tension between duties to shareholders and financial safety and soundness in the case of banks'. If following the suggested consultation on amendment to the 2006 Act the law remains unchanged they propose that the problem is addressed by the Code, the PRA's principles of business and their own proposal for a Senior Persons Regime to replace the Approved Persons Regime

- '... the UK Corporate Governance Code be amended to require directors of banks to attach the utmost importance to the safety and soundness of the firm and for the duties they owe to the customers, tax payers and others in interpreting their duties as directors'

- '... the PRA principles of business be amended to include a require-ment that a bank must operate in accordance with the safety and soundness of the firm and that directors' responsibilities to share-holders are to be interpreted in the light of this requirement'

- '... that the responsibilities of Senior Persons who are directors include responsibilities to have proper regard to the safety and soundness of the firm'.

iii. The Financial Services (Banking Reform) Act 2013

2.62 The reaction of Parliament to the Commission's strictures on the regulatory oversight of boards was swift. The Financial Services (Banking Reform) Act 2013 introduced the concept of 'senior management function' by inserting new sections in the Financial Services and Markets Act 2000. Section 59ZA defines a 'senior management function' by reference, first, to the function involving responsibility for the management of 'one or more aspects of the . [bank's] ... affairs' and, secondly, to there being inherent in those aspects 'a risk of serious consequences' for the bank or 'for business or other interests in the United Kingdom'. To ensure certainty and a proper record, section 60(2A) requires the application for regulatory approval to include a statement of the particular 'aspects of the affairs' of the bank for which the proposed appointee will be responsible.

5. THE FUTURE

It might be thought that after such prolonged and intense investigation of the **2.63** effectiveness of bank boards that significant changes in the relevant law, the Code and in practice would be envisaged. This is not the case. The exception is the regulatory change described in 2.62 of this chapter which will, in due course, impact on the appointment and responsibility of bank executive directors.

As regards the law the Walker Report gave attention to two fundamental issues **2.64** in company law long debated by academics and practitioners alike: first, should 'enlightened shareholder value' (the concept of the Companies Act 2006, s 172, which expresses the duty of a director to promote the success of the company for the benefit of shareholders) be abandoned and a wider duty (encompassing depositors, employees and others) be adopted; and secondly, should the unitary board be replaced by dual boards, supervisory and executive, on the continental two-tier model. Walker firmly opted for no change.

The Parliamentary Commission, on the other hand, was not so sure. It, as is **2.65** stated above, wanted a consultation on a change to the 2006 Act so that a responsibility to preserve the 'safety and soundness' of the bank ranked ahead of the duty to shareholders.

The Commission was clearly confused and should have followed Walker. Each director's duty is to promote the success of the company. The exact opposite of success is insolvency. At the forefront of every director's mind, in all deliberations, should be the need to avoid insolvency. Any disregard for 'safety and soundness' imperils solvency. There is no need for the director's duty to be reformulated.

The Commission was also confused in its treatment of individual and collective **2.66** responsibility. It appeared to resent the failure of the authorities to visit sanctions on individuals and the deployment by individuals of collective responsibility as a defensive shield. But it is axiomatic that the vesting of ultimate management power in a group, the board of directors, carries with it a collective responsibility: and fundamental principles of the rule of law prohibit group sanctions. So the plea by the Commission for 'personal responsibility for each individual director for the safety and soundness of the firm' is fine-sounding nonsense.

The point applies equally to responsibilities under company law and to regula- **2.67** tory responsibilities, since both are enforceable at law. So the Commission's insistence that all the several responsibilities in a bank must be assigned to a 'specific, senior individual' and that the chairman should be under a direct personal responsibility 'to ensure the effective operation of the board' are equally flawed. All executive directors are responsible to the board and supervised by the board: nothing which is material to the success of a bank can be extracted from the purview of the board as a whole and vested, as a responsibility, exclusively in one individual. And where a board has operated ineffectively, the attribution of blame between a chairman and the rest of the board is an impossibility. After all, the rest of the board can sack the chairman at any time.

2.68 The Walker Report also went back to basic principles when it addressed the Code, asking whether the provision requiring boards of FTSE 350 banks to have at least as many non-executive as executive directors (B.1.2) should be revisited. In practice this has led in the UK to boards broadly balanced between executive and non-executives whereas in the US, Canada and Australia there is a much smaller executive membership. The Report concluded that the evidence did 'not point to any particular board composition as consistently preferable' and so made no proposal for a change to the Code.[57]

2.69 The Commission's approach to the Code was, again, confused. It is glib to characterise the nominations committee system as entailing self-selection, self-perpetuation and the sifting-out of challengers, without proposing an alternative other than, as a preliminary, the use of public advertisements. The Code has always proceeded on the basis that, given the board has all the management's powers and is steeped in the consideration of all the various issues that impact on the long-term success of the bank, it is the body that is best placed to assess the skills and experience that are required to be present at the board table and to take a view on individual applicants. Appointment from outside (an ex officio appointment or a political appointment, for example) is fraught with far greater dangers than selection by the body currently vested with the overall management responsibility. And, in principle, no distinction in this respect can be drawn between an executive and a non-executive appointment.

2.70 All of Walker, the Commission and Salz were agreed on a series of points which are, consequently, assuming much greater practical competence in the execution by bank boards of their roles: and some have led to minor amendments to the Code. (Two other areas, where there was substantial agreement, risk and remuneration, are covered elsewhere in this book).

---

57   The Walker Report 42, para 3.4.

(a) Great emphasis was laid, on the importance of boards *understanding* their businesses. This has led to increased attention to induction, continued development and continued exposure to the various activities at the operating level.

   The significance of understanding means an insistence on relevant banking experience among the NEDs.[58] Of course challenge can often be based on first principles and sometimes be more effective if not softened by knowledge and experience of the difficulties faced by the executive team. So a board, executive and non-executive, wholly comprising bankers might not be desirable.

(b) Executive directors are normally full time but emphasis, again, was placed on the time commitment of NEDs, Walker suggesting that with a major bank some, at least, of them should devote between 30 to 36 days a year. Walker thought that the chairman of a major bank should allocate two-thirds of his time to the role: the Parliamentary Commission believed full-time chairmen should become the norm.

(c) All the reviews recognised the pivotal role of the chairman in securing the effectiveness of the board. (This is why a chairman has an especial interest in the composition of the board.) The quality of decision-making in a group depends not simply on the make-up of the group, the experience, judgement and application of the individual members but also on the quality and length of the material circulated to them, the recognition of what are the salient issues, the allocation of time to items on an agenda and the ordering of that agenda and the encouragement of debate and constructive questioning with the discouragement of quibbling and interference with detail and all of these are the responsibility of the chairman.

(d) Finally the reviewers were agreed on the importance of rigorous, formal evaluation of performance.

The effective discharge of a board of its role and responsibilities depends on **2.71** how it operates in practice. The nature and style of any board gatherings is determined, in part, by the number of individuals sitting round the table.[59] Walker referred to 'an "ideal" size of 10 to 12' but concluded that there could be 'no general prescription as to optimum board size' and made no recommendation. Neither did any of the other reviews. Yet no bank board pondering its role and composition should shut its eyes to the issue of numbers.

---

58 This hardly needs to be said about executive directors although Andy Hornby was appointed CEO of HBOS from a retailing background.

59 See 2.16 above.

2.72 In addition to numbers, the behavioural dynamics of the group is a critical consideration touched on but not developed in the reviews.[60] Annex 4 to the Walker Report deals with 'Pyschological and behavioural elements in board performances'. It asserts, 'Behaviour is the clue to performance because it is learnable ...' and includes the recommendation 'Board members need to be schooled in group relations, power dynamics and the behaviours and processes that are required to maximise the intellectual capability of the group'.

2.73 Neither the law nor regulation are equipped to deal with the discharge of collective responsibility and the banking crisis and the reviews have shown this. In the main the constituency from which bank board members will be drawn comprises individuals who have achieved much and are close to the peak of their respective career paths. Learning does not come easily to such people: and it may not be clear to them that participation in a group with ultimate management responsibility involves any imperative to learn beyond the immediate and significant task of understanding the underlying businesses. But if board effectiveness is to be improved, behaviour within the board must be improved and that may well mean that board members 'need to be schooled ...'.

SELECTED BIBLIOGRAPHY

Financial Reporting Council, *UK Corporate Governance Code 2012.*

Financial Services Authority, *The Failure of the Royal Bank of Scotland* (December 2011), available at http://www.fsa.gov.uk/static/pubs/other/rbs.pdf.

Financial Services Authority, *The Wheatley Review of LiBOR: Final Report* (September 2012), available at https://www.gov.uk/government/uploads/system/uploads/attachment_data/file/191762/wheatley_review_libor_finalreport_280912.pdf.

House of Lords and House of Commons, *Changing Banking for Good* (Report of the Parliamentary Commission on Banking Standards) (12 June 2013).

Salz, Anthony, *The Salz Review: An Independent Review of Barclays' Business Practices* (April 2013).

Walker, David, *A Review of Corporate Governance in UK Banks and other Financial Industry Entities: Final Recommendations* (26 November 2009), available at http://webarchive.nationalarchives.gov.uk/+/http://www.hm-treasury.gov.uk/d/walker_review_261109.pdf.

---

60   See 2.54 above.

3

DIRECTORS' DUTIES AND LIABILITIES: DISQUALIFYING 'UNFIT' DIRECTORS AT BANKS? POLITICAL RHETORIC AND THE DIRECTORS' DISQUALIFICATION REGIME

John Lowry and Rod Edmunds

1. INTRODUCTION

In the wake of the global 2008 banking crisis and the more recent LIBOR **3.01** scandal numerous committees have reported on both the need to improve the governance of banks and the need to construct a more rigorous and responsive regulatory regime for UK financial institutions and one which also holds the potential to sanction directors of banks for reckless mismanagement.[1] The focus has been on achieving two objectives: first, how best to raise standards of directorial behaviour by ensuring that directors of banks accept individual responsibility for engaging in high-risk conduct which not only jeopardises the

---

1 See the Walker Report 2009, *A Review of Corporate Governance in UK Banks and Other Financial Industry Entities*, available at: http://webarchive.nationalarchives.gov.uk/+/http://www.hm-treasury.gov.uk/d/walker_review_261109.pdf, accessed 15 July 2013. See also, the Financial Services Board Report, *The Failure of the Royal Bank of Scotland* (December 2011), available at: http://www.fsa.gov.uk/library/communication/pr/2011/110.shtml, accessed 15 July 2013; and *Changing Banking for Good*, Report of the Parliamentary Banking Standards HL Paper 27; HC Papers 175, available at: http://www.parliament.uk/bankingstandards, accessed 8 August 2013. See further, the House of Commons Treasury Committee's Fifth Report HC 640 (2012–13), *The FSA's Report into the failure of RBS*, available at: http://www.publications.parliament.uk/pa/cm201213/cmselect/cmtreasy/640/640.pdf, accessed 20 December 2013.

financial stability of their institutions but also the wider economy; and, second, on devising effective measures aimed at deterring such conduct. In relation to the latter, little attention has been paid to the potential for the directors' disqualification regime to fulfil this objective, notwithstanding the political rhetoric suggesting its value and relevance. Although, the Business Secretary, Dr Vince Cable, has, in the last few years, been vigorous in canvassing disqualification as a worthwhile response to individual bankers' managerial excesses, this has so far not borne fruit in terms of judicial proceedings. And, somewhat inexplicably, there has been a barely perceptible shift in the political and legal landscape. So much so that recently a new received wisdom seems to have emerged, one that has sidelined the disqualification regime in favour of introducing a new criminal sanction, that includes the possibility of custodial sentences in cases of reckless misconduct in the management of a bank.[2] Whilst it appears that this is now regarded as a superior means of addressing any future incidence of incompetence of a kind that will require restoring public confidence in the banking sector, it is not to apply to past behaviour. More significantly, the new policy direction leaves a deafening silence as to why senior bankers whose conduct caused colossal and widespread economic damage should escape liability under the existing legislative provisions allowing unfit directors to be disqualified.

3.02 The effectiveness of the disqualification regime as a deterrent against abuse has been questioned by some commentators and in some cases dismissed,[3] but examples of it being deployed specifically against directors of 'failed' banks are rare. A notable exception is of course, *Re Barings plc (No 5)*,[4] which pre-dates the latest global financial crisis. Those proceedings resulted in various disqualification periods against a number of directors of the Barings group for failures in their supervisory processes which led to the spectacular collapse of the bank

---

2   See the Financial Services (Banking Reform) Act 2013, s 36(1), discussed below.

3   See R Williams, 'Disqualifying directors: A remedy worse than the disease' (2007) 7 *Journal of Corporate Law Studies* 213; A Hicks, 'Director's disqualification: can it deliver?' [2001] *JBL* 433; R Tomasic, 'Corporate rescue, governance and risk taking in Northern Rock: Part 2' (2008) 29(11) *Comp Lawyer* 330. Reservations about the effectiveness of the regime were acknowledged in the July 2013 discussion paper, *Transparency and Trust: Enhancing the Transparency of UK Company Ownership and Increasing Trust in UK Business*, published by the Department for Business, Innovation and Skills, available at: https://www.gov.uk/government/uploads/system/uploads/attachment_data/file/212079/bis-13–959-transparency-and-trust-enhancing-the-transparency-of- uk-company-ownership-and-increaing-trust-in-uk-business.pdf, accessed 15 July 2013. On the other hand, the majority of respondents to the EU Commission's consultation on harmonising disqualification provisions across Member States viewed disqualification as an effective weapon for combating abuse by directors: Directorate General for Internal Market and Services, 'Consultation on Future Priorities for the Action Plan on Modernising Company Law and Enhancing Corporate Governance in the European Union: Summary Report' available at: http://ec.europa.eu/internal_market/company/docs/consultation/final_report_en.pdf, accessed 22 October 2013. However, a strong majority of respondents, some 70 per cent, opposed any new EU legislation given the existing national legislative frameworks; see p 14 of the report.

4   *Secretary of State for Trade and Industry v Baker (No 5)* [1999] 1 BCLC 433, discussed further below.

following a loss of £827m due to the unauthorised activities of a trader, Nick Leeson, in the bank's Singapore office. As such, the decision affords a salutary reminder of the potential of disqualification orders as a regulatory mechanism in cases of directorial nonfeasance or, indeed, misfeasance. Of particular note for our purposes, is the approach taken by the trial judge, Jonathan Parker J, towards the meaning and determination of 'unfitness' where incompetence rather than dishonesty is in issue. We return to the judgment below.

Notwithstanding the criticisms levelled against disqualification and the short **3.03** shrift it was given by the FSA and the Parliamentary Commission on Banking Standards,[5] our current political masters have nevertheless voiced a markedly higher degree of confidence in the regime insofar as it can lead to directors being barred from holding office in the same way that other officeholders can be struck-off professional registers. Calls of this kind can be traced back to the early days of the crisis, and emanated from leading politicians. Take, for instance, the speech of the then leader of the opposition, the Rt Hon David Cameron MP, delivered at Canary Wharf in December 2008, in which he said:

> Justice is effective only when it is seen to be done, for the thug locked up for mugging people on the streets to the highest executive in the biggest firm who's been swindling the books. Doctors who behave irresponsibly get struck off. Bankers who behave irresponsibly should face professional consequences. And for sure, if anyone is found to have behaved criminally they must be prosecuted. Of course, this requires clear evidence of wrongdoing. But that doesn't mean we should sit on our hands and say it's all a failure of regulation.[6]

Similar sentiments were expressed by the leader of the Liberal Democrats, the **3.04** Rt Hon Nick Clegg MP, in an interview with *The Times* newspaper in which he indicated that directors of failed banks were not fit to oversee companies:

> Directors who were running the banks Northern Rock, HBOS, Royal Bank of Scotland and Bradford & Bingley when they were rescued by the taxpayer should be disqualified from sitting on company boards … . My own view is that anyone who had a senior role in the business model, [which] has been shown to be wrong, is spectacularly irrespons-ible. I think they should be disqualified.[7]

Some might associate such unambiguous views as an understandable initial response to the enormity of unprecedented economic meltdown. It has however been matched in more recent political reaction to official reports into what went

---

5 See above n 1.
6 *The Independent*, 16 December 2008, available at: http://www.independent.co.uk/news/uk/politics/cameron-pledges-to-punish-bankers-1128207.html, accessed 15 July 2013.
7 *The Times*, 6 March 2009.

wrong within UK banks such as Royal Bank of Scotland (RBS) and Halifax Bank of Scotland (HBOS). After the determination of catastrophic management failures by those at the helm of HBOS in the April 2013 Report from the Parliamentary Commission on Banking Standards, the BBC reported Dr Cable's feelings of 'outrage' which accompanied his instruction that the Insolvency Service should consider the sufficiency of the evidence to launch disqualification proceedings against three of the bank's senior managers.[8] The media had previously reported the Secretary of State's similarly hard-line stance favouring disqualification of Fred Goodwin (and some of the bank's other directors[9]) after the FSA's report into collapse of RBS.[10] Dr Cable has not been the lone high-profile proponent of the need for intervention against individuals. Andrew Bailey, head of the bank regulatory body, the Prudential Regulation Authority has also publicly voiced surprise at the lack of moves for individual bankers to be disqualified.[11]

3.05 Yet, while throughout the fall-out from the financial crisis there has been significant political momentum to disqualify the senior managers responsible for bringing the banks to the brink of insolvency, two things stand out. First, thus far such legal proceedings have been conspicuous by their absence as a response to the managerial shortcomings of the senior bankers at RBS and HBOS. The reasons for this lamentably slow progress, which may ultimately be leading nowhere, are unclear (indeed they may have been rendered otiose by a change in tack by the measures that have been included in the Financial Services (Banking Reform) Act 2013). However, one perceived obstacle is whether sufficient evidence for disqualification proceedings to succeed exists.[12] This objection is less than convincing when viewed against the circumstances surrounding the fall of RBS in the wake of its acquisition of ABN AMRO and the 'catastrophic failure of HBOS's management'.[13] It is noteworthy that these

8   Vince Cable 'examines ban for former HBOS directors', BBC News, 7 April 2013, available at: http://www.bbc.co.uk/news/business-22056275, accessed 20 December 2013.

9   Including, it seems, Sir James Cameron, former head of RBS's investment bank.

10   Vince Cable: RBS report recommends prosecution, *The Telegraph*, 17 March 2012, available at: http://www.telegraph.co.uk/finance/newsbysector/banksandfinance/9336327/Vince-Cable-RBS-report-recommends-prosecution.html, accessed 20 December 2013. Vince Cable presses Scottish lawyers on RBS bankers, *Financial Times*, 1 May 2013 available at: http://www.ft.com/cms/s/0/85474cd6-b1b6–11e2–9315–00144feabdc0.html#axzz2qJ88wVMY, accessed 30 December 2013.

11   See Regulator surprised no bank bosses face charges over financial crisis, *The Guardian*, 16 April 2013, available at: http://www.theguardian.com/business/2013/apr/16/regulator-surprised-no-bank-bosses-face-charges, accessed 30 December 2013.

12   See 'Disqualification may be on the horizon for former HBOS directors' available at: http://www.lexology.com/library/detail.aspx?g=3e41deb9–23a2–43dc-9ec2–21011ad02501, accessed 15 July 2013.

13   The Rt Hon Andrew Tyrie MP, commenting on the publication of the Fourth Report of the Parliamentary Commission on Banking Standards, available at: http://www.parliament.uk/business/committees/committees-a-z/joint-select/professional-standards-in-the-banking-industry/news/an-accident-waiting-to-happen-the-failure-of-hbos/, accessed 15 July 2013.

circumstances have been, and in some respects continue to be, a matter of forensic enquiry and public scrutiny in the form of the public reports referred to in this chapter. Second, over the course of the last year there has been a sea-change in the Government's thinking that favours invoking a specific and newly introduced criminal sanction presumably as an alternative to trying to achieve a measure of civil redress in the form of disqualification. This attitudinal shift appears to be premised on what needs to be done prospectively. It takes a view both as to the optimum response, and deterrent, in the event of there being any recurrence of individual banking misconduct on a par with that experienced in the first decade of the current century.[14] Thus, in a speech to the London Reform Conference on 'Responsible capitalism' in July 2013, in which Dr Cable set out proposals designed to increase public trust in business, he said:

> Yet, with people apparently responsible for major corporate failures seemingly going unpunished – particularly the banks – the public has been questioning the adequacy of our disqualification system. This has been brought out most clearly by the analysis of the Parliamentary Commission on Banking Standards, which rightly highlighted specific flaws in the accountability mechanisms for banks. The Government has accepted all of the Commission's major recommendations in this respect, including the creation of a new offence of reckless misconduct.[15]

Indeed, the Government acted with considerable speed. The Financial Services (Banking Reform) Act 2013, which received Royal Assent on 18 December 2013, introduces new criminal sanctions including an offence of 'reckless misconduct in the management of a bank', which carries a custodial sentence.[16]

---

14 Which, it is to be hoped, is a rare prospect suggesting the offence will seldom if ever be invoked. What also seems clear is that the law, which is not retrospective in application, cannot be applied to the senior members of RBS and HBOS. During the parliamentary debates on the new law a government spokesman tentatively suggested that Fred Goodwin might have faced prosecution under the terms of the new offence: Goodwin 'may have been prosecuted' under new plans, *The Scotsman*, 11 December 2013, available at: http://www.scotsman.com/news/uk/goodwin-may-have-been-prosecuted-under-new-plans-1-3229019, accessed 20 December 2013.

15 See Trusted Business: Vince Cable speech – Reform Conference on 'Responsible capitalism', London, Deportment for Business, Innovation and Skills, available at: http://news.bis.gov.uk/Press-Releases/Trusted-business-Vince-Cable-speech-Reform-conference-on-Responsible-capitalism-London-68fd4.aspx, accessed 20 December 2013.

16 Section 36(1) provides:

A person ("S") commits an offence if –

(a) at a time when S is a senior manager in relation to a financial institution ("F"), S –
   (i) takes, or agrees to the taking of, a decision by or on behalf of F as to the way in which the business of a group institution is to be carried on, or
   (ii) fails to take steps that S could take to prevent such a decision being taken,
(b) at the time of the decision, S is aware of a risk that the implementation of the decision may cause the failure of the group institution,

Prosecutions may be initiated by the Financial Conduct Authority, the Prudential Regulation Authority, the Secretary of State, or by or with the consent of the Director of Public Prosecutions.[17] While it signals a political shift in the optimum way to respond to future debacles, it does not offer a satisfying answer to whether, and if so, why, the senior managers of RBS and HBOS will escape the disqualification regime. Further, the new offence also has inherent weaknesses and may not offer the solution to the perceived weaknesses of the disqualification regime for which its proponents hope. For one thing, and as is pointed out by the Law Society's Banking Reform Working Group, '[i]ntroducing recklessness as the basis for an offence means that prosecutors will have to decide, possibly years after a business decision was taken, whether it was reckless or not at the time'.[18]

3.06 The purpose of this chapter is to assess the general scope of the Company Directors Disqualification Act 1986 (CDDA 1986), particularly section 8 which provides for the disqualification of 'unfit' directors. The shortcomings of the regime will be assessed together with the current proposals for its reform which are prompted by the desire to facilitate the disqualification of errant senior bankers such as those who captured the attention of the media and, therefore, the wider public. The most prominent amongst these are HBOS's Andy Hornby, Sir James Crosby and Lord Stevenson, together with the former CEO of RBS, Fred Goodwin. The chapter will first consider the particular circumstances that led to the taxpayers' bailout of the RBS and HBOS. Our focus here is on the culpability of the senior executives of both institutions rather than upon the other contributing factors, such as the shortcomings of the regulatory regime, which led to the failure of the banks. Our aim is to show that in the light of what happened in RBS and HBOS, the current timidity over the initiation of disqualification proceedings under section 8, seemingly prompted, as will be seen, by misgivings over whether there is sufficient evidence against the directors to at least establish a prima facie case, may be far too pessimistic. Second, there will be an assessment of the jurisprudence surrounding disqualification on the ground of 'unfitness'. It will show that the substantive terms of this basis for disqualification contains ample scope to address the conduct of senior executives at HBOS and RBS, not least because the courts have refused

---

(c)   in all the circumstances, S's conduct in relation to the taking of the decision falls far below what could reasonably be expected of a person in S's position, and

(d)   the implementation of the decision causes the failure of the group institution.

17   Section 38.

18   'Law Society warns new criminal sanctions will not stop banks failing', available at: http://www.lawsociety. org.uk/news/press-releases/law-society-warns-new-criminal-sanctions-will-not-stop-banks-failing/, accessed 2 January 2014. The FCA, on the other hand, is generally more supportive of the new criminal offence, see 'The FCA's response to the Parliamentary Commission on Banking Standards', October 2013, paras 16–19 available at: http://www.fca.org.uk/static/documents/pcbs-response.pdf, accessed 3 March 2014.

to strait-jacket the test of unfitness with rigid categorisations. We conclude by considering recent initiatives aimed at providing alternative routes for holding senior bankers liable for reckless behaviour.

2. THE RISE AND FALL OF THE ROYAL BANK OF SCOTLAND[19]

Within a year of Fred Goodwin joining RBS as deputy to its Chief Executive, **3.07** the bank embarked upon a massive expansionary programme by bidding for NatWest plc, an institution three times its size. Following the successful acquisition of NatWest in early 2000 for £20.7bn, RBS became the second largest UK bank after HSBC. In 2001 Mr Goodwin was appointed Chief Executive of RBS Group, and the policy of rapid international expansion began. Over the next four years RBS acquired over 20 businesses including First Active (the Irish mortgage bank), Churchill Insurance, Direct Line Insurance, Commonwealth Bancorp and the retail-banking arm of Mellon Financial Group. In May 2004, RBS purchased the US based Charter One Financial Inc of Cleveland, Ohio for $10.5bn. While the price was generally considered to be too high,[20] RBS's profits soared five-fold. Next, in October 2007, just as the global liquidity crisis was beginning to become apparent, ABN-AMRO (hereafter, ABN), accepted a bid by a consortium led by the RBS which was worth £55bn.[21] RBS's share was £10bn (the cash element was set at 93 per cent). This was Europe's largest ever banking takeover. By 2008 RBS was the fifth-largest bank in the world and during that year it lent $9.3bn, mostly by supporting leveraged buyouts.[22]

The ABN deal proved disastrous for RBS and played a critical part in its **3.08** collapse insofar as it had a major impact on its balance sheet, not least because of ABN's exposure to the US subprime mortgage crisis.[23] However, it was not the sole reason for its failure. RBS's exposure to the liquidity crisis was compounded by other aspects of Goodwin's aggressive takeover strategy. His acquisition of NatWest had carried with it the takeover of a US investment bank, Greenwich

---

19   On the story of the collapse, see, Iain Martin, Making IT Happen: Fred Goodwin, RBS and the Men Who Blew up the British Economy (Simon & Shuster 2013).

20   See, for example, *The Journal*, 26 January 2009, 'RBS's Fred Goodwin: the world's worst banker?', available at: http://www.journal-online.co.uk/article/5295-rbss_fred_goodwin_worlds_worst_banker, accessed 3 March 2014.

21   A proposed merger with Barclays had been abandoned when it failed to obtain 80 per cent of ABN's shares.

22   Please see: 'Royal Bank of Scotland wins buyout-lending crown', available at: http://blogs.wsj.com/deals/2009/01/07/royal-bank-of-scotland-wins-a-buyout-lending-crown/, accessed 2 October 2013.

23   See, S Arnott, *BloombergBusinessweek Global Economics*, 14 October 2008, available at: http://www.businessweek.com/stories/2008-10-14/the-rise-and-fall-of-fred-the-shredbusinessweek-business-news-stock-market-and-financial-advice, accessed 3 October 2013.

NatWest, which in the mid-2000s had expanded into private equity loans and into the subprime mortgage market. It had also become a leading underwriter of collateralised debt obligations and, as such, RBS found itself massively overexposed to the losses consequent on these instruments. The combination of these factors left RBS heavily reliant on external wholesale funding.[24] In December 2007 RBS announced a write-down of £950m of US subprime loans and £250m of leveraged loans. In an attempt to rebuild its balance sheet, a £12bn share issue was completed in June 2008 but the attempted sale of Direct Line and Churchill Insurance for £7bn failed due to a lack of interest caused, no doubt, by the liquidity crisis.

3.09 In October 2008 the government's multi-billion pound bailout was agreed. Had RBS not been granted government support it would 'probably have gone into resolution'.[25] As part of the package, Goodwin was required to leave the bank. At the peak of his career at RBS, around February 2007, the share price reached £18 a share, up from £4. 42p when he became CEO in January 2001. On the day of Goodwin's departure the share price had plummeted to around 65p, representing a 98 per cent fall. In February 2009, RBS reported that during Goodwin's tenure it had posted a loss of £24.1bn: representing the largest loss in UK corporate history.[26]

3.10 While in its 2011 report the FSA acknowledge that the bank's failure resulted from a range of factors, including an inadequate regulatory approach, it also noted that poor management and boardroom decisions were contributing reasons.[27] Of particular note in this regard, was the bank's excessive dependence on short-term wholesale funding which reflected the mistaken belief on the part of RBS that it would be able to continue to fund itself. The policy of aggressive growth led to widespread concerns in the market, first, about the bank's asset quality and, second, as to uncertainties about the size of future loan losses: both of which were proven to be justified concerns in the light of subsequent events.[28] RBS's sizeable fair value losses in its credit trading

---

24   Such reliance was also found to have been a principal cause of the failure of the Northern Rock Building Society. In its report, 'The run on the Rock', the House of Commons Treasury Committee found that the directors of Northern Rock 'were the principal authors' of the bank's failure. They had 'pursued a reckless business model which was excessively reliant on wholesale funding'. See the *Fifth Report of Session 2007–08*, 2008, p 3, available at: http://www.publications.parliament.uk/pa/cm200708/cmselect/cmtreasy/56/56i.pdf, accessed 23 October 2013.

25   See Financial Services Authority Board Report, see above n 1, Part 1, 38: available at: http://www.fsa.gov.uk/pubs/other/rbs.pdf, accessed 3 October 2013.

26   *The Guardian*, 26 February 2009, 'RBS record losses raise prospect of 95% state ownership', available at: http://www.theguardian.com/business/2009/feb/26/rbs-record-loss, accessed 2 October 2013.

27   See above, n 1.

28   Ibid., 39.

activities are attributed to the bank's 'deficient strategy and execution'.[29] The most telling part of the FSA's report into the events leading to RBS's failure states, in part:

> The ABN AMRO acquisition significantly increased RBS's exposure to risky asset categories, reduced an already relatively low capital ratio, increased potential liquidity strains and, because of RBS's role as the consortium leader and consolidator, created additional potential and perceived risks. RBS's decision to proceed with this acquisition was made on the basis of due diligence which was *inadequate in scope and depth given the nature and scale of the acquisition and the major risks involved.*[30]

The finding of lack of due diligence is key, and represents the most damning of indictments against the senior management. Indeed, in his Foreword to the Report, the Chairman noted that of the many poor management decisions made by the board of RBS, the most striking was the decision to acquire ABN which proceeded 'on the basis of due diligence which was clearly inadequate relative to the risks entailed'.[31] The information made available to RBS by ABN in April 2007 amounted to 'two lever arch folders and a CD'.[32] The FSA concludes that 'ultimate responsibility' for the disastrous consequences of RBS's policy of aggressive expansion must lie with the firm. This, in its view, was one of the principal factors which led to the bank's failure and the 'pattern' of poor decision-making undoubtedly points to fundamental deficiencies in the bank's senior 'management, governance and culture'.[33] In this regard, the report highlights Goodwin's decision to fund the ABN acquisition principally through debt rather than equity as a major cause of the bank's precarious capital adequacy position towards the end of 2007.[34]

However, notwithstanding these findings, the FSA Report explains that its **3.11** enforcement lawyers reached the conclusion that proceedings against the RBS board stood little chance of success given the lack of any benchmark for judging the adequacy of due diligence particularly in relation to contested takeovers. Accordingly, the Enforcement Division was therefore unable to identify enforceable breaches of FSA rules. The option of banning the directors from holding office in another financial services firm, all of them in question being 'approved persons' under the Financial Services and Markets Act 2000 (as amended by the Financial Services Act 2012), was not, therefore, pursued (the

---

29 Ibid.
30 Ibid., para 4.5, emphasis added.
31 Ibid., Chairman's Foreword, 7.
32 Ibid.
33 Ibid., para 5.
34 With respect to RBS's precarious capital adequacy, which was exacerbated by the ABN deal, the Report quotes Goodwin's defence of his policy.

case against Mr Johnny Cameron was dropped for the reasons explained in Chapter 1 of this volume).Whatever the merits of the FSA's conclusion in this regard, it nevertheless fails to explain why the alternative option in the form of disqualification proceedings have not been brought against Goodwin and his other colleagues by the Secretary of State.

3.12 It will be argued that the case law surrounding the disqualification regime supports the view that a finding of lack of diligence on the part of a director amounts to incompetence such as to support a finding of unfitness.[35] In this light, it can be seen that the lack of due diligence on the part of RBS when acquiring ABN points to a reckless disregard by the bank's board, and Goodwin in particular, of the risks consequent upon the policy of aggressive takeovers, seemingly, as is suggested in the FSA's report, at any price.

3. HBOS: 'AN ACCIDENT WAITING TO HAPPEN'[36]

3.13 Unlike the problems and errors at RBS (and, or that matter, elsewhere in the UK banking sector), the failure of HBOS in 2008 'stands alone' as 'a home-grown banking failure in traditional banking'.[37] HBOS came into existence in 2001 following a merger between Bank of Scotland and the Halifax, which in 1997 was one of the UK's last building societies to demutualise. The newly created bank represented a 'complimentary merger', by which Halifax's 'significantly enhanced balance sheet, from a capital and funding perspective' became matched with Bank of Scotland's corporate and treasury expertise.[38] By the end of 2001 HBOS's total assets were £275bn making it larger than Lloyds TSB and three-quarters the size of RBS (and Barclays) and, by its own assessment, a 'new force in banking'.[39] However, over the course of the seven or so years of HBOS's existence, its board set an aggressive strategy of rapid asset-led growth across all its divisions,[40] the execution of which resulted in a faster expansion in

---

35 See, in particular, the judgment of Jonathan Parker J in *Re Barings plc (No 5)* [1999] 1 BCLC 433, Ch D, discussed below. See further, *Secretary of State for Trade and Industry v Gray* [1995] 1 BCLC 276 CA (Civ).

36 See 'An accident waiting to happen': The failure of HBOS, Parliamentary Commission on Banking Standards, Fourth Report 2012–13 (April 2013). There is an earlier and brief official assessment in House of Commons Treasury Committee, 'Banking Crisis: dealing with the failure of the UK Banks', Seventh Report HC 416 (2008–09), paras 39–48, available at: http://www.publications.parliament.uk/pa/cm200809/cmselect/cmtreasy/416/416.pdf, accessed 13 January 2014. For a journalistic portrayal of events see, R Perman, *Hubris: How HBOS Wrecked The Best Bank in Britain* (Birlinn 2012).

37 Ibid., para 114. See also the Parliamentary Commission's conclusion that (ibid., para 138): 'the downfall of HBOS was not the result of cultural contamination by investment banking. This was a traditional bank failure pure and simple. It was a case of a bank pursuing traditional banking activities and pursuing them badly'.

38 Ibid., para 14.

39 Ibid.

40 Ibid., paras 15 and 19.

its lending than in deposits in a way that ultimately precipitated the bank's failure and occasioned the need for intervention to save the business from becoming insolvent. Intervention came, first, in October 2008 when HBOS was bolstered by £20.5bn of taxpayers' money via emergency liquidity assistance from the Bank of England, and, second, in a government initiated takeover by Lloyds Banking Group early in 2009. In combination HBOS's rescue depended on an injection of £28bn,[41] and cost the bank's original shareholders 96 per cent of their money.

HBOS's losses predominantly arose in its financial dealings across three **3.14** separate spheres of its operation. The Corporate Division incurred estimated losses of £25bn, while its International and Treasury Divisions sustained losses in the order of £15bn and £7bn respectively.[42] In the view of the Parliamentary Committee's Report each of these three Divisions' performance would in itself have led HBOS to insolvency and to have necessitated recapitalisation. Moreover:

> Both the relative scale of such losses and the fact that they were incurred in three separate divisions suggests a systematic management failure across the organisation.[43]

The managerial deficiencies manifested in a number of ways. They notably included an inability and inadequacy at the most senior tier of HBOS's management in controlling the independent operation of the three loss-making divisions. This systemic weakness in risk management was 'a matter of design, not accident'. While HBOS's downfall highlighted the FSA's 'thoroughly inadequate' control,[44] aspects of which may have reinforced the senior managements' 'misplaced priorities', it is clear that the board rather than the FSA was ultimately responsible for the bank's chosen path.[45] The Parliamentary Commission clearly pinpoints responsibility as being attributable to Sir James Crosby, HBOS's Chief Executive until 2005, Andy Hornby who 'failed to address the matter' and 'particularly' the Chairman, Lord Stevenson.[46] The Report is forthright in repeatedly allocating responsibility to those at the top of HBOS, finding, for instance, that HBOS's problems represented 'a fundamentally flawed business model and a colossal failure of senior management and of the Board'.[47] Yet the only manager who has so far been subjected to personal

---

41 Ibid., paras 107–109.
42 By contrast the impaired performance of the Retail Divisions performance was 'not a material factor in the failure of HBOS.': ibid., para 46.
43 Ibid., para 47.
44 Ibid., para 83. For a full assessment of the shortcomings, ibid., paras 66–86.
45 Ibid., para 86.
46 Ibid., para 65.
47 Ibid., para 134.

accountability is Peter Cummings,[48]and senior management have persisted in maintaining that HBOS's demise was essentially a consequence of the drying up of the wholesale funding markets and not a failure in management.[49] That assessment is robustly rejected by the Parliamentary Commission who saw HBOS management's explanation as 'entirely unconvincing'.[50]

> In the view of this Commission, it is right and proper that the primary responsibility for the downfall of HBOS should rest with Sir James Crosby, architect of the strategy that set the course for disaster, with Andy Hornby, who proved unable or unwilling to change course, and Lord Stevenson, who presided over the bank's board from its birth to its death.[51]

The Report is not meant to be the final word on the failings at HBOS. The Parliamentary Commission identified themes for the FSA to expand upon in the review of the failure of HBOS that the Treasury Select Committee commissioned.[52] However, it seems that the promised report, now being conducted under the aegis of the FCA as the FSA's successor, has been delayed, and at the time of writing is yet to be published.[53]

3.15 It is never easy to be sure of the part any one director plays in the demise of a major banking institution particularly where there is increasing accent on viewing events through the lens of institutional responsibility. What is equally understandable is that there is a public and political appetite to attribute individual responsibility for the failure. This is all the more to be expected when the bank failing proved instrumental in a cataclysmic domestic and global economic meltdown. What is notable is that the tenor of the public reports consequent upon HBOS's and RBS's failure is that in addition to collective deficiencies, the directorial failings of senior bankers are documented. This

---

48 Ibid., paras 129–133. See also the most recent Parliamentary Commission report, 'Changing banking for good', see above n 1, para 1136.

49 Ultimately the Parliamentary Commission rejected the insiders' contention that HBOS's difficulties were solely attributable to funding and liquidity, seeing liquidity as the occasion rather than the cause of the bank's downfall: ibid., paras 113–115.

50 Ibid., para 122.

51 Ibid., para 135.

52 Ibid., para 141. For the Treasury Committee's terms of reference for the review and its appointment of three independent experts to review the report see 'Independent Review of Financial Services Authority report on the failure of HBOS – Terms of Reference', available at: http://www.parliament.uk/documents/commons-committees/treasury/Terms%20of%20Reference%20HBOS%20review.pdf, accessed 20 December 2013.This follows the same model adopted in relation to RBS: see 'Evidence to the Treasury Select Committee by Bill Knight and Sir David Walker, specialist advisers to the Committee in relation to the report by the Financial Services Authority into the failure of The Royal Bank of Scotland', available at: http://www.parliament.uk/documents/commons-committees/treasury/RBS%20Evidence%20to%20TSC%20from%20BK%20and%20SDW.pdf, accessed 20 December 2013.

53 'HBOS report delayed until the end of the year', *The Guardian*, 18 July 2013.

prompts the question whether the terms of the CDDA 1986 could be invoked both to prevent unfit individuals from being directors of banks, albeit for a fixed time up to 15 years, and to deter high-risk behaviour.

4. THE COMPANY DIRECTORS DISQUALIFICATION ACT 1986

Judged against the longevity of other corporate control mechanisms, the **3.16** CDDA has a shorter history, although it does extend further back than the statutory framework introduced in 1986.[54] The Companies Act 1929 prohibited undischarged bankrupts from taking part in the management of a company without the leave of the court,[55] it also gave the courts the power to disqualify directors found to be in breach of its fraudulent trading provisions. These powers were extended by the inclusion in the Companies Act 1948 of provisions for the disqualification of directors who had committed fraud, breach of duty or liquidation offences.[56] The next major legislative development in the form of the CDDA 1986,[57] followed the publication of the Cork Report.[58] It is possible to discern a variety of concerns and aspirations in the introduction of the present provisions for the removal of unfit directors. Broadly speaking the 1986 Act aims 'to maintain the integrity of the business environment', and it can be said to offer 'a powerful tool against those who abuse the privilege of limited liability'.[59] In these ways the legislation sets out to promote the public interest by preventing irresponsible directors from being involved subsequently in the management of other companies. This is designed to remove the risk of future harm whether it be to specific groups such as creditors, employees,

---

54 The Companies Act 1929 had prohibited undischarged bankrupts from taking part in the management of a company without the leave of the court (see now CDDA 1986, s 11); It also gave the courts the power to disqualify directors found to be in breach of its fraudulent trading provisions.

55 See now CDDA 1986, s 11.

56 Section 188.

57 Section 1(1) of the CDDA 1986 provides that a disqualification order against a director is an order that:

   [F]or a period specified in the order:

   (a) he shall not be a director of a company, act as receiver of a company's property or in any way, whether directly or indirectly, be concerned or take part in the promotion, formation or management of a company unless (in each case) he has the leave of the court, and

   (b) he shall not act as an insolvency practitioner.

   The order need not be a total disqualification and he can be allowed to act in relation to certain companies subject to conditions, while being disqualified from acting for any others (see *Re Lo-Line Ltd* (1988) 4 BCC 415). Furthermore, even once disqualified, the legislation effectively enables him to later apply for leave to act in relation to certain companies: CDDA 1986, s 17.

58 The Cork Report (Cmnd 8558, 1982) and the White Paper, *A Revised Framework for Insolvency Law* (Cmnd 9175, 1984) which led to the expansion of the jurisdiction in the Insolvency Act 1985.

59 The Insolvency Service, A Guide to Director Disqualification and Other Action, available at: http://www.bis.gov.uk/insolvency/Companies/insolvent-companies/director-disqualification-and-other-action#3, accessed 27 December 2013.

shareholders or, more broadly, in the form of detriment to the market and the wider economy. One thing the regime is not concerned with is subjecting unfit directors to personal liability. Equally, in the light of the political and public furore about the moral culpability of individual bankers such as Fred Goodwin and the leaders of HBOS, it is important to keep firmly in mind that a disqualification order is effectively punitive.[60] Disqualification will impede, if not extinguish, the entrepreneurial and employment prospects of the director concerned.

3.17 Determining the effectiveness of the legislation in fulfilling its goals is challenging. Admittedly there is statistical evidence showing an increase in the number of disqualification orders made by the courts since the jurisdiction was initially introduced.[61] For example, in 1983–84, there were a total of 89 orders,[62] as compared to 197 in 1987–88. This more than doubled in 1994–95, when 493 orders were made. By 1999–2000 the annual total had risen to 1,509.[63] In the year 2003–2004, disqualifications totalled 1,527.[64] Again, in the year to 31 March 2010, the number of director disqualification proceedings was 17 per cent higher than in the previous year, 2,169 as compared to 1,852. Since then the number of orders made has levelled to around 1,500 per year.[65] How far these trends depend upon the efficiency of the Insolvency Service, acting on behalf of the Secretary of State, in bringing such proceedings is difficult to judge.[66] Besides, even if we leave aside the questionable wisdom of assessing the impact of the regime purely in terms of the volume of annual disqualifications achieved, it is revealing to consider the extent to which the legislative regime is, and can be, an efficacious means of responding to the directorial shortcomings that contributed to the major UK banks failing during the banking crisis.

---

60 See the July 2013 discussion paper, *Transparency and Trust*, see above n 3. See also *Secretary of State for Trade and Industry v Ettinger* [1993] BCLC 896 CA; and *Re Westmid Packing Services Ltd* [1998] 2 All ER 124, [3], *per* Lord Woolf MR.

61 S Griffin, 'The disqualification of unfit directors and the protection of the public interest' (2002) 53 *NILQ* 207.

62 Mainly under the Companies Act 1948, s 188.

63 See *Companies in 1998–99* (London: DTI, 1999) 36, and earlier editions. For analysis of the decision-making mechanisms relating to the bringing of disqualification proceedings, see S Wheeler, 'Directors' disqualification: Insolvency practitioners and the decision-making process' (1995) 15(2) *Legal Studies* 283.

64 See *Companies in 2003–04* (London: DTI, 2004), 44. About two-thirds of these were under the new procedure of disqualification by undertaking.

65 The Insolvency Service *Annual Report 2011–12*, HC 358, at 30.

66 Although it is noteworthy that the increase in disqualification orders under s 6 of the 1986 Act followed severe criticisms of the way the Insolvency Service had been managing the case load, these criticisms had been led by both the Public Accounts Committee and the National Audit Office: see, *Committee of Public Accounts 18th Report* (House of Commons Papers, session 1993–1994, 167); and National Audit Office, *The Insolvency Service Executive Agency: Company Director Disqualification* (House of Commons Papers, session 1992–1993, 907) and National Audit Office, *Insolvency Service Executive Agency, Company Director Disqualification – A Follow-up Report* (House of Commons Papers, Session 1998–1999, HC 424).

There are numerous grounds for disqualification. For present purposes, the two **3.18** that merit particular attention are to be found in sections 6(1) and 8(1)–(2),[67] for which disqualification is made to pivot on a determination of unfitness to manage a company. In some ways the applicability of these provisions differs markedly. For one thing, proceedings under section 8 are not subject to a limitation period – making the passing of time in itself legally irrelevant should proceedings be contemplated against the RBS and HBOS directors. Disqualification is mandatory under section 6 but not under section 8. This means that even where the court is satisfied that the conduct in question makes the director unfit to manage a company, it retains a discretion not to disqualify,[68] although it has been judicially acknowledged that it would be unusual for the court to use its discretion in this way.[69] Another point of departure lies in the minimum penalty of disqualification of two years under section 6 whereas there is no minimum period under section 8.[70] Moreover, by way of pre-requisite, section 6 requires the company to have become insolvent, whereas section 8 is available irrespective of the company's solvency, but requires the Secretary of State's belief that disqualification is 'expedient in the public interest'.[71] Section 6 proves problematical in that the banks did not become technically insolvent because of the then Labour Government's intervention which resulted, in effect, in the taxpayer bailing them out on the basis that the banks were 'too big to fail'. This leaves section 8 as the principal contender in holding banking directors to account via the disqualification regime. The test of unfitness to be applied involves the court having regard to the terms of Part 1 of Schedule 1 to the 1986 Act.[72] Included in the matters to which particular regard should be paid are misfeasance, breach of duty and misapplication of property. In addition, the corpus of case law on the meaning of unfitness is, of course, also pertinent.[73]

---

67 The maximum period of disqualification under both is 15 years.

68 See the judgment of Peter Smith J in *Re JA Chapman & Co Ltd* [2003] EWHC 532 (Ch).

69 See *Re Atlantic Computers plc* 15 June 1998, unreported, Ch D, Lloyd J.

70 See further *Re Sevenoaks Stationers (Retail) Ltd* [1991] Ch 164 (CA); and *Re Samuel Sherman plc* [1991] 1 WLR 1070.

71 The formation of that belief depends upon a report having been made to the Secretary of State and which forms the basis for an application for disqualification.

72 See s 9(1)(a). The Schedule contains a non-exhaustive list of factors.

73 The preponderance of which has been generated by the same term contained in the much litigated s 6(1). Though it has been stressed that the starting point in the determination of unfitness must be the words of the statute rather than the gloss placed upon them by the courts: see *Re Sevenoaks Stationers (Retail) Ltd* [1991] Ch 164 CA, 176, per Dillon LJ.

5. DETERMINING UNFITNESS TO BE CONCERNED IN THE MANAGEMENT OF A COMPANY

3.19   As seen above, the 1986 Act does not provide a definition of what constitutes 'unfitness' beyond providing indicia for its determination. However, the courts have provided some useful and general insights when assessing the question.[74] A hallmark of the case law is the broad approach that is adopted towards defining 'unfitness', and the judges have repeatedly stressed that although the words of the 1986 Act are the starting-point, the statutory language is not exhaustive. This is particularly apparent in the modern case law on disqualification and shows that the conduct of Goodwin and the RBS/HBOS board members might in fact fall within the scope of the disqualification regime. Sometimes the allegations in question rest on dishonesty but this is clearly not the only or a necessary manifestation of the requisite conduct. The older case law seems to suggest that either moral culpability or gross incompetence are the key determinants. For instance, in *Re Dawson Print Group Ltd*,[75] Hoffmann J remarked:

> There must, I think, be something about the case, some conduct which if not dishonest is at any rate in breach of standards of commercial morality, or some really gross incompetence which persuades the court that it would be a danger to the public if he were to be allowed to continue to be involved in the management of companies, before a disqualification order is made. Obviously every case must turn on its own facts.[76]

The reference to 'commercial morality' as a yardstick for determining whether the behaviour in question should render the director unfit has received some deserved criticism in the modern case law, not least because of the nebulous nature of such a standard. In *Secretary of State for Trade and Industry v Goldberg*,[77] for example, Lewison J emphasised the need for a principled approach towards the determination of unfitness so that, among other things, a director knows 'what the law expects of him both before accepting his appointment and while carrying out his duties'.[78] The judge, concluding that actual

---

74   It must also be borne in mind that as disqualification is a civil matter establishing unfitness depends upon the civil standard of proof. That said, the far-reaching and grave implications for the director in being excluded from holding office mean that the court will want the question of unfitness to be unambiguously established: Re *Verby Print for Advertising Ltd* [1998] 2 BCLC 23. Hoffmann J, has observed that s 6 is a penal provision in respect of which the court should give the director the benefit of any doubt: *Secretary of State for Trade and Industry v Ettinger; Re Swift 736 Ltd* [1993] BCLC 896.

75   [1987] BCLC 601. The proceedings here were brought under the Companies Act 1985, s 300.

76   Ibid., 604. Followed by Browne-Wilkinson J in *Re McNulty's Interchange Ltd* (1988) 4 BCC 533, 536.

77   [2004] 1 BCLC 597. See further, S Mortimere QC (ed.) *Company Directors Duties, Liabilities and Remedies* (2nd ed.) (OUP 2013), 31.49.

78   [2004] 1 BCLC 597, [42].

dishonesty is not 'the acid test',[79] called for a 'broad brush' approach: 'In considering whether a director is unfit, it is important to consider the cumulative effect of such of the allegations as are proved against him.'[80] Lewison J's observation is, of course, particularly germane in the light of the multiple factors at play in the downfall of RBS and HBOS.

The judges have also made it clear that by using the word 'conduct', Parlia- **3.20**
ment's intention is that a finding of culpability is not restricted to circumstances where a breach of a common law or statutory company law duty such as those listed in the 1986 Act has occurred. In *Secretary of State for BERR v Sullman* ,[81] where the petition was brought under section 8, Norris J was at pains to point out that the criteria for determining whether a director's conduct rendered him unfit should not be confined within the 'tramlines' of directors' duties:

> I do not regard a breach of an identifiable and independent duty to be a prerequisite for a finding of culpable conduct under the CDDA 1986. The Act uses the broad term 'conduct' (not 'any breach of duty'): and I consider that the authorities establish that unfitness may be demonstrated by conduct which does not involve a breach of any statutory or common law duty, but which, for example, constitutes a failure to achieve an acceptable standard of commercial probity.[82]

Nor is it a prerequisite that the unfit conduct must have resulted in harm to the company. Again, Norris J, responding to the submission that for the purposes of section 8 the conduct of which complaint was made had to be 'conduct in relation to' the company, said:

> It is dangerous to put a gloss upon the words of section 8 or to seek to paraphrase them … in my judgment 'conduct in relation to [a] company' encompasses conduct as a director which bears upon the company's business or its affairs, whether that conduct occasions prejudice to the company itself or to its shareholders or to its customers or funders or anyone else with whom it has commercial relationships. The phrase refers to the way the business is run. I consider this to be a fair meaning of the words themselves, to be consistent with categories of relevant conduct specified in Schedule 1 to CDDA, and to be consonant with the mischief at which the Act is directed.[83]

---

79 Ibid., [40].
80 Ibid.,[44], citing *Re Living Images Ltd* [1996] 1 BCLC 348, 355–6.
81 [2009] 1 BCLC 397, [29]–[30].See also, *Re Amaron Ltd* [2001] 1 BCLC 562, 568, where Neuberger J noted that:

> It seems to me that in setting out specific grounds in Sch. I to the 1986 Act the legislature did not intend other grounds capable, on appropriate facts, of being inherently more culpable than, on other facts, some of the grounds set out in the schedule, to be of less importance. It seems to me that one takes each allegation of unfitness on its merits and considers it, irrespective of whether it falls within Sch. I or not.

82 Ibid., [30].
83 Ibid., [28].

Further, the suggestion that the conduct in question must amount to an abuse of limited liability was roundly dismissed by Lindsay J in *Re Polly Peck International plc (No 2)* on the basis that the words of the statute [including Schedule 1, Pt. 1],[84] are wider and make no such qualification: 'I can think of few tasks less profitable in disqualification cases than an examination of whether a given shortcoming of a director could properly be said to be a consequence of or attendant upon the privilege of trading with limited liability.'[85] For present purposes Lindsay J's remarks are pertinent. They acknowledge that the CDDA regime is, and needs to be, available to respond to abuses that go beyond the typical errant behaviour found on the part of directors of private companies that cause damage to stakeholders such as customers, creditors and employees. In substantive terms it highlights the broader potential of the regime in providing an appropriate mechanism to protect the public interest when the conduct of directors of public corporations leads to market failure and global economic disaster.

3.21   In summary, a finding of unfitness to manage is not restricted to conduct which prejudices the position of creditors so as to amount to an abuse of the privilege of limited liability, nor is dishonesty a requirement. Rather, 'unfitness' has an elastic quality which permits the courts to look at the relevant conduct in the round and not to be high-bound by pre-determined categories of behaviour. It encompasses conduct which, in the words of Norris J, falls below an acceptable standard of commercial probity and it therefore extends, as is demonstrated in the reasoning of Jonathan Parker J in *Re Barings plc (No 5)*,[86] to conduct 'which is merely incompetent'.[87] The circumstances surrounding RBS's acquisition of ABN, particularly in the light of the emphasis given in the FSA's report to the lack of due diligence undertaken by the bank, and the inertia of the HBOS

---

84 [1994] 1 BCLC 574. Such a qualification has been taken to have originated from the judgment delivered in *Re Lo Line Electric Motors Ltd* [1988] Ch 477, in which the judge concluded:

> In my judgment, when all these factors are put together there is no doubt that [the defendant] … has been shown to have behaved in a commercially culpable manner in trading through limited companies when he knew them to be insolvent and in using the unpaid Crown debts to finance such trading. His conduct as a director in the past indicates that, without adequate financial and managerial supervision, he cannot at present be trusted to run a limited company in such a way as not to constitute a risk to his creditors.

> See also, *Re Ipcon Fashions Ltd* (1989) 5 BCC 733, 776, where Hoffmann J said:

> The public is entitled to be protected not only against the activities of those guilty of the more obvious breaches of commercial morality, but also against someone who has shown in his conduct … a failure to appreciate or observe the duties attendant on the privilege of conducting business with the protection of limited liability.

> See, D Arsalidou, 'The banking crisis: rethinking and refining the accountability of bank directors' (2010) 4 *JBL* 284, 289.

85 See above n 84, at 579. *Cf Re Lo Line Electric Motors Ltd*, above n 84.
86 See above n 4.
87 Ibid., 483.

directors in failing to address the lending *versus* deposit deficit must at face value fall within this category of incompetent conduct. And it is on the issue of the linkage between incompetence and unfitness that the judgment of Jonathan Parker J is instructive and, as such, provides a useful starting-point for demonstrating the potential of the CDDA 1986 for holding the RBS and HBOS directors to account. The judge, citing the judgment of Hoffmann LJ in *Secretary of State for Trade and Industry v Gray*,[88] noted that in disqualification proceedings the question for the court (which has been described 'as a jury question'[89]) is to decide whether the conduct in question 'has fallen below the standards of probity and competence appropriate for persons fit to be directors of companies'.[90] Elaborating on this key test, Jonathan Parker J said that in a case based solely upon allegations of incompetence, the Secretary of State bears the burden of proving that the 'conduct complained of demonstrates incompetence of a high degree'.[91] He went on to explain that while the court will take account of the demands made upon a director by his particular role, it 'will recognise incompetence in whatever circumstances and at whatever level of management it occurs, from the chairman of the board down to the most junior director'.[92] The judge went on to observe that:

> [T]he court is concerned only with the conduct in respect of which complaint is made, set in the context of the respondent's actual management of the company. If in his conduct in that role the respondent was guilty of incompetence to the requisite degree, then a finding of unfitness will be made and … a disqualification order must follow.[93]

In a sense, Jonathan Parker J's remarks are prescient. They recognise that there is a close interconnection between the standard of care expected of highly remunerated directors charged with major responsibilities and what is material in determining unfitness for the purposes of disqualification. As such, this is indicative of the potential reach of the CDDA 1986 to those at the helm of RBS and HBOS, a potential that has yet to be mobilised.[94] This makes it all the more intriguing to wonder what lies behind the deficit between the judicial interpretation of the substantive grounds for liability and the continuing failure in the years since the collapse of major UK banking institutions to disqualify

3.22

---

88 [1995] 1 BCLC 276, 284.
89 *Re Sevenoaks Stationers (Retail) Ltd* [1991] Ch 164 (CA), 176, per Dillon LJ.
90 See above n 4, 483.
91 Ibid.
92 Ibid., 484.
93 *Ibid*, 485. In concluding his assessment of the term 'unfitness', Jonathan Parker J, 488, stressed that it must be broadly construed. It is not, therefore, a pre-condition to a finding of unfitness that the director in question should have been guilty of misfeasance or breach of duty. Neither is it a defence in a case where the allegation of unfitness is based upon incompetence for the director to say that 'the errors … can be characterized as errors of judgment rather than as negligent mistakes'.
94 *Ibid*, 488.

any senior member of their management team. Ultimately this must be a matter of speculation. It may well be that even though a prima facie case exists for CDDA proceedings to be brought against these directors, a major reason which may explain the Secretary of State's apparent impotence in moving for their disqualification may lie in the belief that the findings in the various report are somehow evidentially insufficient. Even though the usual civil standard of proof applies, there is some judicial support for the view that where the allegations maintain that 'serious impropriety' has occurred the court will require 'cogent evidence' before it will find that the case has been successfully made. This was certainly the approach favoured by Newey J in *Secretary of State for Business, Innovation and Skills v Doffman (No 2)*.[95] Admittedly, the judge had in mind impropriety relating to financial dealings. However, there is nothing to suppose his remarks do not equally cover the kind of behaviour on the part of the high-profile individuals implicated in the failure of RBS and HBOS. This therefore presumably hints at a major impediment – or perceived impediment – to the bringing of actions under the 1986 legislation.

6. INDIVIDUAL FAILURE AND ENSURING PERSONAL RESPONSIBILITY: OLD WINE IN NEW BOTTLES

3.23   As commented above, there is a danger that when subjecting conduct to ex post facto evaluation, particularly that involving commercial decision-making, the circumstances surrounding (and perhaps justifying) such conduct may be lost in the mist of time. This may explain why the emphasis of the early case law surrounding disqualification gives emphasis to clear abuses of the privileges of limited liability rather than the more nuanced approach towards the determination of unfitness seen in the modern cases. It is also noteworthy that the vast majority of the decisions on disqualification concern directors of often small private companies. This factor may have shaped the contours of the 1986 Act in terms of its scope if not its principal focus. Given the complexities and sophistication of boardroom decision-making in large public companies such as banks, the evidential difficulties of attributing individual responsibility for unfit conduct become apparent. They not only include the sufficiency of the evidence but also the time it may take to gather it.[96] This itself presumably goes some way to explain why disqualification proceedings once promised by prominent politicians, including government ministers, has yet to be fulfilled. However, the forensic approach adopted by the reports into the failure of RBS and HBOS

---

95   [2010] EWHC 3175 Ch, [32].
96   See the view of David Richards J reported in J Loughrey (ed), *Director's Duties and Shareholder Litigation in the Wake of the Financial Crisis*, (Edward Elgar 2012) 343.

readily identify and name the individuals whose conduct brought those institutions to the brink of insolvency. Whether or not the reports provide the necessary 'cogent evidence' the courts require before handing down a disqualification order remains a matter for speculation.[97] They do, however, underline the need to ensure individual responsibility, and they recognise the value of preventing risk-takers from being able to act as directors even if for a limited period of time.

Notwithstanding the political rhetoric, it seems highly unlikely that disqualification proceedings will be initiated by the Secretary of State against the directors identified by the reports into the failure of RBS and HBOS. Rather, almost in recognition of the lack of progress and unlikely prospect of obtaining disqualification orders against them, the political focus has shifted in two distinct directions. First, it has turned towards setting out ways of reforming the CDDA in the belief that the regime is not fit for purpose. As noted above,[98] in July 2013, the Business Secretary published a discussion paper, *Transparency and Trust*, (part of the government's policy 'making companies more accountable to shareholders and the public'), which, among other things, contains recommendations to bolster the disqualification regime by: **3.24**

- giving courts the power to make compensation awards against a director when making a disqualification order and allowing liquidators to sell or assign fraudulent trading actions to creditors;
- offering directors education at the end of their disqualification or a slight reduction in the disqualification period if they take up the offer;
- changing laws to prevent disqualified overseas directors from being directors of a UK company;
- extending the time limit for when disqualification action must be taken against the directors of an insolvent company. Currently standing at two years, the paper proposes a new five-year limit to take into account more complex insolvency cases.

In terms of strengthening the regime the recommendations relating to compensation orders and the limitation period will no doubt serve to reinforce the deterrent value of the CDDA as a whole. However, it is less immediately obvious how they can or will overcome the perceived obstacles, most especially **3.25**

---

97 In assessing the obstacles to litigation that bank directors in the financial crisis may have breached their duty of care and skill, Loughrey, ibid., 21, sensibly acknowledges: 'Obviously for any action to succeed these allegations would need to be proven and the conclusions of, for example, the Committee as to whether this has been achieved may not necessarily coincide with those of a court.'

98 See above n 3.

that concerning the lack of sufficiently cogent evidence of individual wrong-doing, that have so far dogged attempts to institute proceedings in the case of RBS and HBOS. That might be achieved by a more far-reaching overhaul of the current legislative scheme, but even if such a development is needed it does not seem to be on the cards. Besides, as at the time of writing, there is little sign of when, or if, the modest proposals in the Discussion Paper are to be taken forward and enshrined in legislative form.[99]

3.26 In any event a new political agenda has now emerged, one that prefers an alternative legal direction to the taking of civil proceedings under the CDDA. In a radical policy move the government has created a new criminal offence of 'reckless misconduct in the management of a bank' introduced by the Financial Services (Banking Reform) Act 2013.[100] Views will differ on the acceptability of criminalising misconduct and imprisoning reckless bankers. How effective the new crime will be in preventing the type of conduct that led to the banking failures remains to be seen.[101] Suffice it to say that the standard of proof is higher than that required by the CDDA 1986. Ahead of its enactment doubts were expressed about the wisdom of introducing recklessness as the basis of a criminal offence in part because, as seen above,'prosecutors will have to decide, possibly years after a business decision was taken, whether or not it was reckless at the time'.[102] Its effectiveness as a solution to remedy the absence of disqualification proceedings (which if, as we suggest, might be attributable to concerns over the cogency of the evidence available against the directors of unfitness) is therefore open to serious question.

7. CONCLUSION

3.27 The enormity of the banking crisis, together with its dire economic consequences for the UK (and the global) economy, has been widely recognised. It has proved a source of considerable public anger and dismay, one focus of which

---

99   Another proposed reform is to be found in the Deregulation Bill which, if enacted, will amend s 7 of the CDDA Act 1986 so as to increase the power of the authorities to demand information from 'any person' in order to facilitate disqualification proceedings.

100 See above n 16.

101 During the Bill's passage the Financial Secretary to the Treasury, Sajid Javid, expressed the government's 'hope that the new criminal sanction will not have to be used because the offence will act as a genuine deterrent against recklessness': House of Commons, Hansard, 11 Dec 2013, Col 253. However, the Shadow Attorney General, Emily Thornberry, maintained that it was neither a 'credible offence' nor one that will be 'successfully prosecuted'; ibid., cols 272–275.

102 See the statement by D Hudson, Chief Executive of the Law Society of England and Wales, 'Law Society warns new criminal sanctions will not stop banking failing', 9 July 2013, available at: http://www.lawsociety. org.uk/news/press-releases/law-society-warns-new-criminal-sanctions-will-not-stop-banks-failing/, accessed 12 December 2013.

has been upon the risky behaviour of directors, such as those individuals in charge of RBS and HBOS considered in this chapter. Official reports have unequivocally implicated a number of them as authors of their respective banks' financial failure, which, but for the intervention of the taxpayer, would undoubtedly have led to their insolvency. In the Foreword to the FSA's Report on the failure of RBS, Lord Turner notes:

> Banks are different because excessive risk-taking (for instance through an aggressive acquisition) can result in bank failure, taxpayers losses and wider economic harm. Their failure is of public concern, not just concern for shareholders.[103]

One element of assuaging this public concern rests in knowing that when individuals are unfit to hold directorships they can, by law, be barred from doing so in the future. This goal has so far proved elusive.[104] As disqualification is not permanent,[105] it need not be seen as a matter of exacting revenge. It offers a prudent and targeted reaction, one that may assist in restoring trust in the banking system and deter future bankers from indulging in similarly risky behaviour. As this chapter has demonstrated, disqualification is an objective to which leading politicians, including the government's Business Secretary, appeared to be firmly committed. The survey of the case law on the determinants of liability under the CDDA 1986 suggest that the pivotal concept of 'unfitness', as interpreted by the courts, holds the potential to apply to the incompetence of individual banking directors as laid out in the official reports. It may be that it remains the government's intention to seek the disqualification of leading bankers who figured largely in the fall of RBS and HBOS. However, with the passage of time, this begins to look more a case of hope being triumphant over experience. The introduction of a new criminal offence to deal with the reckless conduct of future bankers may well impliedly signal the end of the road of the CDDA as an accountability mechanism against directors such as Goodwin and his counterparts at HBOS. If so, this may be something of a missed opportunity. Moreover, and notwithstanding the relatively minor reform proposals that have been recently mooted, the banking crisis may further illuminate inherent limitations in the utility and operation of the 1986 Act.

---

103   See above n 1, 9.

104   It may be thought that the market will regulate the matter in the sense that the employment prospects for failed bankers will be poor. It seems, however, this is not necessarily true: see, for example, *Changing Banking for Good*, above, n. 1, para 1140.

105   A factor which for some raises a question mark over the adequacy of disqualification as a deterrent: see Loughrey, above n 96, 48. See also n 3, above.

SELECTED BIBLIOGRAPHY

A Review of Corporate Governance in UK Banks and Other Financial Industry Entities (the Walker Report, 2009), available at http://webarchive.nationalarchives.gov.uk/ and http://www.hm-treasury.gov.uk/d/walker_review_261109.pdf.

Arsalidou, D, 'The banking crisis: Rethinking and refining the accountability of bank directors' (2010) 4 *JBL* 284.

Changing Banking for Good, Report of the Parliamentary Banking Standards HL Paper 27; HC Papers 175, available at http://www.parliament.uk/bankingstandards.

Finch, V, 'Disqualification of directors: A plea for competence' (1990) 53 *MLR* 385.

Griffin, S, 'The disqualification of unfit directors and the protection of the public interest' (2002) 53(3) *NILQ* 207.

Hicks, A, 'Director's disqualification: can it deliver?' (2001) *JBL* 433.

Loughrey, J, (ed.), *Director's Duties and Shareholder Litigation in the Wake of the Financial Crisis*, (Edward Elgar, 2012).

Martin, Iain, *Making IT Happen: Fred Goodwin, RBS and the Men Who Blew up the British Economy* (Simon & Shuster, 2013).

Milman, D, 'Personal liability and disqualification of company directors: Something old, something new' (1992) 43 *NILQ* 1.

Mortimere, S, QC (ed.) *Company Directors Duties, Liabilities and Remedies* (2nd ed) (OUP 2013).

Perman, R, *Hubris: How HBOS Wrecked The Best Bank in Britain* (Birlinn, 2012).

The Financial Services Board Report, *The Failure of the Royal Bank of Scotland* (December 2011), available at http://www.fsa.gov.uk/library/communication/pr/2011/110.shtml.

The House of Commons Treasury Committee's Fifth Report HC 640 (2012–13), *The FSA's Report into the failure of RBS*, available at http://www.publications.parliament.uk/pa/cm201213/cmselect/cmtreasy/640/640.pdf.

Tomasic, R, 'Corporate rescue, governance and risk taking in Northern Rock: Part 2' (2008) 29(11) *Comp Lawyer* 330.

Transparency and Trust: Enhancing the Transparency of UK Company Ownership and Increasing Trust in UK Business, Department for Business, Innovation and Skills (July 2013), available at https://www.gov.uk/government/uploads/system/uploads/attachment_data/file/212079/bis-13–959-transparency-and-trust-enhancing-the-transparency-of-uk-company-ownership-and-increaing-trust-in-uk-business.pdf.

Walters, A, 'Directors' Duties: Impact of the CDDA' (2000) 21 *Company Lawyer* 110.

Wheeler, S, 'Directors' disqualification: Insolvency practitioners and the decision-making process' (1995) 15(2) *Legal Studies* 283.

Williams, R, 'Disqualifying directors: A remedy worse than the disease' (2007) **7** *JCLS* 213.

4

THE ROLE OF INSTITUTIONAL SHAREHOLDERS: STEWARDSHIP AND THE LONG-/SHORT-TERM DEBATE

Arad Reisberg[*]

1. INTRODUCTION

A. Background

With the financial crisis came a renewed interest in short-termism and its **4.01** negative implications for growth and development in general, and on equity markets in particular. The responses ranged from independent reviews and

* I am grateful to participants at the seminar on the subject of this chapter jointly organised by Continuing Legal Education and Centre for Law & Business Faculty of Law, National University of Singapore (NUS) held on 27 March 2013, for comments. I am also grateful to Anat Keller for providing excellent research assistance at the final stages and at a very short notice and to Eleanore Hickman for doing the same at the final editing stages. The usual disclaimers apply.

public policy recommendations to private sector-led initiatives.[1] These provide solid evidence for a growing consensus on the need to strike an appropriate balance between short-termism and long-termism.[2] One of the first things Marissa Mayer did as CEO of Yahoo was remove the stock ticker from the homepage of Backyard, the company's internal website.[3] The reason, according to those who have interacted with her, is that she believes employees should be more focused on creating better products and services than on corporate finances.[4] Whether this is a sign that companies are shifting from the prevailing sentiment (i.e. that a company's primary goal is to maximise shareholder value), to a more stakeholder approach, is still open to question.[5] 'Why,' askes Unilever's Paul Polman in an interview with Guardian Sustainable Business, 'would you invest in a company which is out of synch with the needs of society, that does not take its social compliance in its supply chain seriously, that does not think about the costs of externalities, or of its negative impacts on society?'[6] The answer, most likely, lies in the priorities of the businesses of today: bottom line returns and an allegiance to the interests of shareholders.

B.   Short-termism – human nature and culture

4.02   In the 1960s the American psychologist, Walter Mischel, conducted a series of experiments on the drivers of delayed gratification.[7] Mischel took pre-school-age children and put a marshmallow in front of them. He then told them that the marshmallow was theirs, but if they waited to eat it until he returned, he would give them a second one as a bonus for waiting. The experiment, which became to be known as the marshmallow test, found that the waiting time of

---

1   The B-Team founded by Sir Richard Branson and Jochen Zeitz, is a stark example of a practical response to short-termism. It is aimed at promoting a shift of business leadership away from the existing short-term gain towards balancing the long-term benefits for people and the planet. See, http://bteam.org/about/vision/, accessed 13 January 2014.

2   D Marginson and L McAulay, 'Exploring the debate on short-termism' (2008) 29(3) *Strategic Management Journal* 273; C Helms and others, 'Corporate short-termism: Causes and remedies' (2012) 23(2) *International Company and Commercial Law Review* 45.

3   A Efrati, 'A Makeover Made in Google's Image', *Wall Street Journal*, (9 August 2012), http://online.wsj.com/news/articles/SB10000872396390443517104577575420060344832, accessed 13 January 2014.

4   Ibid.

5   On which see, A Reisberg 'Shareholder value after the financial crisis: A dawn of a new era?' (2013) *International Corporate Rescue* 143.

6   J Confino, 'Unilever's Paul Poleman: Challenging the Corporate Status Quo', *Guardian Professional Network*, theguardian.com, http://www.theguardian.com/sustainable-business/paul-polman-unilever-sustainable-living-plan?guni=Article:in%20body%20link (24 April 2012), accessed 13 January 2014.

7   See, *Britannica Academic Edition* http://www.britannica.com/EBchecked/topic/385191/Walter-Mischel, accessed 13 January 2014.

the children varied significantly: some ate the marshmallow straight away, some waited a few minutes and some waited until his return to the room.[8]

The seemingly simple test demonstrates two common manifestations of the **4.03** natural human tendency to short-termism.[9] First, the internal rate of return on waiting a few minutes to get two marshmallows instead of one, is extremely high.[10] In other words, there is an excessive discounting of the future in favour of the present. Secondly, there is an innate bias to action. It is very difficult for small children to sit, even for a few minutes, without doing something.[11] As John Kay puts it, the fundamental question that has to be asked is whether we overcome these biases when we grow up to become corporate executives? And do the institutions of our equity markets aggravate these biases, or help us to resist them?[12] The aim of this chapter is to shed light on these questions and provide a solid foundation for the growing debate about short-termism.

C. Major reports, consultations and papers on the topic since 2010

In the wake of the financial crisis, an increasing number of reports, consult- **4.04** ations and papers on the topic of short-termism, have been published. On 25 October 2010, the UK Government launched its consultation termed 'A long-term focus for Corporate Britain', which looked at whether more can be done to help secure the long-term economic growth needed.[13] When the consultation was announced in September 2010, Dr Vince Cable (the Secretary of State for Business, Innovation and Skills) stated that short-termism and shareholder disengagement are an increasing problem for the economy, and emphasised the need for shareholders to act like long-term owners.[14] As part of the consultation, the call for evidence sought to establish whether the system in which companies and shareholders interact promotes or undermines long-term growth.[15] The call for evidence noted that the publication of the Stewardship

---

8   S Kliff, 'The marshmallow test, revisited', *The Washington Post*, (12 October 2012 http://www.washingtonpost.com/blogs/wonkblog/wp/2012/10/13/the-marshmallow-test-revisited/, accessed 13 January 2014).

9   See, J, Kay, Speech at the Kay Review Launch, 23 July 2012, para 6 at https://www.gov.uk/government/uploads/system/uploads/attachment_data/file/253459/bis-12–996-kay-review-of-equity-markets-speech-and-presentation.pdf, accessed 13 January 2014.

10   Ibid.

11   Ibid.

12   Ibid., para 7.

13   BIS, October 2010 (URN 10/1225). Available at: https://www.gov.uk/government/consultations/a-long-term-focus-for-corporate-britain-a-call-for-evidence, accessed 13 January 2014. The consultation ran for 12 weeks until 14 January 2011.

14   G Mulley, J Palmer and D Paterson, 'Investing for the long-term: government consultation on short-termism in the equity markets' Herbert Smith Freehills LLP 26 October 2010 available at: http://www.lexology.com/library/detail.aspx?g=7e57a0b2-fa76–4016-af3a-180592706cd9, accessed 13 January 2014).

15   BIS, October 2010 (URN 10/1225), see above n 13, 5.

Code by the FRC in July 2011 was a major development in this context. Interestingly, the UK Government asked questions such as: Do UK boards
have a long-term focus – if not, why not? Is short-termism in equity markets a
problem and, if so, how should it be addressed? What action, if any, should be
taken to encourage a long-term focus in UK equity investment decisions? What
are the benefits and costs of possible actions to encourage longer holding
periods?[16] In the words of Vince Cable:

> We need to ask ourselves what are the factors influencing short-term decisions, the
> reasons for the growth of directors' pay and why economically damaging takeovers still
> take place. I recognise that the best solutions will come from businesses and that
> regulation is not the only option. That is why today I am calling on all companies and
> individuals to put forward their ideas.[17]

4.05 The UK Government consultation was the first in a host of reports, both
nationally and on an EU level, as well as in the US, tackling the issue from
various angles. These are highlighted in Table 4.1 below.[18] We will return to
deal with most of these in the next few sections of this chapter.

2. SHORT-TERM V LONG-TERM DICHOTOMY AND THE ELUSIVENESS OF THE TERM 'LONG-TERM'

A. Do we all mean the same thing? How long is 'long-term'?

4.06 Short-termism refers to the excessive focus of some corporate leaders, investors,
and analysts on short-term, quarterly earnings and a lack of attention to the
strategy, fundamentals, and conventional approaches to long-term value creation.[19] It is a natural human tendency to make decisions in search of immediate
gratification, at the expense of future returns.[20] In fact, Professor Mike Burkart
believes that the Kay Review seems to suggest that everyone is 'short-termist':[21]

---

16 Ibid, 34.
17 BIS, 'Review on Corporate Governance and Short-Termism opens' Press Release, 25 October 2010 available
  at: http://news.bis.gov.uk/content/detail.aspx?NewsAreaId=2&ReleaseID=416167&SubjectId=2, accessed 13
  January 2014.
18 I refer here to reports where the topic of short-termism is at the heart of the investigation, rather than an
  incidental part of it. As will be seen below, the list is not meant to be exhaustive but focus only on the major
  initiatives, relevant to the discussion in this chapter.
19 D Krehmeyer, M Orsagh, and K Schacht, 'Breaking the short-term cycle', CFA Institute (2006), 3.
20 J Kay, 'The Kay Review of UK equity markets and long–term decision making: Final Report' BIS/12/917 (July
  2012), Chapter 1, para 1.1. The phrase 'natural human tendency' implies that everybody suffers from it.
21 Gösta Olson Professor of Finance, Stockholm School of Economics in a speech at an academic conference held
  by the ECGI on 23 January 2013 to discuss the European Commission's Action Plan on Company Law and
  Corporate Governance (published on 12 December 2012) and associated policy proposals, available at:
  http://www.ecgi.org/conferences/eu_actionplan2013/report.php, accessed 13 January 2014.

Table 4.1 Major reports, consultations and papers on the topic since 2010

Date published	Title	Published body	Where published
July 2010; September 2012	The Stewardship Code	FRC	🇬🇧 (UK)
25 October 2010	Consultation: A long-term focus for Corporate Britain	BIS	🇬🇧 (UK), EU
April 2011	Green Paper: The EU Corporate Governance Framework	The European Commission (EC)	🇬🇧 (UK), EU
9 May 2011	The short long – Paper by Andrew Haldane and Richard Davies	Bank of England	🇬🇧 (UK)
23 July 2012	Kay Review of UK Equity Markets and Long Term Decision Making	BIS appoints John Kay	🇬🇧 (UK), EU
12 December 2012	Action Plan: European company law and corporate governance	The European Commission (EC)	🇬🇧 (UK)
26 February 2013	Overcoming Short-termism within British Business	An independent review by Sir George Cox commissioned by the Labour Party	🇬🇧 (UK)
1 March 2013	The Uneasy Case for Favoring Long-Term Shareholders'	Jesse M. Fried (U.S Scholar)	🇺🇸 (US)

For instance, in Chapter 1 (point 1.1), it states: 'Short-termism, or myopic behaviour, is the natural human tendency to make decisions in search of immediate gratification at the expense of future returns…'. The phrase 'natural human tendency' implies that everybody suffers from it. The whole structure of the financial industry is about emphasising exit over long-term investment and this is why there is a lack of engagement.

4.07 Short-termism can be said to be part of modern culture existing not only within equity markets but extending to risk management and politics.[22] However, determining whether or not an investment is long term is a subjective matter. A day trader, for instance, would define 'long term' rather differently than a buy-and-hold investor, who would consider anything less than several years to be short-term trading. Accordingly, the *Oxford Dictionary of Finance and Banking* provides different definitions to the term, depending on where it applies. For example, while a 'long-term bond' may denote one that does not mature in less than one year, 'long-term debt', describes loans and debentures that are not due for repayment for at least ten years; long-term investment, however, may extend to a period of 30 years or more.[23]

4.08 It is, therefore, not easy to define or capture the general horizon of an investment in a single formulaic sentence.[24] Consequently, the World Economic Forum's definition is more flexible, aligning long-term investment with the intent of the investor when making the investment and the ability to follow through with it in the face of market pressure. Long-term investment is defined as the expectation of holding an asset for an indefinite period of time, by an investor with the capability to do so, rather than a specific horizon.[25]

4.09 Curiously, even investments that enjoy some level of acceptance as to their long-term horizon, are subject to uncertainty. For instance, it is widely accepted

---

22 A recent global research has found that banks take a short-term view when it comes to risk management priorities, See, http://www.sungard.com/pressreleases/2013/financialsystems072313.aspx 23 July 2013, accessed 13 January 2014. Another recent initiative is by the Oxford Martin Commission for Future Generations, which published a report in October 2013 on the increasing short-termism of modern politics titled, 'Now for the Long Term!' http://www.longfinance.net/groups7/viewbulletin/175-now-for-the-long-term.html, accessed 13 January 2014.

23 *The Oxford Dictionary of Finance and Banking* (4th revised ed, OUP 2008), 248.

24 World Economic Forum Report, 'The future of long-term investing' (2011) available at: http://www.weforum.org/issues/long-term-investing, accessed 13 January 2014.

25 World Economic Forum Report, 'The future of long-term investing' (2011) available at: http://www3.weforum.org/docs/WEF_FutureLongTermInvesting_Report_2011.pdf, accessed 13 January 2014. In this respect, an interesting, but somewhat confused long-term statement is provided by HSBC (see: http://www.hsbc.com/about-hsbc/our-strategy, accessed 13 March 2014), where the bank uses unclear phraseology such as: '[O]ur strategic direction is aligned to two long-term trends', i.e. 'international trade and capital flows' – which is linked to 'the next decade' 'and economic development and wealth creation' which 'we expect … by 2050.' Ibid.

that Sovereign Wealth Funds (SWF) retain their assets despite short-term price fluctuations and therefore, are generally said to be a long-term investment.[26] A survey conducted in 2008 by Norton Rose Fulbright confirmed this view;[27] 71 per cent of SWF respondents said they regarded themselves as longer term investors rather than private equity funds (interestingly, almost exactly the same percentage as all non-SWF respondents)[28]. Respondents observed that SWFs had longer 'time horizons', and that they were not engaged in 'active management'.[29] However, the horizon of the SWF invariably depends on the type of the fund. Savings funds and pension funds set more long-term goals because they are intended for future generations. In contrast, stabilisation funds are intended for risk management and not for long-term purposes,[30] and thus, usually, have short- to medium-term goals. That said, determining which funds are purely 'stabilisation funds', or what counts as 'long-' or 'short-term', is a far from easy task.

3. WHAT'S THE PROBLEM WITH SHORT-TERMISM?

An independent review by Sir George Cox commissioned by the Labour Party in February 2013 (the Cox Review) explored the impact of short-termism on British business.[31] It suggested that short-termism is both statistically and economically significant in the UK capital markets and it appears also to be rising.[32] There was also a remarkable degree of consensus in terms of its effects, which were chiefly: a disincentive to think and plan long term; a constraint on the ambition for the business; a disincentive to invest; a disincentive to develop new products; a disincentive to undertake research; and a disincentive to recruit.[33] **4.10**

---

26 SWFs are pools of assets owned and managed directly or indirectly by governments. Investopedia, available at: http://www.investopedia.com/, accessed 13 January 2014.

27 Sovereign Wealth Funds and the Global Private Equity Landscape Survey (June 2008) available at: http://www.nortonrosefulbright.com/knowledge/publications/15287/sovereign-wealth-funds-and-the-global-private-equity-landscape-survey, accessed 13 January 2014.

28 Ibid.

29 Ibid.

30 Ibid.

31 'Overcoming short-termism within British Business, the Key to Sustained Economic Growth' an independent review by Sir George Cox (February 2013), available at: http://www.yourbritain.org.uk/uploads/editor/files/Overcoming_Short-termism.pdf, accessed 13 January 2014.

32 Ibid., 12. Almost 60 per cent of the business leaders interviewed rated it as a major or significant impediment to the growth and development of British business; a survey of IoD members (made up largely of SMEs) put the figure even higher at 92 per cent; the members of Intellect (the trade body for the ITC and electronics industries) rated it at 67 per cent and a representative group of trade union leaders put it at 86 per cent. Ibid., 13.

33 Ibid.

4.11 In this context it is notable that in their recent research, Andrew Haldane and Richard Davies,[34] drawing on evidence across time and industrial sectors conclude: '[T]his evidence – anecdotal, survey, quantitative – is broadly consistent with popular perceptions. Capital market myopia is real. It may be rising. For at least some of the jury, however, it remains inconclusive.'[35] They proceed to construct a variety of quantitative tests to assess the significance and scale of short-termism in equity markets.[36]

4.12 The empirical tests conducted by Haldane and Davies, suggest there has been significant evidence of short-termism, or 'excess discounting', among UK and US companies over the past few decades. They found that in the UK and US, cash-flows five years ahead are discounted at rates more appropriate for eight or more years hence; ten year ahead cash-flows are valued as if 16 or more years ahead and cash-flows more than 30 years ahead are scarcely valued at all.[37] In addition, one year ahead cash-flows are discounted 5–10 per cent more than would be rational. These effects are more significant in the latter part of the sample, suggesting myopia is increasing over time,[38] in a consistent way across all industrial sectors.[39]

4.13 Returning to the Cox Review, it found similarly that this myopia is a significant impediment to growth and development of British business.[40] It highlighted that, short-termism curtails ambition, inhibits long-term thinking and provides a disincentive to invest in research, new capabilities, products, training, recruitment and skills.[41] It results in drastic cost-cutting and staff-shedding whenever revenue growth fails to keep up with expectation.[42] The most important consequence of short-termism is that it militates against the development of the internationally competitive businesses and industries that are essential to the UK's future economic prosperity.[43]

---

34 'The short long paper' (Bank of England) (09 May 2011), available at: http://www.bankofengland.co.uk/publications/Pages/news/2011/043.aspx and the actual speech by the authors delivered in Brussels in May 20011('speech') at: http://www.bankofengland.co.uk/publications/Documents/speeches/2011/speech495.pdf, accessed 15 January 2014.

35 Speech, ibid, 4.

36 Ibid. This draws on a sample of over 600 firms in the UK and US over the period 1980–2009. The tests assess whether expected future cash-flows paid by a company are discounted 'excessively' in the determination of their share price at the time of the research (2011).

37 Ibid, 1.

38 'The short long paper', see above n 34.

39 Speech, see above n 34, 13.

40 'Overcoming short-termism within British business', see above n 31, 6.

41 Ibid.

42 Ibid.

43 Ibid, 6. On the negative affect of short-termism and an overview of the opinion on this issue in the US see L Bebchuk, 'The myth that insulating boards serves long-term value' (October 2013) 113 *Columbia Law Review* 1637.

In terms of the sources of short-termism, the Kay Review in July 2012 called it **4.14** aptly '[T]he erosion of trust and the misalignment of incentives.'[44] Kay further explained that:

> Short-termism in business may be characterised both as a tendency to under-investment, whether in physical assets or in intangibles such as product development, employee skills and reputation with customers, and as hyperactive behaviour by executives whose corporate strategy focuses on restructuring, financial re-engineering or mergers and acquisitions at the expense of developing the fundamental operational capabilities of the business.[45]

Kay then made some important observations and findings. First, he identified a **4.15** wide variety of examples of companies that have made bad long-term decisions, and consider that equity markets have evolved in ways that contribute to these errors of managerial judgement.[46] According to Kay:

> The quality – and not the amount – of engagement by shareholders determines whether the influence of equity markets on corporate decisions is beneficial or damaging to the long-term interests of companies ... [P]ublic equity markets currently encourage exit (the sale of shares) over voice (the exchange of views with the company) as a means of engagement, replacing the concerned investor with the anonymous trader.

Secondly, Kay discovered that UK equity markets are no longer a significant **4.16** source of funding for new investment by UK companies.[47] He observed that:

> most publicly traded UK companies generate sufficient cash from their day-to-day operations to fund their own corporate projects and that the relatively small number of UK companies which access the new issue market often use it as a means to achieve liquidity for early stage investors, rather than to raise funds for new investment.[48]

Kay concluded that the principal role of equity markets in the allocation of capital relates 'to the oversight of capital allocation within companies rather than the allocation of capital between companies'.[49] It follows, according to him, that promoting good governance and stewardship is therefore a central, rather than an incidental, function of UK equity markets.[50]

---

44 Kay, see above n 20, 10.
45 Ibid.
46 Ibid
47 Ibid.
48 Ibid.
49 Ibid.
50 Ibid.

4.17 Thirdly, Kay charted the evolution of the structure of shareholding in UK equities.[51] He found increased fragmentation, driven by 'the diminishing share of large UK insurance companies and pension funds and by the globalisation of financial markets which has led to increased foreign shareholding'.[52] Kay asserted that this fragmentation has 'reduced the incentives for engagement and the level of control enjoyed by each shareholder'.[53]

4.18 Finally, Kay observed that, at the same time, 'there has been an explosion of intermediation in equity investment driven both by a desire for greater professionalism and efficiency and by a decline in trust and confidence in the investment chain'.[54] He believed that the growth of intermediation has led to 'increased costs for investors, an increased potential for misaligned incentives and a tendency to view market effectiveness through the eyes of intermediaries rather than companies or end investors'.[55] However, questions may continue to be raised as to how long intermediation will continue to grow in light of the emergence of investment mechanisms which cut down on the number of intermediaries, such as crowdsourcing.[56]

4.19 The negative case for short-termism is by no means cut and dried. It is the contention of Mark Roe that short-termism is not necessarily the source of myopic corporate governance.[57] The reasons most pertinent to a UK context include, first, that short-termism has not been proven to be a systematic problem. Whilst some investors may invest for the short term, they are counterweighted by the many who still invest for the long term.[58] Secondly, long-termism is not without its own problems, particularly in relation to its over-valuing of assets as exemplified in the dot-com boom.[59] Thirdly, executive remuneration packages are often of a shorter duration than short-term investor problems and, as such, may present more of an issue.[60]

---

51 Ibid.
52 Ibid. This is evident in Department for Business, Innovation and Skills (BIS, 2010), 'A long term focus for corporate Britain –A call for evidence', 17, available at: https://www.gov.uk/government/consultations/a-long-term-focus-for-corporate-britain-a-call-for-evidence, accessed 17 January 2014.
53 Ibid.
54 Ibid.
55 Ibid.
56 B J Rubinton, 'Crowdfunding: Disintermediated investment banking', Working Paper, (June 9, 2011), McGill University, available at: http://mpra.ub.unimuenchen.de/31649/1/MPRA_paper_31649.pdf, accessed 13 October 2014.
57 M J Roe, 'Corporate short-termism – in the boardroom and in the courtroom' (2013) 68 *Business Lawyer* 981.
58 Ibid, 992.
59 Ibid, 993.
60 Ibid, 996.

4. THE CAUSES OF SHORT-TERMISM

The Cox Review identified a number of causes of short-termism.[61] These can **4.20** be grouped under three headings:[62] (1) the way that equity markets now operate; (2) the lack of a 'funding escalator' for smaller companies (the absence of a series of financing mechanisms to carry UK ventures through the successive stages of development from start-up to large-scale corporation); and (3) the short-term focus of (any) government. We look at each of these next.

First, 'the nature of the equity markets and the way they operate in the UK has **4.21** changed progressively over recent decades'.[63] This seems to reaffirm Kay's findings. As seen above, the Kay Review presented a detailed overview of the various aspects of how the structure of shareholding in UK equities has changed.[64] Kay identified (and the Cox Review noted), the diminution of the role of such markets as a source of funding for UK companies; the diminishing share held by major long-term investors in the form of the large UK insurance companies and pension funds; and the explosion of intermediation in equity investment.[65]

Second, lack of long-term development funding for smaller companies was **4.22** identified as a source for short-termism:[66] '[I]n the UK there are no series of financing mechanisms to carry ventures through the successive stages of development from start-up to large-scale corporation.'[67] UK SMEs are finding it harder to access bank lending than many of their European counterparts.[68] Non-bank lending in the UK paints an even gloomier picture when compared to Europe and even more so when compared to the US where it was estimated

---

61   'Overcoming short-termism within British business', see above n 31, 6.
62   Ibid.
63   Ibid, 20.
64   Kay, above n 20, part 4.3.
65   'Overcoming short-termism within British business', see above n 31, 20. In the US context, it has been recently suggested that executives with short-term orientation attract investors who are fixated on quarterly reporting, and hence, the blame should not solely lie with investors but also with the impact of short-termism by executives. See, D Barton and M Wiseman, 'Focusing capital on the long term' (2014) (Jan–Feb) *Harvard Business Review* 44.
66   Kay, above n 20, 6.
67   Kay, above n 20, 24.
68   'SME Financing: Impact of regulation and the Eurozone crisis', an independent report by Ayres & Co, commissioned by TheCityUK (2012) at: http://www.thecityuk.com/research/our-work/reports-list/sme-financing-impact-of-regulation-and-the-eurozone-crisis/, accessed 17 March 2014, 34. The difference may be due, in part, to the concentrated nature of the UK banking sector when compared with the more regional and diverse banks on the continent, as well as comparatively fewer government entities set up to assist SMEs in the UK.

that around 40 per cent of SME financing was non-bank.[69] This lack of 'financing escalator' has far-reaching consequences and has led to an 'early-exit culture in the UK and, more specifically, it prevented smaller companies from reaching their full potential'.[70]

4.23 Finally, the Cox Review observed that the lack of consistent government long-term strategy is a source for short-termism in equity markets.[71] For example, initiatives like the UK Stewardship Code, seek to create a sense of long-term responsibility within the investor, but the removal of stamp duty on exchange traded funds (ETFs), due in April 2014, is incongruent with this goal. By encouraging investment in ETFs, not only will the tax change remove one of the incentives to retain investment, but it also disenfranchises the investor from the stewardship role, as they become a further step removed from the investment. This lack of long-term strategy results 'in a failure to construct a globally competitive infrastructure within which business can flourish. Furthermore, it creates an inconsistent pattern of government spend against which the relevant supplying industries can plan'.[72]

4.24 The question is, why would governments act in such a way? The Cox Review explained that 'for far too long UK governments have concentrated their economic policies on how to spend the nation's income, not on how to generate it'.[73] The former has produced a vigorous argument on how much government takes out (by way of taxation) and how it allocates it.[74] The review then takes the view that:

> [G]overnment cannot deliver economic growth, but to a large extent it determines the conditions under which growth can or cannot take place. The pursuit of long-term growth can only be addressed by a joint understanding and shared goals between the (various departments of) government and the private sector.[75]

---

69   Ibid, 47. See also, S Bair, 'Short-termism and the risk of another financial crisis' *The Washington Post* (8 July 2011).

70   'Overcoming short-termism within British business', see above n 31, 24–25: It is not surprising, therefore, that Colin Mayer believes that short-termism is a very British problem (with the possible exception of the US) and it is thus 'often difficult to find a foreign translation of the term'. See, C Mayer "Short-termism' is a very British problem' *Financial Times* (19 July 2012).

71   Ibid, 27.

72   Ibid.

73   Ibid, 29.

74   Ibid.

75   Ibid., 30. The review makes an interesting analogy with the world of sport (an area where government certainly cannot pick winners). As the review explains, the approach taken with respect to Olympic sportsmen and sportswomen since 1997 took the form of supporting success. Money was directed to those sports and athletes achieving results in major international competition but was withheld from those that did not. Indeed, the system has been quite brutal in its application. See further, ibid, 30–31.

The review therefore believed that:

> [G]overnment has to provide strategic leadership in building an economy based on high skills, scientific and technological advances, creativity and continuous innovation,'[76] and that '[W]hat is needed is not some one-off 'national plan' or series of initiatives, but the continuing pursuit of coordinated Objectives shared between industry, business, commerce, trade unions and education.[77]

Interestingly, the review also found that despite the often repeated phrase that 'all business wants is for government to get out of the way', there was, in fact, widespread recognition that the issues identified cannot be addressed without government action.[78] Indeed, 100 per cent of the business leaders consulted by the review felt that government had a role to play, with over half believing that government could either fundamentally change the situation or do much to bring about change.[79] **4.25**

5. ADDITIONAL DRIVERS OF SHORT-TERMISM

In addition to the drivers of short-termism, as identified by the Cox Review and discussed above, this section identifies a number of additional, practical drivers. The overall effect of these is to entrench short-termism even further. **4.26**

A. Driver no. 1: Does frequent periodic financial reporting cause short-termism?

There is an ongoing (and, at times, heated) debate over frequent periodic reporting. Those in favour of more frequent reporting of earnings believe it improves transparency and market efficiency among listed issuers.[80] Those in opposition contend that it encourages short-termism, as companies are focused on making the bottom-line numbers attractive to investors at every reporting period, at the expense of the company's long-term strategy.[81] Moreover, these **4.27**

---

76 Ibid, 32.
77 Ibid, 33.
78 Ibid, 32.
79 Ibid.
80 For example see the study by Mazars (December 2009) on 'the application of selected obligations of Directive 2004/109/EC on the harmonisation of transparency requirements in relation to information about issuers whose securities are admitted to trading on a regulated market', Study conducted for the European Commission, available at: http://ec.europa.eu/internal_market/securities/docs/transparency/report-application-annexes_en.pdf, accessed 15 January 2014.
81 For example, see A R Rahman, T M Tay, B T Ong and S Cai, 'Quarterly reporting in a voluntary disclosure environment: Its benefits, drawbacks and determinants' (2007) 42(4) *The International Journal of Accounting* 416.

reporting requirements may foster a 'quarterly results' financial culture characterised by disproportionate reactions among internal and external groups to the downside and upside of earnings surprises.[82]

4.28 The question turns to what are the costs and negative consequences of the current focused, quarterly earnings guidance practices? Arguably, the costs and negative consequences are substantial. First, there are costs associated with the unproductive and wasted efforts borne by companies in preparing such guidance.[83] Secondly, reporting requirement tends to pressure management to 'show positive numbers at every reporting period' at the expense of the company's long-term strategy.[84] Thirdly, the current focus fosters a 'quarterly results' financial culture, characterised by disproportionate reactions among internal and external groups to the downside and upside of earnings surprises.[85] For example, it was reported that HSBC in Hong Kong quarterly reporting 'concentrates sell-side analyst analysis on short periods of time, encouraging the promotion of trading recommendations rather than fundamental analysis'.[86] Finally, complex reporting affects quality: there are complex problems involved in frequent reporting for companies running myriad businesses in countries with different accounting standards.[87] Investors may have a distorted view of the financial position of the issuers. Seasonal factors (seasonal business patterns) such as sales, or lumpy and irregular revenue streams, may adversely impact the financial reports' quality, causing underlying risks for companies and their auditors.[88] Auditors may also face extra risk due to potential stock price swings resulting from quarterly reporting macro-incentives for companies to avoid earnings guidance pressure altogether by moving to the private markets.[89]

4.29 Reflecting these concerns, the legal obligation for issuers of shares to provide quarterly financial information (either quarterly financial reports or interim management statements as defined in Article 6 of the Transparency Directive

---

82 'Apples to apples: A template for reporting quarterly earnings' prepared by the CFA Institute Centre for Financial Market Integrity/Business Roundtable Institute for Corporate Ethics (March 2007), 31 (drawing on their report 'Breaking the short-term cycle' available at: www.cfapubs.org/loi/ccb).

83 CFA Institute, Earnings Guidance, available at: http://www.cfainstitute.org/ethics/topics/Pages/earnings_guidance.aspx, accessed 15 January 2014.

84 CAPA Chronicle (October 2007) available at: http://www.capa.com.my/images/capa/OCT-NOV%2007.pdf, 11, accessed 15 January 2014.

85 CFA Institute, Earnings Guidance, see above n 83.

86 C Chan, 'Debate over quarterly reporting' A+ (December 2007), 21 available at: http://app1.hkicpa.org.hk/APLUS/0712/20–22.pdf, accessed 15 January 2014.

87 Ibid, 22.

88 Ibid.

89 CFA Institute, Earnings Guidance, see above n 83.

2004/109/EC) was subject to a recent review.[90] Consequently, the Transparency Directive was amended and the requirement to produce interim management statements or quarterly reports was *removed*.[91] Arguably, this should not have a negative impact on consumer protection since it is sufficiently guaranteed through the mandatory disclosure of half yearly and yearly financial results, as well as through disclosures required by the Abuse and Prospectus Directives.[92] On the contrary, it should enhance consumer protection, putting emphasis on the quality of disclosure rather than the speed of disclosure.[93]

There is, nonetheless, still a concern that many issuers (in particular large ones) **4.30** will continue to disclose quarterly financial information even in the absence of a legal obligation in EU law.[94] Primarily, this is because the suppression of the obligation under EU law does not automatically entail the suppression of such obligation in national law.[95] Additionally, one should remember that many companies are listed in the US where the requirement of quarterly reporting remains. Finally, the expectation of the market for this transparency may derive large issuers to continue to provide it.[96]

B. Driver no. 2: Shareholders' disengagement

As the dominant owners of listed companies, institutional investors in many **4.31** developed countries have been under increasing pressure to act as responsible shareholders.[97] In the UK, a Stewardship Code has been developed to encourage pension funds, insurance companies, and their asset managers to monitor

---

90 European Commission, COM (2011) 683, Proposal for a Directive of the European Parliament and of the Council amending Directive 2004/109/EC on the harmonisation of transparency requirements in relation to information about issuers whose securities are admitted to trading on a regulated market and Commission Directive 2007/14/EC.

91 On 17 October 2013 the Council adopted the proposal to amend the Transparency Directive. On 19 November 2013 the UK Government published its response to the Select Committee Report on the Kay Review. It stated that the government intends to implement the relevant sections of the revised Transparency Directive as soon as possible.

92 Proposal to amend 2004/109/EC (note 16), 5.

93 This is aligned with the FRC Consultation Paper 'Effective Company Stewardship' which aims to improve the quality of annual reports and accounts by providing better information on business strategy and risk management in narrative reports; being more transparent around the work of the Audit Committee, and improving accessibility to information through the use of technology.

94 European Commission Staff Working Document, The Review of the Operation of Directive 2004/109/EC: Emerging Issues, COM (2010) 243, 11.

95 Ibid.

96 Ibid.

97 S Wong, 'Why stewardship is proving to be elusive for institutional investors' (2010) (July–Aug) *Butterworths Journal of International Banking and Financial Law 406;* I H-Y Chiu, 'Turning institutional investors into 'stewards': Exploring the meaning and objectives of 'stewardship'' (2013) 66 *Current Legal Problems 443*. On the structure of the institutional investment industry in the UK and the particular challenges it faces see, BIS, 'A Long-Term Focus for Corporate Britain', above n 52, 17–24; and P Myners, Institutional investment in the

and engage investee companies actively with the view to protect and enhance shareholder value.[98] However, efforts to convince institutional investors to be active, long-term oriented 'stewards', have fallen short.[99] Indeed, a recent OECD Report of the contributing causes of the global financial crisis concluded that institutional investors were generally not effective in monitoring investee companies.[100]

4.32 Wong argues that stewardship is proving to be elusive for institutional investors since it is not in their genetic makeup.[101] To explain why it is so difficult for institutional investors to act as stewards, Wong identifies a number of structural deficiencies in investment management. The first is inappropriate performance metrics and financial arrangements that promote trading and short-term returns.[102] Many asset managers are evaluated and compensated based on short-term, relative performance.[103] Unsurprisingly, investment managers focus on delivering short-term returns, including by pressuring investee companies to maximise their near-term profits.[104] Secondly, the techniques employed by many institutional investors to manage risk often result in excessive diversification, with equity portfolios containing hundreds or even thousands of stocks.[105] Excessive portfolio diversification makes monitoring

---

United Kingdom: A Review ('The Myners Review') (2001), pp 1 – 38, available at: www.hm-treasury.gov.uk/d/31.pdf, accessed 17 January 2014.

98 The first version was introduced by the Financial Reporting Council (the FRC) as the UK Stewardship Code in July 2010, available at: http://www.frc.org.uk/FRC-Documents/FRC/The-UK-Stewardship-Code.aspx . For its origins see, Sir D Walker, 'A Review of Corporate Governance in Banks and Other Financial Industry Entities' (November 2009), chapter 5. Available at: www.ecgi.org/codes/documents/walker_review_261109.pdf and Institutional Shareholders' Committee, *Improving Institutional Investors' Role in Governance* (2009). The more recent version of the Code, Financial Reporting Council, The UK Stewardship Code (September 2012), available at: http://www.frc.org.uk/Our-Work/Publications/Corporate-Governance/UK-Steward ship-Code-September-2012.pdf, accessed 17 January 2014.

99 On the effectiveness of institutional shareholder (or lack of) engagement through the Stewardship Code see J Lowry and A Reisberg, *Pettet's Company Law* (4th ed Longman 2012) 223–33; B Tricker, *Corporate Governance: Principles, Policies, and Practices* (OUP 2012) 65–67, 90–94; A Reisberg, 'The notion of stewardship from a company law perspective: Re-defined and re-assessed in light of the recent financial crisis?' (2011) 18 *Journal of Financial Crime* 126. B R Cheffins, 'The Stewardship Code's Achilles' Heel' (2010) 73 *Modern Law Review* 1004. A more recent initiative is the guidance published by the ICSA in March 2013 titled 'Enhancing Stewardship Dialogue'. This trend is apparent in other developed countries, such as Japan see http://www.glasslewis.com/blog/establishing-the-japanese-stewardship-code/, accessed 15 January 2014. And more recently, M Cobley, 'Investors demand higher stewardship standards' *Financial News* (25 Jun 2013) available at: http://www.efinancialnews.com/story/2013-06-25/investors-claim-corporate-governance-progress-pensions-protection-fund-ima, accessed 17 January 2014.

100 OECD, 'The role of institutional investors in promoting good corporate governance' [2011] http://www.oecd.org/daf/ca/corporategovernanceprinciples/49081553.pdf, accessed 30 November 2013.

101 Wong, see above n 97.

102 Ibid, 406–7.

103 Ibid.

104 Ibid.

105 Ibid, 407.

difficult.[106] Thirdly, investment management has lengthened the ownership chain of companies by increasing use of intermediaries – investment consultants, 'funds of funds', external asset managers, and others.[107] This process weakens the 'owner' mindset and lessens the sense of accountability between the ultimate investor and investee company.[108] Fourthly, owners and asset managers have a misguided interpretation of fiduciary duty which results in excessive deference to quantifiable data at the expense of qualitative factors.[109] Finally, passive funds, such as ETFs suffer from a flawed business model and governance approach.[110] Research suggests that passive funds tend to focus almost exclusively on their deviation from the benchmark index and correspondingly allocate least resources to stewardship activities.[111]

Wong suggests a number of practices that may encourage both a more active **4.33** ownership by institutional investors and a more long-term perspective.[112] First, eliminating unnecessary intermediation and strengthening internal capabilities may eliminate agency problems and improve performance of investment management.[113] In addition, lengthening the period between performance reviews, reducing the emphasis on relative returns and supplementing the existing comparisons to market indexes with other metrics, such as internal rates of return for exited investments, will encourage long-term-thinking.[114] To incentivise monitoring of investees by institutional investors, portfolio holdings should be slimmed down in order to be less diversified.[115]

With regard to passive investment, Wong suggests refining the business model **4.34** by increasing the emphasis on good stewardship, perhaps by charging clients for

---

106 Ibid.
107 Ibid, 407–8.
108 Ibid, 408.
109 Ibid.
110 Ibid, 409.
111 P Cox, 'Responsible investment in fund management: it works, but when?' University of Exeter Business School, (October 2009). In this respect, Glensiter recently noted that, according to an unnamed source involved in running equity portfolios for institutional investors, asset managers were too frequently failing to allocate suitable, experienced staff to the task of stewardship. The unnamed source is cited as saying:

> Often the people involved are not senior enough … [T]hese people have to go to the boards of major listed companies and highlight concerns, hold a relationship with those boards and try to ensure they are focused on preserving long-term value. That is a difficult thing to do but it is often made harder because the human resources allocated to that role often include relatively junior staff. How can they realistically expect to leave a mark in a meeting with senior managers who are experienced enough to know all the tricks in the book?

Cited in M Glensiter, 'Will the Kay Review have a long-term impact on the investment chain?' (5 April 2013) available at: http://www.myinvestorcircle.com/feature/will-kay-review-have-long-term-impact-investment-chain, accessed 20 March 2014.
112 Wong, see above n 97, 409.
113 J McFarland, 'Canada's pension funds: Stronger returns, at a cost' *Globe and Mail* (5 April 2010).
114 Wong, see above n 97, 410.
115 Ibid, 411.

the expenses incurred in this process.[116] In addition, policymakers should clarify fiduciary duties emphasising the importance of thorough examination of both short- and long-term, considerations.[117]

4.35 A separate, but closely related issue that should be explored is the role of international investors in the short-termism culture.[118] Companies operate in an ever-changing business world, where business practice rapidly changes with ever-increasing pressure and complexity and, critically, the 'players' become more diverse and their interests more conflicted.[119] This raises a number of questions, such as is it reasonable to expect that international investors engage themselves in the affairs of UK companies?[120] Can we still just refer to 'overseas investors' without going further, to find out their sources, diversity or varied interests? And most importantly, would foreign investors voluntarily adhere to a stewardship code, and, if not, how relevant or effective would the code be?[121]

4.36 The need for foreign investors to buy in to a stewardship code is critical for the discussion.[122] The Walker Review recommended that foreign investors should be encouraged to commit to the stewardship code on a voluntary basis in the belief that 'this is likely to be in their own interests and in that of their clients as ultimate beneficiaries'.[123] The FRC observed that many foreign investors, such as sovereign wealth funds and overseas pension funds, already have a long-term perspective, consistent with the underlying objective of the UK's governance framework to promote the long-term success of investee companies.[124] In contrast, the experience in Japan reveals that when foreign investors replaced domestic shareholders they were more interested in investment returns than in long-term relationships.[125]

---

116 Ibid.
117 Ibid.
118 On which see, A Reisberg, 'The notion of stewardship', above n 99.
119 Ibid, 136.
120 These questions are raised ibid.
121 Ibid, 141.
122 Ibid.
123 Sir D Walker, 'A review of corporate governance in banks and other financial industry entities' (November 2009), para 5.41, available at: www.ecgi.org/codes/documents/walker_review_261109.pdf.
124 The FRC itself has acknowledged that the need for foreign investors to buy into a stewardship code is critical. The FRC said it recognises: '[. . .] that not all parts of the (stewardship) Code will be relevant to all institutional investors, while smaller institutions may judge that some of its principles and guidance are disproportionate in their case. In these circumstances, they should take advantage of the "comply or explain" approach and set out why this is the case.' Financial Reporting Council, the UK Stewardship Code (July 2010), 2 available at: http://www.frc.org.uk/FRC-Documents/FRC/The-UK-Stewardship-Code.aspx, accessed 17 January 2014. Sadly, there is no evidence in the September 2012 version of the Code of any meaningful change in approach.
125 C Ahmadjian and G Robbins, 'A clash of capitalisms: Foreign shareholders and corporate restructuring in 1990s Japan' (2005) (June) 70 *American Sociological Review* 451, 459.

This brings to the foreground questions I raised in 2011: 'of what the differing **4.37** approaches to ownership portend for the financial system, for companies, and for policymakers and regulators worldwide'.[126] In particular, there is evidence to suggest that: (1) regardless of the industrial nature of the company, unrelated foreign direct investments are associated with negative announcement effects, and long-term performance;[127] (2) it is likewise important to recognise that the UK constitutes a relatively small market for many foreign investors, in terms of the percentage of their invested assets;[128] and (3) the degree to which foreign investors are able to influence local companies depends on a number of variables, the interaction between the system they come from and the one they invest in (say Japan v the UK).[129]

C. Driver no. 3: Diverse incentives

As the Kay Review made clear, shareholding is increasingly fragmented and this **4.38** reduces the incentives for stewardship.[130] Indeed, Goyder subsequently noted that institutional investors, who own less than 1 per cent of a company, do not have sufficient incentive to become good stewards.[131] It may be that Kay provided the answer when he suggested that institutional investors should work together so that their combined stakes in a company make their engagement imperative.[132] However, this is easier said than done and there is no evidence that investors have been prepared to do this in the past.[133] Instead, the Kay Review proposed that regulation should centre more on the structure of markets, and appropriate incentives, and less on fruitless attempts to control

---

126 Reisberg, 'The notion of stewardship', see above n 99, 137.

127 J Doukas and L Lang, 'Foreign direct investment, diversification and firm performance' (2003) 34 *Journal of International Business Studies* 153, 155.

128 Reisberg, 'The notion of stewardship', see above n 99, 137 (drawing on http://www.governance forowners.com/).

129 Ahmadjian and Robbins, see above n 125, 459.

130 Kay, see above n 20, 10.

131 M Goyder, 'Kay – repurposing the equities markets' (2012) (Aug) 218 *Governance* 5.

132 Kay, see above n 20, 13 (recommendation 3).

133 Goyder, see above n 131, 6. There are those who believe that it would be a mistake to dismiss the investor forum launched by bodies such as the ABI and NAPF in December 2013 as yet another 'City talking shop'. See, M Kleinman, 'Inside Track: It's about time the City's watchdog got its act together' City AM (5 December 2013) available at: http://www.cityam.com/article/1386207770/inside-track-it-s-about-time-city-s-watchdog-got-its-act-together#sthash.3ODRG8Zm.dpuf, accessed 17 January 2014. Kleinman believes that this new panel, borne out of the Kay Review, has the potential to be something meatier. Its two years of up-front funding removes from the table the usual questions about resourcing, but Kleinman believes that more importantly, the buy-in from both sides of the investment equation means it has a chance of escaping the Punch and Judy caricature of much of today's shareholder engagement. In his words: 'That isn't to say it is guaranteed to improve matters. There's little evidence that overseas investors would, for example, devote sufficient time to UK investment affairs to make their involvement worthwhile. What the forum needs to ensure is that its punches land with sufficient weight is a prominent frontman. Could Anthony Bolton, the departing Fidelity star, resist an approach?' Ibid.

behaviour, driven by inappropriate incentives.[134] But, as Bainbridge notes, this seems completely incompatible with the incentives of investors holding short positions: what happens when investors have an economic interest via short-selling, or various derivative investments in seeing the stock price drop?[135]

6. HOW TO BREAK THE SHORT-TERM CYCLE

4.39 As we have seen so far, the global financial crisis has undoubtedly intensified the debate surrounding short-termism and the need for reform. However, the need for reform that strengthens the number and power of long-term share-holders in public corporations, was first acknowledged as early as the 1930s.[136] Various proposals floated on ways to remedy or mitigate the problem. As Tables 4.2 and 4.3 below reveal, these proposals can be categorised into (1) tax reforms and (2) corporate governance modifications. Let us look at each in turn.

A. Tax reforms (Table 4.2 below)

4.40 The first set of proposals utilised the income tax system to make long-term ownership more attractive. In 1936 John Maynard Keynes suggested a tax on transactions in the stock market.[137] As Fried reports this proposal was later endorsed by the economists Joseph Stiglitz and Larry Summers in 1989, on the assumption that a tax on securities 'could lead to an increase in the relative number of long-term investors, causing managers to shift their focus to the long run'.[138] The Aspen Institute, which is 'an educational and policy studies organization based in Washington, DC' (see aspeninstitute.org), followed these proposals in 2009 and suggested, accordingly, a graduated long-term capital gains tax rate, offering the lowest rate only to shareholders owning their shares for a substantial period of time.[139] A year later, John Bogle suggested it would be better to eradicate the tax deductibility of short-term capital losses and instead increase the tax rate on ordinary income generated by share trading.[140]

---

134 Kay. See above n 20, Chapter 11.
135 S Bainbridge, 'A stewardship code for institutional investors' (18 January 2010) available at: http://www.professorbainbridge.com/professorbainbridgecom/2010/01/a-stewardship-code-for-institutional-investors.html, accessed 16 January 2014 (as implied by a question asked by Heineman).
136 J M Fried, 'The uneasy case for favoring long-term shareholders' Harvard Law School; *European Corporate Governance Institute (ECGI) Working Paper No 200* (18 March 2013).
137 J M Keynes, *The General Theory of Employment, Interest Rates and Money* 160 (Harcourt Brace & World 1936).
138 J Fried, see above n 136, 22, citing J Stiglitz, 'Using tax policy to curb speculative short-term trading' (1989) 3 *J Fin Serv Res* 101, 109.
139 Fried, ibid, 5. Aspen Institute, 'Overcoming short-termism: A call for a more responsible approach to investment and business management' (9 September 2009).
140 Fried, ibid, 21 relying on J Bogle, 'The clash of the cultures' (2010) 37 *J Portfolio Mgmt* 14, 25.

Table 4.2   A summary of various reforms to reduce short-termism

(Part 1 – Tax reforms)

Type of reform	Details	Proposed by	Year	Comments
Tax reform	Introduce a tax on securities transactions (which would make short-term share ownership less attractive)	John Maynard Keynes	1936	
Tax reform	Same as above (introduce a tax on securities transactions)	Joseph Stiglitz, Larry Summers	1989	2009: endorsed by the Aspen Institute
Tax reform	Same as above with refinement: A graduated long-term capital gains tax rate, which would offer the lowest rate available solely to shareholders that own their shares for a significant period of time	Aspen Institute (an educational and policy studies organization based in Washington, DC)	2009	
Tax reform	Two-parts: (1) increase the tax rate on ordinary income generated by shared trading; (2) at the same time, eliminate the tax deductibility of short-term capital losses	John Bogle	2010	

Source: Adapted from J M Fried, 'The Uneasy Case for Favoring Long-Term Shareholders' Harvard Law School; *European Corporate Governance Institute (ECGI) Working Paper No 200* (18 March 2013).

B.   Corporate governance modifications (Table 4.3 below)

Turning to corporate governance modifications, these largely concern proposals **4.41** to grant long-term shareholders more voting rights in the firm.[141] As Fried reports, this was supported by an American Bar Association corporate governance task force as a tool to boost long termism.[142] In fact, Fried further reports that these proposals had made a real impact in practice as several European companies voluntarily modified their corporate arrangements to give long-term

---

141   Haldane and Davies, see above n 34; P Bolton and F Samama, 'L-Shares: Rewarding long term investors', *ECGI Finance Working Paper* no 342/2013 (suggesting that long-term shareholders receive L-shares entitling them to additional stock in the firm).

142   Fried, see above note 136, 19, relying on the Report of the Task Force of the ABA Section of Business Law Corporate Governance Committee Delineation of Governance Roles & Responsibilities, (2009) 65 *Bus Law* 107.

Table 4.3   A summary of various reforms to reduce short-termism

(Part 2 – Corporate-governance reforms)

Type of reform	Details	Proposed by	Year	Comments
Corporate-governance modifications	Long-term shareholders are to be given: (1) voting rights; and (2) an entitlement to dividend	Patrick Bolton and Frederic Samama; Andrew Haldane and Richard Davies (BOE)	2012 2011	
Corporate-governance modifications	Companies willingly modified their corporate arrangements to give long-term shareholders more cash-flow than short-term shareholders	Several European companies	2012	An American Bar Association corporate governance task force: similar arrangements be considered in the US
Corporate-governance modifications	Companies to prefer the views of long-term shareholders as a matter of 'best practice'	Kay Review	2012	
Corporate-governance modifications	SEC requiring nominating shareholders for proxy access to keep their shares for at least 3 years uninterruptedly	SEC's 75 FED. REG. 56668 (16 Sept. 16, 2010)	2010	(later-invalidated)

Source: Adapted from J M Fried, 'The uneasy case for favoring long-term shareholders' Harvard Law School; *European Corporate Governance Institute (ECGI) Working Paper No 200* (18 March 2013).

shareholders more cash-flow than short-term shareholders.[143] The Kay Review posed a more fluid approach to increasing the influence of long-term share-holders (as seen above) by urging companies to prefer the views of long-term shareholders as a matter of 'best practice'. Similarly, in the US, the SEC required nominating shareholders for proxy access to keep their shares for at least three years uninterruptedly.[144]

---

143   Fried, ibid, 20, relying on Bolton and Samama, see above n 141, 9–10.
144   Fried, ibid, 19. This was later invalidated. 75 Fed Reg. 56,668 (16 Sep 2010).

C. UK Government sets out steps to change culture in UK equity markets

In November 2012, the UK Government followed the spirit of the reforms **4.42** discussed above, by setting out steps to change the culture in UK equity markets and encourage long-term thinking in companies. It is likely that delivering the government's ambitious agenda would require a sustained joint commitment from overnment, regulators and others.[145] Nonetheless, the agenda appears, at least on paper, to be a step in the right direction. When announcing these plans, Vince Cable stated that:

> Many of us feel that in the past, our public companies and investors have focused on short-term profit at the expense of long-term value. The behaviour of many banks in the run up to the financial crisis is an extreme example of this quick buck mentality, but there is clearly a wider problem. That's why I asked John Kay to look at what could be done to ensure equity markets support good, long-term decision-making. His insightful review calls for a shift in the culture of investment and sets a clear challenge to companies and those who invest in them. …

> His agenda is an ambitious one but I am very encouraged by the level of engagement we have seen already from investors. Not only on Kay's ideas, but through our directors' pay and shareholder voting reforms; in addressing diversity on corporate boards; and through changes to the way companies report their business strategy and results. These actions will help restore trust in markets and in the system of capitalism on which our future prosperity depends.[146]

The government plans to publish an update in Summer 2014 setting out its **4.43** progress in delivering Professor Kay's recommendations and reporting how well companies and investors have stepped up to the plate. More specifically, the UK Government recommendations include a number of important strategies.[147] First, working with EU counterparts to end mandatory quarterly reporting and help reduce the excessive focus on short-term earnings.[148] Second, endorsing clear minimum standards of behaviour for all investment intermediaries to

---

145   See, BIS 'Government sets out steps to change culture in UK equity markets' available at: http://news.bis. gov.uk/Press-Releases/Government-sets-out-steps-to-change-culture-in-UK-equity-markets-683c1.aspx 22 November 2012, accessed 16 January 2014.

146   Ibid.

147   Ibid. For the full government's response to the Kay Review see: http://www.bis.gov.uk/assets/biscore/ business-law/docs/e/12–1188-equity-markets-support-growth-response-to-kay-review, accessed 16 January 2014.

148   Ibid. As we saw above in part 5. above the legal obligation for issuers of shares to provide quarterly financial information (either quarterly financial reports or interim management statements as defined in art 6 of the Transparency Directive 2004/109/EC) was subject to a recent review. Consequently, the Transparency Directive was amended and the requirement to produce interim management statements or quarterly reports was removed.

ensure they act in the long-term best interests of their clients.[149] To deliver this, the Law Commission has been asked to review the legal obligations on intermediaries, to take appropriate long-term factors into account.[150] The FSA (which has since been replaced by the FCA) has also been asked to ensure that the regulatory framework promotes high standards of behaviour throughout the investment chain.[151] Third, encouraging industry to establish an Investors' Forum to champion constructive engagement with companies.[152] And finally, the government endorsed *Good Practice* Statements for company directors,[153] asset managers[154] and asset holders,[155] which emphasise the need for trust-based relationships and advocate more collective action by institutional share-holders; better disclosure of costs in the investment chain; increased transparency and fairness in stock lending; and better alignment between pay and long-term performance.[156] Conversely however, there are moves by the FCA to drive down the fees that investment managers may charge. The effect of a lower level of available income, on the willingness of investment managers to undertake more ownership levels of stewardship, remains to be seen.

D.   Are these steps in the right direction?

4.44   Haldane and Davies suggest that, '[I]t might be time to increase the level of policy ambition. Without intervention, the long could become shorter still.'[157] So it appears that the government is finally rising up to the (uneasy) challenge. This is a market failure which requires intervention. But there is still a long way to go. Indeed, Kay's diagnosis, as Goyder aptly puts it, is not an easy one:[158]

---

149   Ibid. See further the full government's response to the Kay Review, above n 147, – para 3.34.

150   On 22 October 2013 the Law Commission published a consultation paper reviewing how fiduciary duties apply to investment intermediaries. See, Fiduciary Duties of Investment Intermediaries at: http://lawcommission.justice.gov.uk/news/2565.htm, accessed 18 January 2014, which was opened until 22 January 2014. The paper traces a chain of intermediaries from an individual, saving for a pension, to the registered shareholder of a UK company. It looks at the obligations of those in the chain to act in the interests of savers. The Commission's project arose out of the Kay Review of the UK equity market. Published in July 2012, the Kay Review criticised intermediaries for excessive trading on the basis of short-term share movements, rather than investing for the long-term. The Law Commission seeks views on these issues by 22 January 2014. David Hertzell, the Law Commissioner leading the project, said: 'Judge-made laws, such as fiduciary duties, cannot make up for gaps in regulation. We think that there may be gaps in the way that investment consultants and custodians are regulated, and ask whether there is a need to review these areas.' Ibid.

151   See, BIS 'Government sets out steps to change culture in UK equity markets', above n 145.

152   Ibid. And see the recent initiative discussed in n 126 above.

153   See the full government's response to the Kay Review, above n 147, Annex A.

154   Ibid, Annex B.

155   Ibid, Annex C.

156   See, BIS 'Government sets out steps to change culture in UK equity markets' above n 145.

157   Haldane and Davies, see above n 34, 15.

158   Goyder, see above n 131, 6.

[T]he patient's relatives might have been hoping for a more immediate cure. He is telling the patient to eat less fast food and be less hyperactive; to get out and mix more and generally develop a healthier lifestyle with one eye on the years ahead. The regime he is prescribing will, over time, help the patient achieve the right habits. But there are no quick fixes and every part of the patient's system needs adjustment in order to find this new equilibrium.

In 2005, the CFA Centre for Financial Market Integrity/Business Roundtable **4.45** Institute for Corporate Ethics proposed a five-point plan to tackle this problem.[159] Sensibly, it suggested that focus should be given to all groups at the same time, that is, leaders, issuer, analyst, institutional investor, asset manager, and hedge fund manager communities, and that only such a multi-pronged approach could mitigate the current overemphasis on short-term performance and refocus on long-term value.[160]

The five-point plan included the following: First, reform earnings guidance **4.46** practices. All groups should reconsider the benefits and consequences of providing and relying upon focused, quarterly earnings guidance and each group's involvement in the 'earnings guidance game'.[161] Second, develop long-term incentives across the board. This means that compensation for corporate executives and asset managers should be structured to achieve long-term strategic and value-creation goals.[162] Third, demonstrate leadership in shifting the focus to long-term value creation.[163] This should include, for example, supporting analysts and asset managers in using a long-term focus in their analyses and capital investment decisions as well as promoting an institutional investor focus on long-term value for themselves and when evaluating their asset managers.[164] Fourth, improve communications and transparency. In other words, more meaningful, and potentially more frequent, communications about company strategy and long-term value drivers can lessen the financial community's dependence on earnings guidance.[165] Finally, promote broad education of all market participants about the benefits of long-term thinking and the

---

159 Krehmeyer et al 'Breaking the Short-Term Cycle', see above n 19.
160 Ibid.
161 Ibid, 2 and 5–9.
162 Ibid, 9. There is, indeed, evidence that there is, at least, more awareness to this, in recent debates and reforms. See, BIS, 'Government announces far-reaching reforms of directors' pay' available at: http://news.bis.gov.uk/Press-Releases/Government-announces-far-reaching-reforms-of-directors-pay-67b96.aspx, accessed 16 January 2014; and 'Directors' pay: revised remuneration reporting regulations' available at https://www.gov.uk/government/consultations/directors-pay-revised-remuneration-reporting-regulations, accessed 16 January 2014.
163 Ibid, 11–14.
164 Ibid, 2.
165 Ibid.

costs of short-term thinking.[166] This should include encouraging widespread corporate participation in ongoing dialogues with asset managers and other financial market leaders to better understand how their companies are valued in the marketplace. In addition, there should be support for education initiatives for individual investors in order to encourage a focus on long-term value creation.[167]

7. DEBATE IS FAR FROM OVER

4.47 A fundamental question that should be put on the table is as follows: are long-term shareholder interests really aligned with maximising the long-term economic value created by the company? Answering this question would have a direct impact on the need to incentivise long-termism through regulation in the first place and the type and form of regulation that should take place.

4.48 Fried critically challenges the norm that firms should favour long-term shareholders over short-term shareholders.[168] This view is based on a widely held belief that long-term shareholders, unlike short-term shareholders, benefit from managers maximising the long-term economic value generated by the firm. Fried's analysis suggest that this belief is mistaken and that the case for shifting power from short-term to long-term shareholders is substantially weaker than it might appear.[169]

Long-term shareholders, like short-term shareholders, can benefit from managers destroying economic value.[170] Favouring long-term shareholders could thus reduce, rather than increase, the value generated by a firm over time.[171]

4.49 The EU Commission has also supported the view that not all short-termism is negative.[172] The general view of scholars in a discussion on the action plan was

---

166 Ibid.
167 Ibid.
168 Fried, see above n 136.
169 Ibid, 7.
170 Ibid, 4.
171 Ibid.
172 The EU Corporate Governance Framework, Green Paper (April 2011) para 2.3 states:

> The Commission recognises that not all investors need to engage with investee companies. Investors are free to choose a short-term-oriented investment model without engagement. However, the agency relationship between institutional investors (asset owners) and their managers contributes to capital markets' increasing short-termism and to mispricing. This issue is particularly relevant as regards the inactivity of long-term-oriented shareholders.

that the Kay Review did *not* address short-termism in a clear and comprehensive way and that the solutions offered were impractical and undesirable.[173]

In particular, Panunzi suggested that although the Kay Review blamed the **4.50** demands of asset management for short-termism, short-termism might, nevertheless, be correct in a given set of circumstances.[174] He observed that there are many factors that might legitimately create a short-termist view.[175] Share prices, for instance, could sometimes be very 'noisy', thus influencing behaviour. In addition, the desire for liquidity might militate against long-termism.[176] Urtiaga pointed out that the Kay Review could have usefully employed more clarity of direction on short-termism, in general and on how to persuade long-term investors to take the long-term view, in particular.[177] She supported that need for further research on benefits and costs of short-termism and considering loyalty shares as a possible incentive for shareholders to adopt a long-term view in public firms.[178] Franks observed that the Kay Review did not demonstrate that long-term shareholding versus activism was of itself better.[179] In relation to M&A activity, he argued that the evidence seemed to suggest that where shareholder approval was required, the outcome was more profitable than those deals where no consent was required.[180] Burkart highlighted the lack of clarity of the Kay Review pointing out that the review's appeal to more group behaviour is not going to get anywhere.[181]

Similarly, Lee, Director at Hermes Equity Ownership Services Ltd, continued **4.51** this line of criticism of the Kay Review, contending that:[182]

> We struggle to be convinced that the proposed investors' forum to coordinate and encourage more engagement will amount to much – it was last proposed only in 2009 in the Walker Report and the Institutional Investors Committee has not resurfaced substantially since – as it seems to place the bulk of the burden on the shoulders of investment managers, the intermediaries Kay rails against and yet he does not propose

---

173 Professor Maria Gutierrez Urtiaga, Associate Professor, Department of Business and Finance, Universidad Carlos III de Madrid and Professor Fausto Panunzi, Full Professor of EconomicsIstituto di Economia Politica and IGIER, Università Bocconi, at an academic conference held by the ECGI on 23 January 2013 to discuss the European Commission's Action Plan on Company Law and Corporate Governance (published on 12 December 2012) and associated policy proposals, available at: http://www.ecgi.org/conferences/eu_actionplan 2013/report.php, accessed 13 January 2014.
174 Ibid, see his Speech.
175 Ibid.
176 Ibid.
177 Ibid, see her Speech.
178 Ibid.
179 Ibid, see his Speech.
180 Ibid.
181 Ibid, see his Speech.
182 P Lee, 'Kay – repurposing the equities markets' (2012) (Aug) 218 *Governance*, 7.

significantly to change their incentives. It is therefore hard to understand why more would actively seek to rise to the challenge he lays out.

4.52 Wong acknowledges the importance of the Kay Review in analysing what causes short-termism in the UK as well as its recommendations to address these causes.[183] However, he points out that one crucial reform, the reconfiguration of the structure and governance of pension funds, is missing from the Review and will affect several of its recommendations.[184] Wong analyses the need to shorten the chain of intermediaries, eliminate the use of short-term performance metrics for asset managers, and adopt more concentrated portfolios.[185] He argues that, without these reforms at the top of the investment chain, it is doubtful that the key recommendations in the Kay Review can be successfully implemented.[186]

4.53 Wong, rightly notes, that: '[a] major challenge facing pension funds in the UK and elsewhere is the lack of relevant expertise and knowledge at board and management levels.'[187] Consequently, many rely heavily – some would argue excessively – on external advisers.[188] At present, reflecting their trustees' paucity of expertise on investment matters, many pension funds employ crude performance metrics, such as quarterly return against a pre-selected market benchmark, to evaluate fund managers.[189] Furthermore, the trustees do not always understand fully why investment managers are retained or terminated.[190]

4.54 By contrast, Wong mentions that in a large Canadian pension fund the board has been revamped to bolster financial expertise and pays scant attention to short-term investment returns.[191] Instead, they focus on whether investment managers are sticking to agreed investment strategies and continue to possess distinctive capabilities.[192] Therefore, there is a crucial need to strengthen board and management capabilities at pension funds.[193] This reform would bring substantial benefits to the pensions' schemes and to the broader economy.[194]

---

183 S Wong, Guest Blog, 'The Missing Reform in the Kay Review' (26 July 2012) available at: http://blogs.reuters.com/globalinvesting/2012/07/26/guest-blog-the-missing-reform-in-the-kay-review/, accessed 18 January 2014.
184 Ibid.
185 Ibid.
186 Ibid.
187 Ibid.
188 Ibid.
189 Ibid.
190 Ibid.
191 Ibid.
192 Ibid.
193 Ibid.
194 Ibid.

Trustees and executives will be better equipped to make informed decisions on their own, including questioning practices that may benefit intermediaries more than the pensions themselves. In addition, it would improve the ability of trustees and executives in assessing the performance of investment managers.[195] Finally, Wong argues that if investment managers are relieved of the strain to 'outperform' each quarter, they may in turn focus less on short-term performance at investee companies.[196]

8. LOOKING AHEAD

The foregoing discussion suggests that there are more open questions than answered ones. One central issue is how to encourage a position where there are more shareholders who have a long-term interest as well as the presence of short-term holders.[197] There is no doubt that people tend to be optimistic about the future and that optimism is inevitably reflected in the stock markets.[198] At the peak of the financial crisis, the objective in many countries was to preserve the company, but regulation had been short-termist in nature, for example, regulations against 'shorting the market' were first introduced in 2009.[199] The EU Commission indicated that it was also looking at incentives for long-term holding such as loyalty shares, enhanced voting rights, taxation options and increased dividends, but as we saw, there is nothing new about these ideas, which have been floating for a long time. Rightly, the EU Commission also held the view that not all short-termism was negative when it stated that:[200]

4.55

> The Commission recognises that not all investors need to engage with investee companies. Investors are free to choose a short-term-oriented investment model without engagement.
>
> However, the agency relationship between institutional investors (asset owners) and their managers contributes to capital markets' increasing short-termism and to mispricing. This issue is particularly relevant as regards the inactivity of long-term-oriented shareholders.

---

195 Ibid.
196 Ibid.
197 See, Frank's speech in an academic conference held by the ECGI on 23 January 2013 to discuss the European Commission's Action Plan on Company Law and Corporate Governance (published on 12 December 2012) and associated policy proposals, available at: http://www.ecgi.org/conferences/eu_actionplan2013/report.php, accessed 13 January 2014.
198 Ibid.
199 Regulation on short selling and certain aspects of credit default swaps is directly applicable in the UK since 1 November 2012. See, http://www.fca.org.uk/firms/markets/international-markets/eu/short-selling-regulations, accessed18 January 2014.
200 The EU Corporate Governance Framework, Green Paper (April, 2011) para. 2.3.

4.56 Being more realistic as to who can be expected to engage and what incentives there are in place, apart from being a pragmatic approach, is a sensible way forward. It recognises the complexity of the financial markets and the diverse interests at play. But it leaves other questions open, such as, should the EU Commission create enabling legislation that allowed companies to offer choices?[201] Perhaps the more difficult question is: how does one encourage investors to engage with boards also taking the long-term view?[202] This is the difficult issue to resolve.

4.57 Perhaps one view that should be looked at more closely is to recognise that long-term incentives will only be implemented by long-term shareholders.[203] Edmans suggests that the main distinction is *not* between short-term and long-term shareholders but rather between large and small shareholders. So the important question is *not* whether shareholders are long term or short term, but whether they are short or long.[204] He suggests, drawing on previous research, that shareholders who are short-term and uniformed would trade on short-term earnings,[205] whereas only long-term shareholder would implement long-term policies.[206] Another view is to demand long-term metrics from companies to inform investment decisions.[207] Making long-term investment decisions, it is submitted, is hard 'without metrics that calibrate, even in a rough way, the long-term performance and health of companies'.[208] These last two views

---

201 As participants at the conference held by the ECGI on 23 January 2013 to discuss the European Commission's Action Plan on Company Law and Corporate Governance correctly noted, bonus shares for long-term membership militated against the one-share-one-vote principle. The laws of several EU countries made the incentive for long-term holding suggestions illegal, but not in the UK or the US. Available at: http://www.ecgi.org/conferences/eu_actionplan2013/report.php, accessed 13 January 2014.

202 Ibid.

203 A Edmans, 'Corporate governance and short-termism: Challenges and solutions' a presentation at the European Corporate Governance & Company Law Conference in the Convention Centre, Dublin (16 May 2013) available at: http://www.corpgov2013.com/delegate-info.php#PRESENTATIONS, accessed 17 January 2014.

204 Ibid.

205 If they are small and short, looking at earnings, would give incentives to management to boost earnings. Ibid.

206 Larger shareholders have bigger incentives to gather information ('sufficient skin in the game'). Instead of having a portfolio in 200 companies they own portfolios at a larger stake in a few companies. And, if, for example, there is cut in dividends, they will try to understand what's behind it. Maybe this is to finance investment in the long run, which would make them hold the shares, or is it because of management mismanagement, in which case they will sell their shares. Exit, in many cases can be an act of governance of disciplinary management, contrary to what people think. So selling the shares would be a vote of no confidence in the current board. Ibid.

207 See, Barton and Wiseman, above n 65, 47.

208 Ibid, 50. Barton and Wiseman explain that:

> focusing on metrics like ten-year economic value added, R&D efficiency, patent pipelines, multiyear return on capital investments, and energy intensity of production is likely to give investors more useful information than basic GAAP accounting in assessing a company's performance over the long haul. The specific measures will vary by industry sector, but they exist for every company. (Ibid).

deserve the full attention of companies, policymakers and of shareholders of all size and orientation.

SELECTED BIBLIOGRAPHY

Ahmadjian, C, and Robbins, G, 'A clash of capitalisms: Foreign shareholders and corporate restructuring in 1990s Japan' (2005) (June) 70 *American Sociological Review* 451.

Aspen Institute, 'Overcoming short-termism: A call for a more responsible approach to investment and business management' (9 Sept 2009), available at aspeninstitute.org.

Bainbridge, S, 'A stewardship code for institutional investors' (18 January 2010) available at: http://www.professorbainbridge.com/professorbainbridgecom/2010/01/a-stewardship-code-for-institutional-investors.html.

Barton, D and Wiseman, M, 'Focusing capital on the long term' (2014) (Jan–Feb) *Harvard Business Review* 44.

Bebchuk, L, 'The myth that insulating boards serves long-term value' (2013) (October) 113 *Columbia Law Review* 1637.

BIS 'Government sets out steps to change culture in UK equity markets' available at: http://news.bis.gov.uk/Press-Releases/Government-sets-out-steps-to-change-culture-in-UK-equity-markets-683c1.aspx 22 November 2012.

BIS, 'A Long-Term Focus for Corporate Britain: A Call for Evidence' (October 2010) available at: www.bis.gov.uk/assets/biscore/business-law/docs/l/10–1225-long-term-focus-corporate-britain.

BIS, 'Government announces far-reaching reforms of directors' pay' available at: http://news.bis.gov.uk/Press-Releases/Government-announces-far-reaching-reforms-of-directors-pay-67b96.aspx.

BIS, 'Review on corporate governance and short-termism opens' Press Release, 25 October 2010, available at: http://news.bis.gov.uk/content/detail.aspx?NewsAreaId=2&ReleaseID=416167&SubjectId=2.

BIS, October 2010 (URN 10/1225), available at: https://www.gov.uk/government/consultations/a-long-term-focus-for-corporate-britain-a-call-for-evidence.

Bogle, J, 'The clash of the cultures' (2010) 37 *J Portfolio Mgmt* 14.

Bolton, P and Samama, F, 'L-Shares: Rewarding long-term investors, *ECGI Finance Working Paper* no 342/2013.

Britannica Academic Edition available at: http://www.britannica.com/EBchecked/topic/385191/Walter-Mischel.

Business Roundtable Institute for Corporate Ethics (2005) 'Breaking the short-term cycle' available at: http://www.corporate-ethics.org/pdf/Short-termism_Report.pdf.

CAPA Chronicle (October 2007) at: http://www.capa.com.my/images/capa/OCT-NOV%2007.pdf.

CFA Institute Centre for Financial Market Integrity/Business Roundtable Institute for Corporate Ethics, 'Apples to apples: A template for reporting quarterly earnings' (March 2007).

CFA Institute, Earnings Guidance, available at: http://www.cfainstitute.org/ethics/topics/Pages/earnings_guidance.aspx.

Chan, C, 'Debate over quarterly Reporting' A+ (December 2007) available at: http://app1.hkicpa.org.hk/APLUS/0712/20–22.pdf.

Cheffins, B R, 'The Stewardship Code's Achilles' heel' (2010) 73 *Modern Law Review* 1004.

Chiu, I, 'Turning institutional investors into 'stewards': Exploring the meaning and objectives of 'stewardship'' (2013) 66 *Current Legal Problems* 443.

Cobley, M, 'Investors demand higher stewardship standards' *Financial News* (25 Jun 2013) available at: http://www.efinancialnews.com/story/2013–06–25/investors-claim-corporate-governance-progress-pensions-protection-fund-ima.

Confino, J, 'Unilever's Paul Poleman: Challenging the corporate status quo', *Guardian Professional Network*, theguardian.com, available at: http://www.theguardian.com/sustainable-business/paul-polman-unilever-sustainable-living-plan?guni=Article:in%20body%20link (24 April 2012).

Cox, Sir G, 'Overcoming short-termism within British business, the key to sustained economic growth' an independent review by February 2013, available at: http://www.yourbritain.org.uk/uploads/editor/files/Overcoming_Short-termism.pdf.

Cox, P, 'Responsible investment in fund management: it works, but when?' University of Exeter Business School, (October 2009).

Doukas, J and L Lang, 'Foreign direct investment, diversification and firm performance' (2003) 34 *Journal of International Business Studies* 153.

ECGI academic conference held on 23 January 2013 to discuss the European Commission's Action Plan on Company Law and Corporate Governance (published on 12 December 2012) and associated policy proposals. Available at: http://www.ecgi.org/conferences/eu_actionplan 2013/report.php.

Edmans, A, 'Corporate governance and short-termism: Challenges and solutions', a presentation at the European Corporate Governance and Company Law Conference in the Convention Centre, Dublin (16 May 2013) available at: http://www.corpgov2013.com/delegate-info.php#PRESENTATIONS.

Efrati, A, 'A makeover made in Google's image', *Wall Street Journal*, (9 August 2012), available at: http://online.wsj.com/news/articles/SB10000872396390443517104577575420060344832.

European Commission Staff Working Document, 'The review of the operation of Directive 2004/109/EC: Emerging issues', COM (2010) 243, 11.

European Commission, COM (2011) 683, Proposal for a Directive of the European Parliament and of the Council amending Directive 2004/109/EC on the harmonisation of transparency requirements in relation to information about issuers whose securities are admitted to trading on a regulated market and Commission Directive 2007/14/EC.

Fried, J, 'The uneasy case for favoring long-term shareholders' *Harvard Law School; European Corporate Governance Institute (ECGI) Working Paper No 200* (18 March 2013).

Glensiter, M, 'Will the Kay Review have a long-term impact on the investment chain?' (5 April 2013), available at: http://www.myinvestorcircle.com/feature/will-kay-review-have-long-term-impact-investment-chain.

Government's response to the Kay Review, available at: http://www.bis.gov.uk/assets/biscore/business-law/docs/e/12–1188-equity-markets-support-growth-response-to-kay-review.

Goyder, M, 'Kay – repurposing the equities markets' (2012) (August) 218 *Governance* 5.

Haldane, A and R Davies, Bank of England, Speech: The Short Long (11 May 2011) at: http://www.bis.org/review/r110511e.pdf.

Haldane, A and R Davies, (Bank of England) 'The Short-Long' Paper (May 2011).

Helms, C and others, 'Corporate short-termism: Causes and remedies' (2012) 23(2) *International Company and Commercial Law Review* 45.

Institutional Shareholders' Committee, *Improving Institutional Investors' Role in Governance* (2009).

Kay, J, 'The Kay Review of UK equity markets and long-term decision making: Final Report' BIS/12/917 (July 2012).

Kay, J, Speech at the Kay Review Launch, (23 July 2012), available at: https://www.gov.uk/government/uploads/system/uploads/attachment_data/file/253459/bis-12–996-kay-review-of-equity-markets-speech-and-presentation.pdf.

Keynes, J M, *The General Theory of Employment, Interest Rates and Money* (Harcourt Brace & World 1936).

Kleinman, M, 'Inside track: It's about time the City's watchdog got its act together' City AM (5 December 2013) available at: http://www.cityam.com/article/1386207770/inside-track-it-s-about-time-city-s-watchdog-got-its-act-together#sthash.3ODRG8Zm.dpuf.

Kliff, S, 'The marshmallow test, revisited', *The Washington Post* (12 October 2012), available at: http://www.washingtonpost.com/blogs/wonkblog/wp/2012/10/13/the-marshmallow-test-revisited/.

Krehmeyer, D, M Orsagh and K Schacht, *Breaking the Short-Term Cycle*, CFA Institute (2006).

Law Commission, Fiduciary duties of investment intermediaries, Consultation Paper No 215 (October 2013).

Lee, P, 'Kay – repurposing the equities markets' (2012) (Aug) 218 *Governance* 7.

Lowry, J and A Reisberg, *Pettet's Company Law* (4th ed Longman 2012).

Marginson, D and McAulay, L, 'Exploring the debate on short-termism' (2008) 29(3) *Strategic Management Journal* 273.

Mazars (December 2009) on 'The application of selected obligations of directive 2004/109/ec on the harmonisation of transparency requirements in relation to information about issuers whose securities are admitted to trading on a regulated market', Study conducted for the European Commission, available at: http://ec.europa.eu/internal_market/securities/docs/transparency/report-application-annexes_en.pdf.

Mulley, G, J Palmer J and D Paterson, 'Investing for the long-term: Government consultation on short-termism in the equity markets' Herbert Smith Freehills LLP (26 October 2010).

Myners, P, Institutional investment in the United Kingdom: A review (2001) available at: www.hm-treasury.gov.uk/d/31.pdf.

OECD, 'The role of institutional investors in promoting good corporate governance' [2011] available at: http://www.oecd.org/daf/ca/corporategovernanceprinciples/49081553.pdf.

Oxford Dictionary of Finance and Banking (4th revised edition, OUP 2008).

Rahman, A R, T M Tay, B T Ong and S Cai, 'Quarterly reporting in a voluntary disclosure environment: Its benefits, drawbacks and determinants' (2007)] 42(4) *The International Journal of Accounting* 416.

Reisberg, A, 'The notion of stewardship from a company law perspective: Re-defined and re-assessed in light of the recent financial crisis?' (2011) 18 *Journal of Financial Crime* 126.

Reisberg, A 'Shareholder value after the financial crisis: a dawn of a new era?' (2013) *International Corporate Rescue* 143.

Roe, M J, 'Corporate short-termism – in the boardroom and in the courtroom' (2013) 68(4) *Business Lawyer* 977.

Rubinton, B J, 'Crowdfunding: disintermediated investment banking' available at http://mpra.ub.uni-muenchen.de/31649/.

Report of the Task Force of the ABA Section of Business Law Corporate Governance Committee Delineation of Governance Roles & Responsibilities (2009) 65 *Bus Law* 107.

Sovereign Wealth Funds and the Global Private Equity Landscape Survey (June 2008) available at: http://www.nortonrosefulbright.com/knowledge/publications/15287/sovereign-wealth-funds-and-the-global-private-equity-landscape-survey.

Stiglitz, J, 'Using tax policy to curb speculative short-term trading' (1989) 3 *J Fin Serv Res* 101.

TheCityUK, *SME Financing: Impact of regulation and the Eurozone crisis* (2012), ab=vailable at: http://www.thecityuk.com/research/our-work/reports-list/sme-financing-impact-of-regulation-and-the-eurozone-crisis/(visited 17 March 2014).

The EU Corporate Governance Framework, Green Paper (April 2011).

Tricker, B, *Corporate Governance: Principles, Policies, and Practices* (OUP 2012).

Walker, Sir D, 'A review of corporate governance in banks and other financial industry entities' (November 2009).

Wong, S, 'Why stewardship is proving to be elusive for institutional investors' (2010) (July–Aug) *Butterworths Journal of International Banking and Financial Law* 406.

Wong, S, Guest Blog 'The missing reform in the Kay Review' (26 July 2012) available at: http://blogs.reuters.com/globalinvesting/2012/07/26/guest-blog-the-missing-reform-in-the-kay-review/.

World Economic Forum Report, 'The Future of Long-term Investing' (2011) available at: http://www.weforum.org/issues/long-term-investing.

5

DESIGN AND CONTROL OF REMUNERATION IN UK BANKS

Marc T Moore

1. INTRODUCTION

Undoubtedly the most controversial corporate governance issue in UK banks **5.01** over recent years has been the arguably 'excessive' remuneration awarded to senior banking executives and other key bank employees. This chapter will explain the most common forms of directorial and executive remuneration in public companies. It will then document the basic legal principles that govern the determination of directors' remuneration in UK companies, together with the proper procedures for directorial remuneration-setting as provided under both the Companies Act 2006 and UK Corporate Governance Code (The Code), including remuneration committees and 'say on pay' resolutions. The chapter will furthermore examine the various regulatory provisions that are designed to ensure the effective alignment of pay with performance and risk tolerance in public companies, with particular regard to those provisions that are uniquely applicable to banks. These include the rules relating to bonus payments, executive share options, restricted share grants, and severance payments ('golden parachutes'). Regard will be had both to the general rules in this regard, and also to the specific requirements that apply to banks under the Financial Conduct Authority/Prudential Regulation Authority Remuneration Code (Remuneration Code). Of particular concern will be the extensive and detailed regulatory restrictions on the payment of bonuses to high-level bank employees today, including the controversial new EU 'bonus cap'. The chapter's principal focus will be on the legal and regulatory framework applicable to those (typically larger) UK-incorporated banks operating as public companies, and which are listed on the London Stock Exchange. However, it is envisaged that many of the chapter's insights will still be relevant to banks that fall outside of this particular category.

2. PRINCIPAL FORMS OF DIRECTORIAL AND EXECUTIVE REMUNERATION

5.02 This section sets out the principal forms of remuneration typically awarded to directors and senior executives of UK public companies. Since the dominant forms of remuneration are for the most part determined privately by companies themselves, there will inevitably be a significant degree of variation amongst prevailing practices in this regard. For this reason, the list below cannot claim to be exhaustive. Furthermore, the extent to which each of the main pay components factor into any particular officer's remuneration package will differ depending on the company and candidate concerned. Subject to the above provisos, though, the following provides a general outline of the most common norms in this regard.

A. Basic director's service fee

5.03 The director's service fee is the basic remuneration that is due to a company director in return for fulfilling their official directorial functions. This is distinct from any further functions carried out by a director for the company in an additional capacity, such as a senior executive office. In public companies, directorial functions typically include attending and participating in periodic board meetings and any associated board committee meetings, assessing relevant documentation both during and in advance of meetings, acquiring any requisite expertise or knowledge in advance of meetings, and – where necessary – consulting with relevant third parties such as professional legal and financial advisers. The director's service fee will ordinarily be paid in the form of a fixed salary. In the case of a director who simultaneously holds a paid executive position in the same company (e.g. as Chief Executive Officer (CEO), Finance Director (FD) or Chief Operating Officer (COO)), the director's service fee may be of purely nominal value. However, in the case of non-executive directors (NEDs), the service fee will normally constitute the exclusive source of remuneration from an employer company, particularly in light of the Code's influential recommendation that NED remuneration should not include share options or other variable, performance-related elements.[1]

B. Executive salary

This is the basic annual contractual pay due to an executive officer in return for **5.04** fulfilling their official executive functions. In the case of a senior executive who holds an additional office as director of the company, the executive salary (rather than director's service fee) will usually constitute the more significant component of basic remuneration, with the director's service fee being purely nominal in nature. In the case of CEOs and other senior executives of larger publicly traded companies, executive salary will frequently comprise a minority of total remuneration received in any year, with the variable, performance-related components of pay providing the majority of the executive's overall annual award.

C. Bonus payments

A bonus payment is an additional increment on pay, normally awarded on an **5.05** annual basis. While the word 'bonus' suggests an element of unexpectedness on the part of the recipient, in practice frequent bonuses are both customary and entirely expected within many environments, and most notably in the banking and financial services sectors. A bonus can be contractual in nature, in which case its award will be triggered by the relevant employee meeting a pre-specified periodic performance target. Alternatively, a bonus can be discretionary in nature, in which instance it may be awarded on the initiative of the employer additionally to, and also independently of, an employee's pre-specified forms of contractual remuneration. In many market sectors including banking and financial services, annual employee bonuses are a fairly common practice at most levels within the organisation. However, in the case of employees fulfilling senior executive functions within public companies (and, in particular, CEOs), the award of an annual pecuniary bonus in recognition of exceptional (or, at least, satisfactory) corporate performance has become a culturally ingrained expectation today. Whilst it was traditionally common practice for executive

---

1   See UK Corporate Governance Code (September 2012), Provision D.1.3, available at: www.frc.org.uk/Our-Work/Codes-Standards/Corporate-governance.aspx.

bonuses to be paid in cash form, in the case of larger public traded companies it is now increasingly the case that bonuses are paid in the form of shares in the employer company, or as restricted share grants (on which, see 5.06 below).

D. Shares and restricted share grants

5.06 The rationale for remunerating senior executives in the form of shares in their employer company is manifestly self-evident: that is, to provide executive officeholders with a direct pecuniary incentive to seek to maximise shareholder wealth.[2] In this way, executive remuneration can (theoretically at least) be deployed so as to mitigate the so-called 'agency problem' in publicly traded companies, whereby individual shareholdings are too widely dispersed to provide effective incentives for direct proprietary oversight by shareholders of managerial decisions and conduct.[3] In recent years, concern about the apparent freedom enjoyed by many executives – particularly in banks – to liquidate personal shareholdings in their employer company in advance of share price falls, has prompted growing scepticism about the effectiveness of unrestricted shares as a form of remuneration.[4] Consequently (and largely in response to ensuing regulatory developments[5]), restricted share grants have become increasingly popular as a form of executive remuneration (especially for the payment of annual bonuses) within larger publicly traded companies and most notably in the case of banks.

5.07 In essence, such schemes prohibit the disposal of some or all shares granted thereunder for a contractually pre-determined period of time. The relevant time period could be a specific number of years, or else could be determined by reference to a specified event such as the retirement of the relevant officeholder or the company's satisfaction of a particular financial-performance target. Alternatively, restrictions on share disposal may be disapplied on a phased basis over the length of the recipient employee's tenure in office, with disapplication of restrictions rendered contingent on the satisfaction of periodic performance objectives. Insofar as restricted share grants are designed to align executives' personal monetary incentives with the long-term performance of their employer firm, they are commonly referred to in practice as a type of long-term incentive scheme (LTIS).

---

2   See M C Jensen and K J Murphy, 'Performance pay and top-management incentives' (1990) 98 *Journal of Political Economy* 225.
3   See MC Jensen and W Meckling, 'Managerial behavior, agency costs and ownership structure' (1976) 3 *Journal of Financial Economics* 305.
4   See, e.g. L A Bebchuk and J M Fried, 'Paying for long-term performance' (2010) 158 *University of Pennsylvania Law Review* 1915; L A Bebchuk, A Cohen and H Spamann, 'The wages of failure: Executive compensation at Bear Sterns and Lehmann 2000–2008' (2010) 27 *Yale Journal on Regulation* 257.
5   On this, see 5.51–5.53 below.

E. Executive share options

Executive share options (or, to use the more common US terminology, 'stock **5.08** options') have undoubtedly been the dominant form of executive performance pay within Anglo-American public companies in recent decades. Share options are designed to provide a more powerful pecuniary incentive on the part of executives to elicit improvements in shareholder wealth (as reflected in the market price of a company's shares) in comparison to standard share grants. Essentially, a share option is a realisable right to purchase a share in a company at a future date, and at a price that is customarily set at the time the option is granted (known as the exercise or 'strike'[6] price of the option). In its most straightforward (so-called 'vanilla') form, the exercise price will be the market price of the underlying share on the date of granting of the option (known in shorthand as 'at-the-money'[7]). This means that, to the extent that the market price of the underlying share on the eventual date of exercise of the option is greater than the market price on the earlier grant date, the option holder will be able to make a corresponding profit on exercising the option and then immediately selling the underlying share (known as 'unwinding'[8] of the option). Where a large number of options to acquire shares in the one company are unwound simultaneously, the resulting personal profit for the options holder can be considerable. In a more sophisticated variant on the standard vanilla option, the exercise price might alternatively be set at a price materially above the market price on the grant date (i.e. 'out-of-the-money'[9]), with the intended effect of eliciting increased levels of devotion by managers to improving share price performance.

The main motivational value of share options resides in the fact that – unlike **5.09** the case with standard share grants (which are essentially 'free' awards of shares) – the realisation of share options entails the options holder making a financial outlay in order to acquire the underlying shares. Hence share options provide a specific incentive to increase a company's share price over and above the relevant options' exercise price. Otherwise, the options holder stands to make no pecuniary gain whatsoever. This is in contrast to (standard or restricted) share grants, where *any* instances of share price appreciation after the grant date (even in the context of a broader pattern of price depreciation) is of some material benefit to the grant beneficiary. Like restricted share grants (described above), share options are a common form of LTIS. However, the extent to

---

6 This term is attributable to L A Bebchuk, J M Fried and D I Walker, 'Managerial power and rent extraction in the design of executive compensation' (2002) 69 *University of Chicago Law Review* 751.

7 Ibid.

8 Ibid.

9 Ibid.

which any option scheme is actually conducive to aligning its beneficiary's personal incentives with long-term firm performance depends on the specific design of the scheme itself. Where options can be readily exercised, and the shares obtained thereunder readily disposed of on an unrestricted basis, the intended long-term incentivising effect of the scheme in question will be undermined. Therefore remuneration committees and external consultants must consider carefully the ease (or, conversely, difficulty) with which options can be unwound by their recipients under alternative future market conditions.

F. Pension allowance

5.10 In addition to basic salary and further performance-related components, a senior executive compensation package will also customarily include a pension allowance. In the standard case, this will be calculated on a defined benefit basis as a contractually specified proportion of the officeholder's final salary.

G. Gratuities

5.11 A gratuity is essentially a discretionary payment made to an employee (most commonly a senior executive officeholder) independently of any pre-existing contractual undertaking on the part of the employer to do so. The most common and well-known forms of gratuity are inducement payments (so-called 'golden handshakes') and severance payments (so-called 'golden para-chutes'). A golden handshake is a (normally one-off) discretionary payment made to a new recruit in order to entice them initially to take up a vacancy. A severance payment or 'golden parachute' is a (likewise normally one-off) discretionary payment made to an outgoing employee as part of the agreed termination of their employment. In this context, a severance payment serves the dual function of: (i) from the *employer's* perspective, encouraging the outgoing employee to acquiesce in the termination of their employment on generally co-operative terms, so as to preclude any future dispute between the parties; and (ii) from the *employee's* perspective, mitigating the likely short-term financial blow from loss of office, thereby metaphorically facilitating a 'soft landing' from the initial 'fall' of job termination.

H. Expenses and perquisites

5.12 A further notable but relatively inconspicuous component of senior executive remuneration in public companies is the common general entitlement to indirect and/or non-pecuniary benefits of office. These include the right to charge reasonable expenses incurred in fulfilment of official executive functions to the employer, with the bounds of 'reasonableness' for this purpose often defined in somewhat liberal terms to include such particulars as business class air travel and fairly lavish corporate hospitality. Additionally, an executive's monetary remuneration may be supplemented by the direct receipt of various non-pecuniary benefits of office, such as the use of a company-owned car or free accommodation in a company-owned apartment. Whilst not impacting directly on measurable levels of pecuniary pay, such 'soft' entitlements nonetheless tend to be important components of a senior executive officeholder's overall remuneration package.

3. WHO DETERMINES DIRECTORS' REMUNERATION?

A. Fundamental principles

As the most senior decision-making body within the corporate hierarchy, the **5.13** board of directors has ultimate responsibility for determining enterprise-wide remuneration policy, and also for ensuring that such policy is implemented throughout the organisation. In large-scale public companies or groups, administrative exigency normally dictates that the vast majority of decisions concerning the practical application of enterprise remuneration policy to individual employees are delegated by the board to subordinate managerial or human resources personnel. In such instances, the board's input is typically restricted to 'arm's length' oversight only. However, where determination of the pay of senior executive officers is concerned, the board naturally has a more compelling incentive to play an active role in the process. From a governance point of view, though, the determination of senior executive pay gives rise to certain unique and significant positional conflicts of interest. Not least amongst these is the fact that many senior executives – most notably CEOs, FDs and COOs – are almost always members of the board of directors *themselves*. Moreover, such individuals – and, in particular, CEOs – frequently wield considerable personal influence over boards due to a combination of hierarchical, informational, personal and psychological factors.[10] For these reasons, absent countervailing legal and/or regulatory controls on their decisions, the objectivity and functional independence of boards with respect to executive compensation issues is a legitimate cause of concern.

Additionally, there remains the outstanding question of who determines the pay **5.14** of the board members themselves, particularly the nominally 'independent' NEDs who have no complementary managerial position in their employer

---

10   On this issue generally, see D Langevoort, 'The Human Nature of Corporate Boards: Law, Norms and the Unintended Consequences of Independence and Accountability' (2001) 89 *Georgetown Law Journal* 797.

company. To this, the answer is at once both simple and counterintuitive: it is that *the board itself* conventionally has ultimate formal responsibility for determining the pay of its members, by virtue of its more general constitutional authority over corporate managerial affairs (which ordinarily includes decisions on employee remuneration policy).[11] Furthermore, companies' articles of association customarily entrust boards with a broad ambit of discretion as to the specific forms and design of remuneration awarded to directors. Indeed, articles normally permit any form or level of pay deemed appropriate for the relevant individual's contribution to the company, whether in a 'pure' directorial or, alternatively, a dual executive-directorial capacity.[12] The only standard procedural constraint in the articles with respect to potential positional conflicts is that any director whose pay is in question should not be counted as participating and voting in the relevant board meeting.[13] With the (limited) exception of this provision, though, articles are typically silent on the matter.

B. The (limited) role of the courts

5.15 Likewise limited is the capacity of the English (and Scottish) courts to exert external judicial control over directorial and executive remuneration in public companies, whether from a substantive or procedural perspective.

5.16 The most obvious potential basis for substantive judicial control over remuneration is the director's duty of loyalty under section 172 of the Companies Act 2006. Section 172(1) requires generally that a director, in discharging his official functions, acts in a way that he considers, in good faith, would be most likely to promote the success of the company for the benefit of its shareholders as a whole. Any director found to be in contravention of this section, whether as a result of an individual or collective (board) decision that they were involved in, will be civilly liable to the company (and, indirectly its shareholders) for breach of duty. Notwithstanding, the prospect of section 172(1) being successfully invoked against a public company board that approves an allegedly excessive executive remuneration award is highly unlikely for a number of reasons. First, given the basic fiduciary nature of the director's equitable duty of loyalty (from which the section 172 duty is historically derived), the ambit of discretion afforded to directors under the section is very broad to say the least.[14] The innately subjective status of the duty means that, so long as a defendant

---

11   See The Companies (Model Articles) Regulations 2008 (SI 2008/3229), Sch 3 ('Model Articles for Public Companies'), art 3.
12   Ibid., art 23.
13   Ibid., art 16.
14   On this, see AR Keay, 'Good Faith and Directors Duty to Promote the Success of the Company' (2011) 32 *The Company Lawyer* 138.

director's purportedly honest commitment to promoting the company's success is irrefutable, it follows that the propriety of any specific strategic or operational decisions that they make is beyond judicial reproach.[15] The only conceivable situation outside the self-dealing context where a remuneration decision might put a board in breach of section 172 is where an approved award is so egregious under the circumstances that no intelligent and honest person could reasonably have deemed it conducive to advancing the company's interests.[16] Even then, determining a specific threshold of pay 'excess' for this purpose would likely be a virtually intractable judicial task, and it would certainly be a bold bench that sought to posit an authoritative view on this matter.[17]

An arguably more likely scenario where the duty of loyalty could potentially be **5.17** invoked in the remuneration context is where a company's board approves an arguably exorbitant executive remuneration package at a time when the company's solvency is threatened. In this regard, section 172(3) expressly retains the pre-2006 common law duty of directors to take account of creditors' interests in addition to those of shareholders, in situations where a company is either insolvent or facing an imminent risk to its continuing solvency.[18] This requires, in particular, that the board refrains from dissipating the company's cash flows

---

15 See *Re Smith and Fawcett* [1942] Ch 304 (CA), 306, per Lord Greene MR (emphasis added): '[Directors] must exercise their discretion bona fide *in what they consider – not what a court may consider –* is in the interests of the company, and not for any collateral purpose.' See also *Regentcrest plc v Cohen* [2001] BCC 494, 513, per Jonathan Parker J (emphasis added):

'The question is not whether, viewed objectively by the court, the particular act or omission which is challenged was in fact in the interests of the company; still less is the question whether the court, had it been in the position of the director at the relevant time, might have acted differently. Rather, the question is *whether the director honestly believed that his act or omission was in the interests of the company. The issue is as to the director's state of mind.*'

16 Pennycuick J's so-called 'intelligent and honest man' test arguably provides a basic objective component to the (otherwise subjective) director's duty of loyalty, with the outcome that a decision which is simply incapable of being deemed conducive to advancing the company's interests by any reasonable estimation will put a director in breach of his duty of loyalty irrespective of whether absence of good faith on his part has been established. See *Charterbridge Corp v Lloyds Bank* [1970] Ch 62, 74.

17 Interestingly, while English courts have been notoriously reluctant to confront this issue directly, the Delaware courts in the US have made tentative inroads into determining the propriety of arguably exorbitant executive remuneration awards under the auspices of the judicial doctrine of 'corporate waste', which denotes 'an exchange of assets [including the remuneration of employees] for consideration to disproportionately small as to lie beyond the range at which any reasonable person might be willing to trade'. See *Lewis v Vogelstein* 699 A 2d 327 (Del Ch 1997), 366, per Chancellor Allen. For a high-profile instance where this test was (ultimately unsuccessfully) applied in practice with respect to a remuneration award, see *Brehm v Eisner* 746 A 2d 244 (Del 2000). While there is no explicit 'waste' doctrine in English company law, the above 'intelligent and honest man' test (see ibid.) could be said to elicit broadly similar outcomes in determining the propriety of board remuneration approval decisions.

18 On this aspect of the director's duty of loyalty, see *West Mercia Safetywear v Dodd* [1988] 4 BCC 30 (CA); *Kinsela v Russell Kinsela Pty* (1986) 10 ACLR 395 (NSW CA); AR Keay, 'The duty of directors to take into account creditors' interests: Has it any role to play' (2002) *Journal of Business Law* 379.

on discretionary business expenses (including exorbitant executive remuneration arrangements) without at least giving prior consideration to the alternative option of preserving such funds in the company, in order to mitigate the potential losses to unsecured creditors in the event of its future liquidation.[19] Due to their concentrated and largely autonomous control over an insolvent company's affairs, coupled with the absence of restrictive rules of standing governing liquidator- (as opposed to shareholder-) initiated enforcement actions against directors, liquidators tend to be much better positioned than shareholders to act as a prospective claimant in actions for breach of directorial duty. For this reason, it is conceivable that the collective interests of a company's *creditors*,[20] rather than its shareholders, may in practice turn out to be the more common criterion by which the fiduciary propriety (or otherwise) of boards' remuneration approval decisions under section 172 is judicially determined in practice.

5.18 Besides the director's general duty of loyalty, an additional (albeit structurally limited) substantive judicial control over exorbitant remuneration awards was identified in the case of *Re Halt Garage (1964) Ltd.*[21] Here it was established that a company director, whose pay was significantly and manifestly out of keeping with her corresponding contribution to managing the company's business, could not genuinely claim to be receiving the money in question as remuneration for directorial services. Rather, on the given facts it was more appropriate, in the court's view, to regard the payments received as an effective disguised gift to the director in her alternative capacity as a company shareholder. Since the company in question did not have sufficient distributable profits at the relevant time to cover these payments, the court consequently found ground to strike down the awards in question as improper payments to a shareholder out of capital. Whilst the *Halt Garage* decision could be construed as a creative judicial attempt to impose an uppermost limit on remuneration awards (at least where the director or executive in question is simultaneously a company shareholder), its significance in this regard for public companies should not be overestimated. Not only was the *Halt Garage* case concerned with the very different context of a family-owned private company, but it involved the somewhat extreme scenario of a director who had effectively carried out no material functions for the company at all over a number of years (albeit on

---

19　However, in more serious cases of corporate financial instability, where there exists no reasonable prospect of the company avoiding going into insolvent liquidation, it is incumbent upon the board to cease the company's trading operations entirely, and thereafter to take all reasonable efforts to mitigate the potential losses to creditors. This is the essence of the wrongful trading rule under s 214 of the Insolvency Act 1986.

20　Or, at least, the *unsecured* segment of its creditors whose collective interests the liquidator is formally appointed to safeguard.

21　[1982] 3 All ER 1016.

account of ill health). Hence this case should be understood as having a very marginal impact on corporate remuneration practices at best, and as doing little to limit the customarily broad sphere of discretion vested in boards with respect to the design and approval of remuneration awards.

Alongside the above substantive judicial controls on directorial and executive **5.19** remuneration, there exists some (limited) further scope for *procedural* control by courts over the board's pay-setting practices. Strictly speaking, remuneration awards could be said to constitute the most common and obvious instance of a directorial conflict of interest, insofar as the relevant officer's personal interest in receipt of the award is directly averse to his fiduciary responsibility to ensure compensation of labour by the company on the most cost-effective available terms. However, unlike other forms of conflicted interest transaction, which should be formally declared by the relevant director to the board,[22] conflicts arising from the terms of directors' service contracts (including pay arrange-ments) are exempted from this requirement where (as is customary) they are already susceptible to consideration by the board or a formally appointed committee of directors (e.g. a remuneration committee).[23] This is subject to the important common law proviso that the board's constitutional powers to determine the remuneration of directors will – on account of the manifest conflicts of interest at play – be construed strictly and narrowly by the courts, so as to preclude directors from exercising discretion in this regard outside the bounds of their formal mandate from shareholders under the articles.[24]

C. Remuneration committees

Ordinarily, the board is freely entitled under the articles to delegate any of its **5.20** powers to specialised committees.[25] In public companies today, the delegation of key board functions to sub-board committees is generally perceived as a practical imperative. This is from the dual perspective of: (i) improving the functionality of directorial decision-making on certain crucial issues; and also (ii) mitigating (albeit not entirely removing) conflicts of interest that would otherwise undermine the formal legitimacy of board decisions on such matters. Alongside director nominations, financial audit and – increasingly – enterprise risk oversight, executive remuneration is almost universally regarded today as

---

22 This general procedural requirement is imposed by sections 177 and 182 of the Companies Act 2006. The former provision establishes the director's duty to declare an interest in a proposed or existing transaction, while the latter sets out the corresponding requirement for a director to declare an interest in a pre-existing transaction or arrangement.
23 See Companies Act 2006, ss 177(6)(c) and 182(6)(c).
24 On this, see *Guinness plc v Saunders* [1990] 2 AC 663 (HL).
25 See Model Articles for Public Companies, see above fn 11, art 5(1)(a).

being one such issue on which the input of a specialised sub-committee of directors is indispensable. There is no express statutory requirement for remuneration committees in the UK, whether generally or for any specific category of companies. Notwithstanding, the Code[26] – whose main principles are enforceable on a relatively informal, 'comply or explain' basis[27] – recommends that FTSE 350 companies with a Premium listing[28] should establish a specialised remuneration committee comprised of at least three independent NEDs.[29] Under the terms of the Code, independent remuneration committees are forwarded as the principal structural means for achieving the important policy objective to the effect that '[n]o director should be involved in deciding his or her own remuneration'.[30] Accordingly, by requiring the absence of any executive presence on the body that is formally entrusted with responsibility for determining senior executive remuneration arrangements, the Code seeks to ensure that this problematic scenario is avoided. To this end, the Code further recommends that remuneration committees be vested with delegated responsibility for setting remuneration for all executive directors and the chairman, including pension rights and any compensation payments for loss of office.[31] The committee is also expected to recommend and monitor the level and structure of remuneration for at least the first layer of senior management below board level,[32] which – in the case of banks – will conventionally comprise functional divisional heads such as the head of investment banking or head of retail banking operations. In addition, the committee should take responsibility for the appointment of any independent remuneration consultants to provide external advice on executive pay arrangements, so as to mitigate the obvious conflict of interest that would otherwise arise where executives have a direct influence over such appointments.[33] To ensure as best as possible that the deliberative dynamic of the remuneration committee does not replicate that of the full board, it is recommended that the chairman of a company's board does not simultaneously act as chair of the remuneration committee (although he may still be a member of the committee).[34]

---

26 See above fn 1.

27 On this, see ibid., 4–5; MT Moore, '"Whispering Sweet Nothings": The Limitations of Informal Conformance in UK Corporate Governance' (2009) 9 *Journal of Corporate Law Studies* 95, 104–07.

28 On this notion, see FCA Handbook, Listing Rule 7 ('Listing Principles and Premium listing'), available at: http://fshandbook.info/FS/html/FCA/LR.

29 In the case of Premium listed companies below FTSE 350 level, the corresponding recommendation is for the establishment of committees consisting of at least *two* independent NEDs. See above fn 1, Provision D.2.1.

30 Ibid., Main Principle D.2.

31 Ibid., Provision D.2.2.

32 Ibid.

33 Ibid., Supporting Principle D.2.

34 Ibid., Provision D.2.1.

While there are no specific requirements with respect to the skills or expertise **5.21**
that should be possessed by remuneration committee members in non-banking
companies, the expectations of bank remuneration committee members in this
regard are notably more onerous. Under the Remuneration Code, remuneration
committees in the banking sector must be sufficiently equipped to exercise
competent and independent judgement on a firm's remuneration policies and
practices, with particular regard to the incentives created for managing risk,
capital and liquidity.[35] Bank remuneration committees must be particularly
alert to any decisions on remuneration that have implications for the firm's
overall risk exposure and/or risk management, which should ultimately be
referred for approval by the group board as a whole as part of its general
strategic remit (although, in such instances, the committee retains responsibility for initially preparing the decision in question for referral to the full board).[36]
A further unique demand that is placed on remuneration committees in banks
today is their regulatory responsibility to take directly into account in their
decision-making not only the long-term interests of shareholders (as is the case
with committees in non-banking companies), but also the interests of the bank's
other stakeholders (most notably its depositors) together with the public
interest as a whole.[37] This places a broad and onerous responsibility on bank
remuneration committees today, with the implication that serving on such a
committee in the post-crisis era is by no means a job for the uninformed or
light-hearted.

In the case of banks and other financial industry entities (so-called 'BOFIs'), Sir **5.22**
David Walker's government-commissioned 2009 Review of Corporate Gov-
ernance[38] – likewise enforceable on a 'comply or explain' basis[39] – recommends
that remuneration committees should furthermore assume responsibility for
determining the overall structure and framework of remuneration policy across
the entity as a whole, with particular regard to the risk factors affecting
prospective performance outcomes in different parts of the business.[40] In
performing this broad and important function, the committee should have
particular regard to the remuneration conditions of any 'high end' employees in
the company, meaning those individuals performing a significant influence

---

35 See Financial Conduct Authority / Prudential Regulation Authority Handbook, Senior Management
    Arrangements, Systems and Controls (SYSC), SYSC 19A.3.12(2), available at: http://fshandbook.info/FS/
    html/FCA/SYSC/19A; http://fshandbook.info/FS/html/PRA/SYSC/19A.
36 Ibid., 19A.3.12(4).
37 Ibid., 19A.3.12(5).
38 See Sir D Walker, 'A Review of Corporate Governance in Banks and Other Financial Industry Entities: Final
    Recommendations' (26 November 2009), available at: http://webarchive.nationalarchives.gov.uk/+/http:/
    www.hm-treasury.gov.uk/d/walker_review_261109.pdf.
39 See above fn 27.
40 See Walker above fn 38, para 7.7 and Recommendation 28 (p 108).

function in the entity or whose activities or decisions could have a material impact on the entity's risk profile.[41] This is in acknowledgement of the fact that, somewhat extraordinarily in the case of banks, many of the most influential employees from an enterprise risk perspective – such as senior traders – are commonly positioned below the board or senior managerial levels of the corporate hierarchy, meaning that they fall outside the scope of the remuneration committee's purview as it is conventionally understood and defined. However, for pragmatic reasons bank remuneration committees are not expected to determine the specific pay arrangements of individual employees below top executive level, which remains the responsibility of the responsible managerial personnel within the organisation.[42]

5.23 Due in no small part to the abovementioned regulatory developments, remuneration committees are now a virtually universal element of UK public company board structures, both in the banking sector and also more generally. While such committees have undoubtedly played a crucial role in increasing the objectivity and formal legitimacy of the executive pay-setting process in public companies, they are by no means the governance panacea insofar as directorial conflicts of interest are concerned. The basic fact remains that remuneration committee members, in spite of their formally independent status, are – like any director – ultimately employed and remunerated by the company itself, under the ultimate leadership of its board and senior management. Against this background, a remuneration committee that adopts an apparently overzealous stance to constraining perceived executive pay excess could risk alienating itself from other board members, thereby undermining the board's collective decision-making dynamic and – in turn – destabilising the committee members' position within the company. It is thus essential that the remuneration committee is supplemented by other legal and institutional mechanisms which are designed to ensure the effective alignment of executive remuneration levels with the corresponding levels of performance of the officers in question.

D. Determination of non-executive directors' (NEDs') remuneration

5.24 Since the remuneration committee is typically comprised entirely of independent NEDs, it would obviously be improper for the committee to determine the pay of the non-executive members of the board. Accordingly, responsibility for determining NEDs' remuneration is – under the UKCGC – vested in the board as a whole, or alternatively the shareholders where the articles make provision to

---

41 See ibid., paras 7.8–7.10 and Recommendation 29 (pp 109–10).
42 Ibid., para 7.

this effect.[43] Exceptionally, a company is permitted under the Code to appoint a specialised committee for this purpose,[44] although it is unlikely that a committee with any more than a minority of non-executive representatives would be deemed acceptable for this purpose from the point of view of a company's institutional investors. The Code further recommends that levels of remuneration for NEDs should reflect the time commitment and responsibilities of the role.[45] Crucially, though, remuneration for NEDs should not include share options or other performance-related elements.[46] This is in view of the risk (exemplified most notably in the 2001 collapse of Enron in the US) that NEDs with a vested personal interest in a company's share price performance might be discouraged from raising concerns about latent enterprise risk exposures, which might in turn have an adverse impact on share price if publicly exposed. The Code does, however, provide exceptional dispensation to grant share options to a NED where this is deemed necessary for recruitment, retention or incentivisation purposes. In such an instance, shareholder approval should be sought in advance of the options award, and any shares acquired by the exercise of the options should be held until at least one year after the relevant NED leaves the board.[47] It is additionally specified that the holding of share options could be deemed relevant to the determination of a NED's independence for the purposes of the Code,[48] thereby insinuating that investors and proxy advisory agencies should be particularly cognisant of this fact when evaluating a company's annual regulatory disclosures.

E. Directors' service contracts open for inspection by shareholders

It should finally be noted that – alongside the above rules governing the **5.25** determination of directorial and executive remuneration in public companies – there is the additional statutory requirement that a company keeps available for inspection a copy of every director's service contract (including those relating to subsidiaries of the company).[49] The contracts should normally be accessible at the company's registered office,[50] and each contract should remain accessible until at least one year after the relevant director leaves office.[51] Any shareholder of the company is entitled to inspect the directors' service contracts – including

---

43   See The Code, above fn 1, Provision D.2.3.
44   Ibid.
45   Ibid., Provision D.1.3.
46   Ibid.
47   Ibid.
48   Ibid.
49   See Companies Act 2006, s 228(1).
50   Ibid., 228(2)(a).
51   Ibid., s 228(3).

any remuneration provisions included therein – without charge.[52] Furthermore, any shareholder is entitled to be provided by the company with any or all of the directors' service contracts on request,[53] and failure by the company to make such provision within seven days will render any officers of the company responsible for the default liable to a fine.[54] There is no minimum share ownership threshold for the purpose of triggering either of these entitlements. Therefore it is technically possible for an individual to purchase a single share in a public company for the purpose of gaining access to contractual information pertaining to directors' remuneration arrangements. Since most meaningful data on directorial pay in public companies will be specified in the annual statutory directors' remuneration report[55] in any event, the practical value to shareholders of the above provisions today is somewhat limited. Notwithstanding, they still provide an extra layer of transparency for shareholders with respect to a company's high-level remuneration policy and practices, particularly where a shareholder – for whatever reason – requires immediate access to such information before publication by the company of that year's remuneration report.

4. THE DIRECTORS' REMUNERATION REPORT AND 'SAY ON PAY' VOTE

A. Background

5.26 The last two decades of the twentieth century witnessed a stratospheric rise in general levels of executive pay in UK public companies, fuelled in part by the spate of large-scale privatisations, and subsequent flotations, of former public utilities. A particular cause of concern in the recessionary years of the 1990s was a widespread public perception of so-called 'rewards for failure', denoting lucrative pay awards to senior executives that apparently were unreflective of corresponding corporate performance levels. The principal industry response to these concerns was the landmark Greenbury Report on directors' remuneration, which was published in 1995.[56] Initially, the Report took the form of a self-regulatory body of principles promulgated by an industry-representative study group. However, many of Greenbury's key recommendations were subsequently incorporated within the inaugural Combined Code on Corporate Governance (now the UK Corporate Governance Code), whereupon they fell

---

52 Ibid., s 229(1).
53 Ibid., s 229(2).
54 Ibid., s 229(3)–(4).
55 On this, see 5.29 below.
56 See 'Directors' Remuneration: Report of a Study Group chaired by Sir Richard Greenbury' (17 July 1995) ('the Greenbury Report'), available at: www.ecgi.org/codes/documents/greenbury.pdf.

under the regulatory purview of the UK's main corporate governance regulatory body, the Financial Reporting Council. One of the central themes that emanated from the original Greenbury Report – and also its more recent guises – is the significance of effective transparency in combatting perceived directorial pay excess. Hence Greenbury professed to 'attach the highest importance to full disclosure of Directors' remuneration as a means of ensuring accountability to shareholders and reassuring the public'.[57] To this end, Greenbury recommended that companies furnish their shareholders with 'all the information they may reasonably require to enable them to assess the company's general policy on executive remuneration and the entire remuneration packages of individual Directors'.[58] It was recommended that this information be included within a report of the remuneration committee, provided on behalf of the board, and to which shareholders would be invited to give their approval at any General Meeting where this was deemed by the board to be appropriate.[59]

The Greenbury Study Group strongly favoured providing companies with **5.27** considerable flexibility regarding how they implemented its recommendations on pay transparency, and correspondingly disfavoured a formal legislative approach to the matter.[60] However, this position became increasingly untenable as the new millennium approached, due to perceived poor standards of compliance with the original 'soft law' framework, coupled with a fresh spike in exposed pay levels triggered by the bull market of the late 1990s.[61] In view of these factors, the Department for Trade and Industry (now Department for Business Innovation and Skills) deemed it necessary to put Greenbury's main recommendations on pay transparency on a formal statutory footing, in the form of the Directors' Remuneration Report Regulations 2002 ('the Regulations').[62] The Regulations placed a mandatory obligation on quoted company boards to prepare a directors' remuneration report for each financial year, to be laid before shareholders alongside the company's standard annual accounts and reports.[63] In every Annual General Meeting, a company's shareholders were given the opportunity to pass an advisory (i.e. non-legally binding) approval resolution on the report (known in US terminology as a 'say on pay' vote). In

---

57   Ibid., para 5.2.
58   Ibid., para 5.3.
59   Ibid., para 5.4.
60   See ibid., para 1.13: 'The way forward as we see it lies not in statutory controls, which would be at best unnecessary and at worst harmful, but in action to strengthen accountability and encourage enhanced performance.'
61   C Villiers, 'Controlling executive pay: Institutional investors or distributive justice?' (2010) 10 *Journal of Corporate Law Studies* 309, 317.
62   (SI 2002/1986). See also Department of Trade and Industry, 'Directors' Remuneration: A Consultative Document' (July 1999).
63   The board's basic statutory obligation in this regard is set out today in s 420 of the Companies Act 2006.

essence, the report was required to contain a detailed explanation of the company's remuneration policy with respect to its directors, including notice periods, termination arrangements, the specific remuneration of each individual director over the most recent financial year, plus any performance conditions relating to each director's entitlement to share options. Additionally, the report was required to detail the membership and role of the company's remuneration committee.[64]

B. The new (post-2013) two-tier procedure for 'say on pay' voting

5.28 The original 'say on pay' model introduced by the 2002 Regulations operated for a decade thereafter, until its replacement in 2013 with a more complex 'two-tiered' framework of remuneration reporting and voting. This was influenced in large part by a perception that the original system had largely failed to curb the continually spiralling rate of public company executive pay, and also the long-standing malaise of 'rewards for failure' within many firms.[65] Indeed, it was widely felt by commentators that – if anything – the greater scope for cross-company pay comparisons facilitated by 'say on pay' disclosures over the past decade has actually prompted a further general 'ratcheting' up of UK plc executive pay levels in recent years.[66] Accordingly, in the Government's view, more stringent legislative action in this area was needed.[67]

5.29 Under the new post-2013 framework,[68] the directors' remuneration reporting (and corresponding voting) system now comprises two separate components. These are: (i) a legally binding shareholder vote (and corresponding report) on a company's reported general *policy* for annual directorial remuneration-setting vote, which must be administered by quoted companies at least once every three years ('the policy report');[69] coupled with (ii) an annual, non-binding advisory vote by shareholders on the company's ongoing *implementation* of its directorial remuneration policy, as reported on by the board at the end of each year ('the implementation report'). Moreover, a company's shareholders are, for the first

---

64 See the Regulations, ibid.
65 See Department for Business Innovation and Skills (BIS), 'Directors' pay: Consultation on revised remuneration reporting regulations' (June 2012), para 12, available at: https://www.gov.uk/government/consultations/directors-pay-revised-remuneration-reporting-regulations.
66 See A Dignam, 'Remuneration and riots: Rethinking corporate governance reform in the age of entitlement' (2013) 66 *Current Legal Problems* 401.
67 See BIS, above fn 65, 5 ('Foreword from the Secretary of State').
68 See, generally, The Large- and Medium-sized Companies and Groups (Accounts and Reports) Amendment Regulations 2013 (SI 2013/1981), substituting new Sch 8 to the previous Companies and Groups (Accounts and Reports) Regulations 2008 (SI 2008/410).
69 That is unless interim changes to an existing remuneration policy are proposed, in which case a vote on those changes should be held either at the company's next AGM, or at a specially convened General Meeting beforehand.

time, entrusted with the formal legal power to directly strike down directorial remuneration awards that are out of kilter with their expectations concerning the future trajectory of directorial pay growth within any company. In promulgating the new UK 'say on pay' system, the Department for Business Innovation and Skills envisaged that the reforms would encourage remuneration committees and external consultants to take a longer-term strategic approach when developing a company's remuneration policy, based on an extended three-year (as opposed to annual) time horizon.[70] At the time of writing, whether the reforms will have the desired effect in this regard remains to be seen.

Crucially, a company is prohibited under the new system from making a **5.30** remuneration payment to a director in breach of its own pre-established remuneration policy. Any contractual arrangement entered into with a director for the future receipt by him of such a payment will have no legal effect, unless the relevant payment is specifically authorised by shareholders via a resolution to this effect. Accordingly, since shareholders now have the final formal say on whether a company's proposed remuneration policy should be rendered legally effective in problematic cases, remuneration committees must correspondingly ensure that any major shareholder concerns in relation to pay are recognised and addressed proactively at the initial policy design stage.

Under the post-2013 framework, moreover, special attention is afforded to the **5.31** controversial issue of directorial severance payments or 'golden parachutes' (on which, see 5.11 above). A company's policy on severance payments must be clearly set out in its tri-annual remuneration policy report. Any such payments can now only validly be made within the ambit of the company's pre-existing policy in this regard, or – failing that – with the specific prior approval of shareholders thereto. Notably, the board's annual implementation report is required to show, inter alia, a single total remuneration figure for every director each year, comprising: salary, benefits, pension, bonus, plus earnings from any long-term incentive scheme. This figure should cover only remuneration actually received by a director during the previous year, and is calculable by reference to an official formula that has been developed by the Financial Reporting Council's Financial Reporting Lab based on consultation with investors and industry.[71] The implementation report must also provide a graphical correlation of CEO remuneration with recent company performance, highlighting the extent to which periodic variations in a CEO's pay are

---

70   See BIS, above fn 65, para 15.
71   See Financial Reporting Lab, 'Lab project report: a single figure for remuneration' (June 2012), available at:
     www.frc.org.uk/Our-Work/Publications/Financial-Reporting-Lab/A-single-figure-for-remuneration.aspx.

reflective of corresponding variations in the total shareholder return generated by his employer company.

C. Expected impact of the 2013 reforms

5.32 The partial upgrading of the directorial remuneration vote onto a legally binding footing is in itself likely to have only a marginal effect on prevailing standards of board accountability. One should not underestimate the coercive impact of the existing 'advisory' vote from a board's perspective, especially when it is mobilised alongside complementary corporate governance tools currently available to shareholders, such as their collective rights of appointment and dismissal over directors. However, the reforms will almost certainly give rise to a materially higher degree of compliance and contracting costs, as companies seek to insure against the risk of individual directors' and officers' contracts being rendered invalid, and thus legally ineffective, on the ground of substantive non-compliance with a firm's currently-applicable remuneration policy.

5.33 A further and related cause of concern is the reduced flexibility afforded to remuneration committees, who must refrain from making any extraordinary awards to new or continuing officeholders outside the bounds of a company's remuneration policy, at least without first convening a General Meeting of shareholders (or, alternatively, awaiting the company's next AGM) in order to obtain the necessary approval. This could potentially make it more difficult for UK firms to attract high-quality leaders from overseas jurisdictions (especially the US) where such regulatory burdens are less onerous. In particular, the requirement to hold a General Meeting where a one-off amendment to a company's pay policy is deemed exigent risks undermining the competitiveness of UK plc in the often fast-moving environment of international executive recruitment markets.

5.34 An additional important question concerns the actual legal mechanics of how the new procedure will work, particularly in cases where a payment awarded to a director is deemed invalid on the ground of non-compliance with a company's remuneration policy. The intended civil consequences in such cases are specified under section 226E of the Companies Act 2006. Under this provision, any director in receipt of such a payment is deemed to hold the relevant payment on trust for the company. It is not automatically clear, though, who will have legal capacity to initiate an action for recovery of the invalid payment on the company's behalf. Where there is a subsequent change of control or business failure, this will presumably be the new board, or liquidator, respectively. However, where the existing board remains in control, it would appear that recovery action in respect of the improper remuneration payment will have to be instigated by a disgruntled minority shareholder via a derivative claim, on the ground that the payment in question amounts either to a 'default' or 'breach of trust' within the meaning of section 260(3) of the Companies Act 2006. Since the key information necessary to prompt such an action is likely to be contained in the company's annual implementation report, remuneration committees must be vigilant and ensure that there are no possible grounds for an awarded payment to be seen as in breach of the company's remuneration policy. At the very least, in instances where a material non-compliance risk exists it falls upon the committee (and, in turn, the board) to ensure that an appropriate approval resolution is sought from shareholders at the company's next General Meeting. Notably, where a company is subject to a takeover involving a wholesale transfer of control over its share capital, the outgoing shareholders (rather than the company itself) will collectively be entitled to any exit payment received by an outgoing director as part of the takeover arrangements. Presumably, the right to initiate a recovery action in this regard against the recipient ex-director will be vested in each individual former shareholder as an effective beneficiary of the payment held on trust by that person.

Finally, the intended effect of the above reforms in encouraging enhanced **5.35** periodic evaluation of the directorial pay-performance nexus could be said to sit somewhat uneasily alongside the UK Government's contemporaneous policy objective (as emphasised most recently in the Kay Review[72]) to combat short-termism in UK equity markets, in particular by removing structural impediments to long-term strategic planning by managers.[73] Frequent direct-orial pay evaluation necessarily entails the corresponding evaluation of ongoing managerial performance, especially where (as within a company's annual implementation report) CEO pay and total shareholder return are explicitly and graphically correlated with one another each year. This could potentially increase the incentives of some CEOs to engage in creative earnings manage-ment practices aimed at proactively 'correcting' expected pay-performance non-correlations, so as to legitimate year-on-year pay increases in the eyes of investors and their corporate governance advisors. As an aside, moreover, the special attention afforded to CEO pay within the proposed implementation report risks 'individualising' the monitoring focus of investors, thereby detract-ing from the innately *collective* nature of the board's responsibility for corporate management and performance.

---

72 See the 'Kay Review of UK Equity Markets and Long-Term Decision-Making' (July 2012), available at: www.bis.gov.uk/assets/biscore/business-law/docs/k/12–917-kay-review-of-equity-markets-final-report.pdf.
73 On this, see M Moore and E Walker-Arnott, 'A Fresh Look at Stock Market Short-Termism' (2014) 41 *Journal of Law and Society* 416.

5. ALIGNING PAY WITH PERFORMANCE AND RISK TOLERANCE: THE REGULATORY FRAMEWORK APPLICABLE TO BANKS

A. Introduction

5.36 With the exception of the very limited instances outlined above (see 5.15–5.19), UK company law has traditionally been silent regarding the appropriate structure and design of directorial and executive remuneration contracts, which were conventionally regarded as private concerns within the internal managerial remit of boards. Since the 1990s, though, the discretion conventionally enjoyed by boards over questions of executive pay policy and practice has been progressively curtailed by an expanding body of non-statutory principles. Moreover, in the aftermath of the 2007–08 financial crisis the regulatory treatment of banking and non-banking companies respectively in this regard has diverged along largely different paths. Accordingly, banks are now subject to a growing deluge of highly complex, industry-specific requirements from which their non-banking counterparts are exempt. The considerably greater scope of regulatory control over executive pay-setting in banks today is attributable principally to the impact of the Remuneration Code,[74] which first came into force in 2010 and applies to all UK banks, building societies and investment firms, plus certain overseas financial services firms as defined by the Code.[75] Notably, the Remuneration Code applies at group-wide level, and thus covers the remuneration policies of both the parent and subsidiary undertakings within a banking company group.[76] The substantive content of the Remuneration Code has been influenced by a variety of policy initiatives over recent years at both domestic and international level, including – in particular – the abovementioned Walker Review[77] and also the Financial Stability Board's Principles for Sound Compensation Practices,[78] which were both published in 2009. While the Code is non-statutory in nature, as part of the FCA and PRA Handbooks its provisions are potentially subject to administrative enforcement. Thus, unlike the corresponding provisions of the UK Corporate Governance Code, the Remuneration Code's requirements are formally binding on firms, in effect rendering the latter Code 'hard law' in nature. Where any provision of a remuneration agreement is deemed to contravene any requirement of the

---

74 See Remuneration Code, above fn 35.
75 Ibid., SYSC 19.A.1.1.
76 Ibid., SYSC 19.A.3.1–19.A.3.2.
77 See above fn 38.
78 See Financial Stability Forum, 'FSF Principles for Sound Compensation Practices' (2 April 2009), available at: www.financialstabilityboard.org/publications/r_0904b.pdf; Financial Stability Board, 'FSB Principles for Sound Compensation Practices: Implementation Standards' (25 September 2009), available at: www.financial stabilityboard.org/publications/r_090925c.pdf.

Remuneration Code, the relevant provision will be rendered void and, in turn, any payment (or transfer of non-pecuniary property) made under that provision will be recoverable by the employer firm (which, moreover *must* take reasonable steps with a view to recovering the payment in question from its recipient).[79]

Under recent reforms to the Financial Services and Markets Act 2000, both the **5.37** FCA and its counterpart financial regulatory authority, the PRA, are jointly vested with general rule-making powers with respect to the activities of authorised persons (including banking firms), which expressly include the power to prohibit certain forms of remuneration within regulated firms.[80] Consequently, the Code has recently been included within the new PRA Handbook, in addition to its existing status within the FCA Handbook. This is in reflection of the fact that both bodies now have statutorily delegated responsibility for regulating on remuneration matters concerning banks, insofar as any such issue falls within their respective regulatory remits[81] (for this reason, future textual references to 'the regulator' are intended to denote either of these bodies). Furthermore, both regulatory bodies are now empowered to provide in future rules that any provision of a remuneration agreement contravening such a prohibition is void, and also that any payment previously made thereunder should be recoverable from the recipient employee.[82] Enforcement action to this effect may be taken by the appropriate regulator either independently, or on the direction of the Treasury where this is deemed appropriate.[83] Therefore the likelihood is that the regulatory framework with respect to remuneration design in banks is likely to increase further in future years, particularly given the potential involvement of the PRA as an additional rulemaking body. However, no such rules made by either body can have retrospective effect and therefore will not undermine the validity of pre-existing remuneration agreements entered into prior to the relevant rules' implementation date.[84]

B. Fundamental principles

As regards the UK's listed company community in general (i.e. both banking **5.38** *and* non-banking companies), the Code stipulates that '[l]evels of remuneration should be sufficient to attract, retain and motivate directors of the quality

---

79 See Remuneration Code, above fn 35, SYSC 19A Annex 1.
80 See Financial Services and Markets Act ('FSMA') 2000, ss 137A and 137G, as substituted by Financial Services Act 2012, s 24(1).
81 Whereas the FCA is formally charged with regulatory responsibility for, inter alia, protecting and enhancing the integrity of the UK financial system, the PRA's corresponding remit is, inter alia, to promote the safety and soundness of banks, building societies, credit unions, insurers and investment firms.
82 FSMA 2000, s 137H(2).
83 Ibid., s 137I.
84 Ibid., s 137H(3).

required to run the company successfully'.[85] This is, however, subject to the important provisos that '[a] company should avoid paying more than is necessary for this purpose', and also that '[a] significant amount of directors' remuneration should be structured so as to link rewards to corporate and individual performance'.[86] Such performance-related aspects of executive pay should be 'stretching' and 'designed to promote the long-term success of the company'.[87]

5.39 In banking groups, moreover, boards must balance these general concerns with their sector-specific requirement under the Remuneration Code to establish, implement and maintain remuneration policies, procedures and practices that are consistent with and promote sound and effective risk management.[88] This is in recognition of the typically greater degree and scope of risk to which banking groups are exposed relative to their non-bank counterparts, including the unique systemic interdependencies between (formally independent) firms in the banking sector, and the consequent risk of a sector-wide 'contagion effect' in the event of any one firm's failure or financial instability. Thus, while maintaining the relative attractiveness of remuneration awards to prospective executive candidates, and also ensuring effective incentives for executive officeholders to maximise shareholder wealth, are by no means irrelevant considerations for banking groups; such considerations must not undermine the board's potentially countervailing responsibility to ensure that key decision-makers are not incentivised to pursue enhanced firm profitability at the expense of the entity's longer-term financial sustainability. Moreover, as regards those executives or other employees engaged in control functions within the firm (and, in particular, compliance and risk management roles) remuneration awards should be sufficiently high so as to attract qualified and experienced staff, but should not be linked in any way to the performance of the business areas that the relevant individuals control.[89] Rather, such employees should be remunerated exclusively in accordance with the achievement of objectives linked to their specific control functions, and independently of wider business performance factors,[90] predominantly via a fixed salary with relatively limited scope for bonuses or other variable rewards.[91] The practical rationale for this requirement (as outlined expressly in the Remuneration Code itself) is to mitigate the potential conflicts of interest that might arise in cases where the pay of control personnel

---

85   The Code, see above fn 1, Main Principle D.1.
86   Ibid.
87   Ibid., Supporting Principle D.1.
88   Remuneration Code, see above fn 35, SYSC 19A.2.1.
89   Ibid., SYSC 19A.3.14(3).
90   Ibid.
91   Ibid., SYSC 19A.3.17(3).

in banks is unduly influenced by other business areas,[92] which could risk undermining the relevant employees' willingness to expose or challenge managerial strategies or policies on legal, risk, or other non-performance-based grounds.

Prior to determining its remuneration policy, a banking group must decide on **5.40** the entity's accepted overall level of risk tolerance, and both the group (and, where relevant, subsidiary company) board(s) is responsible for ensuring that applicable remuneration policy is consistent with this threshold,[93] and also with the entity's pre-determined business strategies, objectives, values and long-term interests.[94] Furthermore, the group board (or, where separate therefrom, the firm's central management body) must periodically oversee the firm's general remuneration policy, and also monitor its implementation at least annually.[95] The implication is that high-level decisions on a banking group's remuneration policy and practices should not be delegated or compartmentalised within the firm's governance structure, but rather should be regarded as a core and inextricable element of the firm's overall entrepreneurial strategy and vision. Additionally, the bank's risk management and compliance functions should have an appropriate input into setting the remuneration policy for other business areas, particularly where risk management and/or compliance personnel have concerns about either the behaviour of certain individuals working within those areas, or the general riskiness of the business that is being undertaken therein.[96] In this way, concerns about key enterprise risk exposures can be factored directly into the a priori monetary incentives of employees engaged in potentially problematic business areas, enabling (in theory at least) a proactive approach to risk management in banking groups focused on curtailing excessively risky activities or behaviours at source.

C. Bonus payments

Bonus payments remain a pervasive element of the executive pay culture in **5.41** public companies today, in banking and non-banking companies alike. However, at least insofar as banks are concerned, the wide discretion formerly enjoyed by boards over matters of bonus policy has been bounded considerably by regulation over recent years, with the outcome that determining the form and level of bankers' bonuses today has become a highly complicated and specialised governance function in itself. The basic corporate governance

---

92 Ibid., SYSC 19A.3.17(1).
93 Ibid., SYSC 19A.3.7.
94 Ibid., SYSC 19A.3.8.
95 Ibid., SYSC 19A.3.10–19A.3.11.
96 SYSC 19A.3.15(1).

principles with respect to bonus payments are relatively general and straight-forward. The Code recommends simply that directors' eligibility for annual bonuses should be assessed by the remuneration committee, which should ensure that performance conditions attached to bonuses are relevant, stretching, and designed to enhance shareholder value.[97] The Code further stipulates that bonuses should be subject to defined and transparent upper limits, and also that there may be a case for part payment of bonuses in the form of shares; which, if granted, should be subject to a significant minimum holding period before the recipient employee is entitled to sell them.[98]

5.42 In banking companies, as explained above, the remit of remuneration commit-tees (and, in turn, their external pay consultants) in this regard is much more complicated. This is due to the fact that, in the immediate aftermath of the 2007–08 financial crisis, a number of serious problems were revealed in the ways in which banks had customarily awarded bonuses to their senior executive personnel. Amongst the most problematic exposed practices in this regard were: (i) a tendency of many investment banks to use revenues rather than profits to determine performance-based bonuses; (ii) generally insufficient use of risk-adjustment in the design of bonus policies; (iii) inadequate use of *non*-financial performance (and especially risk-based) measures in assessing employees' elig-ibility for bonuses; (iv) a general sectoral tendency *not* to defer annual bonuses over future years, but rather to render them immediately payable; and (v) a general sectoral tendency to keep the fixed component of executive remunera-tion *too low* to permit a fully flexible policy on bonuses. In response to these (respective) problems, the Remuneration Code now requires that banks adhere to the following key requirements concerning the award of bonuses to senior managers, risk takers, staff engaged in control functions, and any employees situated within the company or group's uppermost pay bracket (not included within the above categories) whose professional activities have a material impact on the firm's risk profile[99] (the above categories of bank employee will be referred to in the discussion below as 'relevant employees').

5.43 First, in assessing a firm or business area's financial performance for the purpose of determining employees' eligibility for and/or level of bonuses, remuneration committees and consultants should have regard principally to a bank's risk-adjusted profits, rather than its revenue streams.[100] This is on the basis that revenues or even non-risk-adjusted profits do not take adequate account of the quality (and, by implication, long-term sustainability) of the business practices

---

97   The Code, see above fn 1, Sch A.
98   Ibid.
99   Ibid., SYSC 19A.3.4.
100 Ibid., SYSC 19A.3.22–19A.3.23, 19A.3.25.

used to generate the ensuing short-term cash flows; and, in particular, any long-term enterprise risks that are not captured by accounting measures of performance alone.[101] In the same vein, the Remuneration Code requires that a bank's bonus policy does not limit the firm's ability to strengthen its capital base in response to a financial shock.[102] This requirement is especially pertinent for those banks that received governmental liquidity support (including outright nationalisation), given that an exorbitant bonus pool could potentially undermine the relevant firms' ability to make a timely exit from that support.[103] To this end, the Remuneration Code further stipulates that no member of the board (or, where separate, senior management body) of a bailed-out bank should be eligible for variable remuneration (including bonuses), unless this can be expressly justified under the given circumstances.[104]

Second, in determining a relevant employee's eligibility for and/or level of bonus, remuneration committees and consultants should ensure that, in addition to using standard financial performance measures, they also have extensive resort to *non*-financial performance measures including adherence to effective risk management and compliance with applicable regulatory requirements.[105] Moreover, in cases where financial and non-financial (especially risk-based) metrics could potentially elicit differing outcomes in determining an employee's bonus entitlement, the non-financial components of the bonus calculus should override the financial ones, so that risk-based factors ultimately take precedence.[106] In addition, the assessment of firm or business area performance for this purpose should be determined on a relatively long-term, multi-year basis, taking account in particular of the firm's business cycle and risks.[107] This is to ensure that the bonus entitlements of key bank decision-makers are determined with regard to the full and ultimate consequences of any business policies or practices for which they are responsible, as opposed to just the immediate or short-term revenue streams accruing therefrom.[108] **5.44**

Third, the Remuneration Code places fairly stringent constraints on the specific *form* that bankers' bonus awards may take, with a particular focus on mitigating the formerly common sectoral practice of paying 'straight' cash bonuses to senior employees without any longer-term provisos attached. Accordingly, banks today must ensure that a substantial portion (and, in any **5.45**

---

101   See ibid., SYSC 19A.3.26.
102   Ibid., SYSC 19A.3.18.
103   Ibid., SYSC 19A.3.20.
104   Ibid.
105   Ibid., SYSC 19A.3.37.
106   Ibid.
107   Ibid., SYSC 19A.3.38.
108   See ibid., SYSC 19A.3.39.

event, at least 50 per cent) of any variable remuneration (including bonus) payable to a relevant employee consists of an appropriate balance of: (i) shares in the employer firm; and (ii) appropriate debt instruments that adequately reflect the employer firm's current credit quality.[109] Furthermore, at least 40 per cent of the variable remuneration (including bonus) payable to a relevant employee must be deferred over a period of three to five years, so as to align senior decision-makers' personal financial incentives with the long-term success and sustainability of the business policies and practices that they are responsible for.[110] Where the amount of remuneration awarded in any case is particularly high (and, in particular, £500,000 or over), or the employer firm in question is particularly large or organisationally complex, the relevant percentage threshold for this purpose is 60 per cent.[111] However, the Remuneration Code expressly provides that the above requirements do not apply in the case of any relevant employee whose total annual remuneration is no more than £500,000, and where the variable component of which (including bonus) comprises no more than 33 per cent of the overall amount received.[112]

5.46 Finally, and in what may initially appear a somewhat counter-intuitive step (given recent public controversy about alleged banker pay excess), the Remuneration Code requires that banks ensure an appropriate balance between the fixed and variable components of a relevant employee's remuneration; and, in particular, that the fixed component of remuneration is sufficiently *high*.[113] The logic here is that, where an annual bonus or other form of variable remuneration constitutes the dominant part of an employee's typical pay package, non-receipt of that payment in any given year will be likely to have a considerably detrimental impact on their overall personal income. In such circumstances, the employer firm will likely face greater pressure to retain bonus entitlements even where not strictly justified by employee performance, leading the relevant employee(s) in turn to regard receipt of a bonus as an ordinary entitlement for fulfilling their basic functions, rather than as an extraordinary reward for truly exceptional individual or firm performance. Hence a relevant employee's fixed remuneration should be sufficiently high to permit a 'fully flexible' policy on bonuses.[114]

---

109   Ibid., SYSC 19A.3.47.
110   Ibid., SYSC 19A.3.49.
111   Ibid.
112   Ibid., SYSC 19A.3.34.
113   Ibid., SYSC 19A.3.44.
114   Ibid.

The regulator initially refrained from specifying any precise uppermost ratio **5.47** between the fixed and flexible components of a relevant employee's remuneration, stipulating only that the former element of pay should be 'sufficiently high' as adjudged by the employer firm.[115] However, on 1 January 2014 the Remuneration Code was amended to incorporate the requirements of the EU Capital Requirements Directive IV ('CRD IV'),[116] which in effect implemented the Basel III Accord within the European Union. Undoubtedly the most controversial provision of the Directive, at least from a UK perspective, has been its prescription of a mandatory 'bonus cap' applicable to EU-based (including UK) banks. The 'cap', which is now in force at domestic level under the Remuneration Code, prohibits the annual variable remuneration (including bonus) of a relevant employee from exceeding 100 per cent of that individual's annual fixed (e.g. salaried) remuneration.[117] The only permissible exceptions to this rule are: (i) that the relevant percentage threshold may be raised to 125 per cent where the additional 25 per cent of variable pay is deferred for a period of least five years from the date of payment;[118] and (ii) that the relevant percentage threshold may be raised to 200 per cent where this is approved by a supermajority of at least 66 per cent of the company's shareholders (where at least 50 per cent of shareholders attend the relevant General Meeting), or by a higher supermajority of at least 75 per cent (where less than 50 per cent of shareholders attend the relevant General Meeting).[119]

Although the above reform formally came into effect in the UK on 1 January **5.48** 2014, it will only apply to remuneration in respect of work undertaken from 2014 onwards. In effect, this means that bonuses awarded over the course of 2014 will not be covered by the cap, so long as they related to work carried out during the previous year. Hence, the full 'bite' of the reform will not be felt until 2015 at the earliest. Notwithstanding, the so-called 'bonus cap' represents a landmark development insofar as executive remuneration culture in UK banks is concerned, given the previous sectoral norm of paying bonuses that were frequently many times the level of an employee's base salary. Somewhat predictably, the reform has been subject to vociferous criticism from many quarters, not least on account of the fact that its intended downward impact on banker pay can be readily counteracted by raising the fixed remuneration levels

---

115   See ibid.
116   See Directive 2013/36/EU of the European Parliament and of the Council of 26 June 2013 on access to the activity of credit institutions and the prudential supervision of credit institutions and investment firms, amending Directive 2002/87/EC and repealing Directives 2006/48/EC and 2006/49/EC Text with EEA relevance.
117   Remuneration Code, see above fn 35, SYSC 19A.3.44(3).
118   Ibid., SYSC 19A.3.44D.
119   Ibid., SYSC 19A.3.44A–19A.3.44B.

of relevant employees accordingly.[120] Insofar as this leads to reduced reliance by banks on performance-sensitive pay, and – correspondingly – an increased risk of underperforming employees receiving 'rewards for failure', its overall impact on corporate governance quality within the sector will undoubtedly be negative. In September 2013, the UK Treasury lodged a legal challenge to the EU bonus cap in the European Court of Justice, based on a number of alleged administrative defects with respect to the provision's introduction and subsequent application.[121] Therefore, at the time of writing, the future status of this controversial provision remains uncertain. Notwithstanding, boards and remuneration committees would be well advised to proceed on the assumption that the bonus cap will be a prominent part of the UK's corporate governance landscape for at least the foreseeable future.

D. Long-term incentive schemes (executive share options and restricted share grants)

5.49 So-called long-term incentive schemes (or 'LSISs') – including share options[122] and restricted share grants[123] – are regarded as highly popular forms of variable executive remuneration in public companies today. Therefore in the case of banks, they are likewise subject to the above regulatory restrictions applicable to annual bonus payments. Indeed, as observed above (see 5.06), restricted share grants are in themselves a very common form of bonus payment today in banking and non-banking companies alike, particularly in the former sector given the aforementioned regulatory requirement for banks to defer at least 40 per cent (or, in appropriate cases, 60 per cent) of a relevant employee's variable remuneration for three to five years.[124] It is notable that bonuses paid by way of restricted share (or option) grant, like cash bonuses, will also be subject to the EU bonus cap, therefore the total value of any shares (or options) granted under such a scheme must similarly not exceed the recipient employee's annual fixed remuneration for the relevant year, unless appropriate shareholder approval is obtained therefor.[125] However, where the specified period of restriction under such a scheme is five years or more, the shares (or options) granted thereunder may together contribute an additional 25 per cent of variable remuneration over and above the recipient employee's normal capped level.[126] In light of the above

---

120 J Treanor, 'Barclays aims to dodge EU bank bonus cap with new top-up payments to staff', *The Guardian*, 23 October 2013.

121 A Barker, S Schafer and G Parker, 'George Osborne takes EU to court over bank bonus cap', *Financial Times*, 25 September 2013.

122 On share options generally, see 5.08–5.09 above.

123 On restricted share grants generally, see 5.06–5.07 above.

124 On this, see 5.45 above.

125 On this, see 5.47 above.

126 On this proviso, see ibid.

factors, it is clear that restricted share (or option) grants are – from a regulatory perspective – regarded as the preferred form of variable remuneration for senior bankers today. Consequently, the pervasive pre-crisis remuneration culture in banks of unrestricted cash bonuses is becoming increasingly regarded today as an outmoded norm. Notwithstanding, the general employee expectation of incremental annual awards (albeit in increasingly complex LTIS form) would appear to remain as culturally entrenched in the sector as ever, especially within the uppermost echelons of management.[127]

In addition to the above bank-specific regulatory provisions pertaining to share **5.50** options and restricted share grants, boards' and committees' discretion in designing the specific terms of such schemes is further constrained by applicable *general* (i.e. non-bank-specific) corporate governance rules on the matter. Accordingly, all UK-listed companies are required as a mandatory listing condition to ensure that any LTIS (including any share option or restricted share grant scheme) is approved by an ordinary resolution of shareholders in the General Meeting before it is adopted.[128] Such a scheme may exceptionally be offered to an incoming or incumbent director without prior shareholder approval where this is deemed necessary to facilitate, under unusual circumstances, the recruitment or retention of that individual. However, where this occurs, the company must later provide its shareholders with a formal explanation as to why the circumstances in which the arrangement was established were unusual.[129] The most obvious example of 'unusual' circumstances meriting dispensation with the need for prior shareholder approval of a LTIS would be the sudden resignation of a company's CEO, necessitating immediate action on the part of the company to recruit a suitable successor on sufficiently attractive terms. In addition, UK Listing Rules prohibit companies from issuing share options 'at a discount': that is, where the relevant options' specified exercise price is *below* the market value of the underlying shares at the time the options are issued, thereby entitling their recipient to an immediate 'windfall' irrespective of performance factors.[130]

There are some further important recommendations with respect to LTISs **5.51** contained in the Code, albeit that these are applicable on a non-binding, 'comply or explain' basis. Most notably, boards and remuneration committees

---

127 In this regard the current RBS chairman, Sir Philip Hampton, recently remarked that, in the banking sector, 'the expectation of a bonus has become embedded in the past 10 to 15 years', creating an 'expectation that the bonus will be high, come what may'. See High Pay Centre, 'Pay for performance – does it work?' (12 November 2013), available at: http://highpaycentre.org/blog/pay-for-performance-does-it-work.
128 See Financial Conduct Authority Handbook, Listing Rule 9.4.1.
129 Ibid., Listing Rule 9.4.2(2).
130 Ibid., Listing Rule 9.4.4.

should ensure that traditional ('vanilla') share option schemes are weighed against other more exacting kinds of LTIS,[131] such as 'out-of-the-money' options and performance-conditional restricted share (or option) grants.[132] Also, in normal circumstances, shares granted or other forms of deferred remuneration should not vest, and options should not be exercisable, in less than three years.[133] In the case of banks, this latter Code recommendation reinforces the abovementioned Remuneration Code rule with respect to mandatory deferral of a significant component of relevant employees' variable remuneration.[134] Further key Code recommendations in this regard are that pay-outs or grants under all incentive schemes are subject to challenging performance criteria reflecting the company's objectives, and should preferably be made on a phased basis rather than awarded in one large block.[135] Meanwhile, consideration should be given to so-called 'clawback' provisions that permit the company to reclaim variable components in exceptional circumstances of accounting misstatement or employee misconduct (on which, see 5.56 below).[136]

E. Severance payments ('golden parachutes') and pension allowances

5.52   Severance payments (or 'golden parachutes') present one of the most galling corporate governance dilemmas on a practical level. In view of the typically short tenure of senior executive positions within larger public companies today,[137] it is frequently necessary to offer new appointees to such positions the security of a fixed term contract or notice period. This will, in effect, entitle the relevant officeholder to contractual compensation in the event of unilateral termination of their service contract (i.e. 'firing') prior to expiration of their agreed term or notice.[138] At the same time, though, contractually determined severance payments risk acting as a protectionist measures for underperforming executives, on the basis that the anticipated expense of compensating an officeholder for loss of position might render their dismissal cost-ineffective. It follows in such circumstances that retention of the relevant officeholder until

---

131   The Code, see above fn 1, Sch A.

132   On these generally, see above 5.08–5.09.

133   The Code, see above fn 1, Sch A.

134   On this, see 5.47 above.

135   The Code, see above fn 1, Sch A.

136   Ibid.

137   In 2012, average CEO tenure in FTSE 100 companies was recorded at 5.91 years, and 6.35 years across the broader FTSE 350. These figures are attributable to research carried out by Thorburn McAllister in conjunction with the University of Southampton. See: www.southampton.ac.uk/mediacentre/news/2012/mar/12_43.shtml.

138   It is notable in this regard that, whilst a company's shareholders are statutorily empowered to dismiss any or all of its directors without cause, this expressly does *not* deprive the outgoing director(s) of any compensation payable to them in respect of the dismissal. See Companies Act 2006, s 168(5).

the expiry of their term may potentially represent the most cost-effective (or, rather, least cost-ineffective) option from the employer firm's perspective. An equally troubling issue is that of discretionary (i.e. non-contractually-agreed) severance payments that are offered with a view to eliciting an outgoing officer's acquiescence in their own effective dismissal.[139] Whilst the practical benefits of such arrangements for the employer firm are understandable, it may be legitimately queried what long-term corporate benefit is achieved by such payments, given that the recipient of the payment is intended to have no future involvement with the firm in question. Hence the performance-based rationale for discretionary pay is entirely absent in these circumstances.

The above problems posed by severance or 'golden parachute' payments, while **5.53** perhaps most publicly conspicuous in the banking sector over recent years, are by no means specific to this category of companies. Rather, they are very much a common governance challenge for public companies in general. In response, the legal and regulatory protections available to companies and their shareholders in this regard have been both expanded and tightened considerably over recent years. Accordingly, under sections 188–189 of the Companies Act 2006, no directors' service contract may be made to run for a period of more than two years without prior shareholder approval in General Meeting. Otherwise the terms of the relevant agreement will be rendered void, while the agreement as a whole will be deemed terminable by the company at any time on the giving of reasonable notice. This basic statutory rule is overlaid by supplementary provisions of the Code, which recommend in particular that notice or contract periods for directors should be set at the more stringent threshold of one year or less.[140] In exceptional circumstances where a longer term or notice period is necessary in order to attract a new outside recruit to the board, the applicable period should reduce to one year or less after expiry of that individual's initially agreed term or notice.[141] Meanwhile, under the Companies Act any discretionary termination payments that are intended to be made to outgoing directors must be submitted for prior approval by a company's shareholders in the General Meeting.[142] Otherwise, the recipient will be regarded as holding the payment on trust for the company, thereby entitling the company (or, potentially, any of its shareholders via a derivative claim) to seek recovery of the relevant sum therefrom.[143] In addition, any directors who authorised the unapproved payment will be held jointly and severally liable to indemnify

---

139   On this generally, see above 5.11.
140   The Code, see above fn 1, Provision D.1.5.
141   Ibid.
142   Companies Act 2006, ss 215–217.
143   Ibid., s 222(1)(a).

the company for any outstanding loss resulting from the payment, regardless of whether they personally benefitted from it.[144]

5.54 A particular cause of concern in the wake of the well-publicised RBS/Sir Fred Goodwin controversy is the arrangements for provision of pension allowances to outgoing directors or executives, especially following early termination of the outgoing officer's tenure. To this end, the Code today recommends that, as a general norm, only a director's basic salary should be pensionable.[145] The implication is that discretionary pension provision of the type observed in the RBS/Goodwin case should be avoided, at least in the absence of extraordinary circumstances. It is further recommended that remuneration committees consider the pension consequences and associated costs to the company of basic salary increases and any other changes in directors' pensionable remuneration.[146] This is particularly so in the case of directors close to retirement,[147] for whom late-career pay increases can have long-term implications for the relevant officers' entitlements under final salary, defined benefit pension schemes.

5.55 Finally, in the specific case of banking companies, the Remuneration Code further requires employer firms to ensure generally that any payments to relevant employees relating to the early termination of their employment contract reflect performance achieved over time, and are designed in a way that does not reward failure or misconduct.[148] Moreover, banks are required under the Remuneration Code to review their existing contractual payments related to early termination of employment, with a view to ensuring that these are payable only where there is a clear basis for concluding that the relevant outgoing employees have acted in a manner consistent with, and conducive to promoting, sound and effective risk management.[149]

F. Clawback and unilateral pay-reduction provisions

5.56 A final crucial component of the Remuneration Code is its requirement that banking companies put in place so-called 'clawback' provisions, which in effect empower them to demand that a relevant employee repays a specified proportion of variable remuneration previously received from the firm in the event of: (i) the employer firm incurring significant losses for which that employee was responsible for, or participated in; and/or (ii) that employee failing to meet

---

144 Ibid., s 222(1)(b).
145 The Code, see above fn 1, Sch A.
146 Ibid
147 Ibid.
148 Remuneration Code, see above fn 35, SYSC 19A.3.45.
149 Ibid., SYSC 19A.3.46; SYSC 19A.2.1.

appropriate standards of fitness and propriety for their position in the firm.[150] In addition, banks are required to make provision for the future unilateral reduction of any unvested variable remuneration due to a relevant employee where, as a minimum: (i) there is reasonable evidence of employee misbehaviour or material error; (ii) the firm or the relevant business unit suffers a material downturn in its financial performance; or (iii) the firm or the relevant business unit suffers a material failure of risk management.[151] Notably, any such contractual pay-reduction provision should be designed so as to apply not just to prospective cash bonus awards, but also to any non-pecuniary forms of variable remuneration that are payable to a relevant employee in future, including deferred share or option grants.[152]

SELECTED BIBLIOGRAPHY

Barker, A, S Schafer and G Parker, 'George Osborne takes EU to court over bank bonus cap', *Financial Times*, 25 September 2013.

Bebchuk, L A, A Cohen and H Spamann, 'The wages of failure: Executive compensation at Bear Sterns and Lehmann 2000–2008' (2010) 27 *Yale Journal on Regulation* 257.

Bebchuk, L A and J M Fried, 'Paying for long-term performance' (2010) 158 *University of Pennsylvania Law Review* 1915.

Bebchuk, L A, J M Fried and D I Walker, 'Managerial power and rent extraction in the design of executive compensation' (2002) 69 *University of Chicago Law Review* 751.

Cheffins, B R and R S Thomas, 'Should shareholders have a greater say over executive pay: Learning from the US experience' (2001) 1 *Journal of Corporate Law Studies* 277.

Department for Business Innovation and Skills, 'Directors' pay: Consultation on revised remuneration reporting regulations' (June 2012).

Department of Trade and Industry, 'Directors' remuneration: A consultative document' (July 1999).

Dignam, A, 'Remuneration and riots: Rethinking corporate governance reform in the age of entitlement' (2013) 66 *Current Legal Problems* 401.

Financial Conduct Authority Handbook, available at: http://fshandbook.info/FS/html/FCA/LR.

Financial Reporting Lab, 'Lab project report: a single figure for remuneration' (June 2012), available at: www.frc.org.uk/Our-Work/Publications/Financial-Reporting-Lab/A-single-figure-for-remuneration.aspx.

Gordon, J N, 'Say on pay: Cautionary notes on the UK experience and the case for shareholder opt-in' (2009) 46 *Harvard Journal on Legislation* 323.

Greenbury Study Group, 'Directors' Remuneration: Report of a Study Group chaired by Sir Richard Greenbury' (17 July 1995), available at: www.ecgi.org/codes/documents/greenbury.pdf.

Jensen, M C and K J Murphy, 'Performance pay and top-management incentives' (1990) 98 *Journal of Political Economy* 225.

---

150   Ibid., SYSC 19A.3.51A.
151   Ibid., SYSC 19A.3.52(1).
152   Ibid., SYSC 19A.3.52(2).

Jensen, M C and W Meckling, 'Managerial behavior, agency costs and ownership structure' (1976) 3 *Journal of Financial Economics* 305.

Kay Review of UK Equity Markets and Long-Term Decision-Making' (July 2012), available at: www.bis.gov.uk/assets/biscore/business-law/docs/k/12–917-kay-review-of-equity-markets-final-report.pdf.

Keay, A R, 'The duty of directors to take into account creditors' interests: Has it any role to play?' (2002) *Journal of Business Law* 379.

Keay, A R, 'Good faith and directors duty to promote the success of the company' (2011) 32 *The Company Lawyer* 138.

Langevoort, D, 'The human nature of corporate boards: Law, norms and the unintended consequences of independence and accountability' (2001) 89 *Georgetown Law Journal* 797.

Moore, M T, '"Whispering sweet nothings": The limitations of informal conformance in UK corporate governance' (2009) 9 *Journal of Corporate Law Studies* 95.

Moore, M T and E Walker-Arnott, 'A fresh look at stock market short-termism' (2014) 41 *Journal of Law and Society* 416.

Treanor, J, 'Barclays aims to dodge EU bank bonus cap with new top-up payments to staff', *The Guardian*, 23 October 2013.

Villiers, C, 'Controlling executive pay: institutional investors or distributive justice?' (2010) 10 *Journal of Corporate Law Studies* 309.

Walker, Sir D, 'A review of corporate governance in banks and other financial industry Entities: Final Recommendations' (26 November 2009) (Walker Report), Ch 7, available at: http://webarchive.nationalarchives.gov.uk/+/http:/www.hm-treasury.gov.uk/d/walker_review_261109.pdf.

6

CORPORATE GOVERNANCE AND RISK MANAGEMENT IN BANKS AND FINANCIAL INSTITUTIONS

Iris H-Y Chiu

1. INTRODUCTION

The global financial crisis in 2008–9 led to serious scrutiny of banking and **6.01** financial institutions in respect of risk mismanagement. The crisis has highlighted poor risk management at banks to be a key factor in the failure of a number of financial institutions,[1] and so regulators have stepped up regulation in this area as part of micro-prudential regulation. This chapter will discuss risk management in banks and financial institutions as a corporate governance issue but, it should be noted that this area is now largely governed by a post-crisis regulatory framework. The pre-crisis regulatory framework at banks and financial institutions was skeletal in nature and it is arguably natural that ramping up its regulation would be perceived as an apt response to the crisis.

---

1   M Brunnermeier, A Crockett, C Goodhart, A D Persaud and H Shin, 'The fundamental principles of Financial Regulation', Geneva Reports on the World Economy (2009); G Sabato, 'Financial crisis: Where did risk management fall?' (2009) available at: http://papers.ssrn.com/sol3/papers.cfm?abstract_id=1460762; A Mikes, 'Risk management at crunch time: Are Chief Risk Officers compliance champions or business partners?' (2008) available at: http://papers.ssrn.com/sol3/papers.cfm?abstract_id=1138615; H J Blommestein, L Hoogduin and J J W Peeters, 'Uncertainty and risk management after the great moderation: The role of risk (mis)management by financial institutions' (2009) available at: http://papers.ssrn.com/sol3/papers.cfm?abstract_id=1489826; M Crouhy, 'Risk management failures during the financial crisis' in R W Kolb (ed.), *Lessons from the Financial Crisis* (John Wiley 2010), 283; E Sheedy, 'The future of risk modelling' in R W Kolb (ed), *Lessons from the Financial Crisis* (John Wiley 2010), 301; F Partnoy, 'On rogues, risk-taking and restoring trust in banks', *The Financial Times* (23 Sep 2011).

6.02 International standards for managing banking risk have been developed in the Basel I Capital Accord[2] (which dealt with credit risk) since 1988, followed by a more comprehensive consideration of banking risks in the Basel II Capital Accord of 2006.[3] However, as the Basel II Capital Accord has recognised, the management of banking risk specific to the profiles of bank assets and trading books cannot be micro-managed by regulatory prescription and significant responsibility lies in banks having robust risk-management systems themselves, subject to supervision and capital markets accountability.[4] The internal control and risk-management organisation of banks and financial institutions were largely subject to organisational design, and in this light, pre-crisis European legislation on banks or credit institutions left it to the regulated firms to define what 'adequate internal control' may be proportionate to the 'nature, scale and complexity' of the firms' activities.[5] The Markets in Financial Instruments Directive (MiFID 2004),[6] which applied to investment firms, mandated the establishment of separate and permanent compliance and internal audit functions in investment firms,[7] but left firms the discretion to decide if a separate risk-management function[8] would be necessary and proportionate to the nature, scale and complexity of the firm's business. In the UK, the regulator applied the European requirements across the board to authorised financial institutions including banks that are not insurers, reinsurance underwriting agents or building societies.[9] Such a form of regulation can be regarded as 'meta-regulation', a regulatory technique that provides for broad framework principles and leaves firms to implement systems and procedures to meet regulatory objectives.[10] 'Meta-regulation' is often used when the regulated have

---

2   http://www.bis.org/publ/bcbs04A.pdf.

3   http://www.bis.org/publ/bcbs128.htm.

4   Pillars 2 and 3 of the Basel II Capital Accord.

5   European Parliament and Council Directive 2006/48/EC of 14 June 2006 relating to the taking up and pursuit of the business of credit institutions (recast) [2006] OJ L177/1 (Capital Requirements Directive 2006), art 22.

6   European Parliament and Council Directive 2004/39/EC of 21 April 2004 on markets in financial instruments amending Council Directives 85/611/EEC and 93/6/EEC and Directive 2000/12/EC of the European Parliament and of the Council and repealing Council Directive 93/22/EEC [2004] OJ L145/1 (Markets in Financial Instruments Directive, MiFID). Now recast as Directive 2014/65/EU of the European Parliament and of the Council of 15 May 2014 on markets in financial instruments and amending Directive 2002/92/EC and Directive 2011/61/EU (MiFID II Directive 2014).

7   Commission Directive 2006/73/EC of 10 August 2006 implementing Directive 2004/39/EC of the European Parliament and of the Council as regards organisational requirement and operating conditions for investment firms and defined terms for the purposes of that Directive [2006] OJ L241/26 (MiFID Commission Directive), arts 6 and 8.

8   MiFID Commission Directive 2006, art 7. Even if firms consider that a separate risk management function is not necessary, art 7 does require firms to put in place effective and adequate risk management policies and procedures.

9   PRA and FCA Handbooks, SYSC 1A.

10   C Coglianese and E Mendelson, 'Meta-regulation and self-regulation' in R Baldwin, M Cave, and M Lodge (eds), *The Oxford Handbook of Regulation* (OUP 2010) 146–168; J S F Wright, P G Dempster, J Keen, P Allen and A Hutchings, 'The new governance arrangements for NHS Foundation Trust Hospitals: Reframing

the incentives, resources and expertise to carry out such implementation as being necessary for the achievement of business objectives and corporate governance accountability. Meta-regulation seems warranted as it is arguably inappropriate to prescribe excessively amounting to a form of micro-management.

Fanto argues that the global financial crisis of 2008–9 highlights a risk management failure in banks and financial institutions. The failures of risk management are in two dimensions, one relating to the weaknesses and limitations of it as a professional discipline in its application to financial risk management in banks,[11] and the second relating to the weaknesses in the organisation and empowerment of the risk-management function in banks.[12] Both of these failures have contributed to excessive risk-taking at a significant number of international universal banks. Excessive risk-taking[13] has been argued by many commentators to be key to the culmination of the systemic crisis seen in 2008–9 when such excessive risks materialised.

6.03

Empirical evidence not only links the quality of risk management in a financial institution to the avoidance of loss/failure, but also to better financial performance, credit ratings and stock market valuations.[14] A number of empirical studies have shown that financial institutions with a higher quality of risk management (based on variables such as the presence of enterprise risk-management systems, the establishment of a risk committee with expertise and time commitment, the profile of a chief risk officer, etc) have not suffered as much in the global financial crisis.[15] On the flipside, financial institutions with

6.04

---

governors as meta-regulators' (2012) 90 *Public Administration* 351; C Parker, *The Open Corporation* (CUP 2002); 'Meta-regulation: Legal accountability for corporate social responsibility' (2006), available at: http://papers.ssrn.com/sol3/papers.cfm?abstract_id=942157; C Scott, 'Regulating everything: From mega- to meta-regulation' (2012) 60 *Administration* 61.

11   J A Fanto, 'Anticipating the unthinkable: The adequacy of risk management in finance and environmental studies' (2009) 44 *Wake Forest Law Review* 731.

12   J A Fanto, 'The role of financial regulation in private financial firms: Risk management and the limitations of the market model' (2009) 3 *Brook J Corp Fin & Com L* 29.

13   M Brunnermeier, et al, see above n 1; N Roubini, 'Ten Fundamental Issues in Reforming Financial Regulation and Supervision in a World of Financial Innovation and Globalization' (31 March 2008); S McGee, *Chasing Goldman Sachs: How the Masters of the Universe Melted Wall Street Down … And Why They'll Take Us to the Brink Again* (Crown Business 2010), 124, 126, 128; G Tett, *Fool's Gold: How Unrestrained Greed Corrupted a Dream, Shattered Global Markets and Unleashed a Catastrophe* (Abacus Books 2010); H Davies, *The Financial Crisis: Who is to Blame?* (Polity Press 2010).

14   See generally the Senior Supervisors' Report, 'Observations on risk management practices during the recent market turbulence' (6 March 2008), analysed in M McKee, 'Financial markets turmoil and the biggest banks: Lessons to be learned' (2008) 23(8) *Journal of International Banking Law and Regulation* 404.

15   A Ellul and V Yerramilli, 'Stronger risk controls, lower risk: evidence from us bank holding companies' (August 2012), available at: http://ssrn.com/abstract=1550361, accessed 13 March 2013.

poorer risk management become entangled in a downward spiral when high risks materialise.[16] Hence, effective risk management seems to be key to loss prevention or mitigation, especially in stressed conditions.[17]

6.05 The meta-regulatory nature of the framework for risk management has allowed firm implementation of risk management to suit firm needs. The inadequate resourcing and empowering of risk management has been highlighted in one bank[18] that failed in the global financial crisis and another that suffered a massive loss due to failure to control a rogue trader.[19] In some banks, risk management may be regarded more as a function that is intended to add business value[20] than as a gatekeeper for prudent or socially optimal levels of risk-taking. Policymakers in the post-crisis reforms seek to enhance the profile of risk management for prudential purposes[21] by introducing more regulation of aspects of corporate governance in banks and financial institutions related to risk management. Risk management in financial institutions is considered to be bound up with corporate governance because corporate governance is perceived to be the framework within which risk management effectively operates.

---

16 W R Wilson, L C Rose and J F Pinfold, 'Examination of NZ finance company failures: The Role of corporate governance' (January 2010), available at: http://papers.ssrn.com/sol3/papers.cfm?abstract_id=1536874 accessed 13 March 2013, examining the consequences of poor risk management in the financial institutions and banks that failed in New Zealand in the wake of the global financial crisis. See also K P V O'Sullivan and S Kinsella, 'Financial and regulatory failure: The case of Ireland' (2013) 14 *Journal of Banking Regulation* 1, examining how poor risk management perpetuated a downward spiral in Anglo-Irish Bank in Ireland.

17 P Li, 'How can corporate governance control enterprise's financial risk?' (December 2009), available at: http://papers.ssrn.com/sol3/papers.cfm?abstract_id=1523519 accessed 13 March 2013; S Lyons, 'In defense of the corporation' (2009) 66 *Internal Auditor* 1; J N Bezis, 'Conceptualizing the failure of financial institutions and the role of risk management in averting failure: The CLS Model' (January, 2013), available at: http:// papers.ssrn.com/sol3/papers.cfm?abstract_id=2196556 accessed 22 March 2014.

18 'Regulator Blasts HBOS for Failures' *The Telegraph* (London, 9 March 2012), referring to the Halifax Bank of Scotland; House of Commons and House of Lords, Parliamentary Commission on Banking Standards, *An Accident Waiting to Happen: The Failure of HBOS* (4 April 2013), para 53ff.

19 E Pichet, 'What governance lessons should be learnt from the Societe Générale's Kerviel affair' (2008) 3 *La revue Française de Gouvernance d'Entreprise* 117.

20 A Resti and A Sironi, *Risk Management and Shareholders' Value in Banking: From Risk Measurement Models to Capital Allocation Policies* (John Wiley & Sons 2007), xxiiff do not argue that solvency concerns are unimportant but a recognition of the balance and trade off between safety and value creation is needed and risk management is important for working out the optimal creation of value.

21 For example see the UK Prudential Regulation Authority's proposal to make effective risk management one of the fundamental rules of banking regulation in the PRA rulebook consultation, 2014, available at: http:// www.bankofengland.co.uk/pra/Documents/publications/policy/2014/rulebookcon214.pdf.

2. CORPORATE GOVERNANCE AS A FRAMEWORK FOR RISK MANAGEMENT

Poor risk management[22] and excessive risk-taking[23] in banks and financial **6.06** institutions have been diagnosed as being closely linked to the nature of corporate governance in those institutions. Failings in risk management identified by commentators relate to narrow-minded conceptions of risk management adopted by firms and the lack of emphasis and leadership in risk management, both of which are high-level issues of corporate governance. There is much commentator support, which will be elaborated upon below, for the perspective that the effectiveness of risk management is dependent on the corporate governance of banks and financial institutions.

In conventional corporate governance best practices, boards are required to **6.07** maintain proper oversight of audit and internal financial reporting. Hence, the general perception of board responsibility for risk management centres upon these areas. Moore[24] points out that UK corporate governance has developed based on the need for audit and accounting integrity in response to the failure at BCCI in 1990.[25] Subsequently, the Turnbull review[26] further emphasised the need to have reliable internal and external reporting systems as part of 'internal control' and 'risk management'. The language of 'internal control' used in the Cadbury and Turnbull reports deals with systems that process financial information and reporting and how to ensure that such systems underlie integrity in financial reporting. Although the Turnbull Guidance[27] views internal control as a form of risk management that 'enable[s] [companies] to respond appropriately to significant business, operational, financial, compliance and other risks to achieving the company's objectives', the more precise language surrounding risk management and internal control targets the prevention of accounting fraud and ensuring the integrity of financial reporting. The previous Codes

---

22 Poor risk management at firms has been argued to be an important contributing factor to firm failure and financial instability, see Brunnermeier et al, above n 1; G Kirkpatrick, 'The corporate governance lessons from the financial crisis' (2009) 96 *OECD Financial Market Trends* 1; M E Murphy, 'Assuring responsible risk management in banking: The corporate governance dimension' (2011) 36 *Delaware Journal of Corporate Law* 121.

23 D H Erkens, M Hung and P Matos, 'Corporate governance in the 2007–2008 financial crisis: Evidence from financial institutions worldwide' (2012) 18 *Journal of Corporate Finance* 389; S A Ramirez, 'Lessons From the subprime debacle: Stress testing CEO autonomy' (2009) 54 *Saint Louis University Law Journal* 1.

24 M T Moore, 'The evolving contours of the board's risk management function in UK corporate governance' (2010) 10 *Journal of Corporate Law Studies* 279.

25 Culminating in Sir Adrian Cadbury's review of corporate governance in general and the promulgation of the Cadbury Code of Corporate Governance 1992.

26 See Financial Reporting Council, 'Internal Control: Revised Guidance for Directors on the Combined Code' (October 2005), available at: http://www.frc.org.uk/Our-Work/Publications/Corporate-Governance/Turnbull-guidance-October-2005.aspx, accessed 13 March 2013 (Turnbull Guidance).

27 Turnbull Guidance, para 19.

(preceding the current UK Corporate Governance Code 2014) always considered 'internal control' to be key to safeguarding shareholders' interests and corporate assets and tasked the audit committee of the board with supervisory oversight. Such an approach indicates that the emphasis is placed on the integrity and accountability of financial reporting. In this sense, corporate governance reforms are very much led by the securities regulation ideology of supporting transparency to facilitate market discipline. Van der Elst[28] argues that the evolution of 'internal control' as a corporate governance issue in the EU has also been led by the need for reliable securities disclosure, as 'risk' is dealt with in disclosure-based regulation in the Prospectus Directive 2004 dealing with public offers and in the Transparency Directive 2005 providing for ongoing reporting. However, the disclosure of 'risk' is seen as a qualitative form of disclosure and is therefore not subject to further precision or standardisation. The emphasis placed on accounting and reporting integrity is also found in the US response to Enron's collapse in 2000, the Sarbanes-Oxley Act, although the Act also prescribes certain forms of internal control (such as controls over auditor appointment[29] and mandatory certifications by chief financial officers).[30]

6.08 The renewed emphasis on the importance of risk management in financial institutions following the global financial crisis is not merely a reiteration of the disclosure-based ideology in securities regulation aimed at ensuring reliable financial reporting and the prevention of securities fraud. Post-crisis, the importance of risk management has arguably moved away from being a facilitator of market discipline, to a more public interest-based concern for preserving the viability of firms that may affect financial stability. Risk management is therefore now looked at in a much more holistic manner encompassing all forms of business, financial, legal, social and other risks that may threaten the viability of the financial institution. Corporate governance is now seen as the framework in which leadership and emphasis can be provided to give risk management a new character and a key place in corporations.[31] This is supported by findings in empirical research[32] carried out to investigate correlations between management leadership, the quality and profile of risk management in financial institutions and the performance of the financial institution in the financial crisis.

---

28   C Van der Elst and M van Daelen, 'Risk management in European and American corporate law' (April 2009) ECGI Law Working Paper No 122/2009, available at: http://ssrn.com/abstract=1399647.
29   Sarbanes-Oxley Act 2002, ss 502, 503.
30   Ibid., s 302.
31   See Moore, above n 24. See also European Banking Authority, 'EBA's Guidelines on Internal Governance (GL 44)' (27 September 2011), para 20.
32   See Senior Supervisors' Report, above n 14.

In general, commentators (as will be discussed below) have identified the **6.09** following corporate governance characteristics that correlate with poorer risk management and adverse bank or financial institution performance:

(a) failure of board leadership due to lack of information and knowledge of risk profiles of departments;

(b) failure of board leadership in giving risk management a sufficiently high-level profile for board attention and strategic direction; and

(c) lack of board emphasis on risk management as being a concern distinct from compliance or audit.

Post-crisis, Sir David Walker was commissioned by the UK Government to **6.10** investigate the aspects of corporate governance in banks and financial institutions that contributed to the failure of several UK banks. Many recommendations of the Walker Review[33] have been implemented in financial regulation and generally influenced amendments to the UK Corporate Governance Code too. These will be discussed below.

3. POST-CRISIS REGULATORY REFORMS IN CORPORATE GOVERNANCE AND RISK MANAGEMENT

A number of commentators opine that the lack of board competence or **6.11** expertise has been correlated with failures and adverse performance at banks and financial institutions. Mehran, Morrison and Shapiro provide a literature review showing that empirical evidence points to a correlation between a lack of meaningful leadership in banks and financial institutions and poorer quality risk management.[34] Hau and Thum's empirical study finds correlations between the lack of financial expertise and experience on the part of supervisory boards in German financial institutions and larger losses suffered by those institutions in the global financial crisis.[35] Draghi's empirical study[36] also

---

33 D Walker, 'A review of corporate governance in uk banks and other financial industry entities: Final recommendations' (Walker Review) (26 November 2009), available at: http://webarchive.nationalarchives. gov.uk/+/http://www.hm-treasury.gov.uk/d/walker_review_261109.pdf.

34 H Mehran, A Morrison, and J Shapiro, 'Corporate governance and banks: What have we learned from the financial crisis?' (June 2011) *Federal Reserve Bank of New York Staff Report* No 502, available at: <http://ssrn.com/abstract=1880009>.

35 H Hau and M P Thum, 'Subprime crisis and board (in-)competence: Private vs. public banks in Germany' (2009) 24 *Economic Policy* 701. Note however that Mehran warns that directors with financial expertise and experience may also favour greater risk-taking and hence could exacerbate risk-taking tendencies in banks and financial institutions. See ibid., Mehran, Morrison, and Shapiro.

36 M Draghi, 'Observations on risk management practices during the recent market turbulence' in M R Turley (ed.), *Reforming Risk in Financial Markets* (NovaScience Publishers 2009) at 131.

showed that banks that have hired senior management teams with trading experience or management of financial market risks have generally fared better in the global financial crisis.

6.12 The UK Walker Review is now explicit on the requirement that the chairman and non-executive directors (NEDs) should have adequate knowledge and skills to enable effective leadership of the business, along with a greater time commitment.[37] EU legislation now requires all directors of banks and investment firms to possess sufficient knowledge, skills and experience for the business although the range of diverse skills and competencies should still be looked at collectively, especially in relation to understanding the risks of the business.[38] The UK has always imposed an approval regime for persons[39] who are appointed to senior management and to boards of financial institutions and is now scrutinising even more closely[40] proposed candidates' skills, expertise and qualifications. As ex ante approval regimes are limited in that they may only go so far in vetting financial expertise and qualifications, the UK Parliamentary Commission[41] has recommended the regulatory imposition of a Banking Code upon senior management and staff at banks to be adhered to on an ongoing basis. This has now been taken up in legislative reforms[42] to be implemented by the banking regulator[43] and supported by the first professional body for Banking Standards[44] that will focus on bottom-up setting of professional and ethical standards for bankers.

6.13 It has been suggested that the boards of failed banks, such as Bear Stearns and Lehman Brothers in the US and Northern Rock and HBOS in the UK, were not well-informed of risky profiles and operations and hence could not have provided leadership in considering the strategic impact of risk management.[45]

---

37   Walker Review, Recommendations 1–5, 7, 8.

38   CRD IV Directive, art 91(1), (7) and Recast MiFID, art 9(1).

39   Financial Services and Markets Act 2000, s 59; PRA and FCA Handbooks (as of 30 April 2013, formerly FSA Handbook) APER and FIT.

40   A Smith, A Gray and K Burgess, 'FSA scrutiny comes under the spotlight' *Financial Times* (London, 5 June 2012).

41   House of Lords and House of Commons, *Changing Banking for Good* (Report of the Parliamentary Commission on Banking Standards) (12 June 2013) at Vol II, para 612ff.

42   Sections 59ZA, 64A, 65A, inserted into the Financial Services and Markets Act 2000 by the Financial Services (Banking Reform) Act 2013.

43   Bank of England Response to the Final Report of the Parliamentary Commission on Banking Standards (2013), available at http://www.bankofengland.co.uk/publications/Documents/news/2013/pcbsresponse.pdf; The FCA's response to the Parliamentary Commission on Banking Standards (Oct 2013), available at: http://www.fca.org.uk/static/documents/pcbs-response.pdf. See PRA and FCA, *Strengthening Accountability in Banking: A New Regulatory Framework* (July 2014).

44   http://www.bankingstandardsreview.org.uk/background/.

45   Kirkpatrick, see above n 22; M Pirson and S Turnbull, 'Corporate governance, risk management, and the financial crisis – An information processing view' (December 2010) Fordham University School of Business

Although financial expertise may have some correlation with leadership in due risk management and the preservation of firm stability, the empirical studies mentioned above have all been confined to this episode of the global financial crisis. Thus, further refinements may be needed in studying what leadership characteristics may promote proper risk management in financial institutions. The Walker Review recommends that the role of NEDs[46] be enhanced in terms of being able and ready to challenge and critically scrutinise proposals for executive decision-making.[47] NEDs should thus be supported to a greater extent in gaining access to information and business advice,[48] and should also enhance their time commitment to the bank or financial institution on whose board they are serving.[49] EU legislation also requires executive directors not to hold another executive directorship elsewhere and more than two other non-executive directorships.[50] NEDs on the other hand are allowed to hold up to four other non-executive directorships elsewhere.[51] These provisions are to ensure that members of the board are able to devote sufficient time and commitment to the management of the relevant bank or financial institution.

Next, the lack of meaningful monitoring or challenge by boards – whether due **6.14** to a weak board or a dominant Chief Executive Officer (CEO)[52] – is also, it has been suggested, a crucial distinguishing corporate governance feature between banks and financial institutions which were in jeopardy and those that remained viable.[53] Chesney, Stromberg, Wagner[54] and Ramirez[55] have all suggested that the weaknesses and lack of independence of risk management in failed banks, such as the Royal Bank of Scotland and Northern Rock, are correlated with the autonomy of risk-taking and aggressive CEOs, driving the banks towards

---

Research Paper No 2011–003, available at: http://ssrn.com/abstract=1723782 accessed 13 March 2013; P M Vasudev, 'Credit derivatives and risk management: corporate governance in the Sarbanes-Oxley world' (2009) 4 *Journal of Business Law* 331.

46 Moore, see above n 24.
47 Walker Review, Recommendation 6.
48 Ibid., Recommendation 2.
49 Ibid., Recommendation 3.
50 CRD IV Directive, Art 91(3)(a).
51 Ibid., Art 91(3)(b).
52 Ramirez, see above n 23, argues that CEO domination in setting a risk-taking strategy has been key in the banks that failed in the financial crisis.
53 A de Simone, 'Crisis, governance and performance: Evidence from the banking sector' (ADEIMF Conference 'Global Financial Crisis and Management of Financial Intermediaries: Old and New Paradigms', Udine, 11–12 June 2010), available at: http://ssrn.com/abstract=1753734 accessed 13 March 2013, who finds that the two-tier board system has provided more monitoring and has mitigated implosions at banks and financial institutions; Parliamentary Commission on Banking Standards, see above n 18, paras 50, 93–94.
54 M Chesney, J Stromberg and A F Wagner, 'Risk-taking incentives, governance, and losses in the financial crisis' (November 2011) Swiss Finance Institute Research Paper Series No 10–18, available at: https://wpweb2.tepper.cmu.edu/wfa/wfasecure/upload2011FINAL/2011_PA_763108_643275_766704.pdf accessed 13 March 2013.
55 Ramirez, see above n 23.

excessive risk-taking and ultimate failure in the global financial crisis. By this time, CEO turnover is no longer a viable corporate governance mechanism as the financial institution rapidly heads into losses.[56] Hence the UK Corporate Governance Code 2012 was amended to take into account the Walker Review, calls for effective leadership by the chairman of the board,[57] sufficient time commitment by the chairman and board members (including NEDs)[58] and critical monitoring of internal controls and systems of risk management by NEDs.[59] The board collectively is responsible for risk-management monitoring and should conduct a review of risk-management effectiveness on an annual basis.[60]

6.15 Poorer quality risk management is also indicated by narrow conceptions of risk management according to business lines. Such narrow conceptions could also result in a silo departmental approach to risk management, where the objectives are often not clearly articulated or reviewed. Many commentators[61] have observed that, in the banks that failed in the crisis, risk management was largely undertaken on a silo-based approach, that is, each department separately managed their distinct risks according to their lines of business. Such narrow-minded approaches do not encourage a holistic appreciation of risks and may have contributed to the lack of discernment and communication. Further, due to the prevailing regulatory concern for accounting integrity as mentioned earlier, many boards also see risk management as confined to the audit committee's remit and as generally distinct from business strategy.[62] Some firms may view risk management as being narrowly confined to legal compliance.[63] Risk management in many financial institutions and in the corporate sector has also suffered from having an uncertain identity: firms treat risk management as being pro-business and hence play down its independent capacity to act as a check and monitor.[64]

---

56 M Čihák and others, 'Who disciplines bank managers?' (December 2009) IMF Working Paper No WP/09/272, available at: http://www.imf.org/external/pubs/ft/wp/2009/wp09272.pdf accessed 13 March 2013.

57 Corporate Governance Code 2010 (UK), paras A.1, A.3.

58 Ibid., para B.3.

59 Ibid., para A.4.

60 Ibid., para C.2. Also in the CRD IV Directive Art 88.

61 M Harner, 'Ignoring the writing on the wall: The role of enterprise risk management in the economic crisis' (2010) 5 Journal of Business Technology and the Law 45; M Harner, 'Barriers to effective risk management' (2010) 40 *Seton Hall Law Review* 1323; Parliamentary Commission on Banking Standards, see above n 18, paras 54–61.

62 I Brown, A Steen and J Foreman, 'Risk management in corporate governance: A review and proposal' (2009) 17 *Corporate Governance* 546.

63 Mikes, see above n 1.

64 Mikes, ibid.; Murphy, see above n 22.

Post-crisis, the kind of risk management that policymakers and regulators wish **6.16** to encourage is closer to the enterprise-wide risk management model,[65] where risk management is led at the strategic level by the board, rolls out into all aspects of business and operations and is considered holistically. Further, risk management should be an independent function, not compromised by conflicts of business interest and should have a sufficiently high profile, perhaps led by a chief risk officer or an independent risk committee on the board.[66] Many of these reforms have been put in place in post-crisis regulatory frameworks which will be shortly discussed.

The Walker Review has recommended raising the profile of risk management **6.17** at banks and financial institutions by recognising its special position as a board function.[67] This is now affirmed in EU legislation.[68] It also recommends the dedication of high-level resources to risk management via the creation of a risk committee.[69] In appropriate financial institutions of a certain scale, size and turnover, the review recommends the appointment of a chief risk officer.[70]

At the EU level, similar attention has been paid to the importance of enhancing **6.18** risk management at banks and financial institutions. The European Banking Authority (EBA) has issued a set of consolidated Internal Governance Guidelines.[71] The guidelines address risk management from the point of view of board leadership, commitment and effective oversight, as well as structural aspects in the organisation of risk management in banks and financial institutions.[72]

The EBA's guidelines[73] call for more effective leadership by the chairman in the **6.19** form of an overall risk appreciation of the business profile,[74] sufficient time commitment by the management body[75] and adequate skills and competence to

---

65   B W Nocco and R M Stultz, 'Enterprise risk management: Theory and practice' (2006) 18 *Journal of Applied Corporate Finance* 8; L K Meulbroek, 'A senior manager's guide to integrated risk management' in D H Chew (ed.), *Corporate Risk Management* (Columbia Business School Publishing 2008); R M Stultz, 'Rethinking risk management' in Chew (ed.).

66   Harner, see above n 61; Murphy, see above n 22; B Simkins and S A Ramirez, 'Enterprise wide risk management and corporate governance' (2007–8) 39 *Loyola University of Chicago Law Journal* 571; Kirkpatrick, see above n 22.

67   Walker Review, Recommendations 4, 6, 9.

68   CRD IV Directive, Art 86.

69   Walker Review, Recommendations 23, 25, 27–32, 35.

70   Ibid, Recommendation 24.

71   European Banking Authority, 'EBA's Guidelines on Internal Governance (GL 44)' (27 September 2011) (EBA Guidelines).

72   Ibid.

73   Ibid.

74   Ibid., para 14.4.

75   Ibid., para 12.

be represented on the board.[76] EU legislation has now directly prescribed for such board responsibilities to be reflected in board qualifications and composition.[77] The guidelines also promote a 'know your structure' requirement that management bodies must be able to monitor the business lines and subsidiaries and ensure that structure does not get too complex to monitor.[78]

6.20 The UK financial regulator has adopted the Walker Review's recommendations on senior management responsibility for risk management,[79] the establishment of a risk committee by the board[80] and the appointment of a chief risk officer,[81] where appropriate, according to the size, scale and complexity of the financial institution business. Such corporate governance reforms are also aligned with the EBA's guidelines.[82] In particular, EU legislation prescribing aspects of corporate governance mandates the establishment of a risk committee on the board.[83]

6.21 The risk committee of the board is to have overall oversight of risk management and internal controls, working with the audit and remuneration committees in terms of providing risk-based input into these high-level board issues. In particular, the responsibilities of the risk committee are as follows:[84]

(a) providing advice to the firm's governing body on risk strategy, including the oversight of current risk exposures of the firm, with particular, but not exclusive, emphasis on prudential risks;

(b) development of proposals for consideration by the governing body in respect of overall risk appetite and tolerance, as well as the metrics to be used to monitor the firm's risk management performance;

(c) oversight and challenge of the design and execution of stress and scenario testing;

(d) oversight and challenge of the day-to-day risk management and oversight arrangements of the executive;

(e) oversight and challenge of due diligence on risk issues relating to material transactions and strategic proposals that are subject to approval by the governing body;

---

76 Ibid., para 13.
77 CRD IV Directive, Article 87.
78 EBA Guidelines, para 18.6. For example, non-transparent or special purpose vehicles should only be used if the risks are clearly understood and there are legitimate reasons, such as operating in a foreign jurisdiction, tax, etc.
79 PRA and FCA Handbooks SYSC 4.1, 12.1.
80 Ibid., 21.1.5, 21.1.6.
81 Ibid., 21.1.2.
82 European Banking Authority, see above n 71 at 29, para 12.A.
83 CRD IV Directive, Article 75(3).
84 PRA and FCA Handbooks SYSC 21.1.5.

(f)   provide advice to the firm's remuneration committee on risk weightings to be applied to performance objectives incorporated in the incentive structure for the executive; and

(g)   providing advice, oversight and challenge necessary to embed and maintain a supportive risk culture throughout the firm.

The chief risk officer is provide oversight and challenge of the firm's systems **6.22** and controls in respect of risk management; oversight and validation of the firm's external reporting of risk; ensure the adequacy of risk information, risk analysis and risk training provided to members of senior management and the board; and report to senior management and the board on the firm's risk exposures relative to its risk appetite and tolerance, and the extent to which the risks inherent in any proposed business strategy and plans are consistent with the governing body's risk appetite and tolerance. The chief risk officer also provides risk-focused advice and information into the setting and individual application of the firm's remuneration policy, and should also alert senior management and the board as to any business strategy or plans that exceed the firm's risk appetite and tolerance.[85]

The chief risk officer should also be fully independent of a firm's individual **6.23** business units and have sufficient authority, stature and resources for the effective execution of his responsibilities. The quality of independence ensures that the specialist risk-management function is not compromised or unduly influenced by business interests so that it can provide critical challenge on business decisions on risk exposures. Empirical research[86] conducted to examine the relation between the quality of risk management at banks and financial institutions has used 'independence' as a quality indicator for strong risk management, and has concluded that strong risk management has a positive relationship with the survival and success of banks and financial institutions in the global financial crisis.

There are many factors that shape the quality of independence – the account- **6.24** ability channel, the setting of remuneration for the chief risk officer and risk managers, and appointment and removal procedures. UK legislation[87] provides for accountability for the chief risk officer directly to the board. Allowing the chief risk officer to report to the board directly or to the audit or risk committee may provide the chief risk officer with independence from possible interference from senior management or intimidation from aggressive CEOs, such as in the

---

85   Ibid., 21.1.2.
86   Ellul and Yerramilli, see above n 15.
87   PRA and FCA Handbooks SYSC 21.1.3.

failed investment bank Lehman Brothers where CEO Richard Fuld, known for his dominating personality, fired the chief risk officer Madelyn Antoncic in 2007 for urging caution in the bank's excessive engagement in the mortgage securitisation business.

6.25 UK legislation further protects the independence of the chief risk officer by ensuring that s/he would not be arbitrarily removed without approval by the board.[88] The chief risk officer's remuneration should also be decided by the board.[89]

6.26 Further, the EBA Guidelines also provide that the chief risk officer should report[90] directly to the board although communication to senior management is also envisaged. The EBA Guidelines protect the independence of the chief risk officer by ensuring that s/he would not be arbitrarily removed without approval by the board.[91] The EBA Guidelines[92] also provide that the remuneration of the risk-management function's staff should not be linked to the performance of the activities the function monitors.

6.27 The chief risk officer should have unfettered access to any parts of the firm's business capable of having an impact on the firm's risk profile.[93] The information mechanisms[94] in the firm provide the framework for the actual work of risk management to be carried out. In an enterprise-wide risk-management framework, information flows should be enhanced and open throughout the organisation,[95] such that information flows are fluid both top-down and bottom-up,[96] in respect of the communication of risk philosophy and appetites by the board and senior management and reporting from bottom-up in respect of implementation, monitoring, stress-testing and feedback. Banks[97] is of the view that enhanced and open communications throughout creates transparency, responsiveness to problems and respect for risk management, allowing the

---

88   Ibid., 21.1.4 (2).
89   Ibid., 21.1.4 (1).
90   EBA Guidelines (2011), para 24.8.
91   Ibid., para 27.6.
92   Ibid., para 24.6.
93   PRA and FCA Handbooks SYSC 21.1.2.
94   See Pirson and Turnbull, above n 45, for a view emphasising the importance of information transmission and processing to facilitate risk management. The author does not however think that widening the information channels to stakeholders in firm-wide risk management on a regular basis is necessarily ideal.
95   CRM Policy Group, 'Containing systemic risk: The road to reform –The report of the CRMPG III' in M R Turley (ed.), *Reforming Risk in Financial Markets* (NovaScience Publishers 2009) at 1; Erik Banks, *Risk Culture* (Palgrave Macmillan 2012) at 21ff.
96   P Carrel, *The Handbook of Risk Management: Implementing a Post-Crisis Corporate Culture* (John Wiley & Sons 2010), Chs 11–15.
97   Banks, see above n 95, 50ff.

risk-management function to be freer in discussing and challenging issues across levels, enhancing the firm's overall capacity to address problems promptly. Such transparency also facilitates co-ordination and co-operation across levels in the firm. Enhanced information flows and transparency in a firm may be facilitated by cross-divisional communications such as meetings and interactions and regular reporting to senior management. Carrel is of the view that in such a framework, risk becomes a language to be used 'to receive instructions as much as giving feedback. It is used for benchmarking, performance measurements and forecasting'.[98] Prager[99] discusses how Goldman Sachs, the investment bank that weathered the global financial crisis in a relatively better shape than many other comparable firms, has implemented a successful risk-management framework, which includes weekly cross-committee meetings involving senior management or NED attendance.

For information to be meaningful, it has to be derived from the comprehensive capture of data and robust methods in data processing. Further, information must also be practically accessible. Hence, the role of data and information technology systems[100] play an important part in supporting the information framework for firm-wide risk management. Cortez[101] recommends that data needs to be captured over a sufficiently long period of time, at least for 15 years or as long as the firm has been in operation, and the integrity and completeness of data must be ensured.[102] The implementation of information flows and data systems in banks and financial institutions are not minutely prescribed in UK legislation. **6.28**

The EBA reconceptualises 'Internal Control' as a structural necessity in all financial institutions, comprising independent compliance, risk control and audit functions that are to be distinct from each other. Compliance and risk control are envisaged as part of a holistic, institution-wide, risk-management system that feeds into business decisions, such as product development and procedures, in what is termed the 'NPAP' (the new product approval procedure), which must be implemented in all financial institutions. The EBA **6.29**

---

98   Carrel, see above n 96, 198ff.

99   J Prager, 'The financial crisis of 2007/8: Misaligned incentives, bank mismanagement, and troubling policy implications' (2012), available at: http://ssrn.com/abstract=2094662.

100   W Kross, *Organised Opportunities: Risk Management in Financial Services Operations* (John Wiley & Sons 2007), 121ff; B Di Renzo, M Hillairet, M Picard, A Rifaut, C Bernard, D Hagen, P Maa and D Reinard, 'Operational risk management in financial institutions: Process assessment in concordance with Basel II' (2007) 12 *Software Process Improvement and Practice* 321.

101   A Cortez, *Winning at Risk* (John Wiley & Sons 2011), 58ff.

102   L Frésard, C Pérignon and A Wilhelmsson, 'The pernicious effects of contaminated data in risk management' (2011), available at: http://ssrn.com/abstract=1537244 argue that a lot of data feeding into risk management may be incomplete or contaminated by distorting information and caution should be used in ensuring the integrity of the data to be captured.

Guidelines also provide a framework for the roles and responsibilities of the specialist risk-management function in the firm that is overseen by the chief risk officer. The specialist risk-management function should be independent such that the function should not perform tasks that fall within the scope of activities the function is supposed to monitor, or be subordinate to persons performing tasks that the function is supposed to monitor.[103] The guidelines also provide the risk-management function with a seat at the table of strategic decision-making, empowering the function to provide information to and advise the board and senior management.[104] Further, the audit function is viewed as a third line of defence, after compliance and risk control, as a check and monitor on the monitoring functions of compliance and risk control. The EBA thus sees the beefing up of multiple layers of internal control and self-discipline within financial institutions as key, all of this functioning within an overall risk culture whose development should be encouraged in financial institutions.[105] The EBA even encourages the development of internal whistle-blower procedures to assist the compliance or audit functions in their monitoring. Internal alert procedures,[106] for example, allow employees to warn and provide information with respect to concerns 'outside regular reporting lines'.

6.30 The EBA Guidelines therefore provide a framework for the institution of an enterprise-wide risk-management framework at banks and financial institutions. Enterprise-wide risk management,[107] supported by many commentators as the way forward, is led at the strategic level by the board, rolls out into all aspects of business and operations and is considered holistically.

6.31 Post-crisis, regulatory reforms have significantly enhanced the organisational positioning, power and resources of the risk-management function at banks and financial institutions and have situated such a function within a framework of enterprise-wide risk management. However some concerns about the efficacy of regulating risk management remain and these will be discussed in the next section.

---

103   EBA Guidelines (2011), para 24.6.
104   Ibid., para 26.2, 26.3.
105   Ibid., para 7, 20.
106   Ibid., para 17.
107   Nocco and Stultz; Meulbroek; and Stultz, all see above n 65; Cortez, see above n 101,142ff.

4. CAN REGULATING RISK MANAGEMENT EFFECTIVELY SECURE RISK-TAKING AT OPTIMAL LEVELS?

In considering whether the regulation of risk management as a corporate **6.32** governance issue may be effective, a fundamental question that arises is this: Can we expect the risk-management framework and function to monitor excessive risk-taking when it is uncertain what optimal risk-taking means? In the aftermath of the global financial crisis, do we accept 'optimal risk-taking' as a business decision defined by firms[108] or is 'optimal risk-taking' determined with reference to wider social appetite?[109] If we accept risk-taking as an essentially firm-based decision, then should regulatory intervention be made into risk management since risk misjudgements are a necessary learning process for firms? If the latter, there may be a collective failure[110] on the part of firms to recognise what may be socially optimal risk-taking. Moore[111] also argues that post-crisis emphasis on risk management intends to shape risk management towards risk moderation but is it desirable for regulators or policymakers to calibrate socially optimal risk-taking given the adverse associations with excessive economic planning which could lead to distortions, perverse outcomes and unintended consequences?

If we accept that optimal risk-taking is to be determined by banks and financial **6.33** institutions as business decisions which should not be micro-managed by regulators, then is a regulatory framework for risk management inherently limited in securing regulatory objectives such as the prudential sustainability of banking businesses? Some commentators view risk management at banks and financial institutions as being able to meet multiple objectives in managing solvency risks, downside risks as well as seizing opportunities for upside gains and adding value to the firm.[112] Banks[113] is of the view that risk management

---

108 R T Miller, 'Oversight liability for risk-management failures at financial firms' (2010) 84 *South California Law Review* 47.

109 K S Okamoto, 'After the bailout: Regulating systemic moral hazard' (2009) 57 *UCLA Law Review* 18 argues that it would be quite impossible to define what optimal risk-taking is from a perspective of social utility.

110 Above, and see S Schwarz, 'Systemic risk' (2008) 97 *Georgetown Law Journal* 193.

111 Moore, see above n 24.

112 M S Pagano, 'How theories of financial intermediation and corporate risk-management influence bank risk-taking behavior' (2001) 10 *Financial Markets, Institutions and Instruments* 277 argues that risk management in financial institutions is both for managing solvency risk as well as for seizing opportunities in capital markets to add value to the firm. Ellul and Yerramilli, see above n 15, examined the relationship between effective risk management and the twin purposes of solvency and performance and found a positive relationship between strong risk management and the twin purposes. This may suggest that the purpose of performance, which is a firm-centric concern, is not misaligned with prudential regulatory objectives. The meta-review of empirical literature carried out in C Smithson and B J Simkins, 'Does risk management add value? A survey of the evidence' (2005) 17 *Journal of Applied Corporate Finance* 8 seems to suggest the same conclusion.

113 Banks, see above n 95, 1ff.

deals with 'pure risks' i.e. risks that have to do with averting disasters so that what is desired to be achieved is a situation of 'no loss' as well as 'speculative risks' i.e. risks that present opportunities for an upside as well as a downside. However, other commentators wonder if there is a trade-off between risk management purposed towards value creation and risk management that is purposed towards prudential management. For example, Blanchard et al[114] argue that risk management is costly and may be seen to affect the financial bottom-line, and hence shareholders and executives rewarded in stock-linked remuneration whose incentives are similar to shareholders may not be keen to invest substantially in risk management. Mikes[115] also argues that risk management is often seen as a 'business partner' and not as 'compliance champion', meaning risk management may take on a substantially business-advisory aspect focused on firm performance and value creation and less emphasis may be placed on regulatory objectives in relation to prudential management and compliance. Hence, it may perhaps not be assumed that risk management which is firm and business-centred is naturally aligned with prudential regulatory objectives. In 1998, the Basel Committee's recommendations on best practices in internal control[116] for international banks specifically made a distinction between risk management that is firm-centric and risk management that is purposed towards prudential regulatory objectives.

6.34 Raising the profile of risk management to the level of corporate governance may not change the orientation of risk-management objectives from firm-centric ones to ones more aligned with public regulatory objectives. Greater prudence as desired by the regulatory objective towards financial stability may be contrary to value creation and maximisation for shareholders.[117] It may be unrealistic for regulators to expect that by raising the profile of risk management to the level of corporate governance, firms would choose risk moderation behaviour as being optimal for the firm. Difficult judgements of trade-off between safety and profit generation would still have to be made at a strategic level.

6.35 There is empirical research that indicates that the pursuit of risk management in activities such as active buying and selling of derivatives does not reduce the

---

114   D Blanchard and G Dionne, 'Risk management and corporate governance', paper presented at 'The Crisis of Corporate Governance: What's Next?' Conference, Montreal, 7 May 2003.
115   Mikes, see above n 1.
116   Basel Committee on Banking Supervision, *Framework for Internal Control in Banking Organisations* (1998), para 20, 17.
117   M Pettis, 'Why the world needs reckless bankers', *Financial Times* (London, 26 March 2013).

level of solvency risk for banks and financial institutions.[118] Even if the motivation for risk management by actively selling and buying derivatives may have stemmed from a desire to manage downside risks,[119] the successful management of downside risk may then entail business decisions to be made to expand exposure so that more risks are taken on.[120] Draghi[121] is however of the view that the levels and magnitudes of risks may not pose an issue from the point of view of prudential regulatory concerns so long as they are managed soundly. In sum, risk management undertaken to manage solvency risk could also be used to further business objectives,[122] and it may remain uncertain whether increased risk-taking (which is usually related to higher returns) supported by increased risk management may reach a tipping point.

Further, the global financial crisis also revealed weaknesses in the professional **6.36** competence of risk management itself. Risk management is still a developing area in terms of expertise and regulators should not place undue faith in the efficacy of regulating risk management at banks and financial institutions in order to secure prudential objectives.

Commentators have described the risk-management function as dealing with **6.37** the measurement and analysis of risks in the form of 'known' risks ('k'), 'unknown risks' ('u') and 'unknowable' risks ('U').[123] 'Known risks' refer to risks that can be identified and quantified. Often past data and statistical infor- mation are used in analytical models which use mathematical probabilities to generate risk measurements.[124] 'Unknown risks' refer to risks that are not entirely unexpected although the likelihood of occurrence is uncertain, and the magnitude of the materialisation of such risk is also uncertain. Hence, 'unknown risks' present problems of objective measurability and the risk- management function, in analysing and attempting to measure such risks,

---

118 A S Cebenoyan and P Strahan, 'Risk management, capital structure and lending at banks' (2001), available at: http://ssrn.com/abstract=293378, although see later contrary findings in C S Buston, 'Active risk management and banking stability' (2012), available at: http://ssrn.com/abstract=2049390 and H Gersbach and J Wenzel- burger, 'Sophistication in risk management, bank equity, and stability' (2010) 10 *International Review of Finance* 63.

119 Buston, ibid., 'finds a positive relationship between bank stability and active risk management'.

120 Gersbach and Wenzelburger, see above n 118.

121 Draghi, see above n 36, 119ff.

122 L Norden, C S Buston and W Wagner, 'Financial innovation and bank behavior: Evidence from credit markets' (2011), available at: http://ssrn.com/abstract=1800162.

123 A Kuritzkes and T Schuermann, 'What we know, don't know and can't know about bank risk: A view from the trenches' in F X Diebold, N Doherty, and R J Herring (eds.), *The Known, The Unknown and The Unknowable in Financial Risk Management* (Princeton University Press 2010); R J Herring, 'The known, the unknown, and the unknowable in financial policy: An application to the subprime crisis' (2009) 26 *Yale Journal on Regulation* 391; P Jorion, 'Risk management lessons from the credit crisis' (2009) 15 *European Financial Management* 923.

124 J Bessis, *Risk Management in Banking* (John Wiley & Sons 2011), xi, sections 4, 5.

would often have to engage in making estimations and constructing models.[125] 'Unknowable risks' refer to risks that are unexpected and therefore not measured at all, and often systemic type events may be regarded as manifestations of 'unknowable risk'.[126]

6.38 The failure of many financial institutions in the global financial crisis was widely attributed to the collapse of asset prices of collaterised debt obligations held by them. The asset price collapse could be regarded as a materialisation of both the 'unknown risks' and 'unknowable risks'. Collaterised debt obligations are novel and complex structured finance products which have not been tested. However the risk of such products has been erroneously judged as low by both financial institutions and credit rating agencies. Further, financial institutions have not at all factored in their risk measurements events of systemic failure in asset prices or other institutions. The 'unknown risks' of collaterised debt obligations have also been erroneously measured because past data for such novel products is lacking and the subjective estimates applied to the measurement of such risks have been overly optimistic.[127] Some commentators[128] opine that the rigour in risk measurements of collaterised debt obligations in the pre-crisis years has been questionable, as proxy forms of information and externally generated information such as by credit rating agencies have been used as bases for risk modelling and measurement, not extensive due diligence.[129] Further, the uncertainties in measuring risk provide room for financial institutions to underestimate such risks when there have been strong incentives to engage in business lines that could generate high returns.[130] For the banks that fared worst in the global financial crisis, flawed input[131] has been used in the subjective estimates of 'unknown risks' which are then built into quantitative models. Reliance on such quantitative models becomes almost automatic and risk managers forget to question the validity of the initial assumptions built into the models.[132] Rebonato is of the view that that dominant quantitative

---

125   Kuritzkes and Schuermann; Jorion, both see above n 123.
126   See above.
127   Fanto, see above n 11; R Stultz, 'Risk management failures: What are they and when do they happen?' (2008) 20 *Journal of Applied Corporate Finance* 58.
128   S L Schwarz and L Chang, 'The custom to failure cycle' (2012) 62 *Duke Law Journal* 767; Jorion, see above n 123.
129   That said, the banks that used a variety of information and generating information in-house to price risks have fared better in the crisis, see Senior Supervisors' Report, above n 14.
130   A Kling, 'The financial crisis: Moral failure or cognitive failure?' (2010) 33 *Harvard Journal of Law and Public Policy* 507; Okamoto, see above n 109; J Kose, A Saunders and L W Senbet, 'A theory of bank regulation and management compensation' (2000) 13 *Review of Financial Studies* 95 is an early paper that has warned that incentives such as in remuneration fundamentally affect risk-taking at banks and financial institutions.
131   D Hubbard, *The Failure of Risk Management: Why It's Broken and How Do we Fix it?* (John Wiley & Sons 2009), Chrs 8 and 9.
132   D O Edwards, 'An unfortunate "Tail": Reconsidering risk management incentives after the Financial crisis of 2007–2009' (2010) 81 *University of Colorado Law Review* 247.

practice in risk management which is based on the frequentist view of probability is too limited in nature when data is lacking, assumptions made are subjective and affected by cognitive biases.[133]

Post-crisis, commentators have provided a variety of suggestions to enhance the quantitative approaches to risk management as the quantitative approaches are still fundamentally useful.[134] In other words, the baby should not be thrown out with the bath water. For example, a more comprehensive suite of risks including low-probability but high-impact risks should be taken into account,[135] and risk assumptions that are based on subjective estimates should be made more prudent and subject to regular review.[136] Ray[137] suggests that a completely new framework could be instituted to mine more data and rely less on the traditional frequentist approaches to mathematical probabilities, so that a wider range of causal possibilities could be taken into account. Jorion[138] also suggests that a completely new framework that maps the risks of real-time trading and asset positions should be constructed for risk measurement and analysis in a dynamic manner instead of using the traditional approach based on past returns data. **6.39**

Further, many risk-management commentators also believe that if quantitative approaches to risk management are flanked by qualitative approaches, such as the regulation of optimal corporate governance structures for effective risk management, then risk management can be improved significantly over time. The qualitative approach to risk management refers to the element of critical scrutiny of the assumptions and the acknowledgement of inherent limitations of quantitative approaches so that they can be regularly reviewed, updated and adjusted to meet changing conditions. In other words, although quantitative approaches remain fundamental and primary to generating risk measurements and analyses, the robustness of the quantitative approach must be checked and evaluated in a framework of enterprise-wide risk management that is embedded in the corporate governance of the bank or financial institution. Commentators[139] are of the view that enterprise-wide risk management provides the framework for a more comprehensive identification of risks to be measured and **6.40**

---

133   R Rebonato, *Plight of the Fortune Tellers: Why We Need to Manage Financial Risk Differently* (Princeton University Press 2007),18ff, 28ff, 43ff, 127ff and 144ff.

134   G Bénéplanc and J-C Rochet, *Risk Management in Turbulent Times* (Oxford University Press 2011), 194ff.

135   J V Rosenberg and T Schuermann, 'A general approach to integrated risk management with skewed, fat-tailed risks', Federal Reserve Bank of New York Staff Reports, 2004; W W Lang and J A Jagtiani, 'The mortgage and financial crises: The role of credit risk management and corporate governance' (2010) 38 *Atlantic Economic Journal* 123.

136   Rebonato, see above n 133, 196ff.

137   C Ray, *Extreme Risk Management: Revolutionary Approaches to Evaluating and Measuring Risk* (McGraw-Hill 2010), 1ff, 52ff, 153ff, 167ff, 176ff and 206ff.

138   Jorion, see above n 123.

139   Carrel, see above n 96; P Sweeting, *Financial Enterprise Risk Management* (CUP 2011).

analysed by the specialist risk-management function, as risks are identified with the help of better information flows and the generation of corporate intelligence, and supported at the highest management levels and engaged with all business and operational units throughout the firm. The galvanisation of enterprise-wide co-ordination within a firm may provide a better chance of mitigating flaws in the primary quantitative approaches to risk management in terms of comprehensiveness, underlying assumptions and identification of correlations.[140]

6.41 Further, regulators in the EU and UK have now introduced mandatory requirements of stress testing upon banks and financial institutions so that they could put their quantitative approaches to risk management to regular back-testing and forward-looking stress testing[141] and mitigate any flaws discovered in the process.[142] The regulatory framework for stress testing emphasises senior management oversight and responsibility and puts risk management right at the heart of corporate governance.

6.42 However, one may query whether the introduction of a regulatory framework to raise the profile of risk management to the level of corporate governance would instead raise anxiety at board level in terms of responsibilities and liability. As the regulatory framework for corporate governance in relation to risk management is meta-regulatory in nature, boards may choose to embark on excessive proceduralisation in firm implementation in order to show due discharge of responsibility. Resorting to proceduralisation[143] is likely an attractive prospect for the board as the existence of processes and systems may provide good evidence of board engagement with risk matters and discharge of responsibility. However systems and procedures could serve as window dressing to please regulators.[144] Boards may also take false comfort from the institution of systems

---

140   Edwards, see above n 132; J R Boatright, 'Risk management and the responsible corporation: How sweeping the invisible hand?' (2011) 116 *Business and Society Review* 145.

141   Also supported in Hubbard, see above n 131, Ch 10; CRM Policy Group, see above n 95, 1; G P Miller, 'Intellectual hazard: How conceptual biases in complex organizations contributed to the crisis of 2008' (2010) 33 *Harvard Journal of Law and Public Policy* 807; Schwarz and Chang, see above n 128.

142   FSA, 'Stress and Scenario Testing: Feedback on CP08/24 and final rules' (December 2009) PS 09/20 http://www.fsa.gov.uk/pubs/policy/ps09_20.pdf; PRA and FCA Handbooks SYSC 20; EBA Guidelines, para 22.4.

143   M Power, *Organized Uncertainty: Designing a World of Risk Management* (OUP 2007).

144   K D Krawiec, 'Cosmetic compliance and the failure of negotiated governance' (2003) 81 *Washington University Law Quarterly* 487. However some empirical research in relation to compliance systems shows that systems and procedures could encourage real commitment and behavioural change too, see C Parker and V L Nielsen, 'Corporate compliance systems: Could they make any difference?' (2009) 41 *Administration and Society* 3.

and procedures when the art and science of identifying and managing risks is still an emerging discipline.[145]

Further, proceduralisation may also be manifest in the adoption of computer- **6.43** ised and automated systems for risk control.[146] Bamberger[147] warns against the tendency of turning risk management into a streamlined, manageable and easy-to-use system in terms of automated processes and mechanisms. These systems and models may run the risk of encouraging automation bias and replacing more discretionary and considered human judgement. Power has warned[148] that the well-established practices in internal audit and financial reporting could influence the design of risk-management systems towards more technical, calculable and quantifiable systems.[149] Although such systems may be easier to use, they may turn risk management into a narrow-minded exercise or a compliance-based exercise, thus undermining the general spirit of an internal critical culture that the regulatory framework intends to stimulate.

5. CONCLUSION

The importance of the risk-management framework and function has been **6.44** flagged up in the global financial crisis. Despite failures detected in many financial institutions' risk-management frameworks and doubts as to the professional competence of the risk-management function, the regulatory reforms post-crisis have chosen to put faith in the role of risk management and have therefore enhanced the organisational positioning, powers and resources of the risk-management function and introduced mandatory requirements for the establishment of risk-management frameworks in the mould of enterprise-wide risk management. However, as discussed above, the meta-regulation of risk management means that banks and financial institutions would have ultimately responsibility for the implementation of risk management although the regulatory framework has become much more detailed and specific as compared to the pre-crisis one. Banks and financial institutions would have to navigate the balance of interests between business and prudential regulatory objectives and it remains to be seen what incentives would be at play against the

---

145   C Van der Elst, 'The risks of corporate legal principles of risk management' (June 2010), available at: http://papers.ssrn.com/sol3/papers.cfm?abstract_id=1623526 accessed 22 March 2013.

146   Power, see above n 143; G H Lee, 'Rule-based and case-based reasoning approach for internal audit of bank' (2008) 21 *Knowledge-Based Systems* 140.

147   K M Bamberger, 'Technologies of compliance: Risk and regulation in a digital age' (2010) 88 *Texas Law Review* 669.

148   A Bhimani, 'Risk management, corporate governance and management accounting: Emerging interdependencies' (2009) 20 *Management Accounting Research* 2.

149   Power, see above n 143.

backdrop of the emerging professional discipline of risk management. As enterprise-wide risk management is premised upon integrating risk management with business, would the regulatory framework actually achieve the effect of enhancing the 'business partner' role of the risk-management function instead of the 'internal gatekeeper' role with a view to supplying a form of prudential governance to meet regulatory objectives?[150] Risk management could become impossible to judge unless contextualised against business decisions and judgement, and ultimately, it is queried what challenges this may pose to regulatory supervision of risk-taking and management in banks and financial institutions in the future.

SELECTED BIBLIOGRAPHY

Bamberger, K M, 'Technologies of compliance: Risk and regulation in a digital age' (2010) 88 *Texas Law Review* 669.

Banks, E, *Risk Culture* (Palgrave Macmillan 2012).

Basel Committee on Banking Supervision, *Framework for Internal Control in Banking Organisations* (1998).

Bénéplanc, G and J-C Rochet, *Risk Management in Turbulent Times* (OUP 2011).

Bessis, J, *Risk Management in Banking* (John Wiley & Sons 2011).

Bezis, J N, 'Conceptualizing the failure of financial institutions and the role of risk management in averting failure: The CLS model' (January, 2013), available at: http://papers.ssrn.com/sol3/papers.cfm?abstract_id=2196556.

Bhimani, A, 'Risk management, corporate governance and management accounting: Emerging interdependencies' (2009) 20 *Management Accounting Research* 2.

Blommestein, H J, 'Risk management after the great crash' (2010) 28 *Journal of Financial Transformation* 131.

Brunnermeier, M K, A Crockett, C Goodhart, A D Persaud and H Shin, *The Fundamental Principles of Financial Regulation* (Geneva Reports on the World Economy, London: Centre for Economic Policy Research 2009).

Buston, C S, 'Active risk management and banking stability' (2012) available at: http://ssrn.com/abstract=2049390.

Carrel, P, *The Handbook of Risk Management: Implementing a Post-Crisis Corporate Culture* (John Wiley & Sons 2010).

Cebenoyan, A S and P Strahan, 'Risk management, capital structure and lending at banks' (2001), available at: http://ssrn.com/abstract=293378.

Chesney, M, J Stromberg and A F Wagner, 'Risk-taking incentives, governance, and losses in the financial crisis' (November 2011) Swiss Finance Institute Research Paper Series No 10–18, available at: https://wpweb2.tepper.cmu.edu/wfa/wfasecure/upload2011FINAL/2011_PA_763108_643275_766704.pdf.

Chew, D H (ed.), *Corporate Risk Management* (Columbia Business School Publishing 2008).

Čihák, M, and others, 'Who disciplines bank managers' (December 2009) IMF Working Paper No WP/09/272, available at: http://www.imf.org/external/pubs/ft/wp/2009/wp09272.pdf.

Coglianese, C and E Mendelson, 'Meta-regulation and self-regulation' in R Baldwin, M Cave, and M Lodge (eds), *The Oxford Handbook of Regulation* (OUP 2010).

---

150   Mikes, see above n 1.

Cortez, A, *Winning at Risk* (John Wiley & Sons 2011).

CRM Policy Group, 'Containing systemic risk: The road to reform – The report of the CRMPG III' in M R Turley (ed.), *Reforming Risk in Financial Markets* (NovaScience Publishers 2009).

Crouhy, M, 'Risk management failures during the financial crisis' in R W Kolb (ed.), *Lessons from the Financial Crisis* (John Wiley & Sons 2010).

Davies, H, *The Financial Crisis: Who is to Blame?* (Polity Press 2010).

De Simone, A, 'Crisis, governance and performance: evidence from the banking sector' (ADEIMF Conference 'Global Financial Crisis and Management of Financial Inter-mediaries: Old and New Paradigms', Udine, 11–12 June 2010), available at: http://ssrn.com/abstract=1753734.

Draghi, M, 'Observations on risk management practices during the recent market turbulence' in M R Turley (ed.), *Reforming Risk in Financial Markets* (NovaScience Publishers 2009).

Edwards, D O, 'An unfortunate "tail": Reconsidering risk management incentives after the financial crisis of 2007–2009' (2010) 81 *University of Colorado Law Review* 247.

Ellul, A and V Yerramilli, 'Stronger risk controls, lower risk: evidence from US bank holding companies' (August 2012), available at: http://ssrn.com/abstract=1550361.

Erkens, D H, M Hung and P Matos, 'Corporate governance in the 2007–2008 financial crisis: Evidence from financial institutions worldwide' (2012) 18 *Journal of Corporate Finance* 389.

European Banking Authority, 'EBA's Guidelines on Internal Governance (GL 44)' (27 September 2011).

Fanto, J A, 'Anticipating the unthinkable: The adequacy of risk management in finance and environmental studies' (2009) 44 *Wake Forest Law Review* 731.

Fanto, J A, 'The role of financial regulation in private financial firms: Risk management and the limitations of the market model' (2009) 3 *Brook J Corp Fin & Co L* 29.

Frésard, L, C Pérignon and A Wilhelmsson, 'The pernicious effects of contaminated data in risk management' (2011), available at: http://ssrn.com/abstract=1537244.

Gersbach, H and J Wenzelburger, 'Sophistication in risk management, bank equity, and stability' (2010) 10 *International Review of Finance* 63.

Harner, M, 'Barriers to effective risk management' (2010) 40 *Seton Hall Law Review* 1323.

Harner, M, 'Ignoring the writing on the wall: The role of enterprise risk management in the economic crisis' (2010) 5 *Journal of Business Technology and the Law* 45.

Hau, H and M P Thum, 'Subprime crisis and board (in-)competence: Private vs. public banks in Germany' (2009) 24 *Economic Policy* 701.

Herring, R J, 'The known, the unknown, and the unknowable in financial policy: An application to the subprime crisis' (2009) 26 *Yale Journal on Regulation* 391.

House of Lords and House of Commons, *Changing Banking for Good* (Report of the Parliamentary Commission on Banking Standards) (12 June 2013).

Hubbard, D, *The Failure of Risk Management: Why It's Broken and How Do we Fix it?* (John Wiley & Sons 2009).

Jorion, P, 'Risk management lessons from the credit crisis' (2009) 15 *European Financial Management* 923.

Kirkpatrick, G, 'The corporate governance lessons from the financial crisis' (2009) 96 *OECD Financial Market Trends* 1.

Kling, A, 'The financial crisis: Moral failure or cognitive failure?' (2010) 33 *Harvard Journal of Law and Public Policy* 507.

Kose, J, A Saunders and L W Senbet, 'A theory of bank regulation and management compensation' (2000) 13 *Review of Financial Studies* 95.

Krawiec, K D, 'Cosmetic compliance and the failure of negotiated governance' (2003) 81 *Washington University Law Quarterly* 487.

Kross, W, *Organised Opportunities: Risk Management in Financial Services Operations* (John Wiley & Sons 2007).

Kuritzkes, A and T Schuermann, 'What we know, don't know and can't know about bank risk: A view from the trenches' in F X Diebold, N Doherty, and R J Herring (eds), *The Known, The Unknown and The Unknowable in Financial Risk Management* (Princeton University Press 2010).

Lang, W W and J A Jagtiani, 'The mortgage and financial crises: The role of credit risk management and corporate governance' (2010) 38 *Atlantic Economic Journal* 123.

Lee, G H, 'Rule-based and case-based reasoning approach for internal audit of bank' (2008) 21 *Knowledge-Based Systems* 140.

Li, P, 'How can corporate governance control enterprise's financial risk?' (December 2009), available at: http://papers.ssrn.com/sol3/papers.cfm?abstract_id=1523519.

Lyons, S, 'In defense of the corporation' (2009) 66 *Internal Auditor* 1.

McGee, S, *Chasing Goldman Sachs: How the Masters of the Universe Melted Wall Street Down … And Why They'll Take Us to the Brink Again* (Crown Business 2010).

McKee, M, 'Financial markets turmoil and the biggest banks: Lessons to be learned' (2008) 23(8) *Journal of International Banking Law and Regulation* 404.

Mehran, H, A Morrison and J Shapiro, 'Corporate governance and banks: What have we learned from the financial crisis?' (June 2011) Federal Reserve Bank of New York Staff Report No 502, available at: http://ssrn.com/abstract=1880009.

Mikes, A, 'Risk management at crunch time: Are chief risk officers compliance champions or business partners?' (2008) 2 *Journal of Risk Management in Financial Institutions* 7.

Miller, G P, 'Intellectual hazard: How conceptual biases in complex organizations contributed to the crisis of 2008' (2010) 33 *Harvard Journal of Law and Public Policy* 807.

Miller, R T, 'Oversight liability for risk-management failures at financial firms' (2010) 84 *South California Law Review* 47.

Moore, M T, 'The evolving contours of the board's risk management function in UK corporate governance' (2010) 10 *Journal of Corporate Law Studies* 279.

Meulbroek, L K, 'A senior manager's guide to integrated risk management' in D H Chew (ed.), *Corporate Risk Management* (Columbia Business School Publishing 2008).

Murphy, M E, 'Assuring responsible risk management in banking: The corporate governance dimension' (2011) 36 *Delaware Journal of Corporate Law* 121.

Nocco, B W and R M Stultz, 'Enterprise risk management: Theory and practice' (2006) 18 *Journal of Applied Corporate Finance* 8.

Norden, L, C S Buston and W Wagner, 'Financial innovation and bank behavior: Evidence from credit markets' (2011), available at: http://ssrn.com/abstract=1800162.

O'Sullivan, K P V and S Kinsella, 'Financial and regulatory failure: The case of Ireland' (2013) 14 *Journal of Banking Regulation* 1.

Okamoto, K S, 'After the bailout: Regulating systemic moral hazard' (2009) 57 *UCLA Law Review* 183.

Okamoto, K S and D O Edwards, 'Risk-taking' (2010) 32 *Cardozo Law Review* 159.

Parker, C, *The Open Corporation* (CUP 2000).

Parker, C and V L Nielsen, 'Corporate compliance systems: Could they make any difference?' (2009) 41 *Administration and Society* 3.

Pichet, E, 'What governance lessons should be learnt from the Société Générale's Kerviel affair' (2008) 3 *La revue française de gouvernance d'entreprise* 117.

Pirson, M and S Turnbull, 'Corporate governance, risk management, and the financial crisis – an information processing view' (December 2010) Fordham University School of Business Research Paper No 2011–003, available at: http://ssrn.com/abstract=1723782.

Power, M, *Organized Uncertainty: Designing a World of Risk Management* (OUP 2007).

Prager, J, 'The financial crisis of 2007/8: Misaligned incentives, bank mismanagement, and troubling policy implications' (2012), available at: http://ssrn.com/abstract=2094662.

Ramirez, S A, 'Lessons from the subprime debacle: Stress testing CEO autonomy' (2009) 54 *Saint Louis University Law Journal* 1.

Ray, C, *Extreme Risk Management: Revolutionary Approaches to Evaluating and Measuring Risk* (McGraw-Hill 2010).

Rebonato, R, *Plight of the Fortune Tellers: Why We Need to Manage Financial Risk Differently* (NJ: Princeton University Press 2007). Rosenberg, J V and T Schuermann, 'A general approach to integrated risk management with skewed, fat-tailed risks' (Federal Reserve Bank of New York Staff Reports, 2004).

Resti, A and A Sironi, *Risk Management and Shareholders' Value in Banking: From Risk Measurement Models to Capital Allocation Policies* (John Wiley & Sons 2007).

Sabato, G, 'Financial crisis: Where did risk management fail?' (August 2009), available at: http://ssrn.com/abstract=1460762.

Schwarz, S L and L Chang, 'The custom to failure cycle' (2012) 62 *Duke Law Journal* 767.

Scott, C, 'Regulating everything: From mega- to meta-regulation' (2012) 60 *Administration* 61.

Simkins, B and S A Ramirez, 'Enterprise wide risk management and corporate governance' (2007–8) 39 *Loyola University of Chicago Law Journal* 571.

Tett, G, *Fool's Gold: How Unrestrained Greed Corrupted a Dream, Shattered Global Markets and Unleashed a Catastrophe* (Abacus Books 2010).

Van der Elst, C and F Bogaert, 'Risk management in financial law' in M van Daelen and C Van der Elst (eds), *Risk Management and Corporate Governance* (Edward Elgar 2010).

Vasudev, P M, 'Credit derivatives and risk management: Corporate governance in the Sarbanes-Oxley world' [2009] *Journal of Business Law* 331.

Wilson, W R, L C Rose and J F Pinfold, 'Examination of NZ finance company failures: The role of corporate governance' (January 2010) available at: http://papers.ssrn.com/sol3/papers.cfm?abstract_id=1536874.

Wright J S F and B Head, 'Reconsidering regulation and governance theory: A learning approach' (2009) 31 *Law and Policy* 192.

Wright, J S F, P G Dempster, J Keen, P Allen and A Hutchings, 'The new governance arrangements for NHS Foundation Trust Hospitals: Reframing governors as meta-regulators' (2012) 90 *Public Administration* 351.

7

CORPORATE REPORTING AND THE ACCOUNTABILITY OF BANKS AND FINANCIAL INSTITUTIONS

Iris H-Y Chiu

1. INTRODUCTION

7.01 Banks and financial institutions are subject to mandatory transparency in order to cater to two objectives. One relates to reporting to capital markets, in respect of quoted and listed firms. In this respect the corporate reporting which is accountable to shareholders and investors is in the same vein as corporate reporting generally applicable to the corporate sector. The second objective relates to reporting to the relevant financial regulator in order to facilitate ongoing supervision, particularly in prudential matters. Increasingly, one may also regard reporting as a form of accountability as a wider concept extending to groups of stakeholders and civic society.[1] This chapter will discuss bank and financial institution accountability in all three and interrelated dimensions – to shareholders, to regulators and to the wider public.

7.02 The two traditional objectives of reporting by banks and financial institutions viz accountability to the capital markets and to regulators have tended to go

---

1 R McCormick, 'What Makes a Bank a "Sustainable Bank?"'(2012) *Law and Economics Yearly Review* 77; R McCormick, 'Towards a more sustainable financial system: The role of civil society Parts 1 and 2' (2012) 6 *Law and Financial Markets Review* 129 and 200.

hand in hand. Corporate reporting to the capital markets, largely dominated by financial reporting,[2] is scrutinised by the financial regulator[3] in order to consider the prudential position of a bank or financial institution. Micro-prudential reporting by banks and financial institutions that is aimed at meeting regulatory requirements, is also used to assist investors in exercising market discipline, reinforcing the regulatory objectives in microprudential regulation. This is known as the Pillar 3 of the Basel II Capital Accord, an internationally agreed template for capital adequacy in banks.[4]

The global financial crisis of 2008–9 has however raised the following question: **7.03** as banks and financial institutions are accountable to regulatory supervisors and the capital markets, why did the disclosures made by banks and financial institutions leading up to the crisis not reveal any signs, resulting in regulators and capital markets being taken by surprise at the onset of the crisis? This question has resulted in discussions and reflections along the following themes which will be explored in this chapter:

(a)   are the disclosures adequate for the purposes of enabling investors and regulators to see signs of stress that may unravel in the ultimately troubled institutions? In particular, is the adoption or otherwise of the fair value standard of valuation for assets appropriate for the disclosures made? A related question is whether auditors should have signed off 'going concern' statements made by directors of the ultimately troubled institutions, and what such 'going concern' certifications mean in the light of subsequent catastrophic collapses;

(b)   are the disclosures inadequate for one or both of the objectives of facilitating investor discipline and micro-prudential supervision carried out by financial regulators? In particular, are there conflicts between the objectives that affect the disclosure regime as such?

(c)   are the disclosures adequate but unable to support either or both investor discipline and regulatory supervision due to weaknesses in investor discipline or regulatory supervision?

It is arguable that the purposes of capital market transparency and regulatory reporting for the purposes of prudential supervision could come into conflict especially at times of stress. Regulatory intervention in resolving a financial

---

2   See generally, C Villiers, *Corporate Reporting and Company Law* (CUP 2006).
3   G Song, 'The benefits of decoupling financial reporting from bank capital regulation' (2012), available at: http://ssrn.com/abstract=1955453.
4   Bank for International Settlements, *Basel II: International Convergence of Capital Measurement and Capital Standards: A Revised Framework – Comprehensive Version* (June 2006), available at: http://www.bis.org/publ/bcbs128.htm.

institution in an orderly manner may be helped by confidentiality, as market disruptions could occur as a result of information release.[5]

7.04 This chapter will first, explore the financial reporting regime imposed on banks and financial institutions, in particular, whether the incurred loss accounting methodology for valuing assets on banks' and financial institutions' balance sheets has contributed to the significant episodes of asset losses experienced by troubled financial institutions in the crisis. The chapter will explore the issue of whether adopting fair value accounting would address the above issue or cause further concerns. The academic debate on the appropriate accounting measure to address the valuation issues that arose in the global financial crisis is a somewhat divided one. This arguably raises a broader issue regarding the nature and adequacy of financial reporting in general, which as will be discussed, is being addressed in the UK via a package of measures led by the government and the Financial Reporting Council to boost narrative reporting (and director stewardship) and shareholder stewardship. This chapter will critically discuss the UK's approach. It will then suggest that accountability to the capital markets and accountability to regulators by banks and financial institutions will in the future develop along somewhat bifurcated lines. This is due to international enhancements in micro-prudential and macro-prudential regulation of banks and financial institutions, creating more comprehensive and detailed regimes for regulatory reporting, supervision and dialogue between regulators and regulatees. These new frameworks are based on specific objectives in mitigating systemic risk and do not necessarily dovetail with the purposes that serve the needs of capital markets. The chapter will explore the implications for banks and financial institution reporting under the new Basel III regime in international micro-prudential regulation[6] and the development of macro-prudential regulation in the EU and UK.[7] Finally, the chapter will critically explore the wider realm of accountability in banks' and financial institutions' sustainability or citizenship reports, largely voluntary disclosures made to discuss 'environmental social and governance issues' (ESG). ESG reporting is

---

5 The thoughts of Michael McKee, consulting editor to this volume, are gratefully acknowledged. Michael refers to this dilemma as being acknowledged pre-crisis when he was Executive Directive at the British Bankers' Association, 2000–2007.

6 BIS, *Basel III: A Global Regulatory Framework for More Resilient Banks and Banking Systems* (June 2011) at http://www.bis.org/bcbs/basel3.htm. This is largely implemented in Directive 2013/36/EU of the European Parliament and of the Council of 26 June 2013 on access to the activity of credit institutions and the prudential supervision of credit institutions and investment firms, amending Directive 2002/87/EC and repealing Directives 2006/48/EC and 2006/49/EC (CRD IV Directive) and Regulation (EU) No 575/2013 of the European Parliament and of the Council of 26 June 2013 on prudential requirements for credit institutions and investment firms and amending Regulation (EU) No 648/2012.

7 See for example, I H-Y Chiu, 'Macro-prudential supervision: Critically examining the developments in the UK, EU and internationally' (2012) *Law and Financial Markets Review* 184.

generally regarded as being relevant to the capital markets, but the audience for such reporting may be wider.[8]

2. FINANCIAL REPORTING BY BANKS AND FINANCIAL INSTITUTIONS

Banks and financial institutions whether listed or otherwise are subject to **7.05** financial reporting as part of corporate reporting.[9] Where banks or financial institutions are listed or quoted, corporate accountability to the capital markets is also underpinned by financial reporting. Company and securities law reporting has been to a large extent harmonised under European legislation[10] requiring yearly and half-yearly financial reporting to the capital markets. Financial reporting in the European Union (EU) has also been standardised[11] by the adoption of the International Financial Reporting Standards[12] (IFRS), making financial reports issued by quoted and listed companies in the EU comparable and in line with the single market objective. The IFRS adoption has generally been perceived as a boost to the corporate transparency regimes, improving reliability of corporate reporting especially in jurisdictions underpinned by strong enforcement regimes.[13]

The adoption of the IFRS for all financial reporting by listed and quoted **7.06** companies in the EU means that quoted and listed banks and financial

---

8 See discussion in I H-Y Chiu, 'Standardization in corporate social responsibility reporting and a universalist concept of CSR?: A path paved with good intentions' (2010/2011) 22 *Florida Journal of International Law* 361.

9 Council Directive of 8 December 1986 on the annual accounts and consolidated accounts of banks and other financial institutions (86/635/EEC).

10 Article 4, Directive 2004/109/EC of the European Parliament and of the Council of 15 December 2004

on the harmonisation of transparency requirements in relation to information about issuers whose securities are admitted to trading on a regulated market and amending Directive 2001/34/EC (Transparency Directive 2004) and art 46, Council Directive 78/660/EEC (Fourth Company Law Directive, 1978) on annual reporting, and art 5, Transparency Directive 2004 on half-yearly reporting. These have been transposed into Listing and Disclosure Rules enacted by the UK Financial Services Authority (1997–2012).

11 The pros and cons of standardisation in accounting standards for reporting purposes are discussed generally in C Roberts, P Weetman and P Gordon, *International Corporate Reporting* (Financial Times/Prentice Hall 2008) and in particular at 15.

12 Commission Regulation (EC) No 1126/2008 of 3 November 2008 adopting certain international accounting standards in accordance with Regulation (EC) No 1606/2002 of the European Parliament and of the Council (latest text) as amended by Commission Regulation (EU) No 475/2012 of 5 June 2012 amending Regulation (EC) No 1126/2008 adopting certain international accounting standards in accordance with Regulation (EC) No 1606/2002 of the European Parliament and of the Council as regards International Accounting Standard (IAS) 1 and International Accounting Standard (IAS) 19.

13 H Daske, L Hail, C Leuz and R Verdi, 'Mandatory IFRS reporting around the world: Early evidence on the economic consequences' (University of Chicago Working Paper 2008), available at: http://ssrn.com/abstract=1024240; M N Houqe, T van Zijl, K Dunstan and A K M Waresul Karim, 'The effect of IFRS adoption and investor protection on earnings quality around the world' (2012) 47 *International Journal of Accounting* 333.

institutions have been adhering to the accounting standards adopted by the International Accounting Standards Board (IASB, which issues the IFRS) since 2002. In the wake of the global financial crisis, it is questioned whether IAS39, which was at that time the accounting standard relating to valuation of loans, receivables and held to maturity instruments, has contributed to the lack of market discipline in the run-up to the crisis. In other words, the reporting effect of IAS39 may have blunted market discipline, which could otherwise have been stepped up earlier. Market discipline could perhaps have provided impetus for adjustments to behaviour by banks and financial institutions, resulting in a softer landing in the global financial crisis.[14]

7.07 IAS39 requires 'loans and receivables' and 'held to maturity investments' to be measured at amortised cost using the effective interest method. This results in interest being recognised in profit and loss based on the financial instrument's original effective interest rate, irrespective of whether there is a change in market interest rates or future cash flows from the instrument. The effect of IAS39 is that any gains or impairments to assets based on changes in market values would not be recognised until incurred. In the global financial crisis, this has mainly resulted in a significant delay in banks reporting their impaired assets, so that banks and capital markets have carried on procyclical behaviour until very late. The global financial crisis is generally regarded to have been triggered by the failure of US investment bank Lehman Brothers, which along with an earlier number of US and European banks had exhibited signs of stress with a large portfolio of impaired assets. These impaired assets were securitised products based on residential mortgages, some tranches of which were sub-prime mortgages in the US which had been granted indiscriminately and defaulted upon.[15] Subprime defaults had started occurring before the onset of the first signs of the global financial crisis. However, as European banks do not need to recognise potential market value impairments to assets held to maturity, bank balance sheets continued to look healthy under the reporting methodology in IAS39.

7.08 The argument is therefore that the IAS39 methodology of not recognising impairment in asset values until incurred is flawed as it delivers transparency to investors only after the fact. If transparency with regard to expected losses to asset values had been made earlier, investors may have been in a better position to exercise market discipline and this could have had an impact on bank

---

14 G Gebhardt and Z Novotny-Farkas, 'Mandatory IFRS adoption and accounting quality of European banks' (2010), available at: http://ssrn.com/abstract=1732166.

15 R E Mendales, 'Collateralized explosive devices: Why securities regulation failed to prevent the CDO meltdown, and how to fix it' (2008), available at: http://ssrn.com/abstract = 1354062, (2009) *University of Illinois Law Review* 1359; R W Kolb (ed.), *Lessons from the Financial Crisis* (John Wiley & Co 2010) generally.

behaviour.[16] Such an 'expected losses' methodology in valuing assets would be the fair value accounting methodology adopted to a larger extent in the US.

The fair value accounting (FVA) methodology of valuing assets requires assets **7.09** held on books to be adjusted for market value changes. Under the US GAAP (FAS 157), fair value is the amount at which an asset could be bought or sold in a current transaction between willing parties, or transferred to an equivalent party, other than in a liquidation sale. This is used for assets whose carrying value is based on mark-to-market valuations; for assets carried at historical cost, the fair value of the asset is not used. It is argued that if FVA had been used to report asset impairments to banks' significant portfolios of mortgaged-based securitised assets, such reporting would have been made earlier, giving fair warning to investors to act and exercise discipline, and also providing regulators with the necessary information to look into the financial health of banks.[17]

However, it may also be argued that FVA, being based on market values (or a **7.10** mark-to-model values where a ready market is not available for the asset concerned) also suffers from certain drawbacks. A European Central Bank study in 2004 identified that FVA suffers from the following weaknesses:[18] first, FVA has to reflect market price volatility in asset prices and precipitates short-termist financial reporting which may not be accurate.[19] Reporting of asset prices in such a manner may reinforce procyclical behaviour, i.e. imprudent or profligate behaviour may be augmented in times when earnings are booked due to inflation of asset prices, but excessive squeezes and contractions, and volatile asset losses reinforced by an illiquid market, can occur in times of asset losses. Inter-temporal shocks are not smoothed out under the FVA approach and systemic risk could more easily entail. Further, the FVA may not encourage consistency in valuation as some assets that are relatively illiquid could be valued under a mark-to-model approach and it is difficult to compare the internal models of valuation adopted by different financial institutions. It is also argued that FVA is more correlated with systemic risk in a model constructed based on systemic risk indicators such as market illiquidity and

---

16 Suggested by a number of commentators e.g. see M E Barth and W R Landsman, 'How did financial reporting contribute to the financial crisis?' (May 2010), available at: http://ssrn.com/abstract=1601519; T J Linsmeier, 'Financial reporting and financial crises: The case for measuring financial instruments at fair value in the financial statements' (2010), available at: http://ssrn.com/abstract=1775141.

17 Linsmeier, ibid.; C Laux, 'Financial instruments, financial reporting, and financial stability' (2012), available at: http://ssrn.com/abstract=1991825.

18 A Enria et al, 'Fair value accounting and financial stability' (ECB Occasional Paper 2004).

19 This argument is strongly supported in J Kay, 'The market is not the best place to set a fair price for assets', *Financial Times* (London, 17 July 2003).

probable failure of a money centre bank.[20] Haldane[21] argues in his personal capacity that FVA encourages procyclical behaviour, which is undesirable from the macro-prudential point of view. He is of the view that FVA allows banks and financial institutions to report significant profits on the back of asset appreciation and hence banks and financial institutions have been very support-ive of FVA in the good times. However, FVA tends to exacerbate ill-health reporting by banks and financial institutions in bad times, and this is particu-larly pertinent to banks as the very nature of their assets and liabilities is more susceptible to volatility. Assets with credit risk generally have no ready market and could be marked down severely in times where there is a general loss of market confidence, and trading assets would be susceptible to marking down as market prices would be artificially depressed in abnormally illiquid conditions. He argues that the very procyclical nature of FVA makes it unsuitable as an accounting standard for the valuation of bank balance sheets. Shaffer[22] also argues that FVA creates undesirable effects of depressed market values in illiquid crisis times for assets that are not held for trading and whose losses are booked and not realised. In such a case, would it be necessary to report artificially high book losses for such assets, and would such reporting result in overly pessimistic market assessments that may affect systemic risk? The arguments against the adoption of FVA show that capital market needs for reporting may diverge from the needs of regulators who are focused on financial stability.

7.11 On the other hand, dissenting commentators argue that the arguments against FVA are based on prudential and regulatory concerns, and not on the needs of the capital markets.[23] Laux[24] in particular argues that the FVA meets the needs of the capital markets that desire timely information for efficient monitoring, and if the FVA gives rise to undesirable behaviour on the part of banks and financial institutions in terms of imprudence and exacerbating institutional and systemic risk, then those effects need to be corrected by regulatory intervention and best practices in corporate governance, and not by discarding the FVA. However, can the champions of the FVA merely rest on the argument that the FVA is valid as it dovetails with efficient capital market needs and not consider any responsibility for the ensuing procyclical behaviour that the FVA reinforces? The debates regarding the FVA have brought into sharp focus the

---

20 U Khan, 'Does fair value accounting contribute to systemic risk in the banking industry?' (2010), available at: http://ssrn.com/abstract=1327596.
21 A Haldane, 'Discussion of "Financial instruments, financial reporting, and financial stability" by Christian Laux (2012)' (2012) 42 *Accounting and Business Research* 261.
22 S Shaffer, 'Evaluating the impact of fair value accounting on financial institutions: Implications for accounting standards setting and bank supervision' (2012), available at: http://ssrn.com/abstract=2006381.
23 Barth and Landsman, see above n 16.
24 Laux, see above n 17.

potential contest and conflict in the objectives of investor and regulatory accountability. However, the ECB paper mentioned above[25] also recognises that FVA could be useful for regulators in terms of delivering timely and forward-looking information for monitoring and supervision. However, can the FVA be adopted in such a way that its potential drawbacks and systemic effects discussed above may be mitigated? Song's research[26] indicates that FVA applied to asset valuations has marked consequences upon the requirements of capital adequacy, and hence the FVA may not be a reporting standard that is apt for regulatory accountability as fluctuating asset values may trigger unexpected capital adequacy requirements and could in turn give rise to greater risk of institutional stress and systemic risk. This also raises the issue of whether financial reporting by banks and financial institutions should be separately prepared and made for the different respective audiences as there seem to be conflicting needs between the capital markets that desire timely disclosure and regulators that need reporting to be carried out in accordance with the needs of financial stability. This could also be an issue of short-termist disclosure in the interests of capital markets efficiency versus relatively longer-termist perspectives taken by regulators regarding the financial health and prudential safety of banks and financial institutions. Song's research suggests that FVA should be devoted only to capital markets reporting and decoupled from regulatory returns.[27]

The potential bifurcation of capital markets accountability and regulatory **7.12** accountability is not the official line as this understandably causes banks and financial institutions to incur more cost and regulatory burden.[28] However, commentators point out that the divergent objectives of accountability to investors and prudential regulation have already been noticed by banks and financial institutions and resulted in dual approaches to reporting. Klumpes and Welch[29] observe empirically that banks and financial institutions do not disclose risk weighted values of assets in reporting to shareholders as asset values may be lower upon the application of risk weights under the Basel II Accord. Hence, balance sheets may appear stronger than they actually are, and one way to correct this impression is to apply FVA and risk weightings jointly in order to provide an accurate picture to both capital markets and regulators. It is thus arguable that banks and financial institutions already do not sufficiently perceive that prudential reporting is also necessary for capital markets. This

---

25 Enria et al, see above n 18.
26 Song, see above n 3.
27 Ibid.
28 Enria et al, see above n 18; Barth and Landsman, see above n 18.
29 P J Klumpes and P Welch, 'Never the twain shall meet? Addressing the disconnect between banks' financial and regulatory reporting' (2011), available at: http://ssrn.com/abstract=1763817.

could give rise to a readier acceptance of a more pronounced bifurcation between capital markets reporting and regulatory returns to regulators in due course. Haldane[30] seems to prefer a dual approach as he advocates a crisis-neutral financial reporting regime unique to banks and financial institutions, and his suggested approach caters most to the needs of financial stability. Having separate accountability regimes legitimates the imposition of unique regulatory requirements for prudential monitoring, which could become more and more pertinent with the rise of micro-prudential and macro-prudential monitoring that will be discussed shortly. Such regulatory requirements may be rolled out more responsively and dynamically without necessarily needing to compromise the needs of capital markets reporting. Another advantage is that regulatory requirements need not be shackled to accounting standards and professional rules.

7.13 Further, the European Banking Authority's ('EBA') proposal[31] to moderate certain fair valued bank assets using a 'prudent valuation' method for calculating capital adequacy needed to support the trading book further reinforces the bifurcation between meeting regulatory requirements and being accountable to the capital markets. Reporting to regulators is being refined so that bank balance sheets may be clear and capable of regulatory scrutiny for the purposes of micro and macro-prudential supervision, but not all such forms of reporting may be suitable for capital markets as there may be implications for stock price and cost of capital.

7.14 On the other hand, separate regimes for financial reporting by banks and financial institutions to investors and to regulators could be an opportunity for arbitrage. Banks and financial institutions could legitimately neglect micro-prudential information in their annual reports and focus on the usual earnings information that capital markets need. However, several commentators[32] have pointed out that as banks and financial institutions have unique asset profiles as distinguished from many other corporate sectors, prudential information is particularly important for investors to assess the strength of the balance sheet, risk profiles and future performance.

---

30 Haldane, see above n 21.
31 European Banking Authority, *Discussion Paper Relating to Draft Regulatory Technical Standards on prudent valuation under Article 100 of the draft Capital Requirements Regulation (CRR)* (13 Nov 2012), BA/DP/2012/03. Final Regulatory Standards were issued on 31 March 2014.
32 B J Hirtle, 'What market risk capital reporting tells us about bank risk' *Federal Reserve Bank of New York Economic Policy Review*, 2003; R P Bartlett III, 'Making banks transparent' (2012) 65 *Vanderbilt Law Review* 293.

At the moment there does not seem to be a marked resolve towards separating **7.15** clearly the financial reporting regimes for capital markets and prudential supervision. In light of the debate on IAS39 versus FVA, the IASB has introduced modifications to IAS39, and to phase out IAS39 by 2015 by replacing with IFRS 9.[33] The interim modification to IAS39 requires expected losses to be accounted for in credit-based assets upon 'objective evidence' of impairment. Ultimately, the IFRS 9 will move towards an expected losses approach[34] to valuing credit-based assets in consultation and compromise with the US-based Financial Accounting Standards Board (FASB).[35] These negotiations will affect the final shape of the IFRS 9 which is ongoing pending final implementation in 2015.

It is clear that the IASB has taken on board criticisms of the amortised cost **7.16** reporting standard in IAS39 and is determined to introduce a standard that '[will] make it easier for users of financial statements to understand the financial reporting information'.[36] The term 'users' is left open, and commentators to the IASB's consultation include the Basel Committee of Banking Supervision that supports the new approach, as well as banks, bankers' associations, central banks and professional bodies all over the world. However, this does not mean that complete reconciliation has been achieved between the objectives sought to be met by financial reporting to investors as well as to regulators. This chapter suggests that the needs of capital markets have been more at the forefront in the accounting standard reform of IAS39, leaving prudential regulators to introduce other measures to deal with systemic risk issues. Further, the accounting standards for reporting are very much based on the values and principles held by professional bodies such as the IASB and FASB,[37] and the final determination of such standards would be shaped by deliberations which are dominated by the professional bodies. It is queried as to what extent professional bodies would be cognisant of the needs for prudential reporting to and monitoring by regulators, and whether this phenomenon provides some support for considering bifurcation in the reporting regimes to investors and regulators. This argument however could equally be countered if we view the professional role of the accounting bodies as providing an objective yardstick for evaluating and understanding the financial profile of banks and financial institutions, balancing against the operation of overly discretionary regulator evaluations and decisions.

---

33 http://www.ifrs.org/current-projects/iasb-projects/financial-instruments-a-replacement-of-ias-39-financial-instruments-recognitio/Pages/financial-instruments-replacement-of-ias-39.aspx.

34 IASB, *Basis for Conclusions: Financial Instruments: Amortised Cost and Impairment* (Nov 2009).

35 IASB, *Financial Instruments: Impairment* (Jan 2011).

36 IASB, *Basis for Conclusions*, see above n 34, para BC2.

37 IASB, *Financial Instruments*, see above n 35.

7.17 Going forward, the chapter suggests that although financial reporting by banks and financial institutions may not be officially split for the purposes of capital markets accountability and regulatory accountability, the rise in micro-prudential and macro-prudential regulation after 2009 means that banks and financial institutions have to make many unique and separate returns to regulators anyway. Such returns include an expanded range of micro-prudential ratios such as liquidity ratios and perhaps the leverage ratio, stress testing reporting, corporate governance and remuneration reporting and other information that may be necessary to assist in macro-prudential supervision, a recently developed and evolving concept.[38] Further, investment banks exposed to market risks will also be required to comply with additional reporting requirements in relation to trading – transaction reporting the Markets in Financial Instruments Regulation and Directive II respectively;[39] and the reporting of over-the-counter derivatives transactions under the European Market Infrastructure Regulation.[40] These expanded requirements would effectively put in place a new and diverging regime for banks and financial institutions dedicated to regulatory accountability.

7.18 Further, the debate between FVA and alternative approaches to valuing financial instruments such as through-the-cycle approaches[41] or a variation of the amortised cost approach gives rise to the broader question of how far hard numbers tell an objective story of financial institution profiles. Lopes[42] argues that numbers represent the intrinsic assumptions and principles built into them and it would be misleading to treat them simplistically as an end in themselves without contextualising them against the assumptions and principles. Ambler et al also argue that '[i]n an era where intangible assets are increasingly dominating, in value terms, the tangible assets, the formal accounts are becoming less reliable indicators of the company's trading and financial position'.[43] In the UK, there is a marked movement towards mitigating the power of communication through numbers in order to encourage capital markets to take more considered views of all information instead of latching on to numbers for

---

38   See for example, Bank of England and Financial Services Authority, *Instruments of Macro-prudential Policy* (Discussion Paper, Dec 2011).

39   See MiIFD II Directive 2014, and Markets in Financial Instruments Regulation 2014.

40   The Regulation (EU) No 648/2012 of the European Parliament and of the Council of 4 July 2012 on OTC derivatives, central counterparties (CCPs) and trade repositories (TRs) (EMIR) entered into force on 16 August 2012.

41   Suggested but rejected in IASB, *Basis for Conclusions*, see above n 34.

42   D S Lopes, 'Making oneself at home with numbers: Financial reporting from an ethnographic perspective' (2011) 19 *Social Anthropology* 463.

43   T Ambler and A Neely, 'Narrative reporting in company annual accounts' (2007), available at: http://ssrn.com/abstract=1030724 at 2.

short-hand assessments. However, it is important to note why financial reporting has become important over the years – financial metrics has become an objective, neutral form of performance assessment,[44] 'financialising' the corporation and correspondingly depoliticising and de-socialising the role of the corporation.[45] In order to move away from the domination of financial reporting, policy initiatives need to be matched with a change in corporate and investment culture.

The rise in narrative reporting is a response to the perceived insufficiency of **7.19** financial reporting. Narrative reporting may be regarded as serving two purposes. One is to improve the quality of engagement with corporate reporting by both senior management and shareholders so that capital markets discipline is meaningful, considered and not merely knee-jerk and responsive to superficial signals. However, one should note that this requires a deeper movement towards changed perspectives by management and investors as to what corporate performance means and the role of shareholder stewardship.[46] Second, narrative reporting may ameliorate any adverse consequences as a result of the move towards FVA or an expected losses approach in financial reporting. Financial reporting could be contextualised against the backdrop of the narrative explanations so that capital markets reactions may be more nuanced and considered, and unnecessarily volatile behaviour that may threaten systemic stability could be prevented. The next section will now turn to the rise of narrative reporting.

3. THE RISE IN THE IMPORTANCE OF NARRATIVE REPORTING

It has been recognised for some time that non-financial narrative reporting that **7.20** complements financial reporting is necessary to provide a fuller picture in corporate disclosure. The pioneering effort in the US is Regulation S-K that prescribed a list of financial and non-financial disclosures. The Regulation was enacted by the US Securities Exchange Commission after the Jenkins Report

---

44 J Morales and A Pezet, 'Financialization through hybridisation: The subtle power of financial controlling' in I Huault and C Richard (eds), *Finance: The Discreet Regulator* (Palgrave Macmillan 2012), 19.

45 P Zumbasen, 'The next "great transformation" of markets and states in the transnational space: Global assemblages of corporate governance and financial market regulation' (2009), available at: http://papers.ssrn.com/sol3/papers.cfm?abstract_id=1415463; P Ireland, 'Financialization and corporate governance' (2012), available at: http://papers.ssrn.com/sol3/papers.cfm?abstract_id=2068478, W Lazonick, 'The financialization of the US corporation: What has been lost, and how it can be regained', paper presented at the Adolf A Berle Symposium, University College London, 14–15 June 2012.

46 BIS, *The Kay Review of UK Equity Markets and Long-Term Decision Making* (Final Report, 23 July 2012).

recommended that non-financial disclosure be prescribed.[47] The relevant financial and non-financial disclosure that companies have to produce are consolidated as the Management's Discussion and Analysis of Financial Condition and Results of Operations ('MD&A') which has to be filed annually with the US Securities Exchange Commission.

7.21 The Jenkins Report produced in 1994 proposes a comprehensive model of business reporting. Its aim is to allow users to better understand corporate disclosure as a whole. Financial data is recommended to be disclosed according to segregated lines of business, and extraordinary items are to be mentioned specifically and treated separately. As for non-financial information, information relating to productivity, innovation; management analysis of the relationships between directors, management and shareholders; forward-looking information; information about management and shareholders; objectives and strategy; description of business and industry structure; and risks associated with financial instruments and off-balance sheet financing, are recommended to be disclosed.[48]

7.22 The EU has also been keen to affirm the position of narrative non-financial disclosure that complements financial reporting, and has provided for a minimum harmonisation framework in the Modernisation Directive 2002[49] and Transparency Directive 2004,[50] requiring narrative management reports to be made in the quarters between half yearly and annual financial reports. Quarterly reporting has however been repealed[51] due to concerns that quarterly reporting

---

47 Item 303 of Regulation S-K has been consolidated with Items 303(b) and (c) of Regulation S-B, Item 5 of Form 20-F and Paragraph 11 of General Instruction B of Form 40-F to form the Management's Discussion and Analysis of Financial Condition and Results of Operations, or MD&A, to be filed with the US Securities Exchange Commission.

48 E L Jenkins, 'The AICPA Special Committee on Financial Reporting: Meeting the information needs of users' (1993) 7 NO 11 *Insights* 8, which summarises the 'Jenkins Report' mentioned above. The actual report, *Improving Business Reporting: A Customer Focus* (AICPA 1994), may be found on http://www.aicpa.org/members/div/acctstd/ibr/chap2.htm.

49 Directive 2003/51/EC of the European Parliament and of the Council of 18.6.2003 amending Directives 78/660/EEC, 83/349/EEC, 86/635/EEC and 91/674/EEC on the annual and consolidated accounts of certain types of companies, banks and other financial institutions and insurance undertakings (the EU Modernisation Directive).

50 Article 6, Directive 2004/109/EC of the European Parliament and of the Council of 15 December 2004 on the harmonisation of transparency requirements in relation to information about issuers whose securities are admitted to trading on a regulated market and amending Directive 2001/34/EC.

51 European Commission, Proposal for a Directive of the European Parliament and of the Council amending Directive 2004/109/EC on the harmonisation of transparency requirements in relation to information about issuers whose securities are admitted to trading on a regulated market and Commission Directive 2007/14/EC (2011); and see Commission press release of 12 June 2013, at http://europa.eu/rapid/press-release_MEMO-13-544_en.htm?locale=en.

may fuel short-termism in capital markets. It is uncertain to what extent the EU may continue to champion for harmonised narrative corporate reporting frameworks.

The UK has however seen steady policy support for narrative reporting despite **7.23** the unfortunate episode regarding the 'Operating and Financial Review'[52] in 2005 which the chapter will not belabour. In its overhaul of company law reform which culminated in the Companies Act 2006, the UK introduced an expanded directors' business review for quoted and listed companies, that requires narrative reporting of non-financial performance as well as information regarding the environmental impact of corporate activities, and stakeholder and community relations.[53]

In the wake of the global financial crisis, the role of narrative reporting has been **7.24** emphatically affirmed. Narrative reporting is seen as a response to the question why corporate reporting by banks and financial institutions leading up to the crisis has failed to flag up serious issues of concern, particularly in relation to 'going concern' certifications. A post-crisis examination into the role and responsibility of corporate reporting leading up to the crisis was undertaken in order to ascertain what corporate reporting could and should have said about the prospects of certain banks and financial institutions carrying on as 'going concerns'. The Sharman Inquiry appointed by the Financial Reporting Council ('FRC) in the UK carried out this review and the final conclusions of the inquiry[54] obliquely criticised the capital markets for latching onto shorthand financial information such as 'going concern' certifications. The inquiry made recommendations towards more narrative reporting by directors in order to contextualise their decisions, account to shareholders and invite shareholders' considered engagement in respect of the disclosures made by each individual institution.

---

52 DTI, *Draft Regulations on The Operating and Financial Review and Directors' Report: A Consultative Document* (May 2004), available at: www.dti.gov.uk/cld/pdfs/ofr-condoc.htm, ('Consultation paper'), the OFR Regulations 2005 which were rapidly repealed in the same year.

53 Companies Act 2006, s 417. See for example, I Havercroft and A Reisberg, 'Directors' duties under the UK Companies Act 2006 and the impact of the company's operations on the environment' (2010), available at: http://papers.ssrn.com/sol3/papers.cfm?abstract_id=1274567. See also I H-Y Chiu, 'The paradigms for mandatory non-financial disclosure: A conceptual analysis – Parts 1 and 2' (2006) *Company Lawyer* 259 and 291, where it is argued that such narrative reporting relates to non-financial disclosure of non-financial performance indicators and evaluation, and is not a fully fledged 'corporate responsibility' report as such.

54 See The Sharman Inquiry, *Going Concern and Liquidity Risks: Lessons for Companies and Auditors, Final Report and Recommendations of the Panel of Inquiry* (June 2012), available at: http://www.frc.org.uk/getattachment/ 591a5e2a-35d7–4470-a46c-30c0d8ca2a14/Sharman-Inquiry-Final-Report.aspx.

7.25   The FRC[55] has implemented most of the Sharman Inquiry recommendations. It acknowledges the importance of the status of a going concern certification as the board's judgement made on the basis of evaluating solvency, liquidity and business risks in the overall context of business strategy and prospects, and internal and external shocks in the foreseeable future. However, the FRC also accepts that the investor community needs more qualititative information regarding longer-term viability of listed companies and has recommended that directors produce a viability statement to discuss the position of the company in a period exceeding 12 months.[56] The Council also clarifies that bank access to liquidity facilities offered by the Central Bank does not immediately mean that the bank is no longer a going concern.[57] This is because such facilities may be regularly available to solvent and viable banks and any access to liquidity facilities provided by the Central Bank must be considered as part of the board's judgement on the overall viability and prospects of the business. There is clearly a greater emphasis on framing corporate transparency as communicating the board's judgements and inviting dialogue and scrutiny. The board's judgement in making going concern certification in all corporates, and not just banks, is contextualised in the narrative reporting[58] that should reflect the board's overall stewardship and accountability to capital markets. Further, the viability statement provides longer-term qualitative signals about the solvency prospects of the company. Although the 'going concern' certification is not to be completely absorbed into a form of narrative reporting and remains a distinct signal in corporate transparency, investors are urged to engage more with the narrative aspects of reporting in the reformed Strategic Report, as will shortly be discussed, and the longer-term viability statement.

7.26   Narrative reporting is arguably seen as a way to present complex and nuanced information that could stem knee-jerk market panics, providing a more holistic discussion than in the presentation of hard numbers. It could also invite capital markets to critically engage in scrutiny, restoring the robust role of shareholders in corporate governance. Narrative reporting is also seen as a way to compel senior management and directors to engage with taking responsibility in reporting. The Sharman Inquiry believes that making the role of narrative reporting robust would be necessary to provide capital markets with more accurate transparency for scrutiny and engagement and the answer to making

---

55   Financial Reporting Council, *Implementing the Recommendations of the Sharman Panel: Revised Guidance on Going Concern and Revised International Standards on Auditing (UK and Ireland)* (January 2013); FRC, *Guidance on Risk Management, Internal Control and Related Financial and Business Reporting* (Sep 2014).

56   FRC, *Guidance on Risk Management, Internal Control and Related Financial and Business Reporting* (Sep 2014).

57   FRC, *Guidance on Going Concern Supplement for Banks* (January 2013).

58   FRC, 'Implementing the Recommendations of the Sharman Panel', see above n 56, 16.

corporate reporting by banks and financial institutions more effective does not lie in a separate financial reporting regime for them.

The Sharman Inquiry has brought to the fore the undesirable tendencies of **7.27** capital markets to rely on shorthand information contained in hard numbers such as earnings and 'going concern' certifications, and is a reminder that corporate financial reporting serves the more comprehensive purpose of engaging shareholders in scrutiny of directors' decision-making, which is the essential corporate governance issue. The inquiry emphatically states[59] that 'going concern' certifications in particular are not an end in themselves but rather the end of a process of deliberation and decision-making by directors using good faith and skilled judgement regarding the strategy, business planning and risks of the company concerned. Directors should substantiate the 'going concern' certification decisions in their directors' review through narrative reporting.[60] The 'going concern' certification should thus not be taken out of context or as a symptomatic piece of shorthand information for simplistic reliance without critical engagement in the comprehensive matrix of corporate reporting.

The Sharman Inquiry affirms the initiative undertaken by the FRC earlier in **7.28** calling for directors' narrative reporting in the directors' business review to be more focused on directors' roles as 'effective company stewards'. In particular, directors should report in narrative on strategic risks and the major operational risks inherent in their business model and their strategy for implementing that business model, explaining how they will address those risks and any obstacles that may be encountered as a result of changes in the business environment.[61] The directors' review should therefore capture how the role of directors has been discharged in stewardship of the company's business. The council also recommends that audit committees be given an expanded role in monitoring directors in their stewardship and risk management roles and should separately report on that.[62] This initiative is of course applicable to the corporate sector generally and not just to the banking and financial sector.

The UK Government is fully supportive of the move towards expanded **7.29** narrative reporting by directors and commenced a process to overhaul the directors' business review in section 417 of the Companies Act 2006 in early

---

59   Sharman Inquiry, see above n 55, paras 5 and 6.
60   Ibid, para 7.
61   FRC, *Effective Company Stewardship: Enhancing Corporate Reporting and Audit* (Jan 2011), available at: http://www.frc.org.uk/Our-Work/Publications/FRC-Board/Effective-Company-Stewardship-Enhancing-Corporate.aspx.
62   See Chapter 4 of this volume.

2012 i.e. to replace the directors' business review with a Strategic Report.[63] The rise in the importance of narrative reporting could compel directors to pay attention to and take responsibility for the disclosures made to capital markets and also forces shareholders to engage in critical and measured scrutiny.[64] Transparency and accountability are not regarded as giving rise to automatic outcomes but as a means to decision-making by participants in the capital markets.

7.30   The government envisages the Strategic Report to be a high-level report for shareholders where the board of directors would set out the strategy, direction and challenges facing the company, evidenced by high-level financial and remuneration information. This report would provide clear information about the company's business strategy, the business model and risks of the company to the financial results and the resulting rewards for the company's directors. Much of this report will incorporate the content from the directors' business review that is currently required by the Companies Act 2006, supplemented by high-level information from the financial statements and other sources. The report therefore includes strategy, risk management and remuneration issues as being integral to risk management. The government would also take the opportunity to require new and simplified disclosures for executive remuneration in single total figures for greater understanding by users.

7.31   In August 2013, the Companies Act 2006 was amended by the Companies Act 2006 (Strategic Report and Directors' Report) Regulations 2013[65] which implements the Strategic Report to replace the directors' business review in the now superseded section 417 of the Companies Act 2006.[66] The Strategic Report now incorporates the former requirements of the superseded directors' business review in section 417 of the Companies Act, as well as a description of the company's strategy, business model and gender diversity on the board, in senior management and in employees. The Strategic Report in its final shape seems to place less emphasis on risk management as the BIS consultation paper suggested. Further, it seems more like the old directors' business review with an added descriptive component. It remains uncertain how far the re-named Strategic Report will actually become a high-level narrative report useful for providing a key overview to shareholders.

---

63   BIS, *The Future of Narrative Reporting* (Consultation Paper, Sep 2011); BIS, *The Future of Narrative Reporting: The Government's Response* (March 2012).

64   UK Stewardship Code 2010; see critical account in I H-Y Chiu, 'Institutional shareholders as stewards: Towards a new conception of corporate governance?' (2012) *Brooklyn Journal of Financial, Corporate and Commercial Law* 387; I H-Y Chiu 'Turning Institutional Investors into "stewards"– Exploring the meaning and objectives in "stewardship"' (2013) *Current Legal Problems* 1.

65   SI 2013/1970.

66   Companies Act 2006, s 414A.

In general, narrative reporting may be criticised[67] as being too subjective and **7.32** qualitative. This issue is still alive even with the current shape of the Strategic Report. The legislation refers to narrative reporting as a 'description' and the key challenge for narrative reporting is how it could be unique, conveying information pertinent to the company concerned and yet objective, allowing investors to find such information meaningful and comparable. Recent research has shown that investors value narrative reporting as traditional forms of financial reporting are less able to capture the changing asset profiles of businesses,[68] and they frequently make forward-looking assessments on earnings potential based on narrative reporting.[69] But the scope for comparability[70] as well as more information that contributes to forward-looking assessments, such as brand equity,[71] could be improved.

However, research has also shown that narrative corporate reporting engages in **7.33** 'impression management',[72] which relates to the way information is presented in order to be perceived favourably. There are various drivers for impression management in corporate reporting, such as the desire on the part of corporations to maintain the legitimacy of certain corporate actions or decisions, to manage investor relations, or even to explain away negative information. Corporations engage in various communication formats, selective detail of disclosure, frames of expression and language manipulation to achieve impression management.[73] The reliability of narrative reporting is thus affected by management's self-serving bias in impression management. The FRC seems keenly aware of the perennial issues surrounding narrative reporting and has therefore issued a guidance for the Strategic Report.

---

67 L Holder-Webb, 'The question of disclosure: Providing a tool for evaluating managements' discussion and analysis' (2007) 10 *Advances in Accounting Behavioral Research* 183.

68 P Yeoh, 'Narrative reporting: The UK experience' (2010) 52 *International Journal of Law and Management* 211; S Mouselli and K Hussainey, 'Disclosure quality and stock returns in the UK' (2009), available at: http://ssrn.com/abstract=1499258; D Campbell, M Ridhuan and A Rahman, 'A longitudinal examination of intellectual capital reporting in Marks & Spencer annual reports, 1978–2008' (2010) 42 *British Accounting Review* 56.

69 T Ambler and A Neely, 'Narrative reporting in company annual accounts' (2007), available at: http://ssrn.com/abstract=1030724.

70 Holder-Webb, see above n 6; A C Beck, D Campbell and P J Shrives, 'Content analysis in environmental reporting research: Enrichment and rehearsal of the method in a British–German context" (2010) 42 *British Accounting Review* 207.

71 Ambler and Neely, see above n 70.

72 D M Merkl-Davis and N Brennan, 'Accounting narratives and impression management' in L Jack, J Davison, R Craig (eds), *The Routledge Companion to Communication in Accounting* (2013) at Ch 4; and at http://ssrn.com/abstract=1873188; Merkl-Davis and Brennan, 'A conceptual framework of impression management: New insights from psychology, sociology, and critical perspectives' (2011) 41(5) *Accounting and Business Research* CHK PAGE; D M Merkl-Davis, N Brennan and S Macleay, 'Impression management and retrospective sense-making in corporate narratives: A social psychology perspective' (2010) 24 *Accounting, Audit and Accountability Journal* 315.

73 Merkl-Davis and Brennan, 'Accounting narratives and impression management', ibid.

7.34 The FRC's Guidance[74] provides that the Strategic Report should be fair, balanced and understandable, these being overriding principles applicable to annual reporting as a whole. To achieve these qualities, the council recommends that Strategic Reports contain only concise and material information unique to the company that is relevant to investors, a fair balance of positive and negative information that would affect investors' assessment of the company's performance, be forward-looking in orientation where relevant and written in plain language and clearly signposting how the narrative reporting relates to other parts of the annual report and financial statements.

7.35 The Guidance also provides more detailed recommendations on how each element in the Strategic Report can be reported in a narrative but meaningful manner. In terms of the objectives of the company, the Strategic Report should explain what the objectives are and why they are established, and financial as well as non-financial objectives. The element relating to 'description of business model' should relate to how the company generates and preserves value. In particular, information should be provided regarding how the company is structured, the market in which it operates, its main products, services, customers and its distribution methods, the nature of its relationships and resources, its external environment and future trends and its internal factors and trends such as research. In terms of principal risks and uncertainties, companies should report on the key risks that may affect future performance or threaten viability, in such a way that the range of risks covered are both comprehensive and specifically explained so that investors may be able to make the connection between the identification of certain risks and their likely impact on the company. The risks that should be discussed comprise the full range of business risks including commercial, operational and financial risks. Next, the Guidance recommends that the key performance indicators of the company that should be disclosed are the ones that the directors judge to be the most relevant to the objectives and strategy of the company, and narrative reporting should explain what they are and how they are used to calculate and measure performance. The Guidance also provides on how narrative reporting can be used to meaningfully explain financial statements. The Strategic Report should provide narrative explanations of the cash flow, liquidity positions of the company and how the company intends to fund its strategies. It should also report on the tangible and intangible assets including brand, intellectual property rights and human capital. Finally, in relation to stakeholder matters such as the environment, customer and supplier matters that have been included in the previous directors' business review, the FRC's position is that such matters should be reported in a way that relates them to the performance of the company and the relevance

---

74   FRC, *Final Guidance on the Strategic Report* (Sep 2014).

should be explained. Hence these matters are to be contextualised within the overall objectives, strategy and key performance indicators of the company and are not sustainability reports as such.

The FRC's endeavours in providing rather detailed guidance for the Strategic **7.36** Report highlights its concerns relating to making the narrative report useful and meaningful by improving its objectivity and comparability. The guidelines also highlight the need for directors to be more critically engaged with what is narratively reported as explanations for relevance are often required, compelling firm-specific information to be provided to investors.

The move towards placing more emphasis on narrative reporting as the **7.37** mainstay of capital markets accountability may also mean that less expectations should be placed on the financial auditors' role in vetting financial reporting, as an 'expectations gap'[75] between auditors and users has always existed. This does not mean that the accuracy of financial reporting is no longer important but that some of the perverse effects of over-reliance on financial reporting are sought to be mitigated – such as the desire for shorthand information through hard numbers, superficial market reactions and short-termist market behaviour in response to quarterly financial disclosures.[76] The emphasis on narrative reporting is intended to counter these perverse incentives although the usefulness of narrative is still developing.

There also seems to be a contemporaneous move in the UK towards emphasis- **7.38** ing the primary responsibility of the corporate disclosers, instead of looking for surrogate responsibility in the role of auditors.[77] The new section 414D of the Companies Act compels the board to approve of, and one specific director to sign off, the Strategic Report and every director who knows that the report is non-compliant or is recklessly indifferent as to whether the report is non-compliant and fails to take reasonable steps to secure compliance could be convicted of a criminal offence and subject to a fine. The next section of this chapter will briefly discuss the role of the audit committee as internal gatekeepers for the corporate responsibility in reporting, following which the role and liability of auditors in corporate reporting and the post-crisis developments will be discussed.

---

75   M Ojo, 'Eliminating the audit "expectations gap": Reality or myth?' (2005), available at: http://ssrn.com/abstract=1407199.

76   The disease of 'short-termism' which is reinforced by over-reliance in the investment markets on quarterly earnings disclosures is heavily criticised by A Rappaport, *Saving Capitalism from Short-Termism* (McGraw-Hill 2011) and J C Bogle, *The Clash of the Cultures: Investment vs Speculation* (John Wiley & Sons 2012).

77   I H-Y Chiu, 'The role and liabilities of auditors in financial regulation: Addressing the "expectations gap"' (2012) *International Business Law Journal* 545, but this approach in the UK is contrary to the EU's view of the role of auditors.

4. THE AUDIT COMMITTEE

7.39   Since the 1970s, boards of companies have instituted the audit committee, a separate committee of the board, to be dedicated to monitoring the integrity of financial reporting.[78] In the UK, the fall of BCCI and the scale of its fraudulent financial reporting prompted a review into the integrity of corporate reporting. The Cadbury Review of 1992 reached into corporate governance to call for more non-executive directors (NEDs) to monitor the board, and for the audit committee to comprise of NEDs who would oversee the integrity of internal controls, and the appointment of external auditors, and review financial statements.[79]

7.40   The audit committee has remained a staple feature of best practice in corporate governance in the UK, now enshrined in successive versions of Corporate Governance codes since the Cadbury Code. The Corporate Governance Code now requires that an audit committee should comprise of at least two independent directors, and at least one director should have recent and relevant financial experience.[80] The audit committee is tasked with reviewing the integrity of the financial statements, the internal controls and internal audit in the company, and reviewing the independence of the external auditor to make recommendations with regard to appointment or removal, and to engage with the external auditor.[81] The special role of the audit committee has been emphasised by the Basel Committee, which recommends that the audit committee should have an engaged relationship with the financial institution's external auditor and to maintain robust oversight over the external auditor.[82] However, the primary responsibility for financial reporting lies with the board collectively.[83]

7.41   There is no marked pattern of imposing liability upon audit committee members in cases of financial misreporting.[84] In the UK, individual directors' liability may be established only upon the satisfaction that an individual director has breached his/her duties under the Companies Act 2006.[85] The standard of care expected of executive or NEDs does not appear to differ.[86] Directors are

---

78   See S C. Vera-Muñoz, 'Corporate governance reforms: Redefined expectations of audit committee responsibilities and effectiveness' (2005) 62 *Journal of Business Ethics* 115.

79   The Cadbury Committee, *The Financial Aspects of Corporate Governance* (1992), para 4.33ff.

80   UK Corporate Governance Code 2010, para C.3.1.

81   Ibid., para C.3.2.

82   Basel Committee, *External Audits of Banks* (March 2014).

83   UK Corporate Governance Code 2010, para C.1.1–C.1.3.

84   See also more generally on the position of non-executive directors in B Black, B Cheffins and M Klausner, 'Liability risk for outside directors: A cross-border analysis' (2005) 11 *European Financial Management* 153.

85   Companies Act 2006, ss 171–177, 182.

86   *Dorchester Finance Co. v. Stebbing* [1989] BCLC 498.

however generally expected to have a reasonable level of competence to understand the basic financial position of the company,[87] although financially trained directors may be expected to do more.[88] Where directors persist with trading when the company clearly cannot stave off insolvency, wrongful trading liability may ensue.[89] Under the new section 414D as discussed earlier, the new criminal liability for directors who fail to secure compliant reporting in the Strategic Report would also apply to all directors and not audit committee directors in specific. However, individual directors should bear in mind that changes are afoot in terms of regulatory accountability and the regulator can subject directors to discipline under the new senior persons regime in the Financial Services and Markets Act 2000, as amended by the Financial Services (Banking Reform) Act 2013.[90] Under the new regime, each director would be tied to certain specified responsibilities as agreed with the regulator, and could be held to account for failures in those responsibilities.[91] In exceptional circumstances, senior persons may also be made criminally liable for financial institution failures. The Prudential Regulation Authority, Financial Conduct Authority, Secretary of State or Director of Crown Prosecutions could institute criminal proceedings against senior management who have knowingly taken a decision for the business being aware of the risk of failure that could ensue, and in so doing have fallen below the standard of a reasonable person in his/her shoes and has caused the failure of the financial institution. Hence, additional risks loom for audit committee members in view of the senior persons regime.

7.42 In the US, a number of early millennium corporate scandals involving fraudulent financial reporting such as the fall of Enron have also prompted an overhaul of corporate governance relating to financial reporting. The Sarbanes-Oxley Act 2002 in particular provides that audit committees should consist of largely independent directors, and they are tasked with overseeing the external auditor and whether non-audit services may be provided to the company, and they may have independent powers of investigation into the company's financial affairs at the expense of the company.[92]

7.43 The presence of an audit committee has been empirically documented to have an actual positive effect upon the monitoring of internal controls and systems in

---

87   *Re Brian D Pierson (Contractors) Ltd* [2001] 1 BCLC 275; [1999] BCC 26.
88   *Re Produce Marketing Consortium (No.2)* [1989] BCLC 520.
89   Insolvency Act 1989, s 214.
90   PRA and FCA, *Strengthening Accountability in Banking: A New Regulatory Framework* (July 2014).
91   The Financial Services and Markets Act 2000, as amended by the Financial Services (Banking Reform) Act 2013, ss 66A, 66B.
92   Sarbanes-Oxley Act 2002, s 301.

the company.[93] Further, a string of empirical research also points out that audit committee characteristics such as independence and competence in financial affairs are negatively correlated with financial misreporting or earnings mis-management.[94] Hence, the presence of an audit committee that is engaged with its responsibilities does not merely improve the perception of the integrity of corporate reporting but is likely to have a real positive effect upon corporate accountability in financial reporting to capital markets.

7.44 However, the audit committee's role does not extend to critically considering whether the financial reporting framework itself may be inadequate, as discussed in the FVA debate above, or the issue of whether financial reporting has become too narrowly focused. The audit committee's role only monitors that corporate reporting adheres to the prevailing frameworks and standards. The issue that has arisen in the global financial crisis regarding bank and financial institution reporting is that the financial reporting does not capture a comprehensive picture of risk and risk profiles could have better highlighted the future viability or performance of the financial institution concerned. This is a gap that has been acknowledged not only at the level of corporate reporting, but also at the level of corporate governance.[95] The emerging importance of risk management has sometimes been dealt with at the governance level as a peripheral issue for boards and audit committees,[96] or only dealt with by a department within the corporation as a technical and not strategic matter.[97] The UK Corporate Governance Code was amended in 2012 to require boards to review risk control and management annually.[98] However, the reporting of risk management remains to be developed. The next section considers the role and liability of auditors in corporate reporting, and the debate on whether auditors could provide leadership in enhanced corporate reporting such as in risk reporting.

---

93   Y Gendron and J Be'dard, 'On the constitution of audit committee effectiveness' (2006) 31 *Accounting, Organizations and Society* 211.

94   F DeZoort, D Hermanson, D Archambeault and S Reed, 'Audit committee effectiveness: A synthesis of the empirical audit committee literature' (2002) 21 *Journal of Accounting Literature* 38 and Vera-Muñoz, see above n 79 contain summaries of a string of previous research affirming this position.

95   Sir David Walker, *Review of Corporate Governance in UK Banks and Financial Institutions* (Final, 26 Nov 2009), available at: http://www.hm-treasury.gov.uk/walker_review_information.htm.

96   G Kirkpatrick, 'The corporate governance lessons from the financial crisis' (OECD Report 2009), available at: http://www.oecd.org/dataoecd/32/1/42229620.pdf; M E Murphy, 'Assuring responsible risk management in banking: The corporate governance dimension' (2011) 36 *Delaware Journal of Corporate Law* 121.

97   J V Rizzi, 'Behavioral basis of the financial crisis' in R W Kolb (ed.), *Lessons from the Financial Crisis* (John Wiley & Sons, 2010), 277; M Crouhy, 'Risk management failures during the financial crisis' in Kolb (ed.), 283.

98   UK Corporate Governance Code 2010, para C.2.1.

5. THE ROLE OF AUDITORS

In the financial sector, auditors perform the traditional role of vetting corporate reporting and vetting compliance with rules in financial regulation relating to client money and asset handling. This role has been described by Coffee as a role of 'gatekeeping'.[99] Auditors provide a form of reputational assurance to the market that overcomes the information asymmetry between the market and firm, generating expectations with regard to the 'governance' potential on the part of auditors. **7.45**

One of the expectations linked to the audit is that auditors may be able to detect fraud in corporate reporting. Fraud detection serves as a platform for facilitating market discipline of management. It is argued that there is a significant public perception of the auditor's role as fraud detector,[100] although auditors do not see this as a primary role. Power refers to the audit as a ritual of verification, akin to a label that confirms the integrity of corporate disclosure so that those obscured by the information asymmetry may have the comfort of safety in investment.[101] There is arguably an 'expectations gap' between how auditors and the public see the auditors' role. An 'expectations gap' is a gap between what the auditor does and what users expect the auditors to have done, such as in fraud detection or insolvency prediction for a company. **7.46**

Empirical research shows that auditors may not be able to detect fraud with ease or regularity,[102] although there are also arguments that they are insufficiently incentivised[103] so to do. Further, the limited regime of auditors' civil liability in the UK reinforces the legitimacy of the 'expectations gap'. The limitation of gatekeeper liability is seen as sound as gatekeepers are not directly involved with the causation of loss. The EU's position in the 2008 Commission recommendation[104] is also to limit auditors' civil liability in order not to impede the discharge of auditing functions. **7.47**

---

99 J C Coffee, *Gatekeepers* (OUP 2004); 'Understanding Enron: "It's about the gatekeepers, Stupid"' (2002) 57 *Business Lawyer* 1403.

100 Ojo, see above n 77.

101 M Power, *The Audit Society: Rituals of Verification* (OUP 1999) Chs 1 and 3.

102 Discussed in Chiu, 'The role and liabilities of auditors', see above n 79.

103 C Corona and R S Randhawa, 'The auditor's slippery slope: An analysis of reputational incentives' (2010) 56 *Management Science* 924; Coffee, 'Understanding Enron'; *Gatekeepers*, for both see above n 99: G Fooks, 'Auditors and the permissive society: Market failure, globalisation and financial regulation in the US' (2003) 5 *Risk Management* 17; R C Smith and I Walter, 'The auditors' in *Governing the Modern Corporation* (OUP 2006), 159 and 277.

104 Commission Recommendation of 5 June 2008 concerning the limitation of the civil liability of statutory auditors and audit firms, 2008/473/EC.

7.48 In the UK, civil law imposes severe limitations on which persons could call auditors to account in respect of the financial audit. In the classic case of *Caparo Industries plc v Dickman*,[105] a potential takeover bidder who had built up a shareholding large enough to launch a takeover bid in Fidelity plc sued the auditors Dickman when it was subsequently discovered that a negligent audit had allowed the financial statements to paint a rosier picture of Fidelity's financial health than thought. The House of Lords dismissed the action, on the basis that the auditors did not owe a duty of care to the shareholders at large, and the duty would only be owed in a situation of sufficient proximity between the auditors and the shareholder whose purpose for consulting the financial statements was made known to the auditors in advance. Hence, even if existing and potential investors are reasonably likely to consult and rely on audited financial statements, the civil liability of auditors would not arise at large, a more special relationship has to be established for a duty of care to arise.

7.49 The limitations placed on the parameters of auditors' civil liability have continued in *Stone & Rolls v Moore Stephens*.[106] In that case, the controlling shareholder S of a company Stone & Rolls Ltd sued the auditors Moore Stephens for failing to detect fraud in sham transactions the company had carried out, ultimately causing the company to enter into liquidation. The auditors proceeded to strike out the claim and this was ultimately upheld by the House of Lords. The House reasoned that auditors would owe a duty of care to the company and the body of shareholders as a whole. However, S was the only shareholder and controlling mind of the company and knew that fraud was being carried out. S therefore could not rely on an action against auditors to benefit from his own fraud. The auditors are entitled to the defence of ex turpi causa against S. The majority decision in the House of Lords also suggested that fraudulent acts of persons in the course of business could be imputed to the company itself, such that the company was also precluded from suing its auditors for failure to detect fraud. Watts has criticised this part of the judgment as going too far as companies are an abstraction that act through natural persons, and hence, an imputation of fraud should not easily be made to undermine the separate legal personality of the company.[107] This would prevent liquidators from suing for the company. However, where there may be other innocent shareholders, there is still a possibility for calling auditors to account,

---

105 [1990] 2 AC 605.
106 [2009] 1 AC 1391.
107 P Watts, '*Stone & Rolls Ltd (In Liquidation) v Moore Stephens (A Firm):* Audit contracts and turpitude' (2010) 146 *Law Quarterly Review* 14.

subject to the test of proximity above.[108] The judgment however rejected that a wider remit of care was owed to creditors.

The tenor of private law jurisprudence has placed many limitations on the **7.50** characterisation and enforcement of auditors' duties of care. This reinforces the position that auditors should not be regarded as surrogates for the performance of primary obligations that firms should perform.

After the global financial crisis, UK policymakers are arguably addressing the **7.51** 'expectations gap' by limiting the expectations attached to the auditor's role. This means that the expectations gap is being managed by reducing expectations instead of putting pressure on auditors to close the gap.

The Sharman Inquiry looked into whether auditors should have expressed **7.52** more scepticism in signing off 'going concern' statements in UK banks that failed in the global financial crisis. This is because such assurance could mislead the market into assuming the financial health of the entities concerned. The inquiry[109] was of the view that the directors are responsible for 'going concern' opinion taking into account the risks and profile of the bank, and it is directors' disclosure that should be strengthened to account to the market. The onus should not be placed on auditors to guarantee the financial health of assured entities to the market. The UK Government[110] and FRC[111] generally support auditors' ability to have an enhanced role in assisting audit committees with more detailed reports which could be available to regulators for supervisory purposes, but not to further reinforce any undue reliance by users on auditors instead of on the primary disclosers which are the corporates.

The EU initially proposed to expand the role of auditors and this could give rise **7.53** to increased reliance by users of corporate reporting and a bigger instead of a minimised 'expectations gap' between users and auditors. In the EU, the European Commission Green Paper[112] flagged up the possibility of enhancing auditors' role in gatekeeping the financial health and risk profile of financial sector firms they audit. In particular, it has opined that auditors should be more

---

108 Roach acknowledges that the ex turpi causa defence would not likely not work for large firms with dispersed shareholding, see L Roach, 'Auditor liability: The case for limitation: Part 1' (2010) 31 *Company Lawyer* 136.

109 Sharman Inquiry, see above n 55.

110 Business, Innovation and Skills Department, *The Future of Narrative Reporting: A Further Consultation* (Sep 2011).

111 FRC, *Effective Company Stewardship*, see above n 62.

112 European Commission, *Proposal for a regulation on the quality of audits of public-interest entities and proposal for a directive to enhance the single market for statutory audits* (Green Paper) (November 2011) available at: http://ec.europa.eu/internal_market/auditing/reform/index_en.htm.

sensitive to risk issues and perhaps be asked to provide assurance statements in respect of prudential and risk compliance.

7.54 The legislation[113] that finally came into force however dropped the Commission's idea of an expanded role for auditors. It has dovetailed with the UK's approach of using auditors in an intelligence capacity and imposed obligations to make auditors more independent and robust.

7.55 The EU Regulation imposes a prohibition on auditors of 'Public Interest Entities' not to engage in the provision of non-audit services and hence be affected by conflicts of interest.[114] Further there would be a mandatory rotation of auditors working for Public Interest Entities every 10 years.[115] This would be accompanied by the carrot of allowing auditing firms an EU passport to provide services across Member States.[116]

7.56 This chapter agrees that it is the right move not to expect auditors to be able to provide prudential compliance assurance. As risk management is a highly technical area, it is uncertain if auditors can actually provide meaningful assurance of a financial sector firm's strategy, processes and policies for risk management. The demands of such assurance would merely result in a wide 'expectations gap'.[117]

7.57 One also queries if it is desirable to enhance auditors' role in the prudential assurance of banks and financial institutions as this role may reinforce some of the perverse incentives on the part of investors mentioned above – relying on shorthand information and not being sufficiently concerned with detailed scrutiny and engaging in meaningful market discipline.

7.58 The UK has also considered[118] whether the auditors' role should be expanded for prudential and risk management matters in financial institutions, but has concluded that auditors should not be mandatorily enrolled into vetting the prudential and risk management disclosures made by financial institutions, as

---

113 Regulation (EU) No 537/2014 of the European Parliament and of the Council of 16 April 2014 on specific requirements regarding statutory audit of public-interest entities and repealing Commission Decision 2005/909/EC.

114 Art 5.

115 Art 17.

116 Directive 2014/56/EU of the European Parliament and of the Council of 16 April 2014 amending Directive 2006/43/EC on statutory audits of annual accounts and consolidated accounts.

117 M Magnan and G Markarian, 'Accounting, governance and the crisis: Is risk the missing link?' (2011) 20 *European Accounting Review* 215, arguing that auditors are poor at incorporating risk profiles into traditional accounting.

118 Financial Services Authority, *Enhancing the Auditor's Contribution to Prudential Regulation* (Discussion Paper, June 2010).

such disclosures vary too much across different business lines and would be costly to undertake.[119] Such assurance work may give rise to wider and undue 'expectations gaps'.

Auditors' accountability to regulators and supervisors look set to be improved. **7.59** The accounting profession's regulator, the FRC took disciplinary proceedings against auditors of companies that had gone insolvent such as Farepak and MG Rover,[120] resulting in a £1.2m fine for Ernst & Young as auditors of Farepak,[121] and a £14m fine and severe reprimand for Deloitte & Touche as auditors of MG Rover, with the lead audit partner in that case disqualified for three years and fined personally as well.[122] Although civil liability for auditors continues to be difficult to establish, the accounting regulator is stepping up to provide disciplinary governance to improve the standards of the profession. Further, the Basel Committee[123] envisages that auditors work closely with financial regulators to supply them with relevant supervisory information in order to assist in the prudential regulation process. Auditors' insights into the robustness of internal control systems maintained by financial institutions are especially relevant.

6. REGULATORY ACCOUNTABILITY, MICROPRUDENTIAL REPORTING AND REGULATORY SUPERVISION

The post-crisis reforms in enhancing the prudential regulation of financial **7.60** institutions would entail increased reporting by financial institutions to regulators in the UK and EU. Such reporting is not necessarily tied to publicly visible corporate transparency, but would be regarded as part of the supervisory framework in banking and financial regulation, generating adequate and accurate intelligence[124] in order to assist regulators in considering pre-emptive or early intervention actions[125] to safeguard the safety and soundness of financial institutions.

---

119 FSA, *Feedback Statement to Enhancing the Auditor's Contribution to Prudential Regulation* (March 2011), 28ff.
120 'Watchdog hits at E&Y over Farepak', *Financial Times* (16 Nov 2012).
121 See http://www.telegraph.co.uk/finance/newsbysector/banksandfinance/10527882/EY-to-pay-1.2m-over-Farepak-audit-failings.html.
122 FRC, *Final Report of Disciplinary Hearing: MG Rover Group, Deloitte & Touche and Mr Maghsoud Einollahi* (Sep 2013), available at: https://www.frc.org.uk/News-and-Events/FRC-Press/Press/2013/September/FRC-publishes-Final-Report-of-Disciplinary-Hearing.aspx.
123 Basel Committee, *External Audits of Banks* (March 2014).
124 I H-Y Chiu, 'Transparency regulation in financial markets – moving into the surveillance age?' (2011) 3 *European Journal of Risk and Regulation* 303.
125 See principle 8, Basel Core Principles (Revised Edition 2012), Bank of England and FSA, *Our Approach to Banking Supervision* (2011); PRA, *Our Approach to Banking Supervision* (Oct 2012), available at: http://www.fsa.gov.uk/static/pubs/other/pra-approach-banking.pdf; FCA, *Journey to the FCA* (Oct 2012).

7.61 Pursuant to Pillar 2 of the Basel Capital Accord II (2006), banks and financial institutions have to make regulatory returns on how credit, market and operational risks are managed in order to adhere to the capital adequacy framework in the Accord. EU-level resolve to enhance the quality of such reporting is expressed through the European Banking Authority's (EBA) harmonised disclosure framework[126] that would be imposed on all Member State regulators, and would ultimately be imposed on banks and financial institutions subject to the capital adequacy regime adopted in European legislation.[127]

7.62 As prudential regulation has expanded greatly post-crisis to include scrutiny over bankers' remuneration and short- and long-term liquidity positions, regulatory reporting would correspondingly increase. Bankers' remuneration reporting is subject to EBA harmonisation,[128] while the frequency and intensity of liquidity reporting depends on the individual supervisory assessment of each financial institution as is determined by the Prudential Regulation Authority (PRA) or Financial Conduct Authority (FCA) whichever is applicable.[129]

7.63 The development of macro-prudential regulation in the EU and UK[130] also means that financial regulators may require additional reporting from banks and financial institutions for the purposes of monitoring financial sector trends on a macro basis. For instance, the macro-prudential regulator in the UK, the Financial Policy Committee, which is nested within the Bank of England, may monitor banks' and financial institutions' leverage ratio in order to determine the risk profiles of banks for systemic risk monitoring. Such monitoring may

---

126 EBA, *Technical Implementing Standards on Supervisory Reporting Requirements for Institutions* (9 July 2013).

127 Capital Requirements Directive 2006/48/EC; 2006/49/EC, and CRD IV which will recast the 2006 Directives incorporating the capital accord known as Basel III in due course.

128 EBA, *Guidelines on Remuneration Benchmarking, Guidelines on Data Collection regarding High Earners* (July 2012), collecting two standardised reports on remuneration benchmarking and high earners' remuneration composition, see FSA's implementation in *Data Collection on Remuneration Practices* (Policy Statement: Nov 2012). See EBA's first report on data on high earners, EBA, *Report on High Earners 2010–11 Data* (15 July 2013).

129 FSA, *Policy Statement on Strengthening Liquidity Standards*, available at: http://www.fsa.gov.uk/pubs/policy/ps09_16.pdf; PRA, *Our Approach to Banking Supervision* (Oct 2012), available at: http://www.fsa.gov.uk/static/pubs/other/pra-approach-banking.pdf; FCA, *Journey to the FCA* (Oct 2012).

130 Chiu, see above n 7; P N Pooran, 'Macro-prudential supervision – A panacea for the global financial crisis?' (2009) *Law and Financial Markets Review* 534. For the EU, the European Systemic Risk Board is the macro-prudential body nested within the European Central Bank, see European Parliament legislative resolution of 22 September 2010 on the proposal for a regulation of the European Parliament and of the Council on Community macro prudential oversight of the financial system and establishing a European Systemic Risk Board (COM(2009)0499 – C7–0166/2009 – 2009/0140(COD)), hereinafter referred to as the 'ESRB Regulation 2010'; E Ferran and K Alexander, 'Can soft law bodies be effective? Soft systemic risk oversight bodies and the special case of the European systemic risk board' (2010) *European Law Review* 751; and the UK has instituted the Financial Policy Committee nested within the Bank of England to be responsible for macro-prudential supervision, see Bank of England and Financial Services Authority, *Instruments of Macro-prudential Policy* (Discussion Paper, Dec 2011).

mean that additional reporting is imposed on banks. European legislation has also left it open[131] as to whether or not a leverage ratio may be imposed but banks and financial institutions are to regularly report their leverage ratios. Further, the UK PRA has also indicated that in imposing additional capital planning buffers as part of the capital adequacy regime applicable to banks and financial institutions, the PRA may require additional reporting on individual banks' risk management, internal controls, stress testing and governance profiles in order to determine whether surcharges may be imposed.[132] The enhanced powers for financial regulators generally in implementing prudential regulatory reforms would mean that additional reporting may be required of any aspect that may have a bearing on safety and soundness of institutions.

Further, regular stress-testing[133] imposed on banks and financial institutions **7.64** also entail regular reporting to and dialogue with regulators, such information is unlikely to become part of corporate transparency, but is relevant for ongoing supervisory monitoring, adjustments to individual institution prudential regulation and possibly enforcement action taken by regulators. Across-the-board stress-testing for European banks such as carried out by the EBA[134] may however be subject to public reporting, although public reports may omit the most sensitive details, presenting the authority's broad-based conclusions only.

Further the international convergence[135] on the importance of recovery plans **7.65** for financial institutions also means that banks and financial institutions have to draw up contingency plans for recovery in case of severe stress[136] and maintain a

---

131 Art 156 as amended by Art 38, Directive 2009/111/EC of The European Parliament and of The Council of 16 September 2009 amending Directives 2006/48/EC, 2006/49/EC and 2007/64/EC as regards banks affiliated to central institutions, certain own funds items, large exposures, supervisory arrangements, and crisis management; and CRD IV Directive Art 429, 430.

132 PRA, *Our Approach to Banking Supervision* (Oct 2012), available at: http://www.fsa.gov.uk/static/pubs/other/pra-approach-banking.pdf.

133 FSA, *Stress and Scenario Testing* available at: http://www.fsa.gov.uk/pubs/policy/ps09_20.pdf and FSA Handbook SYSC 20.

134 EBA's *Principles for Stress-testing*, available at: http://www.eba.europa.eu/EU-wide-stress-testing.aspx (accessed CHK).

135 Principle 8, *FSF Principles for Cross-border Cooperation on Crisis Management*, available at: http://www.financialstabilityboard.org/publications/r_0904c.pdf. See CRD IV Directive, arts 37–55.

136 See FSA, *Recovery and Resolution Plans, Consultation Paper* (Aug 2011) available at: http://www.fsa.gov.uk/pubs/cp/cp11_16.pdf, and FSA Handbook FINMAR 4; Directive 2014/59/EU of the European Parliament and of the Council of 15 May 2014 establishing a framework for the recovery and resolution of credit institutions and investment firms and amending Council Directive 82/891/EEC, and Directives 2001/24/EC, 2002/47/EC, 2004/25/EC, 2005/56/EC, 2007/36/EC, 2011/35/EU, 2012/30/EU and 2013/36/EU, and Regulations (EU) No 1093/2010 and (EU) No 648/2012, of the European Parliament and of the Council.; but see R J Feldman, 'Forcing financial institution change through credible recovery/resolution plans: An alternative to plan-now/implement-later living wills' (2010), available at: http://papers.ssrn.com/sol3/papers.cfm?abstract_id=1608023.

dialogue with regulators as to the viability and review of such plans. Information in these plans feed both into the prudential supervision of financial institutions on an ongoing basis, as well as the consideration of resolution options for the financial institution if a crisis cannot be avoided.

7.66 The above snapshot of the scope of increased regulatory reporting would likely result in a bifurcation between regulatory reporting and corporate transparency, with regulatory reporting serving more explicitly the needs of prudential supervision, and unlikely to be made available for public scrutiny. However, Basel III is also premised on Pillar 3 which is market discipline based on transparency and disclosure and so there is an international movement[137] towards making risk-related information that is both quantitative and qualitative more transparent to capital markets. This chapter is of the view that micro-prudential and macro-prudential reporting will however not completely dovetail with capital markets transparency. Regulatory reporting serves systemic risk monitoring objectives which may not be helped by capital markets discipline and could in some circumstances be undermined by reactions in the capital markets. The needs of corporate transparency and prudential supervision diverge somewhat.[138] It also remains uncertain if accounting standards that apply to valuation of bank assets for prudential reporting should be different from that applicable for corporate transparency.[139] The application of different sets of accounting standards may cause confusion and increased cost in compliance. However, it is to be noted that some commentators[140] are more optimistic about the potential of market discipline and argue that regulatory returns for prudential supervision should be made equally available as corporate transparency generally, as this may improve stakeholder discipline. In the immediate term, it is unlikely that micro and macro-prudential reporting will dovetail completely with capital markets reporting.

7. CORPORATE TRANSPARENCY IN ESG MATTERS, SUSTAINABILITY AND INTEGRATED REPORTING

7.67 It is observed that the accounting profession, business and policymakers are increasingly keen on reforming corporate transparency as the dominant model

---

137 Financial Stability Board, *Enhanced Disclosure Task Force Survey* (July 2013), available at: http://www.financialstabilityboard.org/publications/r_130821a.pdf.

138 P J Klumpes and P Welch, 'Never the twain shall meet? Addressing the disconnect between banks' financial and regulatory reporting' (2011), available at: http://ssrn.com/abstract=1763817.

139 Haldane, see above n 21.

140 A Bourgain, P Pieretti, and Z Skerdilajda, 'Financial openness, disclosure and bank risk-taking in MENA countries' (2012) 13 *Emerging Markets Review* 283; R P Bartlett III, see above n 32.

of financial reporting has become increasingly complex, difficult to access[141] and short-termist.[142] Corporate reporting has come under criticism as being less than useful[143] or achieving only an impression of accountability[144] since the occurrence of a number of corporate scandals such as Enron and Parmalat in the early 2000s, and the global financial crisis which has taken investor communities by surprise.

Many corporations have in the last decade voluntarily adopted forms of **7.68** sustainability or citizenship reporting, which would allow a range of stakeholder, environmental, social and governance (ESG) and contextual information broadly affecting the corporation to be presented.[145] Such reporting tends to place the corporation within the context of the social fabric of its operations and ameliorate unfavourable impressions of self-interested profit-chasing behaviour, irresponsibility or disregard for the wider context. Banks and financial institutions, especially the large universal banks, have all produced annual sustainability reports voluntarily to complement mandatory reporting.[146]

However, sustainability reports, which are narrative in nature and susceptible to **7.69** subjective and incomparable reporting, may still lack credibility as forming the basis of a useful and material information platform for investors. Roberts et al opine that much of corporate sustainability reporting is 'values-based' i.e. high level and pandering largely to social expectations or 'compliance-based' i.e. saying the right things in order to address particular issues that are in the media spotlight or social scrutiny such as environmental compliance and carbon footprint.[147]

---

141 H T C Hu, 'Too complex to depict? Innovation, "pure information", and the SEC Disclosure Paradigm' (2012) 90 *Texas Law Review* PAGE CHK, available at: http://papers.ssrn.com/sol3/papers.cfm?abstract_id= 2083708; D Weil, A Fung, M Graham and E Fagotto, 'The effectiveness of regulatory disclosure policies' (2006) 25 *Journal of Policy Analysis and Management* 155.

142 BIS, *The Kay Review*, see above n 47, paras 5.16ff.

143 R P Bartlett III, 'Inefficiencies in the information thicket: A case study of derivative disclosures during the financial crisis' (2010) 36 *Journal of Corporation Law* 1.

144 U Rodrigues and M Stegemoller, 'Placebo ethics: A study in securities disclosure arbitrage' (2010) 96 *Virginia Law Review* 1.

145 KPMG International, *KPMG International Survey Of Corporate Responsibility Reporting 2008*, at 13 (2008), available at: http://www.kpmg.com/US/en/ IssuesAndInsights/ArticlesPublications/PressReleases/ Documents/Corporate_Sustainability_Report_US_Final.pdf.

146 D De-Felice, 'Sustainability reporting by banks', empirical research presented at the International Comparative Legal Risk workshop, LSE, 31 Oct 2012.

147 Roberts, Weetman and Gordon, see above n 11, 137.

7.70 The European Commission[148] is also spearheading a movement to reform corporate reporting so that publicly quoted companies in the EU that employ more than 500 employees or have assets exceeding 20 million euros on their balance sheet or have a net turnover exceeding 40 million euros must prepare a non-financial statement on their policies and risk management in relation to containing information relating to environmental, social and employee matters, respect for human rights, anti-corruption and bribery matters. This is similar to but exceeds the UK requirements for the directors' business review as discussed earlier. The utility of such narrative forms of disclosure may depend on whether there are standardised reporting standards that could underpin the quality of such reporting.

7.71 The development of international voluntary templates for ESG reporting such as the Global Reporting Initiative's G3 standards[149] has assisted greatly in corporate adoption of sustainability reporting. Reports adhering to the G3 standards have been perceived to be more credible, especially for socially responsible investing.[150] However, it remains debatable[151] whether sustainability reports genuinely engage in useful contextual reporting of a corporation's role and responsibility or acts as a form of impression management to appeal to investors and economic stakeholders in order to improve financial performance.

Nevertheless, the achievements of standardisation may also not be overstated, as standardisation has tended to occur at broad levels and issues of methodology and metrics are still in developing stages.[152]

---

148 European Commission, Proposal for a Directive of the European Parliament and of the Council amending Council Directives 78/660/EEC and 83/349/EEC as regards disclosure of non-financial and diversity information by certain large companies and groups (16 April 2013), available at: http://ec.europa.eu/internal_market/accounting/docs/non-financial-reporting/com_2013_207_en.pdf. This was adopted by the European Parliament on 15 April 2014, but has not yet come into force as law.

149 Available at: https://www.globalreporting.org/reporting/latest-guidelines/Pages/default.aspx.

150 A G F Hoepner and D G Mcmillan, 'Research on "responsible investment": An influential literature analysis comprising a rating, characterisation, categorisation and investigation' (2009), available at: http://ssrn.com/abstract=1454793; F Hung-Gay, S A Law and J Yau, *Socially Responsible Investment in a Global Environment* (Edward Elgar 2010); N Eccles, 'New values in responsible investment' in W Vanderkerckhove, J Leys, K Alm, B Scholtens, S Signori and He Schäfer eds, *Responsible Investment In Times of Turmoil* (Springer 2011), at 20–3; B J Richardson, *Socially Responsible Investment Law* (OUP 2008), Chs 2ff.

151 J Brown and Fraser, 'Approaches and perspectives in social and environmental accounting: An overview of the conceptual landscape' (2006) 15 *Business Strategy and the Environment* 103; D Hess, 'The three pillars of CRS reporting in new governance regulation' (2008), available at: http://papers.ssrn.com/sol3/papers.cfm?abstract_id=1176882.

152 Chiu, 'Standardization', see above n 8.

Empirical research[153] also seems to suggest that banks and financial institutions **7.72** engage in or regard sustainability or citizenship matters as more peripheral than integrated into core business. Effort is spent on such matters following good performance, and performance does not seem driven by these matters. McCormick[154] has also criticised banks for failing to integrate the notion of sustainability into core banking business, in light of the spate of misselling scandals such as payment protection insurance, and the social cost of the global financial crisis.

A new development which has captured professional, corporate and policy **7.73** attention is the integrated report, a form of corporate reporting that integrates financial and contextual ESG information in order to present a high-level integrated view of the corporation in terms of its long-term vision and 'value-creation' (moving away from the hackneyed term of 'performance').[155] Brockett et al[156] from Ernst & Young argue that investors are demanding reporting along the lines of five areas of multiple bottom-line performance: economic, governance, social, ethics, and environmental. In order to report along multiple bottom lines, corporations need to engage in holistic risk management, and corporate reporting should be based on materiality, stake-holder inclusiveness, the sustainability context and completeness. The International Integrated Reporting Committee (IIRC) has recently been formed by the IFAC (International Federation of Accountants), the Global Reporting Initiative (GRI), and The Prince's Accounting for Sustainability Project in order to develop an international template for integrated reporting.

The integrated report envisages that both financial and non-financial reporting **7.74** should be put into one place, but the delivery of information should itself be an integrated whole, developed from business strategy and risk considerations, and a holistic consideration of long-term value creation.[157] Hence the IIRC draft framework[158] proposes for the basic elements of integrated reports to contain the following elements:

- Organisational overview and business model
- Operating context, including risks and opportunities

---

153 M-G Soana, 'The relationship between corporate social performance and corporate financial performance in the banking sector' (2009), available at: http://papers.ssrn.com/sol3/papers.cfm?abstract_id=1325956.
154 McCormick, see above n 1.
155 IIRC, *Towards Integrated Reporting: Communicating Value in the 21st Century* (Sep 2011, Discussion Paper and Summary of Responses).
156 A Brockett and Z Rezaee, *Corporate Sustainability: Integrating Performance and Reporting* (John Wiley & Sons 2012).
157 R P Eccles and M Krzus, *One Report: Integrated Reporting for a Sustainable Strategy* (John Wiley & Sons 2010).
158 IIRC, *Draft Framework Outline: Integrated Reporting* (July 2012).

- Strategic objectives and strategies to achieve those objectives
- Capitals and resources and relationships
- Governance and remuneration
- Performance; and
- Future outlook.

Further, the principles of reporting should be guided by the following considerations and more detailed prescriptions may in time emanate from the IIRC:

- Strategic focus
- Connectivity of information
- Future orientation
- Responsiveness and stakeholder inclusiveness; and
- Conciseness, reliability and materiality.

7.75 The IIRC developments are in an embryonic stage and it is acknowledged that more research and challenges lie ahead in terms of securing acceptable definitions of high-level terms such as 'business model', 'capitals' and 'value creation'. Further, questions remain as to the internal processes, technology and cost-benefit associated with implementing integrated reporting, as well as the development of assurance methodologies and standards.[159] However, the European Commission has considerable faith in the integrated report and proposes to exempt quoted companies from the abovementioned proposal of preparing a non-financial statement if companies issue integrated reports.

7.76 In terms of applying the integrated report to banks, integrated reporting may force banks to consider the sustainability of their business practices in product distribution and risk management. However, the benefits of the integrated report may be overstated if the integrated report results in over-standardisation, failing to capture specific industry particulars that are important to stakeholders. For example, issues of asset risks, liquidity and accountability to regulators may be important due to the systemic nature of certain banks. It is hoped that the implementation of integrated reporting may over time entail changes to corporate behaviour and culture in banks – that integrated reporting may force integrated oversight and leadership responsibility[160] for risk management, sustainability of business models and long-term value creation for stakeholders and shareholders. The nascent steps in the UK towards more

---

159 Ibid.
160 E G Hansen and R Reichwald, 'CSR Leadership study: Leading corporate responsibility in multinational corporations – A study in Germany's biggest firms. Final report.' (Institute for Information, Organization and Management, TUM Business School, Technische Universität München, Munich, Germany, 2009).

senior management responsibility for going concern reports and directors' business reviews as discussed earlier are a starting step that may converge towards a model of integrated reporting.

8. CONCLUSION

The regulatory regime for financial reporting has developed and matured in the **7.77** UK and EU through the substantial legal integration achieved in the EU Company Law and Transparency Directives, and the adoption of the IFRS. Although the global financial crisis has sparked off critical reflection of the corporate transparency regime, there remains a fundamental belief in the usefulness of corporate transparency. Reforms have dealt largely with how disclosure is made, with emphasis placed on increased narrative reporting that is infused with insight from the highest levels of management in the corporation. These reforms reflect a cherished belief in the necessity of shareholder engagement as a means to check and scrutinise corporate behaviour and performance based on the receipt of useful and timely information. Thus, there are corresponding reforms to enhance the stewardship of shareholders.[161] The post-crisis era however also ushered in developments such as macro-prudential regulation and the empowerment of regulators to conduct more regular and intrusive scrutiny into banks and financial institutions. Regulatory requirements in micro- and macro-prudential regulation will generate further informational demands on banks and financial institutions, and this chapter predicts that these informational demands would be unlikely to dovetail completely with corporate transparency, hence imposing an additional burden on them. Although such bifurcation may impose additional burdens on banks and financial institutions, the needs of corporate transparency and systemic risk monitoring may diverge.

SELECTED BIBLIOGRAPHY

Ambler, T and A Neely, 'Narrative reporting in company annual accounts' (2007), available at: http://ssrn.com/abstract=1030724.

Bank for International Settlements (BIS), *Basel II: International Convergence of Capital Measurement and Capital Standards: A Revised Framework – Comprehensive Version* (June 2006), available at: http://www.bis.org/publ/bcbs128.htm.

Bank for International Settlements (BIS), *Basel III: A Global Regulatory Framework for More Resilient Banks and Banking Systems* (June 2011), available at: http://www.bis.org/bcbs/basel3.htm.

---

161   BIS, *The Kay Review*, see above n 47, Chiu, 'Turning institutional investors into "stewards"', see above n 65.

Bank for International Settlements (BIS), *The Kay Review of UK Equity Markets and Long-Term Decision Making* (Final Report, 23 July 2012.

Barth, M E and W R Landsman, 'How did financial reporting contribute to the financial crisis?' (May 2010), available at: http://ssrn.com/abstract=1601519.

Bartlett, R P III, 'Making banks transparent' (2012) 65 *Vanderbilt Law Review* 293.

Beck, A C, D Campbell and P J Shrives, 'Content analysis in environmental reporting research: Enrichment and rehearsal of the method in a British–German context' (2010) 42 *British Accounting Review* 207.

Black, B, B Cheffins and M Klausner, 'Liability risk for outside directors: A cross-border analysis' (2005) 11 *European Financial Management* 153.

Bogle, J C, *The Clash of the Cultures: Investment vs Speculation* (John Wiley & Sons 2012).

Bourgain, A, P Pieretti and S Zanaj, 'Financial openness, disclosure and bank risk-taking in MENA countries' (2012) 13 *Emerging Markets Review* 283.

Brockett, A and Z Rezaee, *Corporate Sustainability: Integrating Performance and Reporting* (John Wiley & Sons 2012).

Campbell, D, A Rahman and M Ridhuan, 'A longitudinal examination of intellectual capital reporting in Marks & Spencer annual reports, 1978–2008' (2010) 42 *British Accounting Review* 56.

Chiu, I H-Y, 'The paradigms for mandatory non-financial disclosure: A conceptual analysis – Parts 1 and 2' (2006) *Company Lawyer* 259, 291.

Chiu, I H-Y, 'Standardization in corporate social responsibility reporting and a universalist concept of CSR?: A path paved with good intentions' (2010/2011) 22 *Florida Journal of International Law* 361.

Chiu, I H-Y, 'Transparency regulation in financial markets – moving into the surveillance age?' (2011) 3 *European Journal of Risk and Regulation* 303.

Chiu, I H-Y, 'Macro-prudential supervision: Critically examining the developments in the UK, EU and internationally' (2012) *Law and Financial Markets Review* 184.

Chiu, I H-Y, 'The role and liabilities of auditors in financial regulation: Addressing the "expectations gap"' (2012) *International Business Law Journal* 545.

Chiu, I H-Y, 'Institutional shareholders as stewards: Towards a new conception of corporate governance?' (2012) *Brooklyn Journal of Financial, Corporate and Commercial Law* 387.

Chiu, I H-Y, 'Turning institutional investors into "stewards" – Exploring the meaning and objectives in "stewardship"' (2013) *Current Legal Problems* 1.

Coffee, J C Jnr, 'Understanding Enron: "It's about the gatekeepers, stupid"' (2002) 57 *Business Lawyer* 1403.

Coffee, J C Jnr, *Gatekeepers* (OUP 2004).

Corona, C and R S Randhawa, 'The auditor's slippery slope: An analysis of reputational incentives' (2010) 56 *Management Science* 924.

Daske, H, L Hail, C Leuz and R Verdi, 'Mandatory IFRS reporting around the world: Early evidence on the economic consequences' (University of Chicago Working Paper 2008), available at: http://ssrn.com/abstract=1024240.

DeZoort, F, D Hermanson, D Archambeault and S Reed, 'Audit committee effectiveness: A synthesis of the empirical audit committee literature' (2002) 21 *Journal of Accounting Literature* 38.

Department of Business Innovation and Skills, *The Kay Review of UK Equity Markets and Long-Term Decision Making* (Final Report, 23 July 2012).

Department of Trade and Industry, *Draft Regulations on The Operating and Financial Review and Directors' Report: A Consultative Document* (May 2004), available at: www.dti.gov.uk/cld/pdfs/ofr-condoc.htm.

Eccles, N, 'New values in responsible investment' in W Vanderkerckhove, J Leys, K Alm, B Scholtens, S Signori and H Schäfer (eds) *Responsible Investment In Times of Turmoil* (Springer 2011).

Eccles, R P and M Krzus, *One Report: Integrated Reporting for a Sustainable Strategy* (John Wiley & Sons 2010).

Enria, A, et al, 'Fair value accounting and financial stability' (ECB Occasional Paper 2004).

European Banking Authority, *Discussion Paper on Template for Recovery Plans* (May 2012).

European Banking Authority, *Guidelines on Remuneration Benchmarking, Guidelines on Data Collection Regarding High Earners* (July 2012).

European Banking Authority, *Discussion Paper Relating to Draft Regulatory Technical Standards on prudent valuation under Article 100 of the draft Capital Requirements Regulation (CRR)* (13 Nov 2012).

European Banking Authority, *Technical Implementing Standards on Supervisory Reporting Requirements for Institutions* (9 July 2013).

European Banking Authority, *Report on High Earners 2010–11 Data* (15 July 2013).

Ferran, E and A Kern, 'Can soft law bodies be effective? Soft systemic risk oversight bodies and the special case of the European Systemic Risk Board' (2010) *European Law Review* 751.

Financial Reporting Council, *Effective Company Stewardship: Enhancing Corporate Reporting and Audit* (Jan 2011), available at: http://www.frc.org.uk/Our-Work/Publications/FRC-Board/Effective-Company-Stewardship-Enhancing-Corporate.aspx.

Financial Reporting Council, *Implementing the Recommendations of the Sharman Panel: Revised Guidance on Going Concern and Revised International Standards on Auditing (UK and Ireland)* (January 2013).

Financial Reporting Council, *Guidance on Going Concern Supplement for Banks* (January 2013).

Financial Services Authority, *Enhancing the Auditor's Contribution to Prudential Regulation* (Discussion Paper, June 2010).

Fooks, G, 'Auditors and the permissive society: Market failure, globalisation and financial regulation in the US' (2003) 5 *Risk Management* 17.

Gebhardt, G and Z Novotny-Farkas, 'Mandatory IFRS adoption and accounting quality of European banks' (2010), available at: http://ssrn.com/abstract=1732166.

Gendron, Y and J Be'dard, 'On the constitution of audit committee effectiveness' (2006) 31 *Accounting, Organizations and Society* 211.

Haldane, A, 'Discussion of "Financial instruments, financial reporting, and financial stability" by Christian Laux (2012)' (2012) 42 *Accounting and Business Research* 261.

Hirtle, B J, 'What market risk capital reporting tells us about bank risk' (Federal Reserve Bank of New York Economic Policy Review, 2003).

Hoepner, A G F and D G Mcmillan, 'Research on "responsible investment": An influential literature analysis comprising a rating, characterisation, categorisation and investigation' (2009), available at: http://ssrn.com/abstract=1454793.

Holder-Webb, L, 'The question of disclosure: Providing a tool for evaluating managements' discussion and analysis' (2007) 10 *Advances in Accounting Behavioral Research* 183.

Houqe, N, T van Zijl, K L Dunstan and A K M Waresul Karim, 'The effect of IFRS adoption and investor protection on earnings quality around the world' (2012) 47 *International Journal of Accounting* 333.

Hung-Gay, F, S A Law and J Yau, *Socially Responsible Investment in a Global Environment* (Edward Elgar 2010).

IASB, *Basis for Conclusions: Financial Instruments: Amortised Cost and Impairment* (Nov 2009).

IASB, *Financial Instruments: Impairment* (Jan 2011).

IIRC, *Towards Integrated Reporting: Communicating Value in the 21st Century* (Sep 2011, Discussion Paper and Summary of Responses).

IIRC, *Draft Framework Outline: Integrated Reporting* (July 2012).

Khan, U, 'Does fair value accounting contribute to systemic risk in the banking industry?' (2010), available at: http://ssrn.com/abstract=1327596.

Kirkpatrick, G, 'The corporate governance lessons from the financial crisis' (OECD Report 2009), available at: http://www.oecd.org/dataoecd/32/1/42229620.pdf.

Klumpes, P J and P Welch, 'Never the twain shall meet? Addressing the disconnect between banks' financial and regulatory reporting' (2011), available at: http://ssrn.com/abstract= 1763817.

Kolb, R W (ed.), *Lessons from the Financial Crisis* (John Wiley & Sons 2010).

KPMG International, *KPMG International Survey Of Corporate Responsibility Reporting 2008*, at 13 (2008), available at: http://www.kpmg.com/US/en/ IssuesAndInsights/Articles Publications/PressReleases/Documents/Corporate_Sustainability_Report_US_Final.pdf.

Laux, C, 'Financial instruments, financial reporting, and financial stability' (2012), available at: http://ssrn.com/abstract=1991825

Linsmeier, T J, 'Financial reporting and financial crises: The case for measuring financial instruments at fair value in the financial statements' (2010), available at: http://ssrn.com/ abstract=1775141.

Magnan, M and G Markarian, 'Accounting, governance and the crisis: Is risk the missing link?' (2011) 20 *European Accounting Review* 215.

McCormick, R, 'What makes a bank a "sustainable bank"?' (2012) *Law and Economics Yearly Review* 77.

McCormick, R, 'Towards a more sustainable financial system: The role of civil society Parts 1 and 2' (2012) 6 *Law and Financial Markets Review* 129, 200.

Mendales, R E, 'Collateralized explosive devices: why securities regulation failed to prevent the CDO meltdown, and how to fix it' (2008), available at: http://ssrn.com/abstract = 1354062, (2009) *University of Illinois Law Review* 1359.

Merkl-Davis, D M and N Brennan, 'Accounting narratives and impression management' in L Jack, J Davison, R Craig (eds), *The Routledge Companion to Communication in Accounting* (2013) at Ch 4 available at: http://ssrn.com/abstract=1873188.

Merkl-Davis, D M, N Brennan and S Macleay, 'Impression management and retrospective sense-making in corporate narratives: A social psychology perspective' (2010) 24 *Accounting, Audit and Accountability Journal* 315.

Morales, J and A Pezet, 'Financialization through hybridisation: The subtle power of financial controlling' in I Huault and R Chrystelle (eds), *Finance: The Discreet Regulator* (Palgrave Macmillan 2012).

Mouselli, S and H Khaled, 'Disclosure quality and stock returns in the UK' (2009), available at: http://ssrn.com/abstract=1499258.

Murphy, M E, 'Assuring responsible risk management in banking: The corporate governance dimension' (2011) 36 *Delaware Journal of Corporate Law* 121.

Ojo, M, 'Eliminating the audit "expectations gap": Reality or myth?' (2005), available at: http://ssrn.com/abstract=1407199.

Power, M, *The Audit Society: Rituals of Verification* (OUP 1999).

Rappaport, A, *Saving Capitalism from Short-Termism* (McGraw-Hill 2011).

Richardson, B J, *Socially Responsible Investment Law* (OUP 2008).

Roach, L, 'Auditor liability: The case for limitation: Part 1' (2010) 31 *Company Lawyer* 136.

Roberts, C, P Weetman and P Gordon, *International Corporate Reporting* (Financial Times/ Prentice Hall 2008).

Rodrigues, U and M Stegemoller, 'Placebo ethics: A study in securities disclosure arbitrage' (2010) 96 *Virginia Law Review* 1.

Seabra Lopes, D, 'Making oneself at home with numbers: Financial reporting from an ethno-graphic perspective' (2011) 19 *Social Anthropology* 463.

Shaffer, S, 'Evaluating the impact of fair value accounting on financial institutions: Implications for accounting standards setting and bank supervision' (2012), available at: http://ssrn.com/abstract=2006381.

Sharman Inquiry, *Going Concern and Liquidity Risks: Lessons for Companies and Auditors, Final Report and Recommendations of the Panel of Inquiry* (June 2012), available at: http://www.frc.org.uk/getattachment/591a5e2a-35d7–4470-a46c-30c0d8ca2a14/Sharman-Inquiry-Final-Report.aspx.

Soana, M-G, 'The relationship between corporate social performance and corporate financial performance in the banking sector' (2009), available at: http://papers.ssrn.com/sol3/papers.cfm?abstract_id=1325956.

Song, G, 'The benefits of decoupling financial reporting from bank capital regulation' (2012), available at: http://ssrn.com/abstract=1955453.

Vera-Muñoz, S C, 'Corporate governance reforms: Redefined expectations of audit committee responsibilities and effectiveness' (2005) 62 *Journal of Business Ethics* 115.

Villiers, C, *Corporate Reporting and Company Law* (CUP 2006).

Walker, Sir D, *Review of Corporate Governance in UK Banks and Financial Institutions* (Final, 26 Nov 2009), available at: http://www.hm- treasury.gov.uk/walker_review_information.htm.

Watts, P, '*Stone & Rolls Ltd (In Liquidation) v Moore Stephens (A Firm):* Audit contracts and turpitude' (2010) 146 *Law Quarterly Review* 14.

Yeoh, P, 'Narrative reporting: The UK experience' (2010) 52 *International Journal of Law and Management* 211.

Zumbasen, P, 'The next "great transformation" of markets and states in the transnational space: Global assemblages of corporate governance and financial market regulation' (2009), available at: http://papers.ssrn.com/sol3/papers.cfm?abstract_id=1415463.

8

SYSTEMS AND CONTROLS IN ANTI-BRIBERY AND CORRUPTION

Anna P Donovan[*]

1. INTRODUCTION

8.01 A critical challenge facing banks (and those responsible for their governance) is the implementation of effective anti-bribery and corruption (ABC) systems and controls. Regulatory developments and, in particular, the Bribery Act 2010 (the Bribery Act or the Act) have renewed interest in (and scrutiny of) a firm's internal governance as a key component of its ABC initiatives. An organisation's internal systems and controls are, of course, a central tenet of its' ABC

---

[*] The author is grateful to Dr Iris Chiu and Michael McKee for their commentary and generosity of time in reviewing this chapter. Any errors of course remain my own.

236

response (particularly in light of the Act's requirement that a firm implement adequate procedures to prevent bribery being committed on its behalf). However, these internal procedures are just one aspect of a board's ABC responsibility; regulation and industry guidance make it clear that boards are also required to develop and instil a culture of compliance within the bank.[1] Drawing on the Bribery Act as the key driver of recent governance attention, this chapter considers the impact of the Act on a board's responsibility to implement both adequate internal procedures and a broader ethical culture within the bank's governance framework.

Banks and other financial institutions occupy an interesting position regarding **8.02** the Act and the governance response that it demands. They are, of course, already subject to complex risk-management, compliance and wider financial crime[2] obligations and sanctions.[3] Therefore, they are ostensibly better equipped to respond to the Act's somewhat nebulous requirement that a firm implement 'adequate procedures'[4] to prevent a third party from paying a bribe on its behalf (or for its benefit). However, banks operate within a high-risk environment from a bribery perspective[5] and are vulnerable both to an internal breach (by their own employees) and an external threat arising from third parties utilising the bank as a conduit to further financial crime. This exposure, combined with the opacity of recent regulatory requirements (which still await

---

1   Financial Reporting Council, *The UK Corporate Governance Code* (September 2012), principle A.1; Basel Committee on Banking Supervision, *Principles for the Sound Management of Operational Risk* (June 2011), principle 1; Basel Committee on Banking Supervision, *Principles for Enhancing Corporate Governance* (October 2010) (BCBS Principles), principle 1.

2   Financial crime in this context is defined by FSMA 2000, s 6 as including;

    any offence involving

      (a)   fraud or dishonesty;
      (b)   misconduct in, or misuse of information relating to, a financial market; or
      (c)   handling the proceeds of crime.

  The use of the word 'include' means that this is not an exhaustive list and the Financial Conduct Authority (FCA) has, understandably, taken s 6 to include bribery and corruption, see: Financial Services Authority, *Anti-bribery and Corruption in Commercial Insurance Broking, Reducing the Risk of Illicit Payments of Inducements to Third Parties* (May 2010) (CIB Guidance), para 8.

3   Pursuant to the Financial Conduct Authority (FCA) Handbook's Principles for Businesses, authorised firms are required to 'act with integrity' (Prin 1), conduct their business 'with due skill care and diligence' (Prin 2) and 'organise and control its affairs responsibly and effectively, with adequate risk management systems' (Prin 3). Furthermore, under the FCA Handbook's Senior Management Arrangements, Systems and Controls (SYSC) provisions, a firm must 'take reasonable care to establish and maintain effective systems and controls ... for countering the risk that the firm might be used to further financial crime' (SYSC 3.2.6R) and to 'establish, implement and maintain adequate policies and procedures sufficient to ensure compliance of the firm including its managers, employees and appointed representatives...with its obligations under the regulatory system and for countering the risk that the firm might be used to further financial crime' (SYSC 6.1.1R).

4   Bribery Act, s 7(2).

5   These business risks (or 'red flags') are considered further in paragraphs 8.42 and 8.43 but include engaging with third parties (including public officials), territorial risks and government interaction.

judicial interpretation), mean that uncertainty nevertheless abounds as to what constitutes 'adequate' procedures in this context. It is perhaps not surprising therefore that, even within an already highly regulated industry, the Financial Services Authority (FSA) found that certain banks had 'been slow and reactive in managing bribery and corruption risk' with most failing to 'ensure adequate systems and controls to identify, manage and control the bribery and corruption risks to which they were exposed'.[6]

8.03   This chapter proceeds as follows. Section 2 examines the two provisions of the Bribery Act that have driven the latest focus on internal governance controls and culture. The first is the corporate offence of failing to prevent bribery[7] and the second is the concomitant defence of 'adequate procedures',[8] a term that the Act deliberately omits to define. Thereafter, Section 3 considers the six principles set out in the Ministry of Justice's guidance (the MOJ Guidance)[9] on the interpretation of the adequate procedures defence. In doing so, it draws on guidance that applies specifically to banks and other financial services firms, including the Financial Conduct Authority's 'Financial Crime Guide' (the FCA Guidance)[10] and the British Bankers' Association 'Anti-Bribery and Corruption Guidance' (the BBA Guidance)[11] to demonstrate how these principles may manifest in practice.

8.04   The analysis of the Act and the MOJ Guidance distils a common theme, namely the importance of a zero-tolerance culture to bribery as a defence under the Act. As such, Section 4 explores the wider role of culture as a component of a firm's ABC governance measures. In doing so, it has regard to both the UK Corporate Governance Code (applicable to all companies with a premium listing) together with industry-specific guidance including the Basel Committee on Banking Supervision's 'Principles for Enhancing Corporate Governance' (the BCBS Principles).[12]

---

6   Financial Services Authority, *Anti-bribery and Corruption Systems and Controls in Investment Banks* (March 2012) (ABC Guidance), para 4.

7   Bribery Act, s 7(1).

8   Ibid., s 7(2).

9   The Ministry of Justice, *Bribery Act 2010: Guidance About Procedures which Relevant Commercial Organisations can put into Place to Prevent Persons Associated with them from Bribing (section 9 of the Bribery Act 2010)* (March 2011).

10   FCA, *Financial Crime: A Guide for Firms, Part 1: A Firm's Guide to Preventing Financing Crime* (April 2014) (FCA Guidance, Part 1), available at: http://media.fshandbook.info/Handbook/FC1_Full_20140401.pdf; and FCA, *Financial Crime: A Guide for Firms, Part 2: Financial Crime Thematic Reviews* (April 2013) (FCA Guidance, Part 2), available at: http://media.fshandbook.info/Handbook/FC2_Full_20130401.pdf (together: the FCA Guidance).

11   British Bankers' Association, *Anti-Bribery and Corruption Guidance* (May 2014).

12   See above n 1.

A comment on the scope of this chapter is prudent from the outset. Bribery and **8.05** corruption are global phenomena and many banks will find themselves subject to a wide array of international regulations and conventions.[13] While an overview of key international conventions is set out in Annex 8.1, the chapter's primary focus is on the consequences of the UK Act and its associated guidance. Nevertheless, the principles discussed are likely to be relevant to banks subject to a wider regulatory regime.

2. THE BRIBERY ACT 2010: A CATALYST FOR INTERNAL CONTROLS

Bribery and corruption[14] have, in various guises, been unlawful in the UK for **8.06** centuries.[15] Nevertheless, the implementation of the Bribery Act was a significant regulatory development and is undoubtedly the motivation behind the recent (and widespread) attention on ABC systems and controls. Whilst the Act's primary offences are far-reaching (and arguably go beyond the UK's international obligations)[16] they are not the cause of the substantial controversy generated by the Act.[17] Rather, the genesis of the debate surrounding the Act is

---

13   In particular, the provisions of the Foreign Corrupt Practice Act 1977, the related guidance to which is instructive when seeking to implement robust internal controls. See: Criminal Division of the US Department of Justice and the Enforcement Division of the US Securities and Exchange Commission, *A Resource Guide to the US Foreign Corrupt Practices Act*, (November 2012) (FCPA Guidance); US Sentencing Commission, *Guidelines Manual*, §8 (November 2013); Department of Justice, *US Attorney's Manual – Principles of Federal Prosecution of Business Organizations*, §9–28.00.

14   Bribery and corruption are terms of art that are often used interchangeably across the international arena. Within the UK, the term 'corruption' arguably incorporates a broader range of behaviours beyond bribery and, historically, this was the case at common law, see below n 15. The FCA Guidance, see above n 10, 58 defines corruption as 'the abuse of public or private office to obtain an undue advantage. Corruption includes bribery'. For a wider discussion of the historic crimes of bribery, corruption and the distinction between the two see: R Lissack and F Horlick, *Lissack and Horlick on Bribery* (LexisNexis 2011) Chs 1 and 3.

15   The UK has a long legislative and common law history of prohibiting bribery and broader corruption offences. Common law offences included misconduct in public office and embracery (the offence of attempting to influence a juror corruptly). Anti-corruption legislation included: the Sale of Offices Act 1551; the Sale of Offices Act 1809; the Public Bodies Corrupt Practices Act 1889; the Prevention of Corruption Act 1906; the Prevention of Corruption Act 1916; Honours (Prevention of Abuses) Act 1925; Licensing Act 1964, s 178; Criminal Law Act 1967, s 5; Local Government Act 1972, s 117(2); Customs and Excise Management Act 1979, s 15; Representation of the People Act 1983, ss 107, 109 and 111–115; and, more recently, the Anti-Terrorism, Crime and Security Act 2001 (ss 108–110). The Act repealed the common law offences of bribery and embracery together with the whole of the Public Bodies Corrupt Practices Act 1889, the Prevention of Corruption Act 1906 and the Prevention of Corruption Act 1916 (the Bribery Act 2010, s 17 and Sch 2).

16   The OECD Convention (see Annex 8.1) only required legislation addressing the bribery of foreign public officials to be implemented.

17   It would be difficult to suggest that the offences in the Act themselves are unreasonable as they simply prohibit: (i) the offer, promise or grant of a bribe intending the recipient to (or rewarding the recipient for) improperly performing a relevant function or activity (s 1); (ii) the request, receipt or acceptance of a bribe intending that as a consequence a relevant function or activity will be performed improperly or where the request, receipt or

the introduction of the corporate[18] offence of failing to prevent bribery[19] and the associated 'adequate procedures'[20] defence.

A.   Failure of commercial organisations to prevent bribery

8.07   The Act was introduced following significant international pressure.[21] In particular, there was widespread condemnation that the operation of the UK's identification doctrine[22] rendered corporate prosecutions under the pre-2010 law 'extremely unlikely'.[23] Acceding to demands that the UK implement regulatory reform to meet its international obligations, the Act eventually introduced a strict liability corporate offence of failing to prevent bribery.[24] In doing so, the Act effectively (and deliberately) increased the risk of corporate prosecution by removing the protection obliquely offered by the identification doctrine.[25]

8.08   Under the Act, a corporation is liable if an associated person[26] commits an act of bribery with the intention of obtaining, or retaining, business for the benefit of the organisation.[27] It creates a strict liability offence as prosecutors do not have

---

acceptance is itself an improper performance of such function (s 2); and (iii) the bribery of a foreign public official with the intent to influence that person in his or her capacity as a foreign public official (s 6).

18   For ease of reference, this chapter refers to a 'corporate' offence. However, the Act extends the offence to 'bodies corporate' and therefore includes certain partnerships (see Bribery Act, s 7(5)) but excludes sole traders and other unincorporated organisations.

19   Bribery Act, s 7.

20   Ibid., s 7(2).

21   On which, see Annex 8.1 and, in particular, the activities of the OECD.

22   In brief, the identification doctrine (or principle) stipulates that for a corporation to satisfy the mens rea of a criminal offence, the prosecutor needs to identify a natural person connected (or identified) with the corporation who committed the offence. The inherent difficulty with this doctrine is identifying a single individual who satisfies the principle's requirements, especially in a globalised economy. See: *Tesco Supermarkets Ltd v Nattrass* [1972] AC 153, [1971] 2 All ER 127; *R v Andrews-Weatherfoil Ltd* [1972] 1 All ER 65; *Meridian Global Funds Management Asia Ltd v Securities Commission* [1995] 2 AC 500, [1995] 3 All ER 918.

23   Director of Public Prosecutions, Joint Committee Report Vol II (n 44), BB48, Ev 273. Although note that difficulties in establishing corporate liability do not apply to individuals, who may still be liable.

24   There is some debate as to whether s 7 can properly be defined as a strict liability offence, given the availability of a defence. However, debates on the Act commonly refer to the nature of the offence as one of strict liability, which is not surprising given the absence of mens rea. On this see: E O'Shea, *The Bribery Act a Practical Guide* (Jordan Publishing Ltd 2011), 132–3.

25   Law Commission, *Reforming Bribery* (Law Com No 313, 2008) (Reforming Bribery), paras 6.25–6.39.

26   The Bribery Act, s 8 provides a broad definition of 'associated person' and captures any person (including a legal person) that 'performs services for or on behalf of' the organisation. The Act does not define what constitutes the performance of services but the MOJ Guidance suggests that this test is intended to give s 7 broad scope (see MOJ Guidance, above n 9, para 37). The Act expressly states that the capacity of the 'relevant person' is irrelevant in determining whether they are caught by the provision (Bribery Act, s 8(2)) and therefore it is a matter to be determined on the facts of any given situation. Thus, an associated person could include a subsidiary, agent or other representative of the organisation (ibid., s 8(3)). There is a rebuttable presumption (s 8(5)) that an organisation's employee is an associated person for the purpose of s 7.

27   Ibid., s 7(1).

to establish mens rea (or intent) on the part of the corporation, the mere act by a third party of making a bribe with the intention of obtaining or retaining business for the corporation gives rise to a liability.[28] Crucially, the corporation does not even need to be aware that the bribery took place, a claim will be maintained simply if it failed to prevent the bribery from occurring, subject only to the adequate procedures defence (considered in paras 8.13–8.18).[29]

By structuring the Act in this way, corporations are potentially liable for the acts **8.09** of a wide range of individuals, far beyond their direct employees. This breadth of scope has, understandably, given rise to legitimate concern as to the extent of an organisation's liability for the acts of third parties within their supply chain (beyond their direct counterparty). This exposure is particularly problematic for the financial services sector, where the use of third parties in day-to-day business is commonplace. Indeed, third-party liability has been a prominent factor in recent FCA enforcement actions, even where the regulated firm had seemingly robust policies in place (albeit where they had not adequately implemented them).[30]

The scope of the corporate offence has also ignited concerns as to subsidiary **8.10** liability. It is a cornerstone of English company law that a subsidiary is a separate entity, distinct from its parent.[31] However, as expressly envisaged by section 8 of the Act, a subsidiary may qualify as an associated person, giving rise to the possibility of parent liability for subsidiary activities. If, as a matter of fact, the subsidiary is found to be performing services for or on behalf of its parent, then the parent (subject to the adequate procedures defence) will be liable if the subsidiary pays a bribe with the intention of retaining or obtaining business for the parent. As with other third parties, the determination of the status of a

---

28 Although note that intention needs to be established on the part of the individual paying the bribe. Also, see n 24 above as to the debate over the correct classification of the strict liability offence.

29 The identification doctrine will still apply to corporate prosecutions pursuant to ss 1, 2 and 6 of the Act, only section 7 is structured in this way.

30 By way of example, in 2012 the FCA fined the specialist insurance broking firm JLT Speciality Ltd (JLTS) over £1.8m for failing to have in place appropriate procedures to guard against the risk of bribery or corruption in making payments to third parties. The FCA held that JLTS's failure amounted to a breach of its obligation to manage business and risks responsibly and effectively. In particular, the company failed to undertake appropriate due diligence before entering into relationships with overseas introducers. In a salient warning, the FCA explained that whilst JLTS had ABC policies in place they failed to implement them effectively, notwithstanding previous warnings by the FCA. In its final notice, the FCA made clear that whilst it did not conclude that JLTS authorised the illicit payments, it nevertheless failed to undertake the necessary due diligence, or implement its own ABC policies, thereby giving rise to an unacceptable level of risk that such payments would be made. The MOJ Guidance places similar importance on the effective implementation of ABC policies and the JLTS prosecution is indicative of the risks that firms face if they fail to do so. The FCA's final notice, 19 December 2013 is available at: http://fca.org.uk/static/documents/final-notices/jlt-specialty-limited.pdf, accessed 20 January 2014.

31 *Adams v Cape Industries* [1990] Ch 433; 2 WLR 657; [1991] 1 All ER 929.

subsidiary in this matter will be a substantive one, looking at the facts of the case and the substance of the relationship.[32] To be clear, a parent company cannot avoid liability simply by entering into contractual relationships stipulating that its subsidiaries are not performing services on its behalf.

8.11 The MOJ Guidance sought to respond to fears of excessive supply chain liability, intimating that a commercial organisation will only be liable for the acts of its direct counterparty in the chain.[33] However, this is a departure from previous (albeit draft) guidance and the MOJ Guidance itself is non-binding. Thus, the determination of supply chain liability remains a contentious one and, ultimately, will be a question of fact in each case. As with subsidiary liability, the substance of the relationship is likely to be critical together with the extent to which an organisation sought to impose ABC controls on its direct counterparty (with a concomitant obligation that these be passed further down the supply chain).

8.12 The consequence of the broad scope of the Act's corporate offence is that it drives an equally broad response. Thus, even organisations that are accustomed to risk management controls need to reconsider the reach of their governance programmes. Pending judicial determination of this issue, organisations would be prudent to proceed conservatively in determining who is an associated person. While the Act's offence influences the potential scope of a firm's internal systems and controls, it is the concomitant defence of 'adequate procedures', considered in the next section, that generated the widespread scrutiny of corporate governance in the context of ABC compliance.

B.   The adequate procedures defence

8.13 The only defence to a claim under section 7 (failure to prevent bribery) is that the commercial organisation had in place 'adequate procedures' to prevent an associated person from making (or offering) a bribe with the intent to retain or obtain business for the corporation.[34] It is important to note from the outset that the defence relates to 'procedures', namely policies and their implementation, not simply 'policies'. In common with FCA enforcement action in this area, it will not suffice for a corporation to draft detailed written policies that are not then embedded throughout the organisation in an effort to achieve a genuine culture of compliance.[35] Unsurprisingly, the adequate procedures

---

32   Reforming Bribery, see above n 25, para 6.120. See also: MOJ Guidance, above n 9, para 42.
33   MOJ Guidance, see above n 9, para 39.
34   Bribery Act, s 7(2).
35   Reforming Bribery, see above n 25, para 6.6.

defence raises a number of concerns, primarily that the term is too uncertain and that those subject to it are unclear as to their regulatory obligations.

The criticism that the adequate procedures defence was too uncertain was **8.14** anticipated from the outset[36] and the Joint Committee on the Draft Bribery Bill agreed that 'centrally issued'[37] guidance on the meaning of adequate procedures would be essential.[38] This obligation was enshrined in section 9 of the Act, which resulted in the issue of the MOJ Guidance as to procedures that organisations can implement to prevent associated persons from bribing. However, the production of the guidance itself has attracted controversy, with the final text issued in March 2011 being substantially different to that initially released for consultation. Notwithstanding these changes, although perhaps not surprisingly, the final guidance has received mixed reactions; the Executive Director of Transparency International UK described it as 'deplorable', arguing that parts of it read more like a 'guide on how to evade the Act, than how to develop company procedures that will uphold it'.[39]

One important impact of the adequate procedures defence is its reversal of the **8.15** traditional burden of proof in criminal cases; that is, it is not for the prosecutor to prove guilt under section 7 but for the corporation to prove it has implemented 'adequate procedures'.[40] Therefore, the question (currently untested) arises as to whether this reversal is lawful.[41] While scope does not permit a detailed consideration of this issue a few observations are merited at this

---

36   The lack of definition is interesting (although it must be noted that here we are discussing a defence), given the Law Commission's acknowledgement when discussing the term 'corruptly' that for 'a term which is not statutorily defined to be included in the definition of an offence, we must be confident that its generally understood meaning is unequivocal and that the common meaning is the meaning we would like imported into the offence', Law Commission, *Legislating the Criminal Code: Corruption* (LC 248, 3 March 1998) (Legislating the Criminal Code), para 5.65. It remains to be seen whether a commercial organisation will attempt a defence premised on the incompatibility of the adequate procedures defence with the European Convention requiring certainty of law. Although maintaining a claim that the law is too uncertain to be enforceable is a difficult task, see: *Kokkinakis v Greece* (1993) 17 EHRR 397, [1993] ECHR 14307/88 and *Handyside v United Kingdom (application 5493/72)* (1976) 1 EHRR 737, [1976] ECHR 5493/72.

37   House of Lords, House of Commons, Joint Committee on the Draft Bribery Bill, *Draft Bribery Bill, First Report of Session 2008–09 Vol I, Report, together with formal minutes* (HL Paper 115-I, HC 430-I 28 July 2009) (Joint Committee Report), para 109.

38   Ibid., para 91.

39   Chandrashekhar Krishnan, Executive Director of Transparency International UK, 'UK: Government Guidance "Deplorable" and will Weaken Bribery Act' (30 March 2011), available at: http://www.transparency.org/news/pressrelease/20110330_guidance_weakens_bribery_act, accessed 17 December 2013.

40   Ordinarily, it is for the prosecutor to prove the defendant's guilt. See: the ECHR, art 6(2), which dictates that everyone charged with a criminal offence shall be presumed innocent until proven guilty. Furthermore, the 'golden thread' of the English criminal law is that 'it is the duty of the prosecution to prove the prisoner's guilt', see *Woolmington v Director of Public Prosecutions* [1935] AC 462, 481 (Viscount Sankey LC).

41   For a general discussion of the authorities on the reversal see: Legislating the Criminal Code, see above n 36, paras 4.22–4.30.

juncture.[42] The parameters of a lawful reversal of the burden of proof draw a distinction between, inter alia, the evidential and legal burden of proof. The evidential burden of proof requires the defendant to assert reasonable doubt as to an issue or fact whereas the legal burden requires the defendant, on a balance of probabilities, to disprove the key elements of the offence. The former is less likely to violate the European Convention on Human Rights (ECHR), whereas it is the latter that has been reversed by the Act.[43]

8.16 The Joint Committee on the Draft Bribery Bill received evidence on the legality of the Act's proposed reversal of the burden of proof. In particular, the Chairman of the Joint Committee on Human Rights[44] gave evidence and referred to the government's view that the reversal of the legal burden was compatible with ECHR, art 6(2).[45] It was noted that the government argued that the reversal pursued (in a proportionate manner) the legitimate aim of ensuring that an organisation was responsible where it failed to prevent a person from committing an act of bribery on its behalf, subject to the adequate procedures defence. Furthermore, the government relied on the fact that the procedures that an organisation had in place to prevent bribery were particularly within the knowledge of the corporation. As a consequence, it would be difficult to place the legal burden on the prosecution to establish the contrary position.[46] The Chairman, in giving evidence, reported that his committee felt

---

42 The lawfulness of the reversal of the burden of proof was considered more fully by the Court of Appeal in *Attorney General Reference (No 1 of 2004), R v Edwards* [2004] EWCA Crim 1025, [2004] 4 All ER 457, which held that the reversal of the burden of proof was permissible pursuant to both the English common law and ECHR, art 6(2). In considering the question, the court issued guidance to the Crown and magistrates courts, which is instructive to consider (in part) in this context. The guidance stipulated that, inter alia: (i) courts should strongly discourage the citation of authority to them other than the decision of the House of Lords in *R v Johnstone* [2003] 3 All ER 884; (ii) reverse legal burdens would probably be justified if the overall burden of proof was on the prosecution, but there could be a situation where there were significant reasons why it was fair and reasonable to deny the defendant the general protection normally guaranteed by the presumption of innocence; (iii) where the exception went no further than was reasonably necessary to achieve the objective of the reverse burden (i.e. it was proportionate) it was sufficient if the exception was reasonable in all the circumstances; (iv) the reversal of an evidential burden only would not breach art 6(2); (v) when ascertaining whether an exception was justified, the court had to construe the provision to ascertain the realistic effects of the reverse burden; in doing so the court should be concerned more with substance than form and if the provision created an offence plus an exception that would, in itself, be a strong indication that there had been no contravention of art 6(2); and (vi) the easier it was for the accused to discharge the burden the more likely it was that the reversal was justified.
43 Ministry of Justice, *Bribery Draft Legislation* (Cm 7570) (MOJ Draft Legislation), para 103.
44 House of Lords, House of Commons, Joint Committee on the Draft Bribery Bill, *Draft Bribery Bill, First Report of Session 2008–09 Vol II, Oral and Written Evidence* (HL Paper 115-II, HC 430-II 28 July 2009), (Joint Committee Report Vol II), BB 61, Ev 328.
45 The government's view was set out in the explanatory notes on the draft bill, MOJ Draft Legislation, see above n 43, para 101.
46 Ibid., para 105.

that this analysis was 'broadly correct' and that the Act's reversal of the burden of proof did not lead to a significant risk of incompatibility with art 6(2).[47]

It is clear that the government would not adopt a reversal of such a fundamental **8.17** principle of criminal law lightly, or without first taking significant counsel. However, this reversal is an important departure from established principles and it remains to be seen if a corporation tests its legality in due course.

The clear (and intended) outcome of the adequate procedures defence is that **8.18** boards are left to determine what procedures are required and whether those adopted by a particular organisation are adequate for the purposes of the Act. Pending judicial determination, which may be increasingly scarce given the introduction of deferred prosecution agreements in the UK,[48] UK banks and financial institutions will be restricted to considering the guidance issued by, inter alia, the MOJ and the FCA together with enforcement decisions by overseas jurisdictions.

3. THE BRIBERY ACT 2010: THE MOJ GUIDANCE

It is clear that the requirements of the Act's adequate procedures are exacting: **8.19** the procedures must 'prevent' bribery, not simply identify and respond to it. While this cannot be an absolute standard, and an incident of bribery is not ipso facto evidence that procedures were inadequate, it is nevertheless a high threshold to meet. However, those corporations that adhere to (as a minimum) the MOJ Guidance, which promotes a risk-based approach to compliance supported by genuine top-level commitment to cultural change, will be better placed to satisfy the defence than those who engage in a mere box-ticking exercise. This section considers the recommendations of the MOJ Guidance and, in doing so, also draws on the corresponding industry guidance that is relevant to each of its principles.

The MOJ Guidance sets out six general principles (each followed by commen- **8.20** tary and examples) that should inform the procedures that corporations put in place to prevent bribery. It is not legally binding and nor does compliance with the principles provide a safe harbour from prosecution. To be clear, whether an organisation satisfies the adequate procedures defence in any given situation 'is

---

47   Joint Committee Report Vol II, see above n 44, BB 61, Ev 329.
48   Crime and Courts Act 2013, Sch 17.

a matter than can only be resolved by the courts taking into account the particular facts and circumstances of the case'.[49]

8.21 The principles set out generally established norms (which typically align with industry risk-management requirements) for identifying risks and implementing a compliance programme that responds to them. However, while the principles are not necessarily surprising, organisations need to distil them and understand how they apply to their own operations taking into account their industry, territorial reach and organisation size. The content of any ABC programme will be highly industry- and organisation-specific and must, as will be seen, respond to a bespoke risk-assessment undertaken by the corporation.

8.22 The MOJ Guidance is the centrally issued guidance concerning the requirements of section 7 and is therefore the focus of this chapter. However, regulated firms should, of course, also consider, inter alia, the FCA Guidance (which is referred to in the ensuing sections to add industry-specific expectations to the six principles).[50] The FCA Guidance provides banks and other FCA authorised firms with practical guidance on how to counter the risk of being used to further financial crime and draws on earlier FSA thematic reviews to do so. As such, the FCA Guidance provides practical insight into how a risk-based approach may be adopted and applied proportionately given the size and the complexity of the organisation, making distinctions between, inter alia, a global retail bank and a small local building society.[51] It also sets out self-assessment questions together with examples of good and poor practice, and is a useful resource for all organisations within the financial services industry when looking to review and implement internal anti-bribery and corruption policies.[52]

A.   Principle 1: Proportionate procedures[53]

8.23 An organisation must implement ABC procedures that are proportionate to the bribery risks it faces and to the nature, scale and complexity of the corporation's activities. Reflecting the requirements of the FCA Handbook,[54] the procedures should be clear, practicable, accessible, understood by all relevant staff,[55] effectively implemented and enforced. The effective implementation of the

---

49   MOJ Guidance, see above n 9, para 4.
50   FCA Guidance, see above n 10.
51   Ibid., para 1.14.
52   Outside specific financial services guidance, Transparency International UK has issued 'The 2010 UK Bribery Act Adequate Procedures: Guidance on Good Practice Procedures for Corporate Anti-bribery Programmes' (July 2010), which is also a helpful resource.
53   MOJ Guidance, see above n 9, 21.
54   FCA Handbook, SYSC 3.2.6R and SYSC 6.1.1R.
55   FCA Guidance, see above n 10, box 2.4.

procedures is, of course, paramount and has been the subject of previous FSA action, with fines being levied against several firms for failing to properly enforce their own policies.[56]

By demanding proportionality, this first principle alludes to the overarching **8.24** theme of the MOJ Guidance, namely that any ABC programme needs to be premised on a bespoke risk-assessment,[57] the requirements of which are considered further in paragraphs 8.39 – 8.46. However, in very high-level terms an initial risk-assessment to determine the proportionality of any ABC policies will need to consider, as a minimum, factors such as the size of the organisation (subject to the caveat that size is not determinative of risk),[58] the nature and extent of its third-party relationships (in particular overseas relationships and those with politically exposed persons), and the nature, location and complexity of its business.

The exact content of an organisation's ABC policies will vary depending on the **8.25** outcome of the risk-assessment, as it is imperative that these policies (to be effective) are tailored to the risks that the organisation is exposed to. The failure to comply with this fundamental principle is cited by the FCA as a specific example of poor practice in a case where an IFA had its policies drawn up by an external consultant but these had not been tailored to the business.[59] Nevertheless, common components of an ABC policy (or stand alone policies incorporated by reference to the ABC policy) are likely to include:[60]

a.   a broad, high level statement of the board's commitment to bribery prevention and a zero-tolerance to bribery. Specifically, any ABC policy should start with this overarching commitment, providing the normative framework the ensuing, more detailed, provisions will operate within. A zero-tolerance to bribery is the standard expected by organisations subject to the Bribery Act[61] and is increasingly the expected norm from wider international efforts in this regard[62] regardless of whether the organisation is operating in other jurisdictions with a more permissive ABC regime;

---

56   JLTS final notice, see above n 30, paras 2.2(3) and 4.34–4.40.
57   The risk-assessment requirement is detailed in MOJ Guidance, see above n 9, principle 3.
58   Ibid., 21 para 1.2.
59   FCA Guidance, see above n 10, Part, 2 box 10.7.
60   This list also reflects the recommendations of the OECD, *Good Practice Guidance on Internal Controls, Ethics, and Compliance* (February 2010) (OECD Good Practice Guidance), para A(5).
61   MOJ Guidance, see above n 9, 23.
62   See Annex 8.2, para A2. 13.

b.   an overview of its implementation strategy (detailed in paras 8.27 and 8.80–8.94);[63]

c.   gifts and hospitality (a more detailed analysis of which is set out in Annex 8.2);

d.   the use of intermediaries (including lobbyists): this is a particularly high risk area for authorised firms and third party relationships should only be entered into following compliance with a risk-based approvals process premised on appropriate due diligence, details of which are set out in paras 8.47–8.53. The policy needs to make clear that deviations from this due diligence (including any escalation and approvals process) will not be permitted;[64]

e.   employee/HR matters: employees are deemed to be associated persons under the Act and therefore need to be included within the firm's ABC policies. Recruitment and employment policies need to ensure that employees are aware of, and properly trained in, the ABC policies, that there is a clear, easy and accessible reporting procedure for any ABC concerns that an employee may have and that remuneration packages are structured to avoid excessive risk-tasking within the ABC arena. Many organisations also incorporate by reference their ABC policy (including the disciplinary consequences of a breach) into employee contracts;

f.   financial reporting and controls: these include 'adequate bookkeeping, auditing and approval of expenditure',[65] and serve not only as an ABC prevention mechanism but also play an important role in its detection;

g.   sponsorship, donations and political contributions: each of which could conceal bribes and will need to be subject to clear thresholds, approval processes and business case requirements;

h.   whistle-blowing, reporting and escalation procedures: to challenge non-compliant cultures employees must feel that they are both able to report corrupt behaviour and, moreover, that there will not be adverse, personal repercussions for doing so. To achieve this objective, organisations need to consider implementing confidential systems by which employees can raise concerns. As part of the firm's training programme, these whistle-blowing mechanisms need to be explained and their confidentiality emphasised; and

i.   ABC investigations, with roles and responsibilities clearly allocated.[66]

8.26 Principle 1 relates to both an organisations' anti-corruption policies together with the procedures that implement them. In doing so, it makes it clear from

---

63   MOJ Guidance, see above n 9, 22

64   This is of particular concern for authorised firms and is considered further in paras 8.47–8.53.

65   MOJ Guidance, see above n 9, 22.

66   BBA Guidance, see above n 11, para 4.11.1.

the outset that to comply with the Act corporations need to effectively embed an anti-corruption ethos within their culture. The MOJ Guidance includes the following, non-exhaustive, list of considerations (which overlap in part with the policies themselves) that those responsible for implementing the ABC policies should consider:

a.   involvement of senior management;
b.   risk-assessment;
c.   due diligence for existing and prospective associated persons;
d.   the provision of gifts, hospitality, promotional expenditure, political or charitable donations and demands for facilitation payments;
e.   employment;
f.   governance of business relationships;
g.   financial and commercial controls;
h.   transparency and disclosure;
i.   decision-making, including delegation and the separation of functions;
j.   enforcement and discipline for breaches of anti-bribery policies;
k.   whistle-blowing;
l.   implementation strategy;
m.   communication and training; and
n.   monitoring and review.[67]

It is instructive that the MOJ Guidance emphasises the importance of properly **8.27** implementing ABC programmes. Well-resourced organisations will be able to produce procedures that, ostensibly, comply with best practice requirements. Nevertheless, where the real test of 'adequacy' is likely to stand or fall is how these are rolled out across the organisation, aligning with the elusive question of 'culture'. Procedures should detail clear and unambiguous consequences for breach,[68] which are consistently enforced thereby enhancing the legitimacy of (and therefore compliance with) the programme. Furthermore, these policies must be tailored to the organisation in response to its own risk-assessment.

An organisation should have in place group-wide policies and procedures for **8.28** anti-bribery and corruption.[69] This raises difficulties for global organisations operating within complex and sometimes conflicting legal and cultural frame-works. However, a firm adopting a zero-tolerance policy to corruption needs to implement this normative framework throughout its operations, regardless of location, reinforcing this culture to both its employees and third parties that it

---

67   MOJ Guidance, see above n 9, 22.
68   FCA Guidance, see above n 10, box 6.3.
69   Ibid., Part 2, box 8.3.

engages with. Notwithstanding this universal policy, how it is rolled out throughout the firm will need to be tailored depending on the local context and this is considered further in paragraphs 8.54–8.60.

8.29 The implementation of UK-equivalent standards across an entire group was one aspect of the FSA's enforcement action against the HSBC Group in respect of deficiencies in its anti-money laundering (AML) procedures (which were also the subject of a $1.9bn settlement with US authorities). This action is instructive both to demonstrate the regulators' expectation that UK equivalent standards be adopted on a group-wide basis and also to gain insight into the governance structures that can be adopted (or may be expected) for high-risk banking and financial institutions. In brief, in 2012 the FSA took action against HSBC Holdings plc (HSBC plc) in response to, inter alia, HSBC's compliance with AML rules. As part of the action, the FSA stipulated (with the intent that these requirements would ensure compliance across the whole group) that HSBC plc:

a.   establish a committee of the board to oversee matters relating to, inter alia, AML;

b.   review HSBC Group policies to ensure equivalent compliance with UK standards;

c.   appoint an FSA approved, group money laundering reporting officer; and

d.   appoint an independent monitor to oversee the group's compliance with UK AML and related rules and to report to the HSBC board committee and regulators.[70]

B.   Principle 2: Top-level commitment[71]

8.30 A fundamental objective of the Act is to instil a more ethical compliance culture within organisations.[72] Central to achieving this objective is a governance structure that is supported by top-level commitment to a zero-tolerance approach to corruption. Without this commitment, genuine cultural change will not be possible, as ABC policies will be operating within a corporate environment that tacitly, if not expressly, fails to support their objectives. It is not surprising therefore that Principle 2 of the MOJ Guidance identifies the importance of management communication and supervision of the ABC programme and requires that the top-level management of the corporation 'are

---

70   See FSA, *FSA requires action of the HSBC Group* FSA/PN/111/2012 (11 December 2012), available at: http://www.fsa.gov.uk/library/communication/pr/2012/111.shtml>, accessed 20 January 2014.

71   MOJ Guidance, see above n 9, 23.

72   The role of culture within an ABC programme is considered further in paras 8.66–8.94.

committed to preventing bribery by persons associated with it. They foster a culture within the organisation in which bribery is never acceptable'.[73]

The notion of 'tone from the top' is now pervasive in literature in this field. **8.31** However, its familiarity should not undermine its practical importance. The creation of detailed ABC policies are going to be of little value if the board and senior management set business strategies and remuneration policies that undermine the programme's norms. In most cases, employees are going to be more influenced by the actions of their management team (and the norms that they promote) rather than those of a corporate policy that has not been embedded within the corporation's culture and decision-making framework. To be clear, an ostensibly compliant ABC policy is unlikely to sustain an adequate procedures defence if it is operating within a culture that promotes business objectives over ABC standards and/or that marginalises the corporation's compliance function. Moreover, while ethical culture is a key component of reducing misconduct,[74] it is prudent to note that key metrics of such a culture include tone from the top and supervisor reinforcement of ethical behaviour.[75]

The exact nature of the governance structure adopted will depend on the **8.32** demands of, and risks faced by, the organisation. Nevertheless, regardless of the approach taken, it is essential that senior management[76] takes 'clear responsibility' for managing financial crime risks and that there should be 'evidence that senior management are actively engaged' in the firm's approach to addressing these risks.[77] Specifically, the FCA suggests that good practice would include a single manager having clear, documented responsibility for anti-bribery and corruption measures or a committee with appropriate terms of reference and senior management membership, with reporting responsibility to the board.[78] As a minimum, the senior management team should be able to demonstrate a clear understanding of the bribery risks faced by the organisation, how they adopt a risk-based approach to corruption[79] and the steps taken by the company to respond to these.[80]

---

73 MOJ Guidance, see above n 9, 23. See also FCPA Guidance, see above n 13, 57. The importance of 'tone from the top' is also recognised in the OECD Good Practice Guidance, see above n 60, para A(1).

74 Ethics Resource Centre, *2009 National Business Ethics Survey: Ethics in the Recession* (2009), 41.

75 Ethics Resource Centre, *2011 National Business Ethics Survey: Workplace Ethics in Transition* (2012), 19.

76 A senior manager is defined in the FCA Handbook Glossary as an individual other than a director to whom the governing body of the firm (or a member thereof) has given responsibility (jointly or alone) for management and supervision and who reports directly to the governing body (or a member thereof), or the chief executive or the head of a significant business unit

77 FCA Guidance, see above n 10, box 2.1.

78 Ibid., Part 2, box 9.1.

79 Ibid.

80 FCA Handbook, SYSC 2.1.3.

8.33 The FCA Handbook sets out specific requirements regarding individual responsibility for internal systems and controls. In particular, SYSC 2.1 mandates that a board member or senior manager be allocated responsibility to oversee the establishment and maintenance of systems and controls under SYSC 3.1.1 R.

8.34 To enable this oversight role and responsibility to be properly discharged, it is imperative that the firm ensures that the compliance function is properly resourced in terms of time, money, independence and access to the board. Further, they must be supported in their work by clear, appropriate and co-ordinated reporting, information sharing and escalation procedures across the business.[81] To ensure that they receive appropriate information, the management team should establish suitable reporting principles, so that it can be properly informed of those risks that need to be factored into any compliance programme (and thereafter monitored). For this reporting line to be effective, the corporation needs to operate within a culture where employees feel able to report potential problems, rather than withhold them from the management team. In its 2012 report, the FCA found that in response to the Act many firms had improved policies on, inter alia, gifts and hospitality but they had failed to complement these with suitable management information processes, that would, for example, enable a review of hospitality on a cumulative basis.[82]

8.35 Management information should include, as a minimum, an overview of the bribery and corruption risks faced by the organisation, the systems and controls implemented to mitigate the risks, information about the effectiveness of those systems, any breaches or potential breaches, information on third-party relationships,[83] together with legal and regulatory developments.[84] Senior management should then document how they have responded to any issues included within the management information provided.[85]

8.36 Creating a culture of compliance is difficult and needs to mitigate many industry, cultural and legal norms. However, a key step in introducing cultural change is a clear management commitment to zero-tolerance to bribery,[86] which is consistently enforced throughout the organisation.[87] In this regard, the

---

81 FCA Guidance, see above n 10, box 2.1 and 6.1; US Sentencing Guidelines, see above n 13, §8B2.1(b)(2)(B).
82 ABC Guidance, see above n 6, para 3(g).
83 The CIB Guidance, see above n 2, 13 suggests that such third-party information could include (but is not limited to): new third-party accounts, their risk classification, higher risk third-party payments for the preceding period, changes to third-party bank account details and unusually high commission payments.
84 ABC Guidance, see above n 6, paras 29 and 33.
85 FCA Guidance, see above n 10, Part 2, box 9.1.
86 MOJ Guidance, see above n 9, 23.
87 BBA Guidance, see above n 11, para 4.3.1.

FCA lists narrow compliance with minimum regulatory standards as an example of poor governance practice in combatting financial crime.[88] This commitment should be expressed internally and externally but, moreover, reflected obliquely in remuneration structures and procurement methods to ensure that they do not tacitly create pressures or incentives that could encourage high-risk activities. For example, firms should adopt a 'balanced scorecard' approach to appraisals and bonus decisions, which consider a wide range of factors including compliance standards, rather than simply concentrating on pure profit generation.[89] Firms should also consider including a deferral and claw-back element to bonus arrangements, which may impact on individual risk-taking.[90]

The senior leadership team needs to be visible in implementing anti-corruption policies, an objective that is increasingly possible through the use of technology. Corporations can utilise videos and podcasts from board members when introducing training programmes. Also, organisations should clearly identify and communicate who has board-level responsibility for compliance and the compliance team needs to be accessible by employees and other third parties that are subject to an obligation to report ABC violations. **8.37**

The importance of top-level commitment within a compliance programme (and other MOJ Principles such as due diligence and training) was apparent from the evidence of the former director of the SFO to the Joint Committee on the Draft Bribery Bill. The director indicated that he would want to see a robust compliance toolkit that would help assess how successful a company had been in mitigating risk including: **8.38**

(i)   a clear statement of an anti-corruption programme fully and visibly supported at the highest levels in the company;
(ii)   a clear and personalised reporting structure from the CEO down to all managers;
(iii) a code of ethics;
(iv)   principles that are applicable regardless of local laws or culture;
(v)   individual accountability;
(vi)   a policy on gifts and hospitality and facilitation payments;
(vii) a policy on outside advisors/third parties, including vetting and due diligence;

---

88   FCA Guidance, see above n 10, box 2.1.
89   Ibid., box 9.7.
90   CIB Guidance, see above n 2, paras 134–135.

(viii) training – to enable staff to comment and input; and

(ix) robust maintenance – auditing/updating/evaluation/actions.[91]

C. Principle 3: Risk assessment[92]

8.39 It is critical that a firm's ABC policy is premised on a thorough and bespoke risk assessment of its 'exposure to potential external and internal risks of bribery on its behalf by persons associated with it'.[93] The need for a risk-based approach to bribery and corruption is prevalent throughout the Act, the international anti-bribery conventions and the Handbook. Without a proper risk assessment an organisation will not be able to design a programme that would 'prevent' bribery or that would satisfy the FCA's systems and controls requirements.[94] An organisation needs to know what risks it faces, where they are most likely to arise and, moreover, how to design and implement adequate procedures to be effective within their particular organisation. Without a clear risk assessment it is unlikely that a corporation (or its officers on cross-examination) will be able to defend the adequacy of any procedures that it adopts. Moreover, without properly understanding the risks it faces, a corporation will not know where to best direct its resources with the outcome that resources are spread too thinly, reducing the effectiveness of its programme.[95] It is salient that one of the primary findings of the FSA in its CIB Guidance was that there was a general failure to adopt a risk-based approach to anti-bribery and corruption in practice.[96]

8.40 Crucially, the risk assessment is not a one-off or isolated event. It needs to be tied into the firm's ABC policies and renewed periodically and/or in response to a trigger event, such as a new acquisition or product offering, extending operations into a new territory or any other material business change or change in external and internal bribery and corruption risks.[97] Fundamental to any effective risk assessment is that it is not undertaken in abstract, but rather in consultation with people 'on the ground' who are aware of the tensions and risks that can arise on a day-to-day basis. It is likely that a simple, questionnaire based assessment will not be sufficient to identify any control weaknesses that

---

91 Joint Committee Report, see above n 37, BB47, Ev 269.
92 MOJ Guidance, see above n 9, 25.
93 Ibid., 25. This is also reflected in the OECD Good Practice Guidance, see above n 60, para A.
94 It is important to note that the Act's risk-assessment requirements relate to bribery only whereas the FCA requires the assessment to cover the broader definition of 'financial crime' as set out in FCA Handbook, SYSC 3.2.6R and 6.1.1R. See also: BBA Guidance, see above n 11, para 5.1.2.
95 FCPA Guidance, see above n 13, 58.
96 ABC Guidance, see above n 6, 4.
97 Ibid., para 47.

will expose the organisation to a bribery risk.[98] Rather, interviews and focus groups will also need to be undertaken. As with bribery and corruption responsibility more generally, responsibility for carrying out and updating the risk assessment should be clearly allocated to a senior individual or relevant committee.[99]

The MOJ Guidance recommends that the basic characteristics of the risk **8.41** assessment include: (i) the oversight of the risk assessment by top management; (ii) that it is adequately resourced; (iii) that it identifies the internal and external information sources that need to be engaged with; (iv) that it undertakes due diligence inquiries (discussed further in principle 4); and (v) that the risk assessment and its conclusions are properly documented. Documenting the risk assessment will be essential should an organisation need to demonstrate that it has complied with this principle. Records should be taken to demonstrate, inter alia, the scope of the risk assessment, the personnel involved (including those interviewed), the risks identified and why, the involvement of any outside counsel, the findings of the assessment and the action taken as a result.

To help identify the source of external risk factors, the MOJ Guidance lists the **8.42** following commonly encountered factors that would need to be considered as part of the risk assessment:

a. jurisdictional: in particular whether the firm engages in business in high-risk territories. When considering whether a particular jurisdiction should be considered high risk, it is important to engage with actual risks based, for example, on Transparency International's Corruption Perception Index[100] and not assumptions. Factors to consider include the strength of the territory's domestic anti-bribery regulation;

b. sectoral: some industries are considered to be higher risk than others (such as the extractive and pharmaceutical industries);

c. transactional: with particular consideration given to high-risk transactions such as charitable or political donations, license and public procurement contracts;

d. business opportunity risks: which may arise in high-value projects, those at non-market prices or involving third parties; and

---

98   BBA Guidance, see above n 11, para 3.4.9.
99   ABC Guidance, see above n 6, para 50.
100 Transparency International's Corruption Perception Index will be of assistance here.

e.   business partnership risk: with higher risks potentially arising from relationships with foreign public officials, consortia, joint venture partners or
politically exposed persons.[101]

8.43 The BBA Guidance identifies, inter alia, the following additional risk factors
that may be considered:

a.   the lack of clear ABC messages from top-level management;[102]

b.   route to market, particularly those involving third parties, commission
structures and interactions with public officials;[103]

c.   product and business opportunities such as project finance, mergers and
acquisitions and high value projects or those involving many intermediaries;[104]

d.   lobbying;[105]

e.   advisory and consulting activities;

f.   remuneration structures and incentives;[106]

g.   people/HR risks including the existence and application of disciplinary
policies, ethics and conduct, deficiencies in employee training, skills and
knowledge;

h.   the risk of missing data.[107]

8.44 The risk assessment (both the initial undertaking and its periodic review) is
going to be the foundation of any defence under the Act. It must therefore be
clearly documented together with any ad hoc reviews undertaken in response to
a breach. The BBA Guidance includes a helpful schematic, which suggests one
possible approach for banks undertaking a risk assessment.[108]

8.45 Traditionally, risk assessments undertaken by banks and financial institutions,
have been very technical. Enforcement action, such as that taken against HSBC
(see paragraph 8.29) but replicated by regulators on a global scale, means that
financial crime compliance is now elevated 'to the highest level within the
bank's structure and reinforces the notion that, over the years, it has emerged

---

101   MOJ Guidance, see above n 9, 26.
102   BBA Guidance, see above n 11, para 5.1.4
103   Ibid., para 5.2.1.3.
104   Ibid., para 5.2.1.2.
105   Ibid., paras 5.2.2.4 and 5.2.1.6.
106   Ibid., para 5.1.4. The FCA Guidance, see above n 10, Part 2, box 9.7 also recommends that organisations
subject their remuneration structures to risk assessment to ensure that they do not increase the risk of bribery
and corruption. See also the CIB Guidance, see above n 2, paras 129–135.
107   BBA Guidance, see above n 11, para 5.2.1.5. See also the FCA Guidance, see above n 10, box 6.3.
108   BBA Guidance, ibid., 30.

form a backwater function to one of the most significant compliance challenges facing major financial institutions'.[109]

It is clear that a firm's ABC policy needs to respond to and reflect the outcome **8.46** of the risk assessment. The threat arising from identified risks will be subjective for each organisation and a firm will need to weight the identified risks and design its internal systems and controls accordingly. Furthermore, properly understanding the risks faced by the firm will then enable the organisation to determine how best to allocate its resources, focus training and concentrate due diligence. It will also highlight those areas that will be subject to local differences and where an element of local, managerial discretion will be warranted (provided this discretion is clearly subject to the broad principles set out in the global code of conduct and/or ABC policy, such as a zero-tolerance to bribery).

D.   Principle 4: Due diligence[110]

A particular risk for banks and other financial firms is the exposure arising from **8.47** engagement of third parties. This is reflected in principle 4 of the MOJ Guidance, which requires commercial organisations to undertake due diligence on 'persons who perform or will perform services for or on behalf of the organisation, in order to mitigate identified bribery risks'.[111] This is a deliberately broad definition, which corporations should interpret as such (pending judicial interpretation) and includes, but is not limited to, consultants, lobbyists, contractors, lawyers, introducers and other third parties. For many organisations, it is the acts of third parties that may expose them to liability and it is important that due diligence of new 'associated persons' is firmly embedded as standard business practice (together with ongoing monitoring once the relationship has been entered into). It is imperative that authorised firms have a clearly documented policy detailing what constitutes a third party, the criteria for selecting third parties, the commercial rationale for doing so together with a detailed due diligence process to approve and thereafter monitor any specific third party.[112]

---

109   Peter Djinis, former regulatory policy official with the US Treasury Department's Financial Crimes Enforcement Network cited by Brett Wolf, 'HSBC board-level committee may prompt other banks to focus on enterprise-wide risk management' (Thomson Reuters *The Knowledge Effect*, 4 February 2013), available at: http://blog.thomsonreuters.com/index.php/hsbc-board-level-committee-may-prompt-other-banks-to-focus-on-enterprise-wide-risk-management/, accessed 20 January 2014.
110   MOJ Guidance, see above n 9, 27.
111   Ibid.
112   ABC Guidance, see above n 6, para 71. For examples of poor third-party due diligence see CIB Guidance, see above n 2, para 4, which also contains detailed information on appropriate third-party due diligence in section 3.3.

8.48 This due diligence requirement complements the proportionate, risk-based, procedures that are endorsed by the other principles. By undertaking appropriate due diligence on new relationships firms are able to identify and avoid (or properly manage) potentially high-risk, third-party relationships. The extent of the due diligence itself should be informed by a risk-based approach,[113] taking into account the jurisdiction in question, the nature of the relationship (including the ease of termination) and the risks associated with the counterparty (such as whether they are a politically exposed person).[114] Further 'red flags' indicating higher risk third parties include those relationships where the third party is an individual (or a company that is, in reality, a mere nominee for an individual), where there is no convincing business case for the engagement, if any commission is paid on the instructions of another party in the transaction, if the third party asks for secrecy concerning payment or where the third party asks for a commission payment prior to premiums being paid.[115] As red flags arise, so to should the scrutiny to which the third party is subject.[116]

8.49 The BBA Guidance provides helpful information on the content of any due diligence exercise on third parties, depending on the outcome of the risk assessment. First, it is necessary to determine the identity (including beneficial ownership) and potential risks of the third party (for example whether they have a relationship with a foreign public official) together with the scope of services that they are to be performing. Thereafter, the contract with any third party should include, inter alia, warranties that the third party is not a foreign public official (or working on behalf of one) and that the third party has not been guilty of corruption in the past, together with obligations to report any change that may give rise to a bribery risk and commitments to implement and maintain anti-bribery policies and procedures (predicated on the firm's own policies and training).[117]

8.50 The OECD Good Practice Guidance contains specific advice concerning third-party (referred to as 'business partners') due diligence, recommending that policies include:

(i) properly documented risk-based due diligence pertaining to the hiring, as well as the appropriate and regular oversight of business partners;

(ii) informing business partners of the company's commitment to abiding by laws on

---

113   MOJ Guidance, see above n 9, 28.
114   BBA Guidance, see above n 11, para 6.2.3.
115   CIB Guidance, see above n 2, para 61.
116   FCPA Guidance, see above n 13, 60.
117   BBA Guidance, see above n 11, 31–38; MOJ Guidance, see above n 9, para 39.

the prohibitions against foreign bribery, and of the company's ethics and compliance programme or measures for preventing and detecting such bribery; and

(iii) seeking a reciprocal commitment from business partners.[118]

A firm's ABC policies should make it clear that a relationship with a third party **8.51**
should only be entered into when the organisation is satisfied that appropriate
due diligence has been undertaken (and documented)[119] in accordance with its
internal policies. Moreover, the firm should be satisfied that there is a legitimate
commercial reason for engaging the third party in the circumstances[120] and that
it is comfortable that the terms of engagement (which should clearly define the
scope of work to be undertaken) do not pose an ABC risk. For example, an
organisation should be comfortable that remuneration terms reflect industry
norms,[121] whilst being cognisant that remuneration structures that rely heavily
on commission payments may increase the risk of exposure. Further, as recommended by the OECD (see para 8.50), organisations should elicit ABC
commitments from counterparties (including, but not limited to, conduct,
training, books and records and onward engagement of third parties). Ideally,
these ABC commitments should be contained within the written terms of
engagement that a firm has with a third party.

If any red flags are raised during the due diligence process these must be **8.52**
addressed before the company proceeds with the relationship. Accordingly,
ABC policies should include an escalation procedure to be followed if any
concerns are identified. More generally, organisations should consider requiring
that a member of its legal or compliance team is included in the sign-off process
for third-party relationships. Once a firm enters into a relationship with a third
party this should then be monitored on an ongoing basis with the firm's
compliance function having oversight of all third-party relationships.[122] The
FCA recommends that organisations, as part of their due diligence ask third
parties to complete initial forms that ask relevant, mandatory, questions the
responses to which should then be carefully verified.[123] Firms should always

---

118   OECD Good Practice Guidance, see above n 60, para A(6).
119   The FCA has made it clear that it expects authorised firms to document third-party due diligence ABC
      Guidance, see above n 6, para 70.
120   The lack of commercial justification to support payments to third parties was one aspect of the FCA's
      enforcement action against Willis Ltd, an insurance intermediary. Pursuant to this action a penalty of
      £6.895m was levied against Willis Ltd for, inter alia, failing to establish and record a commercial rationale to
      support its payments to overseas third parties. See: FSA Final Notice to Willis Ltd (21 July 2011), available at:
      http://www.fsa.gov.uk/pubs/final/willis_ltd.pdf, accessed 20 January 2014.
121   FCPA Guidance, see above n 13, 60.
122   FCA Guidance, see above n 10, box 6.4.
123   Ibid., Part 2 box 9.3.

undertake their own due diligence and not rely on the fact that another organisation may have performed due diligence on the party in question.[124]

8.53 The risk of failing to properly monitor and control third-party relationships can be significant. In January 2009 the FSA fined Aon Ltd £5.25m for failing to implement strong controls over payments to intermediaries. In its findings, the FCA found that Aon failed to properly assess the risks associated with its third-party relationships and thus failed to implement effective controls to mitigate them. Of note is that Aon's failing related both to due diligence prior to entering into the relationships and also to the ongoing monitoring of the relationships after they had been entered into.[125]

E. Principle 5: Communication (Including training)[126]

8.54 The first principle of the MOJ Guidance requires that a firm's ABC procedures are 'effectively implemented' and instrumental to achieving this is ensuring that the corporation adopts a comprehensive training and communication programme. It is clear that even the most carefully drafted policies will be of limited value (and certainly unlikely to be 'adequate') if they are not properly communicated and embedded within the organisation. In this regard, the FCA cites a failure to adequately communicate a firm's policies and procedures as an example of poor practice.[127]

8.55 All members of staff and associated persons will need to be subject to mandatory basic training (given by people with specialist knowledge)[128] with further, bespoke, training given to certain sectors of the workforce in response to particular risks identified as part of the risk assessment.[129] In addition, the organisation will need to determine a policy on mandating and managing third-party and supply chain training, namely whether they will conduct the training themselves or include contractual requirements that the third party

---

124 Ibid.
125 Ibid., box 6.5; ABC Guidance, see above n 6, para 86. See also the FSA's final notice against Aon Ltd. Aon was fined £5.25m for, inter alia, failing to maintain effective systems and controls for countering the risks of bribery and corruption associated with payments to overseas third parties. See: FSA Final Notice to Aon Ltd (6 January 2009), available at: http://www.fsa.gov.uk/pubs/final/aon.pdf, accessed 20 January 2014.
126 MOJ Guidance, see above n 9, 29.
127 FCA Guidance, see above n 10, box 2.4.
128 This may seem to be an obvious point but the FSA found, as recently as May 2010, that the staff responsible for financial crime training had generally not received specialist training themselves on anti-bribery and corruption, see CIB Guidance, above n 2, para 126.
129 FCA Guidance, see above n 10, box 2.5.

undertake such training itself. Staff records should detail what training was undertaken and when.[130]

Corporate policies will need to be communicated both internally and externally **8.56** (although the extent of disclosure will differ). Part of the communication programme should include unequivocal management support for the training programme, clear explanations as to why such training is important and what it is designed to achieve. Organisations can (and should) use different mechanisms for doing this. Hard copies of policies can be sent to staff or made available on the intranet, but this is unlikely to suffice in isolation. The MOJ Guidance emphasises the importance of training in not only informing 'associated persons' of the terms of the compliance programme but also in deterring bribery by making people aware of its harmful effects and the corporation's commitment to enforcing its anti-bribery stance.[131] This second objective is unlikely to be achieved by a purely passive, paper-based exercise. Thus, organisations should explore a variety of methods of communication including face-to-face meetings, online training and testing and regular bulletins on relevant developments.

The content of training will be organisation-specific. As a minimum, the **8.57** training will need to detail the firm's policies and procedures, define and explain the term bribe, highlight that the request/payment of a bribe may not be immediately obvious, explain individual duties and responsibilities under the law including the repercussion of a breach and an explanation of how and when to seek advice.[132]

To be successful, training needs to engage individuals in understanding the **8.58** harm caused by corruption, including its impact on the individual. Individual liability should be raised together with practical examples that highlight how an individual could unintentionally transgress the requirement of the Act. Training should also focus on the difficult decisions (and competing norms) that an individual may be faced with but emphasise that the organisation requires, and will support, ethical decision making i.e. what will happen if an employee is asked to pay a bribe to win a contract that will result in a significant personal bonus. The FCA Guidance suggests that training should include a strong practical dimension, such as using case studies, and that it should also include some form of testing.[133] Training hypotheticals should be tailored to the

---

130　Ibid., box 9.6.
131　MOJ Guidance, see above n 9, 29.
132　BBA Guidance, see above n 11, para 4.15.10.
133　FCA Guidance, see above n 10, box 2.5; ABC Guidance, see above n 6, para 135.

audience reflecting their line of work, cultural environment and the situations that they are likely to incur in real life.[134]

8.59 Effective training programmes need to be rolled out to all parties who may be 'associated persons', which is likely to involve many different levels of staff across multiple jurisdictions. The training needs to be tailored to its audience to reflect the nature of the work undertaken by the individuals concerned and their territory of operation (including any cultural sensitivities, for example not using 'standard' training videos that include social situations involving alcohol where this would be offensive to the audience). The nature of the training should include a mixture of online and in-person training, adopting a combination that is likely to be the most effective.

8.60 This training will, of course, need to be recorded, updated (including associated training materials) and repeated on a regular basis and in response to trigger events (such as a complaint, change in business offering or regulatory development).[135] It is advisable for individuals to certify their attendance at a training event and many organisations include a test at the end of ABC training to ensure individual understanding. A failure to attend ABC training is often cited as a disciplinary matter.

F.   Principle 6: Monitoring and review

8.61 Regardless of the adequacy of the initial risk assessment, concomitant guidance and training, if it is not regularly reviewed it will struggle to comply with the Act.[136] The business environment (incorporating political, social and personnel factors), can change rapidly and compliance programmes need to reflect this fluidity. Therefore, principle 6 requires that the organisation monitors its compliance programme and makes changes where necessary.[137] In addition to a periodic review, an organisation should identify a list of factors (such as an acquisition) that will trigger an extraordinary review.

8.62 The MOJ Guidance suggests several mechanisms that can be adopted to monitor the adequacy of internal controls. These include: internal financial control mechanisms, staff surveys, client questionnaires and periodic reviews

---

134   FCPA Guidance, see above n 13, 59.
135   OECD Good Practice Guidance, see above n 60, A8.
136   In the US, the DOJ will also require evidence that compliance programmes have been reviewed and, where necessary, updated. See FCPA Guidance, see above n 13, 58.
137   See also: OECD Good Practice Guidance, above n 60, A; OECD, *Guidelines for Multinational Enterprises (2011 Edition)*, Section VII Combatting Bribery, Bribe Solicitation and Extortion, para VII(2).

and reports for (and by) top-level management.[138] This is in addition to the possibility of external review. Any internal review will need to be subject to careful scrutiny to ensure that it can be properly objective (given the risk of commitment bias, amongst others) or that a conflict of interest does not otherwise arise to undermine the effectiveness of the review. If an organisation feels that it lacks the appropriate skills or resources to undertake an internal review then it should seek external assistance.[139]

Reviews of internal policies and procedures should not be limited to whether **8.63** the current governance structure has been followed but also whether it has been effective. The BBA guidance acknowledges that banks may treat financial crimes as a combined risk (bribery, money laundering, etc) and that they should consider the structure of their existing financial crime committees to review and develop their anti-bribery policies and procedures.[140] As part of the review process, firms should consider feedback from staff and third parties, any complaints that the firm has received, together with enforcement action by the Serious Fraud Office (SFO), FCA and/or other relevant regulatory bodies.[141]

Monitoring red flags include: excessive gift giving/hospitality, unexplained **8.64** changes to a third-party relationship, unusually high requests for commission payments (or isolated requests), over invoicing within current payment controls and exclusive dealings by one employee with a single third party.[142]

Organisations need to determine who will be responsible for the ongoing **8.65** monitoring of the programme and how/when reviews will be undertaken. For example, will a review committee be appointed, comprised of stakeholders from the compliance, legal, business and HR teams? Those responsible for the ongoing review must be given clear parameters as to the scope of, and triggers for, review including periodic reviews (at least annually) and extraordinary events (such as a breach or new business acquisition). This review process will form an integral part of the cycle of continuous review and improvement of an organisation's ABC culture.

---

138   MOJ Guidance, see above n 9, 31.
139   FCA Guidance, see above n 10, part 2, box 6.15.
140   BBA Guidance, see above n 11, 4.17.1–4.18.1.
141   ABC Guidance, see above n 6, para 62.
142   BBA Guidance, see above n 11, p 34.

4. CULTURE AS A BULWARK AGAINST CORRUPTION?

8.66 The previous sections of this chapter identified the critical importance that regulators and industry bodies have placed on creating a zero-tolerance culture towards bribery.[143] Creating a responsible culture is not simply an ethical ideal or 'nice to have'. It plays an instrumental role in supporting a compliance programme[144] and changing individual behaviours, providing 'an essential foundation of good governance'.[145]

8.67 The responsibility for creating, implementing and maintaining this culture lies with the board as part of their core leadership duties.[146] Put another way, culture begins and ends with the board.[147] However, the creation of 'culture' is often an elusive ideal and this section considers why culture is so fundamental to a firm's ABC response and, thereafter, how it may be achieved.

A. Identifying culture's functionality

8.68 Culture and, moreover, a culture of 'integrity' will be a core value of most organisations' code of conduct. Nevertheless, defining culture and identifying its instrumental role in shaping corporate behaviour can be a challenging proposition. Notwithstanding these difficulties, it is imperative that senior management understand the vital role that culture performs within organisational behaviour. In doing so, they can endorse and implement cultural change, which this chapter has identified, forms both the basis of a defence under the Bribery Act and part of the board's broader governance obligations.[148]

8.69 What do we mean by culture? At its most basic, a firm's culture reflects 'the way we do things'. There are many definitions of the term, but most encompass the notion of a set of shared norms and values that are strongly held throughout the organisation.[149] Often, firms expressly state that they seek to embed a culture that sees external regulation as a minimum compliance standard and 'doing the

---

143   See paragraphs: 8.25, 8.28, 8.30, 8.36 and 8.46.
144   FCPA Guidance, see above n 13, 57.
145   BCBS Principles, see above n 1, para 26.
146   See above n 1.
147   K J Hopt, *Better Governance of Financial Institutions* (April 1 2013), ECGI – Law Working Paper No. 207, 31, available at SSRN: http://ssrn.com/abstract=2212198: 'Corporate governance of banks and other financial institutions after the financial crisis', *Journal of Corporate Law Studies* (2013) 13(2) 219–53 (Part B); 'Corporate governance of banks after the financial crisis', in E Wymeersch, K J Hopt, G Ferrarini (eds), *Financial Regulation and Supervision, A post-crisis analysis* (OUP 2012), 33–767 (Part A).
148   Bribery Act, s 7(2). As to the board's governance duties see above n 1.
149   C O'Reilly and J A Chatman, 'Culture as social control: Corporations, cults and commitment,' in B M Staw and L L Cummings (eds) *Research in Organizational Behavior*, Vol 18 (JAI Press Inc 1996), 160.

right thing' as the ultimate arbiter of any decision (although it can be questioned whether other internal policies, such as promotion and remuneration, support this ideal). Regardless of the exact values enshrined in an organisation's culture, in each case the firm's culture 'tell[s] employees what to do under a wide variety of unimaginable circumstances'[150] and on this basis, culture creates a normative standard and order. From an institutional perspective, a resilient culture creates a sense of identity, against which its strategic aims should be measured.[151]

The effective integration of a culture of integrity performs three key roles **8.70** within an ABC regime (each of which are discussed further below). First, it constrains (not eradicates) a pure profit maximising focus within the organisation's decision-making framework, effectively operating as a structure within which potentially conflicting normative demands can be ordered. Secondly, it helps individual employees identify the appropriate course of conduct when faced with multiple equilibria and/or unforeseen circumstances (both of which are considered in more detail in paragraphs 8.74–8.76). Put another way, it acts as a panacea to help employees determine the appropriate decision where the correct course of action is unclear. Finally, it acts as a social ordering mechanism, which complements and enhances the formal ordering required by individual policies.

i.   Culture as a normative ordering mechanism

A topical debate in corporate ethics is why it is that individuals who are **8.71** seemingly law-abiding citizens in their private capacity engage in high-risk, unethical and sometimes illegal conduct within the organisation. The debate is a vast one and outside of the scope of this chapter. However, it is introduced here to make the observation that within a corporate environment there are, inter alia, powerful drivers of individual decision-making. One particularly pervasive influence is the profit-maximising objective derived from the dominant Anglo-American paradigm of shareholder wealth maximisation.[152]

---

150   C Camerer and A Vepsalainen, *The Economic Efficiency of Corporate Culture* (1988) 9 *Strategic Management Journal* 115.

151   This notion of corporate identity also raises interesting normative questions as to the impact of that identity. In particular, the status of identity as a commitment to (and from) its employees.

152   This reflects the dominant Anglo-American norm that the corporation 'is carried on primarily for the profit of the stockholders', *Dodge v Ford Motor Co* 170 NW 668, 684. This principle is reinforced by a suite of shareholder governance rights in the Companies Act 2006 see: s 168 (right to remove directors); s 172 (duty to promote the success of the company for the benefit of its members); s 239 (ability to ratify acts of directors); s 260 (derivative claims); ss 302–305 and 338 (convening general meetings); s 314 (power to circulate statements); s 510 (power to remove auditors); s 551 (authorisation of share allotment); and s 561 (rights of pre-emption). The literature on shareholder primacy is vast. Key works include: S Bainbridge, 'In defense of the shareholder wealth maximization norm: A reply to Professor Green,' (1993) 50 *Washington and Lee Law*

8.72 In the ABC context, individuals are therefore asked to make ethical decisions that may conflict with this prevalent normative position of profit-maximisation. One function of a robust corporate culture is that it can introduce an express value or norm within the organisation, which supersedes that implied by the wider corporate environment. For example, while a shareholder wealth-maximising norm pervades a large part of corporate regulation and practice, a firm can instil a culture that makes it clear to individuals that responsible decision-making (such as compliance with a zero-tolerance approach to bribery) takes priority over profit.[153] In doing so, the culture effectively orders, or ranks, normative values. Thus, culture serves as both a normative order[154] and a normative ordering mechanism. In turn, this enables employees faced with conflicting normative pressures to know which one to prioritise.

8.73 For culture to work effectively as an ordering mechanism it is clear that an employee needs to be confident that he or she can rely on the normative order as expressed by the board (this notion of predictability is central to all aspects of culture's functionality within a firm). Without the certainty that a particular course of behaviour will be rewarded, recognised and followed by others an individual is unlikely to pursue an ethical code of conduct in favour of, for example, a profit maximising one. Thus, it is essential that the culture is reflected and reinforced throughout the firm's internal governance mechanisms. For example, on a very basic level, if a culture asks for ethical decision-making but an employee is incentivised by a remuneration structure that rewards risk-taking then the cultural ordering function is likely to fail.

ii.   Culture as a panacea

8.74 There are two key difficulties that arise when designing a governance response to combat bribery. First, it is not possible to identify ex ante all of the circumstances in which the opportunity to bribe, or the environments in which employees may be faced with 'ethical' challenges, may arise. Therefore, a firm designing its systems and controls is not able to anticipate all of those situations

---

Review 1423; D G Smith, 'The shareholder primacy norm', (1997) 23 *Journal of Corporation Law* 277; L Stout, 'Bad and not-so-bad arguments for shareholder primacy', (2009) 75 *Southern Californian Law Review* 1189.

153   R F Hurley, N Gillespie, D L Ferrin and G Dietz, 'Designing trustworthy organizations', (2013) (54) 4 *MIT Sloan Management Review* 77.

154   C O'Reilly, 'Corporations, culture, and commitment: Motivation and social control in organizations', (1989) 31(4) *California Management Review* 12.

and behaviours that will be judged (and sanctioned) ex post. This is what Kreps[155] identified as the problem of 'unforeseen circumstances'.[156]

Secondly, when faced with an ethical conundrum an employee is likely to have a **8.75** range of options available to him, options that often sit at the apex of regulation, personal gain, individual safety and corporate strategy with potential opacity as to which course of action should be taken. In these circumstances, we cannot be certain as to which of the options the employee will elect (and nor will the employee have certainty as to which he should choose). This second scenario is a form of what Kreps defined as the problem of 'multiple equilibria'.[157]

By their very nature, the problems of unforeseen circumstances and multiple **8.76** equilibria cannot, efficiently or at all, be individually negotiated or contracted for ex ante.[158] Nevertheless they reflect significant, practical, difficulties in managing organisational bribery. However, both can be powerfully mitigated by the implementation of a robust, predictable and resilient culture. A clear and unambiguous culture, which introduces and enforces an ordered value system provides the broader framework of principles in which decisions can themselves be analysed and ranked. These values can narrow the scope of options available or help identify the principles that need to be met when decision-making in new or novel situations. In essence, culture helps individuals choose which course of action to take when faced with multiple options or situations not otherwise addressed by firm policy.

iii. Culture as a social order

Over time, the implementation of culture will create a continuity and predict- **8.77** ability of behaviour that helps to generate consensus as to the values of the firm and, as a corollary, a type of social order.[159] Once consensus is achieved, culture starts to become an informal control system, premised on the powerful social pressures that arise from acting in accordance with a group's norms and expectations.[160] As individuals start to conform to the culture, they will expect others to act in a similar manner; those that fail to conform will start to attract opprobrium from those that do.

---

155 D M Kreps, 'Corporate culture and economic theory', in J E Alt and K A Shepsle (eds), *Perspectives on Positive Economy* (CUP 1990).
156 Ibid., 92.
157 Ibid., 103.
158 B E Hermalin, Economics and corporate culture (2000) *University of California* 2 available at: http://faculty.haas.berkeley.edu/hermalin/cultchds.pdf, accessed 9 June 2014.
159 Ibid., 13.
160 O'Reilly, see above n 154, 12.

8.78 Thus, the firm's culture acts as an informal, social control structure. This structure embodies a shared view about appropriate (and expected) behaviours and gains momentum when individuals are cognisant of the judgement of their peers, should they deviate from the accepted norms of the community.[161] Often, this social exposure and judgement is often a more powerful behavioural control than formal managerial demands.

8.79 These three characteristics arising from a consistently enforced culture converge to highlight the powerful co-ordination role that culture plays within an organisation. It helps to determine and define those actions that are legitimate within the firm and that will be rewarded (both through direct remuneration or acceptance by peers). In doing so, culture reinforces and legitimises the specific ABC policies that have been implemented, whilst filling any gaps that may arise.

B. Implementing culture

8.80 The previous section examined culture as a powerful driver of behaviour and a guide to decision-making, one that has greater potential to persuade than express strategy statements or managerial diktats (although it is undeniably informed by them).[162] The objective for any firm will be for a culture to become a self-perpetuating value system that is readily adopted by its employees. However, to instigate a culture and to ensure its maintenance within a competitive normative environment, carefully designed strategies are required to embed the desired value system within the organisation.

8.81 To be effective, an implementation strategy will need to be tailored to the specific needs of each organisation. Nevertheless (to the extent not addressed earlier in the chapter) this section considers the key components that are likely to inform any implementation strategy, namely: (i) tone from the top; (ii) communication; (iii) employee participation; and (iv) enforcement.[163]

---

161 Ibid.

162 C Jarnagin and J Slocum, 'Creating corporate cultures through mythopoetic leadership', (January 22, 2007), SMU Cox School of Business Research Paper Series No. 07–004, 289, available at: SSRN: http://ssrn.com/abstract=1004565.

163 These broadly reflect O'Reilly's four-stage implementation mechanism of: (i) participation; (ii) tone from the top; (iii) information from others and particularly co-workers; and (iv) a reward system that promotes recognition. See: O'Reilly, above n 154, 20–22.

i.   Tone from the top

In a now familiar concept, tone from the top is essential if a culture is to be **8.82** embedded within the firm. Whilst this principle is discussed in depth in paragraphs 8.30–8.38 it is prudent to emphasise several points in the context of creating corporate culture. It should also be noted that whilst the MOJ Guidance concentrates on the board in this context, the FCA extends the principle to senior management and 'tone from the middle'.[164] Moreover, boards will need to determine (and clearly document) who will have ultimate responsibility for ABC measures.

A board must be seen to make a genuine commitment to adhering to the values **8.83** it sets out, which includes allocating a sufficient quality and quantity of resources dedicated to ABC work.[165] As with policy implementation, a culture that is not fully embraced by the board is simply a paper-exercise with very little traction. Moreover, board commitment contributes to an important behavioural function, as the rest of the firm will look to the board to determine their own commitment to the values and norms that it espouses.[166]

By committing to the firm's culture, the board contributes to the essential **8.84** consensus of norms and predictability of behaviour that is required if a value system is to perform the ordering function discussed in the previous section. Central to establishing this consensus and predictability is a clear leadership commitment that is reflected in all board decisions. The board must be cognisant of (and reflect) the firm's stated values in every decision it makes; culture is not created by simply dictating what a firm's culture is but rather by what a firm's management (and, as a consequence, its employees) do.[167] Thus, the creation of a value system and a firm's internal control mechanisms are mutually reinforcing.

By observing the firm's culture in a clear and consistent way, the board helps to **8.85** promote certain characteristics to the position of a 'value' to be observed at all times, rather than 'a goal that is traded off against other goals'.[168] In doing so, the value becomes a commitment in respect of which compromises will not be

---

164   BBA Guidance, see above n 11, para 4.1.5.
165   Ibid., para 4.1.3.
166   Hermalin, see above n 158, 40.
167   L Guiso, P Sapienza and L Zingales, 'The value of corporate culture', (2013) Chicago Booth Research Paper No. 13–80, 1.
168   Ibid., 5.

tolerated and, in particular, one that will not be subject to economic calcula-tions.[169] Thus, the value becomes enshrined as a social norm that does not rely on legal (or other formal) sanctions for enforcement.[170] These norms become embedded through their observation by the wider organisation and, in particu-lar, the managers setting the tone and culture of the firm.

8.86 A firm needs to support its board (and senior management) in performing this role. The board needs to be clear on the values it sets and their consequences, together with the lines of responsibility for ABC measures within the organ-isation. As such boards themselves will require dedicated training, including workshops and discussion forums, where the culture and the consequences of failing to follow it can be fully and frankly discussed.[171]

ii.   Communication

8.87 Communication of culture is key; it is axiomatic that a person cannot comply with values that they are not aware of. However, the method of communication is important. The first step in the communication strategy is often the value statement or code of conduct discussed in paragraph 8.25. This statement provides a broad set of principles that guide employee decision-making in the unforeseen circumstances that are not governed by an express policy. These principles create the DNA that is then embedded throughout the firm[172] and reflected in the specific ABC policies (acting to legitimise each other). If properly instilled, this code of conduct becomes a common belief between employees and binds them to a common purpose.

8.88 The code of conduct is an important first step in the communication strategy. However, it is not enough for a firm's culture to be stipulated in a policy, supported by a single training session and then forgotten about. It must be communicated by permeating the decisions, strategies and policies of the firm.[173] Needless to say, it is vital that the firm's systems and controls, remuneration strategies, broader board decisions and strategic objectives align, normatively, with the general code of conduct. Without this normative cohe-sion, the expressed culture will fail to embed within the firm. Employees must recognise the stipulated culture as a fundamental part of the identity of the corporation that permeates everything that they do.

---

169   Ibid., 6.
170   Ibid.
171   BBA Guidance, see above n 11, 24.
172   Jarnagin and Slocum, see above n 162, 292.
173   Ibid., 293.

One important part of cultural communication is publicity of decisions taken to **8.89** enforce that culture – be it to reward good behaviour or punish bad.[174] For example, the famous IBM scenario where an employee was rewarded after refusing to admit Chairman Thomas Watson into a restricted area without a badge.[175] This anecdote is not purely for entertainment though. It represents an important commitment to enforce the firm's internal policies. Individuals rely on 'anecdotes as implicit definitions of cultural rules'[176] and they serve as a key training opportunity, one that enforces the firm's willingness to enforce its stated values.

iii. Employee participation

Internal governance, if implemented effectively, is not simply a policy drafted by **8.90** senior management and then performed at set periods of time.[177] It needs to pervade the entire organisation and become part of its DNA. One method of achieving this is to ensure that employees engage with the policy through genuine participation with the design, implementation, review and monitoring process. Participation creates a sense of volition that increases commitment and is an effective method of transmitting the firm's values throughout the organisation.[178] Furthermore, by being included within the system an individual feels valued,[179] which has a powerful impact on their commitment to the organisation and its cultural objectives. This concept of participation should therefore pervade the structure of training and consultation surrounding ABC systems.

One part of generating engagement with, and commitment to, a corporation's **8.91** culture is to give individuals a certain degree of authority and autonomy within that culture.[180] In doing so, this provides a sense of ownership and responsibility that helps to internalise the values of the firm. Importantly, once adopted, the firm's cultural framework can act as a mechanism to delineate that authority, supported by clear reporting lines should senior input be required.

---

174 BBA Guidance, see above n 11, para 4.2.4.
175 Camerer and Vepsalainen, see above n 150, 120.
176 Ibid.
177 Basel Committee on Banking Supervision, *Framework for Internal Control Systems in Banking Organisations* (September 1998), 8.
178 O'Reilly, see above n 154, 20.
179 Ibid.
180 Jarnagin and Slocum, see above n 162, 288.

iv. *Enforcement*

8.92 Enforcement of the culture is essential to its success. A strong culture emerges when there is both consensus as to the firm's values and an intensity attached to peoples' belief in those values.[181] One mechanism by which the board and senior management can contribute to both consensus and intensity is ensuring active and consistent enforcement of the value system. However, it is important to ensure that enforcement strategies reward compliant behaviour as well as sanction those in breach. It is critical that no individual can be considered 'too valuable'[182] to discipline should this be warranted. A culture that embodies a zero-tolerance to corruption requires a zero-exception approach to enforcement. As outlined in the previous section, enforcement decisions should (where appropriate to do so) feed into the internal ABC communication strategy to reinforce the predictability of, and commitment to, the firm's core values.

8.93 When considering positive enforcement, personal incentives play a pivotal role in creating a pervasive culture within an organisation. A robust compliance programme, code of conduct and corporate responsibility statement will do little if operating within a framework of personal incentives that establish a conflicting set of norms. In particular, bonus, appraisal and promotion criteria that promote high-risk profit maximising behaviours will transcend any statements or tone from the top that seek to embed broader, ethical norms.[183]

8.94 Ultimately, culture is a question of identity and there is no shortcut. It is a system of values and norms that permeate every decision of the organisation and thus must be the reference point against which strategic decisions are made, from business relationships to personal remuneration. Moreover, they are values that need to be enforced. In this way, the identity of the firm becomes synonymous with this normative framework and that individuals who transgress this identity do so knowingly.

5. CONCLUSION

8.95 In response to widespread international pressure, the Act has adopted a novel regulatory approach to corporate liability in what is ultimately a successful endeavour to avoid the difficulties raised by the identification doctrine. In doing so, it has successfully concentrated the attention of 'relevant commercial

---

181 O'Reilly, see above n 154, 13.
182 FCPA Guidance, see above n 13, 60.
183 See also: ibid.

organisations' on the need to implement adequate internal procedures in an endeavour to prevent the commission of bribery on their behalf.

For banks and financial services industries the Act has added a layer of **8.96** complexity to the existing regulatory requirements imposed on them by the FCA together with the expectations of the media and general public. It is important for such organisations to understand that the Act does not simply require a light-touch revision of existing policies but a thorough risk-assessment led change to the way in which the business identifies and manages corruption risks. Paramount to effective compliance is achieving a cultural change that embeds an anti-bribery and corruption ethos within the organ-isation, a change that is likely to require analysis of the norms that the organisation promotes (expressly or tacitly) through the other aspects of its business discussed elsewhere in the book (such as remuneration policies).

While the MOJ Guidance is helpful, the question of the 'adequacy' of an **8.97** organisation's procedures remains one for the corporation itself. However, those corporations that engage in a genuine attempt to introduce a culture of ethical compliance will, at least, have made significant steps to achieving that objective. In the meantime, those organisations subject to the Act's broad remit will need to wait for judicial determination of contested cases to better understand how the defence will be interpreted in practice.

ANNEX 8.1: SUMMARY OF KEY INTERNATIONAL CONVENTIONS

8.98 The Act was the product of intense international pressure from the wider anti-bribery community and it is helpful to understand this provenance when considering the Act's application. Most notably, the Organisation for Economic Co-operation and Development (OECD)[184] pursued a rigorous campaign to encourage UK regulatory reform, observing that it was 'disappointed and seriously concerned with the unsatisfactory implementation of the Convention by the UK'.[185]

8.99 In particular, the OECD (in common with the other international bodies discussed in this Annex) was concerned that the UK's corporate identification doctrine rendered effective corporate prosecutions impossible.[186] It was in response to this criticism that the Act, together with its strict liability offence and related defence of adequate procedures, received Royal Assent. Scope does not permit a detailed analysis of these, or the many other global initiatives designed to fight corruption.[187] Rather, this Annex provides an overview of the key conventions that influenced the Act's architecture.

A. OECD Convention on Combating Bribery of Foreign Public Officials in International Business Transactions (the OECD Convention)[188]

8.100 The OECD Convention imposes legally binding obligations on its signatories to, inter alia, implement domestic legislation that criminalises the bribery of foreign public officials (FPOs) in business transactions.[189] It governs the 'active'

---

184 The OECD Working Group first expressed 'serious concerns' as to the UK's foreign bribery legislation in 1999, when it issued its Phase 1 Report: OECD Working Group, *United Kingdom, Review of the Implementation of the Convention and the 1997 Recommendation* (December 1999), 24–25.

185 OECD Working Group, *United Kingdom: Phase 2bis Report* (October 2008) (Phase 2*bis* Report), 4.

186 See: the OECD Working Group, *United Kingdom: Phase 2 Report on the Application of the Convention on Combating Bribery of Foreign Public Officials in International Business Transactions and the 1997 Recommendations on Combating Bribery in Business Transactions* (March 2005), paras15–18; the OECD Working Group, *United Kingdom: Phase 2 Follow–Up Report on the Implementation of the Phase 2 Recommendations* (June 2007), para 20, and the Phase 2*bis* Report. The Law Commission itself acknowledged that, if not strictly required by law, it was in the spirit of the UK's international obligation to 'do more to prevent bribery, by providing enhanced means of deterring and punishing companies indifferent to the commission of bribery on their behalf' Law Commission, Reforming Bribery, see above n 8, para 6.14.

187 Other organisations undertaking significant work in this field include: Global Integrity, Global Witness, International Corporate Governance Network, Transparency International, TRACE International, UK Anti-Corruption Forum and the World Bank. The influence of the US fight against corruption is, of course, significant. In particular the Foreign Corrupt Practices Act 1977, the US Sentencing Commission, Guidelines Manual (November 2013), chapter eight – sentencing of Organizations; and the Inter-American Convention Against Corruption (March 1996).

188 The OECD Convention came into force on 15 February 1999 and was signed by all 24 OECD members together with Argentina, Brazil, Bulgaria, Colombia, Russia and South Africa.

189 OECD Convention, art 1.

bribery of FPOs, that is, the payment of bribes (in contrast to passive bribery, which refers to the receipt of bribes).[190]

However, it was the OECD Convention's provisions regarding corporate **8.101** liability that were instrumental in the Act's regulatory design. In particular, the requirement that signatories introduce an effective regime to ensure the liability of legal persons for the bribery of FPOs.[191] The difficulty for the UK in meeting this demand was its identification doctrine, which made the effective enforcement of criminal sanctions against a corporation 'almost impossible'.[192] Nevertheless the unrelenting scrutiny of the OECD (and concomitant public pressure) resulted in the UK incorporating the section 7 strict liability offence as a means of addressing the conflict between the requirements of the OECD Convention and the identification doctrine.

The OECD was also responsible for the focus on corporate governance as an **8.102** effective measure to combat bribery. In terms that are reflected in the Act, the OECD 'Recommendation for Further Combating Bribery of Foreign Public Officials in International Business Transactions' (the OECD Recommendation)[193] suggested that member states encourage corporations to implement adequate internal controls to prevent and detect bribery. Moreover, the annex to the OECD Recommendation, the 'Good Practice Guidance on Internal Controls, Ethics and Compliance' (the OECD Good Practice Guidance),[194] advocates that ABC policies should be incorporated within a company's overall compliance framework and established in response to a corporation-specific risk-assessment.[195] These recommendations are largely mirrored by the MOJ Guidance[196] and help to provide context to the principles set out therein.

The focus on internal systems and controls as a bribery prevention mechanism **8.103** was reiterated in the OECD's non-binding guidance on anti-corruption measures, the Guidelines for Multinational Enterprises (OECD Guidelines for MNEs).[197] These emphasise the need for 'adequate internal controls, ethics and

---

190 OECD Convention, Commentaries on the Convention on Combating Bribery of Foreign Public Officials in International Business Transactions (OECD Commentaries), para 1.

191 OECD Convention, art 2. See also: OECD Commentaries, ibid., para 20.

192 Joint Committee Report Vol II, see above n 44, BB16, Ev 197, para 9. This further exposed the UK to a breach of the requirement that sanctions under the OECD Convention are to be 'effective, proportionate and dissuasive', OECD Convention, art 3(1).

193 Issued on 26 November 2009. Available at: http://www.oecd.org/investment/anti-bribery/anti-bribery convention/44176910.pdf, accessed 17 December 2013.

194 OECD Recommendation, Annex II.

195 Ibid., para A.

196 MOJ Guidance, see above n 9, 25.

197 OECD, Guidelines for MNEs, see above n 137.

compliance programmes'[198] supported by robust books and records measures to mitigate the risk of concealing bribery.

B. United Nations Convention Against Corruption (UNCAC)[199]

8.104 UNCAC called for signatory states to 'establish and promote effective practices aimed at the prevention of corruption',[200] and is 'mutually supporting and complementary'[201] to the OECD Convention. In contrast to the OECD Convention, UNCAC includes mandatory and voluntary provisions and covers a broader range of corruption offences than other international conventions.

8.105 From a bribery perspective, UNCAC imposed mandatory requirements for the criminalisation of the bribery of a public official,[202] while leaving the decision to criminalise bribery in the private sector to the discretion of the signatories. In this regard, it simply encourages signatories to 'consider adopting such legislative and other measures'[203] that are necessary to establish, as a criminal offence, both active and passive bribery in the private sector. Nevertheless, UNCAC endorses the promotion and development of codes of conduct by corporations for the correct and proper performance of the business.[204] Further, and perhaps not surprisingly given that UNCAC was written in the wake of the Enron scandal, it includes a robust books and records requirement as means of preventing and detecting bribery.[205]

8.106 As with the OECD Convention, the identification doctrine created a conflict with the UK's UNCAC obligation to 'establish the liability of legal persons'.[206] In particular, UNCAC required that legal persons be subject to 'effective' sanctions, mitigating arguments that under UK law corporations could, technically, be held to account and adding to pressure for UK law reform.

---

198   Ibid., para VII(2).
199   United Nations Office on Drugs and Crime, United Nations Convention Against Corruption (New York 2004), which came into force on 14 December 2005.
200   UNCAC, art 5(2).
201   OECD, Guidelines for MNEs, see above n 137, Section VII, para 79.
202   UNCAC, arts 15–16. See also UNCAC, arts 5–11 for preventative measures in the public sector.
203   Ibid., art 21. See also UNCAC, art 12 concerning preventative measures to prevent corruption in the private sector (although not that UNCAC omits to define 'corruption').
204   UNCAC, art 12(2)(b).
205   Ibid., art 12(3).
206   Ibid., art 26(1).

C. Council of Europe and the Group of States Against Corruption (GRECO)

The Council of Europe adopts a multidisciplinary approach to combatting **8.107** corruption through, inter alia, setting and monitoring European norms and standards. One way it seeks to achieve this is the adoption of the Twenty Guiding Principles for the Fight Against Corruption (the Twenty Principles).[207] The Twenty Principles are not legally binding but set out a potential framework for international coordination in the fight against corruption. From a corporate perspective, the Twenty Principles raised a now common concern for the UK, namely the prevention of 'legal persons being used to shield corruption offences'.[208]

The Committee of Ministers also established GRECO, designated to monitor **8.108** the observation of the Council of Europe's anti-corruption standards, including the Twenty Principles. In addition, GRECO is responsible for monitoring the Council of Europe's Criminal Law Convention on Corruption (the CoE Criminal Convention),[209] the Additional Protocol to that Convention (the Additional Protocol)[210] and the Council of Europe's Civil Law Convention on Corruption (which requires Member States to introduce legislation to enable victims of corruption to sue for compensation; the UK has signed but not yet ratified this convention).[211]

The parties to the CoE Criminal Convention are required to criminalise both **8.109** active and passive bribery in both the public[212] and private sector.[213] In accordance with the OECD Convention and UNCAC, each signatory state must adopt legislative and other measures to ensure legal persons are liable for active bribery.[214] In contrast to other conventions, the CoE Criminal Convention offence applies when a person with a 'leading position' within the corporation committed the bribery, creating an offence that is more aligned with the

---

207 Council of Europe Committee of Ministers, Resolution (97) 24 On the Twenty Guiding Principles for the Fight Against Corruption (6 November 1997), available at: http://www.coe.int/t/dghl/monitoring/greco/documents/Resolution(97)24_EN.pdf, accessed 17 December 2013.

208 Ibid., principle 5.

209 The Council of Europe, Criminal Law Convention on Corruption (ETS 173), 27 January 1999 (in force 1 July 2002).

210 The Council of Europe, Additional Protocol to the Criminal Law Convention on Corruption (ETS 191) 15 May 2003.

211 The Council of Europe, Civil Law Convention on Corruption (ETS 174) 4 November 1999 (in force 1 November 2003).

212 CoE Criminal Convention, arts 2–6.

213 Ibid., arts 7–10.

214 Ibid., art 18(1).

identification doctrine than the OECD Convention and UNCAC. The Additional Protocol extends the CoE Criminal Convention to bribery of jurors and arbitrators. In a clear correlation with the Act, the CoE Criminal Convention prioritises corporate supervision by introducing an offence where a 'lack of supervision or control … has made possible the commission of the criminal offences'.[215] Again, the sanctions implemented into national law need to be 'effective, proportionate and dissuasive'.[216]

---

215   Ibid., art 18(3).
216   Ibid., art 19(1). See para A1.9 for a discussion of the UNCAC requirement that sanctions be 'effective'.

ANNEX 8.2: THE BRIBERY ACT 2010: CORPORATE HOSPITALITY AND FACILITATION PAYMENTS

The Act has raised significant industry concern regarding two aspects of **8.110** commercial life. The first, gifts and hospitality. That is, at what point could gifts and hospitality be deemed to be concealed bribes? The second is the use of facilitation payments, which are prohibited by the Bribery Act but permitted (within a limited scope) under the Foreign Corrupt Practices Act 1977 (the FCPA). This Annex considers the debate arising in these two areas and introduces the current UK position on them both.

A. Gifts and hospitality

The broad scope of the Act raised legitimate concerns among corporations that **8.111** hospitality could fall foul of its remit. The Law Commission, cognisant that bribery could be concealed as hospitality, confirmed that expenditure that was considered to contravene the Act would give rise to prosecution, regardless of its classification as 'hospitality'.[217] That said, the Law Commission tried to clarify its position by explaining: 'we believe that a definition wide enough to catch ordinary corporate hospitality would be too wide. On the other hand we cannot simply exclude *all* corporate hospitality from the offence, because that would open the door to abuse'.[218] Corporations are left therefore to balance the need to comply with the Act with the commercial imperative to engage in hospitality with prospective clients and business partners.

The SFO's latest statement on the issue of hospitality, stated that 'bona fide **8.112** hospitality … is recognised as an established and important part of doing business'[219] but it reserves the right to pursue hospitality that exceeds legitimate boundaries in accordance with prosecutorial guidelines.[220] To breach the Act, hospitality would need to be given with intent to confer a financial or other advantage and there would need to be a reasonable connection between the hospitality and the intention to secure a business advantage.[221] The questions that corporations should ask themselves are, inter alia, what is the reason behind the hospitality and subsequent business? Was the recipient influenced by the

---

217 Reforming Bribery, see above n 25, Appendix D, 190, para D.14
218 Legislating the Criminal Code, see above n 36, paras 5.75 and 5.76.
219 Available at: http://www.sfo.gov.uk/bribery–corruption/the-bribery-act/business-expenditure.aspx, accessed 17 December 2013.
220 See also MOJ Guidance, above n 9, para 26.
221 Ibid., para 28.

hospitality in a way that breached an expectation that he/she would act in good faith or impartially?[222]

8.113 Certain industries do, typically, engage in substantial hospitality. When considering the question of 'legitimate' hospitality, the standards or norms of a particular industry 'may' be relevant.[223] However, there will be a limit to the extent to which a corporation can argue an industry norm in defence of a claim under section 7. The MOJ Guidance itself emphasises that hospitality that is commensurate with industry norms is not evidence that a bribe was not paid, particularly if other evidence to the contrary exists.[224]

8.114 As a minimum, organisations should implement a written, global,[225] hospitality policy, which explains the risks associated with hospitality and a clear procedure to follow when offering or receiving gifts or hospitalities. Commonly, policies set out thresholds where approval is required for corporate hospitality although care needs to be taken that this does not give tacit approval for illegitimate payments, no matter how small. The important point is that the policy sets out clear principles as to acceptable and unacceptable hospitality, not complex formulas that disengage and promote a formalistic approach to compliance.

8.115 Common internal policy approaches require prospective approval of expenses over a certain amount (individually and in aggregate for any one entity or individual) or for all expenses that are irregular. Further, travel expenses should not be paid as cash to the recipient but paid directly to the travel organisation. The policy should detail a clear approvals escalation procedure that involves members from the compliance team where necessary and incorporates some flexibility for unusual cases.[226] Particularly high-risk individuals, such as public officials may be subject to separate approvals processes.

8.116 The policy should include a database (ideally online) where all hospitality and gifts are recorded together with the business case for such expenses, a statement of circumstances where gifts/hospitality are prohibited (such as cash or cash-equivalents) and an escalation procedure for sensitive cases.[227] A clear audit trail of approvals should be kept together with the reasons for giving the approval

---

222 Reforming Bribery, see above n 25, Appendix D, paras D.15–16.
223 Ibid.
224 Ibid.
225 Again, global policies may delegate local discretion but this discretion must be subject to (and exercised within) the global code of conduct that adopts a zero-tolerance to corruption.
226 As to flexibility, see: FCPA Guidance, above n 13, 58.
227 BBA Guidance, see above n 11, para 5.3.2

(large firms typically have an online approvals process).[228] A firm's corporate hospitality policy (and concomitant register) should be regularly assessed for its adequacy and also to provide suitable management information to enable the senior management team to review that firm's hospitality practices as a whole and in respect of individual parties.[229] The particular risks associated with hospitality should play a pivotal role in compliance training so that employees understand the risks (and personal liability) associated with gift giving/receiving and the processes that they need to follow before accepting/offering hospitality.

It is important that the hospitality database is not an abstract process that is kept in isolation. The database has two functions, not only does it force consideration by the relevant employee as to whether hospitality is appropriate but thereafter it enables the corporation to identify patterns of unusual, unacceptable or concentrated expenses. For example, if one particular client is receiving regular hospitality that individually appears to be acceptable but when taken in aggregate gives rise for concern. **8.117**

B. Facilitation payments

The issue of facilitation payments has received significant attention for two reasons. First, the inconsistent treatment of facilitation payments by the Bribery Act and the FCPA (the former prohibiting them, the latter providing an exception), leading to claims that the Act put UK businesses at a competitive disadvantage.[230] Secondly, it has been argued by industry that the reality of doing business in certain territories mean that facilitation payments need to be paid, either commercially (as an accepted means of practice) or for the personal safety of in-territory workers (where such payments are demanded rather than requested). **8.118**

The UK response to these criticisms is unequivocal: facilitation payments are bribes. They are illegal and remain illegal under the Act[231] a point that is emphasised by the FCA.[232] To legalise facilitation payments it was felt would **8.119**

---

228 ABC Guidance, see above n 6, para 108.
229 Ibid., paras 110–111.
230 FCPA, s 78dd–1(b). Although this exception may, in reality, be limited. See K Sheahen, 'I'm not going to Disneyland: Illusory affirmative defenses under the Foreign Corrupt Practices Act' (2010) *Wisconsin International Law Journal* available online at: http://papers.ssrn.com/sol3/papers.cfm?abstract_id=1657675.
231 Bribery Act 2010: Joint Prosecution Guidance of the Director of the Serious Fraud Office and the Director of Public Prosecutions, 8–9. See also, SFO, *Questions and Answers*, available at: http://www.sfo.gov.uk/bribery–corruption/the-bribery-act/questions-and-answers.aspx, accessed 17 December 2013.
232 CIB Guidance, see above n 2, 10.

justify the 'thin end of the wedge' and the broad territorial reach of the Act is cited in support of claims that UK corporations will nevertheless operate on a level playing field. It should be noted that guidance issued under the previous directorship of the SFO, which suggested that facilitation payments would not be pursued provided they met six factors, has been revoked.[233] Thus the current position remains clear: a facilitation payment is a bribe and can be prosecuted as such (subject to prosecutorial guidance).

8.120 Notwithstanding the different territorial treatment of facilitation payments, those organisations trying to embed an anti-corruption culture within their organisation will be best placed to do so when adopting a zero-tolerance approach to corruption. This approach would include a prohibition of facilitation payments and a culture that seeks to adopt the 'right' approach to compliance rather than seeking to identify, and use as a benchmark, the minimum compliance standards. The introduction of exceptions to a zero-tolerance approach allows the introduction of normative inconsistencies and potentially weakens the cultural framework within which strategic and individual decisions are made. The importance of consistency in creating culture cannot be underestimated and the inclusion of exceptions to clear, zero-tolerance rules, can act to erode this culture.

8.121 That said, the reality is that in some circumstances individuals may be placed in exceptionally challenging circumstances. If, following its risk assessment, an organisation identifies a likely risk that facilitation payments will be demanded it needs to consider how it will respond to this and put a support network in place. For example, a procedure whereby individuals can report the demand (and/or payment) enabling the corporation to respond appropriately. In these situations a defence might exist where a facilitation payment is made in response to a genuine, imminent, threat or danger. In that limited case, the existing defence of duress/necessity may apply.[234]

8.122 It is interesting to note that the international arena is similarly toughening (in a relative sense) its stance on facilitation payments. Facilitation payments were excluded from the ambit of the OECD Convention.[235] However, reflecting a potential (albeit slight) change in approach, the OECD Recommendation suggests that signatory states should 'encourage companies to prohibit or

---

233   SFO Press Release, *Revised Policies* (9 October 2012), available at: http://www.sfo.gov.uk/press-room/latest-press-releases/press-releases-2012/revised-policies.aspx, accessed 17 December 2013.

234   Reforming Bribery, see above n 25, para 7.14. See also MOJ Guidance, above n 9, para 48. By relying on existing defences in this way it was felt that the criminal law would not be subject to undesirable inconsistencies, which may arise had the Act introduced new defences in response to facilitation payments.

235   OECD Commentaries, see above n 190, para 9.

discourage the use of small facilitation payments in internal company controls, ethics and compliance programmes or measures'.[236] A similar approach is taken by the OECD Guidelines for MNEs, which suggests that corporations should 'prohibit or discourage' facilitation payments (guideline 3).[237]

In practical terms, boards need to identify where a risk of facilitation payments **8.123** is most likely to arise and develop a plan of action that provides employees with practical support and guidance on how to respond when a payment is demanded together with the response that the organisation will take in response to such a demand.

SELECTED BIBLIOGRAPHY

Arbogast, S V, *Resisting Corporate Corruption: Lessons in Practical Ethics from the Enron Wreckage* (M&M Scrivener Press 2008).

Basel Committee on Banking Supervision, *Principles for Enhancing Corporate Governance* (October 2010).

Basel Committee on Banking Supervision, *Principles for the Sound Management of Operational Risk* (June 2011).

Biegelman, M T and J T Bartow, *Executive Roadmap to Fraud Prevention and Internal Control* (2nd edn, John Wiley & Sons Inc 2012).

British Bankers' Association, *Bribery Act 2010 Guidance on Compliance Practical Implementation Issues for the Banking Sector* (December 2011).

Calder, A, *Corporate Governance: A Practical Guide to the Legal Frameworks and International Codes of Practice* (Kogan Page 2008).

Camerer, C and A Vepsalainen, 'The economic efficiency of corporate culture', (1988) *Strategic Management Journal* 9.

Crown Prosecution Service, *The Code for Crown Prosecutors* (January 2013).

Eicher, S (ed.), *Corruption in International Business: The Challenge of Cultural and Legal Diversity* (Gower 2009).

Financial Conduct Authority, *Financial Crime: A Guide for Firms, Part 1: A Firm's Guide to Preventing Financing Crime* (April 2014).

Financial Conduct Authority, *Financial Crime: A Guide for Firms, Part 2: Financial Crime Thematic Reviews* (April 2013).

Financial Reporting Council, *The UK Corporate Governance Code* (September 2012).

Financial Services Authority, *Anti-bribery and Corruption in Commercial Insurance Broking, Reducing the Risk of Illicit Payments of Inducements to Third Parties* (May 2010).

Financial Services Authority, *Financial Crime: A Guide for Firms* (December 2011).

Financial Services Authority, *Anti-bribery and Corruption Systems and Controls in Investment Banks* (March 2012).

Fleming, P and S C Zyglidopoulos, *Charting Corporate Corruption: Agency, Structure and Escalation* (Edward Elgar 2009).

Guiso, L, P Sapienza and L Zingales, 'The value of corporate culture', (2013) Chicago Booth Research Paper No. 13–80.

---

236   OECD Recommendation, see above n 193, para VI(ii).
237   OECD Guidelines for MNEs, see above n 137, Section VII, para 3.

Hermalin, B E, *Economics & Corporate Culture* (2000) University of California available at: http://faculty.haas.berkeley.edu/hermalin/cultchds.pdf, accessed 9 June 2014.

Hopt, K J, 'Corporate governance of banks and other financial institutions after the financial crisis', (2013) 13(2) *Journal of Corporate Law Studies* 219 (Part B); 'Corporate governance of banks after the financial crisis', in: E Wymeersch, K J Hopt, G Ferrarini (eds), *Financial Regulation and Supervision, A Post-crisis Analysis* (OUP 2012) (Part A); both at ECGI – Law Working Paper No. 207, 31, available at SSRN: http://ssrn.com/abstract=2212198.

Hurley, R, N Gillespie, D Ferrin and G Dietz, *Designing Trustworthy Organizations*, (2013) 54(4) *MIT Sloan Management Review* 74.

Jarnagin, C and J Slocum, 'Creating corporate cultures through mythopoetic leadership' (January 22, 2007). SMU Cox School of Business Research Paper Series No. 07–004, 289, available at SSRN: http://ssrn.com/abstract=1004565.

Kreps, D M, 'Corporate culture and economic theory', in J E Alt and K A Shepsle (eds), *Perspectives on Positive Economy* (Cambridge UP, 1990).

Lissack, R and F Horlick, *Lissack and Horlick on Bribery* (LexisNexis 2011).

Loughman, B P and R A Sibery (Ernst & Young LLP), *Bribery and Corruption: Navigating the Global Risks* (John Wiley & Sons Inc 2012).

Maurer, V G, 'Corporate governance as a failsafe mechanism against corporate crime', (2007) *Company Lawyer* 99.

Ministry of Justice, *The Bribery Act 2010: Guidance About Procedures which Relevant Commercial Organisations can put into Place to Prevent Persons Associated with them from Bribing (section 9 of the Bribery Act 2010)* (March 2011).

O'Reilly, C, 'Corporations, culture and commitment: Motivation and social control in organizations', (1989) 31(40) *California Management Review* 12.

O'Reilly, C and J A Chatman, 'Culture as social control: Corporations, cults and commitment', in B M Staw and L L Cummings (eds) *Research in Organizational Behavior* vol. 18 (JAI Press Inc 1996).

O'Shea, E, *The Bribery Act 2010 A Practical Guide* (Jordans 2011).

Parker, C and V L Nielsen (eds), *Explaining Compliance: Business Responses to Regulation* (Edward Elgar 2011).

Raphael, M, *Blackstone's Guide to The Bribery Act 2010* (OUP 2010).

Securities and Exchange Commission, *Report of Investigation Pursuant to Section 21(a) of the Securities Exchange Act of 1934 and Commission Statement on the Relationship of Cooperation to Agency Enforcement Decisions*, SEC Rel. Nos. 34–44969 and AAER-1470 (23 October 2001)(Seaboard Report), available at: http://www.sec.gov/litigation/investreport/34–44969.htm, accessed 27 April 2014.

Securities and Exchange Commission Division of Enforcement, *Enforcement Manual* (9 October 2013), available at: http://www.sec.gov/divisions/enforce/enforcementmanual.pdf, accessed 27 April 2014.

Serious Fraud Office, *Guidance on Corporate Prosecutions*, available at: http://www.sfo.gov.uk/media/65217/joint_guidance_on_corporate_prosecutions.pdf, accessed 17 December 2013.

Serious Fraud Office, *Bribery Act 2010: Joint Prosecution Guidance for the Director of the Serious Fraud Office and Director of Public Prosecutions*, available at: http://www.sfo.gov.uk/media/167348/bribery_act_2010_joint_prosecution_guidance_of_the_director_of_the_serious_fraud_office_and_the_director_of_public_prosecutions.pdf, accessed 17 December 2013.

Solomon, R C, *Ethics and Excellence: Cooperation and Integrity in Business* (OUP 1992).

Transparency International UK, *The 2010 UK Bribery Act Adequate Procedures: Guidance on Good Practice Procedures for Corporate Anti-Bribery Programmes* (July 2010).

Transparency International, *Business Principles for Countering Bribery* (December 2013).

Transparency International, *Business Principles for Countering Bribery: TI Six Step Process: A Practical Guide for Companies Implementing Anti-Bribery Policies and Programmes* (July 2005).

9

THE MARKET FOR CORPORATE CONTROL IN THE BANKING INDUSTRY

Georgina Tsagas[*]

1. INTRODUCTION

9.01 Failures of monitoring the performance of financial institutions led to over-exposure to high-risk investments and the ultimate collapse of various financial firms marking the beginning of the financial crisis emerging in the autumn of 2008.[1] The fact that the market for corporate control did not lead to share price reductions and subsequent takeovers of financial firms where there was in fact poor risk management and inadequate oversight by the board[2] is an indication of a dysfunctional mergers and acquisitions (M&A) market. Failures in risk-management systems and weaknesses in board composition were a few of the

---

[*] The author would like to thank Professor Andrew Johnston, Edmund Schuster and the Editors Michael McKee and Dr Iris H-Y Chiu for their constructive comments that greatly contributed to improving the final version of the present chapter.

1 G Kirkpatrick 'The corporate governance lessons from the financial crisis' 96, *Financial Market Trends* 61 OECD (February 2009) available at: www.oecd.org/dataoecd/32/1/42229620.pdf.

2 B Clarke, 'Where was the "Market for Corporate Control" when we needed it?' (December 17, 2009). UCD Working Papers in Law, Criminology & Socio-Legal Studies Research Paper No. 23/2009, available at SSRN: http://ssrn.com/abstract=1524785, at 1.

causes of the collapse of several financial institutions.[3] There were however no early signs of such corporate governance inefficiencies. The 2009 Turner Review provides that bank credit default swap (CDS) prices before the crash of 2007 did not provide forewarning of the events that would follow and were only moderately successful in indicating the relative riskiness of different institutions.[4] Bank shares had similarly failed to indicate that risks were increasing and on the contrary delivered positive signals reassuring managers that their aggressive growth strategies were value creating.[5]

9.02 The non-effective function of the market for corporate control in the banking industry is interlinked with the unfair results stemming from the governmental bail-outs of financial firms which followed. The financial crisis had caused '[g]overnments and central banks around the world [to spend] more than $11 trillion to support the financial sector and about $6 trillion on fiscal stimulus programs'.[6] The creation of large financial institutions ingrained in the economy had created 'too-big-to-fail' banks, which required government financial assistance in order to prevent a potential disastrous ripple effect throughout the economy. Although the bail-outs were based on financial institutions' 'systemic role',[7] they can be challenged from a public welfare point of view on the basis that they created an unfair distribution of the burden of adjustment on to taxpayers situated in European Member States to the advantage of private investors and creditors.[8] Banks constitute a special case, not only due to their 'systemic role' in the economy, but also due to the fact that banks are 'opaque firms', meaning that it is difficult for outsiders to understand and control them.[9] The opacity of bank assets makes it hard for the market for corporate control to become an effective means of discipline. Bank securities' prices, such as stock, bonds and CDSs can be used, as Flannery explains, to improve government supervisory processes, but have limitations.[10] The complex corporate structures employed by modern financial institutions limit accurately reflecting bank

---

3   Kirkpatrick, see above n 1, 2; Also see J de Larosière, *Report of the High-Level Group on Financial Supervision in the EU* (2009) (de Larosière Report), available at: http://ec.europa.eu/internal_market/finances/docs/de_larosiere_report_en.pdf. On the broader discussion see K Hopt 'Corporate governance of banks and other financial institutions after the financial crisis-Regulation in the light of empiry and theory', (2013) 13(2) *Journal of Corporate Law Studies* 219–53, at 237–8.

4   The Turner Review, *A Regulatory Response to the Global Banking Crisis* (FSA, March 2009) 46.

5   Ibid.

6   D M Dickson, 'Debate rages over stimulus fallout', *Washington Times*, Feb. 23 2010, A1 (quoting Ruth Stroppiana, chief international economist for Moody's Economy.com).

7   J Armour and W G Ringe, 'European Company Law 1999–2010: Renaissance and Crisis' (December 14, 2010), ECGI – Law Working Paper No. 175/2011, 40, available at: http://ssrn.com/abstract=1691688.

8   L Tsoukalis, 'The Delphic Oracle on Europe', in L Tsoukalis and J A Emmanouilidis (eds) *The Delphic Oracle in Europe: Is there a Future for the European Union?* (OUP 2011).

9   M J Flannery, 'Market discipline in bank supervision', in A N Berger, P Molyneux, and J O S Wilson (eds) *The Oxford Handbook of Banking Online* (OUP 2012) at 1/19.

10 Ibid., at 2/19.

conditions in market prices.[11] The quality of information released by bank managers is also affected by the monitoring supervisors exercise.[12] In fact, supervisors' willingness to support large systemically important banks constitutes the most important impediment to market discipline, as it weakens investors' incentives to gather information on the bank's performance.[13]

Evidence brought forward by the financial crisis has made evident a threefold **9.03** set of issues concerning the operation of the market for corporate control in the banking sector. First, the market for corporate control has specifically in the banking sector proved dysfunctional, secondly, the 'systemic role' of banks and the subsequent governmental bailouts of 'too-big-to-fail' financial institutions reinforce the argument of adopting a more pluralist approach when considering the merits of an acquisition in this sector and thirdly, the 'opaqueness' of banks allows for differential regulation of M&A activity of banks . The general aim of the chapter is to reflect on the efficacy of the legal framework on bank acquisitions by considering: (i) the extent to which the shareholder primacy norm adopted in the case of acquisitions of commercial companies should be similarly followed in the case of bank acquisitions; and (ii) whether regulators should adopt a more interventionist approach in bank acquisitions and on what grounds. The chapter will hence specifically discuss *whether* the market for corporate control in the banking industry is functioning perversely, *how* this function affects and is affected by prudential concerns and *what* aspects of the legal framework on bank acquisitions may potentially need to be the subject of reform.

The outline of the chapter is as follows. Section 2 will report on the most recent **9.04** developments concerning the operation and regulation of the market for corporate control in Europe in general and specifically in the banking sector. Section 3 will reflect on a series of bank acquisition case studies which form a good set of examples on: (i) the role of the supervisory authority in the context of EU cross-border bank acquisitions; (ii) the problems that arise in relation to target company valuations, information and risk assessment, especially in contested bank takeovers; and (iii) financial stability concerns. Section 4 of the chapter will reflect on the UK/EU regulatory framework, by addressing selected provisions of the Qualifying Holdings Directive, the UK City Code on Takeovers and Mergers and the EU Takeover Directive. Section 5 will focus on the peculiarities of the EU market for corporate control in the banking industry. It will refer to the general theoretical assumptions underlying the operation of

---

11   Ibid., 7/19.
12   Ibid., 7/19.
13   Ibid., 7/19.

the market for corporate control and discuss how the market for corporate control in the banking sector specifically defies some of the general assumptions. The chapter supports the argument that less shareholder primacy for takeovers in the banking sector should be opted for, and at the same time considers how best to regulate parties' intervention in the process. Section 6 will focus on controversial aspects related to bank acquisitions by focusing on: A. The role of the Supervisory Authority; B. The role of the board of the bidding company; and C. The role of the target board and target shareholders. Finally, section 7 will provide conclusive remarks and propose possible ways forward.

2. RECENT DEVELOPMENTS

9.05 The expansion of banks through M&A activity is viewed upon unfavourably following the financial crisis.[14] At the turn of the century many policymakers had projected that EU financial integration would prompt a wave of cross-border banking mergers that would boost industry profits.[15] Not only did M&As of such a scale never materialise, but also the bank mergers which did in fact occur turned out to be disasters, the most notable being the takeover of ABN AMRO by RBS.[16] In December 2011, following Royal Bank of Scotland's (RBS) takeover of Dutch Bank ABN AMRO and RBS's subsequent UK Government bailout, the Financial Services Authority (FSA) called for greater powers to veto bank takeovers and suggested that hostile takeovers involving banks should potentially be banned.[17] The business community was however opposed to the proposed measures arguing against state intervention into the board decisions of these entities.[18] It is notable that prior to the emergence of the financial crisis, national supervisory authorities made efforts to frustrate attempts by European banks to acquire financial institutions in other EU Member States by blocking the acquisitions on alleged prudential grounds.[19]

---

14 D Enrich, G Legorano and M Stevis, 'Europe's banks poised to return to acquisition trail', *Wall Street Journal*, 3 February 2014.

15 Ibid.

16 Ibid.

17 R Partington, 'FSA given frosty reception on hostile bank M&A call', *Financial News*, 13 Dec 2011.

18 Ibid.

19 For examples of such intervention refer to: (a) the decision taken by the Portuguese Minister for Finance on 18 June 1999 to oppose the BSCH/Champalimaud merger as not having been 'prudent'; (b) BBVA, a Spanish bank, which was frustrated in its attempt to acquire Italy's Banco Nazionale del Lavoro (BNL) in 2005; (c) ABN Amro's tender offer for Antonveneta, whereby it was alleged that the Bank of Italy had shown unjustifiable difference in the treatment of bidders ABN Amro and BPI respectively; and (d) Poland initially refused to accept the takeover of BPH by Unicredito in 2006.

There have been important developments in the UK and the EU concerning **9.06** the market for corporate control over the past few years. In the UK, changes were made to the UK Takeover Code in September 2011 following the hostile takeover of Cadbury by Kraft, making it harder for hostile M&As to succeed, including M&As in the banking sector.[20] The reform of the UK takeover rules in 2011 introduced a stricter timeline to be followed by the bidder by strengthening the 'Put Up or Shut Up' (PUSUP) rule of the code,[21] added an explanation to the controversial issues surrounding the advisory role observed by the target board by adding an interpretive text on the issue of the factors that the board takes into account in its advice, imposed increased disclosure requirements on the bidder, as well as the target company and amended a series of provisions of the code in order to secure greater recognition of employee rights in the target company and to address problems of enforcement in relation to the bidder's intentions regarding the business of the target.[22] A debate similar to that over Kraft – Cadbury on the efficacy and fairness of the UK takeover rules arose in May 2014, following Pfizer's failed £69bn pursuit of UK-based AstraZeneca, whereby the Labour party in the UK lobbied in favour of even tougher rules on takeovers.[23] The Pfizer/AstraZeneca deal, although falling within the life sciences sector, brought forward the issue of whether government powers to intervene in deals affecting strategic aspects of the UK's industry should be permitted on grounds of 'public or national interest'. The deal failed to go through following the application of the PUSU Rule; political lobbying however undoubtedly played its role in the forestalling of the proposed bid.[24] Proposals for the reform of the UK takeover rules are ongoing. In May 2014, in the context of its possible offer for AstraZeneca plc, Pfizer Inc. had stated that, subject to successful completion of its combination with AstraZeneca, it would make a number of commitments for a minimum of five years. Following the particular set of voluntary commitments, the Code Committee of the Panel issued Public Consultation Document 2014/2 on *Post-Offer Undertakings and Intention Statements*, making proposals to amend the Code in order to make a distinction between actions that parties to an offer *commit* to

---

20 Partington, see above n 17.

21 The Panel on Takeovers and Mergers, 'The Code on Takeovers and Mergers', rule 2.6 of which provides a 28-day limitation period within which a potential bidder must either announce a firm intention to make an offer or announce that he does not intend to make an offer and retreat.

22 For further analysis of the particular reforms see G. Tsagas, 'The revision of the EU Takeover Directive in light of the 2011 UK takeover law reform', (2013) 10(1) *International and Comparative Company Law Journal* 21, at 27–34.

23 E Rigby, 'Labour to push for tougher rules on takeovers before election', *The Financial Times*, 27 May 2014.

24 Ibid., whereby it is, however, correctly noted that arguing in favour of strengthening the government's powers of intervention would be subject to specific grounds mentioned in EU regulations, namely public security, media plurality, and financial stability of financial services.

take and actions that parties to an offer *intend* to take.[25] Another development to note is that in April 2014 the decision on ABN AMRO's claim to challenge[26] the European Commission's 2011 five-year ban on acquisitions imposed on the bank after a Dutch Government bailout was decided, whereby ABN AMRO lost on the legal basis that the bank's priority should be to repay the government aid received ahead of any acquisitions.[27]

9.07 The financial crisis, as well as the questioning of the UK's regulatory framework and the unfair consequences stemming from governmental bail-outs of 'too-big-to-fail' banks have all triggered a stronger awareness that policymakers should adopt a different approach when it comes to regulating the market for corporate control in the EU, specifically in the banking sector. The consequences that flow from the failure of banks emerging from major acquisitions have a spill-over effect on the economy and negatively affect a range of constituencies, from institutions within an economy to taxpayers bearing the burden of adjustment of governments rescuing the otherwise failed bank.

9.08 In order to better address the challenges facing the legislator in regulating the market for corporate control in the banking industry, the following section will report on a series of case studies and the contentious issues that arose in each case respectively. The golden thread connecting issues addressed in the case studies of bank acquisitions boil down to the main topic explored by the present chapter, which is namely what balance needs to be struck between the marketisation and state protection of the banking industry. Specifically, the case studies selected allow for the consideration of: (i) whether there may be acceptable grounds that a supervisory authority of a Member State can intervene in an acquisition on the basis of economic stability concerns; (ii) whether problems relating to target company valuations and special informational problems and risks involved in hostile acquisitions of banks can be rectified by elaborate legal requirements; (iii) whether the law should revisit the shareholder primacy position adopted in the regulation of bank acquisitions on the basis that the position may adversely affect stakeholders' interests and public welfare; and (iv) what safeguards should be set in place in order to guarantee that the newly emerged company will be managed effectively and in a financially prudent way.

---

25 Public Consultation Paper 2014/2, The Takeover Panel Code Committee, 'Post-Offer Undertakings and Intention Statements' (PCP 2014/2, 15 September 2014); also see Response Statement 2014/2, The Takeover Panel Code Committee, 'Post Office Undertakings and Intention Statements' (RS 2014/2, 23 December 2014).

26 T-319/11, *ABN AMRO Group NV v Commission.*

27 A White and M van Gaal, 'ABN AMRO loses court challenge to EU ban on acquisitions', *Bloomberg News* 8 April 2014.

3. BANK ACQUISITION CASE STUDIES

Specific tensions are likely to arise within a bank takeover context between the **9.09** parties that assume a role in determining the outcome of a bid. A triangular relationship which is created during the launch of a takeover bid for a banking group is that between the shareholders of the target company, the board of directors of the target company and the supervisory authority. The question from a corporate governance perspective is how the legal framework can best strike a balance: (i) between the two organs of the company; and (ii) between the two organs and the regulator. Regarding the first relationship, the key tension in the context of a contested takeover exists between the executive directors of the board who typically have a vested interest in defeating the bid and the shareholders that typically have an interest in accepting the bid, provided the price is high enough and the offeror has a compelling enough vision for the business. The problem amounts to the fact that, generally speaking, a high price will prevail, because few shareholders will value longer-term business prospects promised by the existing management above the short-term gains of a high offer price. Conversely, in a recommended bid the board may have more of a vested interest than the shareholders, because the board may be recommending a bid although a higher price could be obtained if a wider range of potential buyers is canvassed. The board may have incentives to recommend a particular bid, because for example a commitment has been made that a director's role within the target will be safeguarded. Regarding the second relationship, the key tension in the context of a takeover exists between the regulator whose interests may be based on sound prudential or even protection-ist grounds and the target company with interests that are normally based on commercial grounds. The chapter reflects on a series of case studies exploring both relationships. On the one hand one must address the issue of whether shareholder decision-making should be followed in bank acquisitions. On the other hand, where the option of state intervention is to be further explored, one must also question how well qualified the regulator is to make the decision instead of shareholders.

A. ABN AMRO and Banca Antonveneta

The takeover of Italian lender Banca Antonveneta by AMRO Holding NV is a **9.10** classic example of the exercise of economic protectionism within the context of cross-border bank acquisitions. In September 2005 ABN AMRO Holding NV prevailed in the takeover battle for Italian lender Banca Antonveneta, making ABN Amro Holding NV the first foreign bank to gain control of an Italian lender. In its acquisition for Banca Antonveneta, ABN AMRO had been up against the domestic bank, Banca Popolare Italiana (BPI), which at the time owned 29.5 per cent of Antonveneta.[28] In July 2005, ABN AMRO's €7.6b tender offer for Antonveneta, offering €26.50 a share in cash, was rejected in favour of a BPI bid for €27.50 in cash and stock.[29] When ABN AMRO eventually acquired BPI's 29.5 per cent stake in Antonveneta, ABN AMRO's stake rose to 59.5 per cent triggering, according to Italian securities law, a mandatory bid for the remaining shares of Banca Antonoveneta.[30] The issue which arose in the particular deal concerned the alleged unfair advantage given by the Italian supervisory authority to the domestic bank's bid over that of ABN AMRO's. Italy's financial sector was alleged to be aggressively protected by the political establishment and its chief regulator, Bank of Italy Governor, Antonio Fazio.[31] In July 2005 the Governor of the Bank of Italy was recorded talking to the chief executive of BPI, Gianpiero Fiorani, about the bidding for Antonveneta and it was alleged that the Governor of the Bank of Italy had deliberately participated in a stalling strategy to try and prevent ABN AMRO from acquiring Banca Antonoveneta. The leaked transcript prompted Italian prosecutors to initiate an inquiry into whether BPI had illegitimately built up its stake in Antonveneta. It was found that in December 2004 BPI had indeed loaned more than €1.1b to several Italian businessmen to buy Antonveneta shares without disclosing the loans.[32]

9.11 Following ABN AMRO's petition alleging that the Bank of Italy had shown unjustifiable difference in the treatment of ABN AMRO and BPI respectively, the Italian Administrative Court was called to examine the stance that the Bank of Italy adopted in relation to the bids made.[33] ABN AMRO specifically alleged that the Bank of Italy had shown preference to BPI by, among others, reviewing BPI's requests for approval significantly faster compared to ABN AMRO's requests, and by initially refusing approval for ABN AMRO to increase its stake without providing for sound reasons for the refusal.[34] Although the Italian court rejected ABN AMRO's petition, the case highlighted the problems associated with the ability a supervisory authority had to refuse authorisation of a bidder's request to increase its holding on vague grounds.[35] The Bank of Italy's protectionist behaviour prompted the EU to

---

28 BBC News, 'ABN AMRO "wins Italy bank battle"', 15 September 2005.
29 A Lagorce, 'ABN AMRO wins Antonventa control', MarketWatch, *The Wall Street Journal*, 15 September 2005.
30 Ibid.
31 BBC News, see above n 28.
32 Lagorce, see above n 29.
33 S Kerjean, 'The legal implications of the prudential supervisory assessment of bank mergers and acquisitions under EU Law', European Central Bank, Legal Working Paper Series No 6, June 2008, at 36.
34 L Curran and F Turitto, 'Antononventa: the challenge of cross-border acquisitions of banks in the EU', (2006) *Journal of International Banking and Financial Law* (2006) 79–82.
35 Kerjean, see above n 33, 36–7.

revisit the prudential considerations followed in cross-border bank acquisitions leading to the adoption of the Qualifying Holdings Directive.

The issue to be considered in the particular case is not only how to deal with **9.12** economic protectionism but also *how* the law can strike a balance between bank safety concerns and protectionism. Banks cannot be completely marketised in view of the fact that banks have a social utility dimension. The unique features that the market for corporate control in the banking sector possesses could justify economic stability concerns that Member States may potentially have. When is protectionism justified and how can this be projected in the legal framework? In order to guarantee a level-playing field in the EU, the grounds for a rejection of authorisation need to be clear and comprehensive for all supervisory authorities. The particular case study prompts one to consider carefully the provisions which regulate the authorisation that the supervisory authority is called to give when there is an increase in holding in a financial institution based in the EU. The provisions of the Qualifying Holdings Directive will be reflected on in section 4.A. of the chapter, where it will be made evident that it is important to further clarify the legal criteria for authorisation.

B. RBS – ABN AMRO

A consortium of banks made up of RBS, Santander and Fortis acquired ABN **9.13** AMRO on 17 October 2007, after seven months of contested bid activity. Prior to the acquisition, Barclays Bank had made a competing bid for ABN AMRO, which had been recommended by the board of ABN AMRO. Barclays' announcement on 19 March 2007 that it was in exclusive preliminary discussions with ABN AMRO concerning a potential merger prompted RBS to consider an acquisition. The minutes of the RBS board meeting on 28 March 2007 record that the acquisition was not seen as a 'must do deal' and that 'execution risk would be high'.[36] The board of RBS had only limited access to confidential information on ABN AMRO and hence conducted 'only a limited due diligence review of ABN AMRO'.[37] In April 2007 the consortium notified ABN AMRO of its intention to make an offer and made a request to be provided with the same information that had been made available to Barclays.[38] RBS eventually acquired ABN AMRO for £49bn in 2007 for approximately three times its market value, making the deal the biggest banking takeover in history. Following the acquisition, ABN's main assets turned out to be seriously

---

36   RBS, 'Continuation of minutes of a meeting of the board of directors', 28 March 2007.
37   The offer memorandum and listing particulars, 20 July 2007, at 15.
38   See Takeover Code, above n 21, rule 20.2 on the equality of information to competing offerors.

impaired, leading to a £45bn bailout of RBS by the UK Government in 2008. In March 2009, following RBS's government bailout, investigations were conducted, which examined among others, the decisions made by RBS during the acquisition. The investigations did not aim to produce a comprehensive report on the causes of the RBS failure, but rather to identify whether there were grounds for bringing enforcement action. Following the acquisition, it was widely accepted that the FSA should have intervened to block the acquisition, especially in light of the fact that the deal was one of the factors which lead to the £45bn government bailout.[39] On 3 April 2009, the then Chairman of RBS, Sir Philip Hampton, reflecting on the acquisition of ABN AMRO, stated: 'With the benefit of hindsight it can now be seen as the wrong price, the wrong way to pay, at the wrong time and the wrong deal.'[40] The particular statement reflects concerns which all too often come up in contested bid situations. Problems associated with the valuation of the target firm, the funding of the bid, the financial circumstances surrounding the potential acquisition, as well as the concern of whether the emerging company will turn out to be a successful deal, are all issues which from a corporate governance perspective deserve further attention.

9.14   The box-ticking approach the supervisory authority followed in this case was inadequate and did not give enough consideration to the risks involved.[41] The FSA took only limited account of the substantial uncertainties and risks involved in the acquisition of ABN AMRO and should have arguably played a more active role concerning the assessment of the bid. When the FSA was informed of the consortium's intention to make a bid for ABN AMRO in April 2007, it did not test in detail the potential capital and liquidity implications of the acquisition, nor did it challenge sufficiently the adequacy of RBS's due diligence.[42] It should be noted however, that the FSA was not legally under the obligation to assess the acquisition. The passive approach adopted by the FSA reflects the philosophy observed by the supervisory authority at the time, which was to encourage supervisors to place reliance on assurances from firms' senior management and boards about strategy, business models and key business decisions.[43]

---

39   J Treanor, 'Regulator should have stopped RBS from buying ABN Amro, say MPs', *The Guardian*, 19 October 2012.

40   RBS Press Release, 'Royal Bank of Scotland Group PLC-Annual General Meeting/General Meeting', 3 April 2009.

41   Ibid.

42   FSA Report, 'The failure of the Royal Bank of Scotland', December 2011, Executive Summary, 25; However it should be noted that the FSA was content in 2007 that RBS would have been able to manage the acquisition of ABN AMRO from a capital perspective, and would face liquidity difficulties only in the 'very unlikely' event of an extreme scenario.

43   Ibid., Executive Summary, 25.

The funding of the acquisition is another aspect of the bid which had not been **9.15** thoroughly examined at the early stages of the bid. RBS's initial decision in 2007 to launch an acquisition and its decision in September 2007 to proceed with the acquisition were made in the face of market deterioration.[44] The acquisition, which was primarily funded by short-term debt, eroded RBS's capital adequacy and increased its reliance on short-term wholesale funding.[45] The way in which the acquisition was financed significantly increased RBS's exposure to structured credit and other asset classes on which large losses were subsequently taken.[46]

RBS proceeded with the acquisition of ABN AMRO without appropriate heed **9.16** to the risks involved and with inadequate due diligence.[47] The information made available to RBS by ABN AMRO in April 2007 amounted to '*two lever arch folders and a CD*'.[48] The Enforcement Division of the FSA, which reviewed the decision-making processes adopted by RBS, concluded that the due diligence was insufficient in its scope and depth and inappropriate in relation to the nature and scale of the acquisition and the risks involved.[49] Despite the inadequate due diligence it was reported that: (i) there was no failure of formal governance process in terms of the relationship between the executive management and the board; the board was aware that the proposal to proceed was made on the basis of very limited due diligence and had been professionally advised on the fact that the proposed transaction required more consideration, (ii) the level of due diligence conducted was in line with market practice for contested bids, bank acquisitions do not require higher standards of due diligence compared to non-bank acquisitions, (iii) even if RBS had had access to a greater level of information, it was unclear whether its due diligence would have resulted in a better estimate of future potential losses anywhere near the losses that actually arose.[50] Hence, according to the report, there was no basis for bringing an enforcement case with a reasonable chance of success.[51]

A point raised in the FSA Report was that the board having proceeded with the **9.17** takeover, despite the inadequate due diligence, was nevertheless evidence that the board was not sufficiently sensitive to the wholly exceptional and unique importance of customer and counterparty confidence that is followed in the

---

44 Ibid., 408.
45 Ibid., Executive Summary, 25.
46 Ibid.
47 Ibid., Executive Summary, 21.
48 Ibid., Introduction, 7.
49 Ibid., 408.
50 Ibid., 33.
51 Ibid., 408.

case of banks.[52] It could therefore be argued that despite limited due diligence being the norm in contested takeover situations, boards of banks in particular should not be free to escape liability if there is evidence of behaviour which amounts to a breach of duty or negligence. The standards against which such behaviour is assessed should be reconsidered. Effective board decision-making is dependent on how well board dynamics are managed at the time the launch of a bid is being considered. The dynamics between the RBS board and its executives at that instance remain unclear. Aspects of RBS's management, governance and culture may have affected the quality of RBS's decision-making. Issues considered by the FSA Report were: (i) whether the board's mode of operation, including a potential challenge to the Executive, was as effective as its composition and formal processes would suggest, (ii) whether the CEO's management style discouraged robust and effective challenge, and (iii) whether RBS's board received adequate information to consider the risks associated with strategy proposals, and whether it was sufficiently disciplined in questioning and challenging what was presented to it.[53]

9.18 The case study of RBS–ABN AMRO provides a good example of the informational problems and the risks involved in bank acquisitions. The deal also highlights the impact that large-scale bank acquisitions may potentially have on the economy and other stakeholders, such as employees, creditors and taxpayers in the event that the 'too-big-to-fail' bank emerging from the acquisition collapses. From a regulatory perspective, the deal specifically highlighted the need to revisit the following issues, which will be specifically addressed in section 6 of the chapter, namely: (i) *the funding* of an acquisition, (ii) the *due diligence* conducted, especially when an acquisition is a contested one, (iii) *the role that the FSA* should play in scrutinising the merits of a deal, (iv) the *shareholder primacy* norm followed in the acquisitions of banks, and (v) *the dynamics* between the board and the management of the bidding company.

9.19 From the overview of the deal it is apparent that by law neither the board, nor the supervisory authority, were under any extensive obligation to assess the merits and the potential impact of the bid. This in turn places more weight on the shareholders called to vote on the acquisition. In the case of RBS–ABN AMRO, shareholders supported RBS because the bid for growth and value creation were seen as boosts to the share price of RBS. In August 2007 RBS received the backing of over 60 per cent of shareholders at a meeting for the proposed acquisition and in October 2007 RBS revealed it had received the

---

52   Ibid., Executive Summary, 25.
53   Ibid., 26–7.

backing of 86 per cent of ABN AMRO shareholders for its €72b bid.[54] In retrospect the failed takeover qualifies as clear evidence that an absolute version of shareholder primacy is not the ideal approach to be followed in the case of takeovers in the banking industry. Decisional powers placed with shareholders that have short-term investment horizons, enables banks to virtually sell themselves, even if the target banks are in fact not worth surviving in the market place. An imposition of more controls on the market for corporate control in the interests of prudence in the banking industry may therefore well be the way forward. What remains a controversial issue however from a corporate governance perspective is to what extent the regulator should intervene in the overall process.

C. BNP – Société Générale

The case study of BNP – Société Générale qualifies as a good example of an **9.20** acquisition that raises concerns regarding the future management of the target company. In 1999 the French Bank BNP made a hostile bid for another French bank, Société Générale. The French competent authority, the CECEI,[55] refused to authorise the acquisition of a minority of 37.15 per cent which qualified as 31.8 per cent of the voting rights in Société Générale.[56] The basis for CECEI's rejection was that the particular percentage of acquisition of stock did not allow for an exercise of effective control over the institution and hence the argument was that this did not allow for a sufficiently stable structure.[57] In view of the fact that the bid was hostile, the CECEI prompted the companies to reconsider a pre-arranged solution.[58]

In today's factual circumstances, following the evidence brought forward by the **9.21** recent financial crisis, concerns of a prospective bid compromising financial stability would perhaps find support as a ground for rejecting a bid. The decision of the CECEI in 1999 however had at that time been viewed unfavourably and had given rise to legal criticism on a dual basis. First, it was argued that CECEI had acted *ultra vires* with regard to imposing a requirement for a friendly bid on the parties involved and second, it was argued that the requirement imposed by CECEI for the acquirer to acquire a percentage which

---

54   'RBS timeline: where it all went wrong', *The Daily Telegraph*, 2 December 2010.
55   Note that according to Article L. 511–10 of the French Financial and Monetary Code, credit institutions must obtain authorisation from CECEI before commencing their activities and in the prescribed assessment the CECEI is called to assess, in accordance with the provisions of the French Financial and Monetary Code and other requirements, the applicant company's ability to realise the development plans in conditions which are compatible with the proper functioning of the banking system and which afford security for customers.
56   Kerjean, see above n 33.
57   Ibid., 59.
58   Ibid.

would enable him to exercise effective control, was not legally imposed, as there was no requirement as such in the European or French rules.[59] Kerjean rightly identifies that if the case were to be considered after the adoption of the new maximum harmonisation standards imposed by the Qualifying Holdings Directive, it is likely that CECEI's refusal dated in 1999 would be in breach of the rules of the Directive; the ground of refusal would not be in line with the detailed prudential assessment criteria laid down in the Directive.[60] The case study of BNP – Société Générale builds an even stronger case in favour of adopting a regulatory framework that clearly outlines the criteria upon which the supervisory authority can intervene, and that better enables the authority to reflect on the competence of the future management of the emerged entity following concerns of financial stability.

4. LEGAL FRAMEWORK

9.22 The Turner Review concluded that market discipline of financial institutions cannot play a major role in constraining bank risk taking, suggesting that primary constraints should come from regulation and supervision.[61] The role that the market or the regulator should respectively play in M&A in the banking sector however remains a contentious matter. The 'systemic risk' element associated with bank acquisitions is intricately linked with the question of who, by law, should decide on the change of control in the banking group and on what grounds. The particular problem facing the legislation concerning the market for corporate control in the banking industry is that the operation of the market for corporate control in this sector can be characterised by mutually conflicting or dependent conditions. On the one hand, banks should be protected from the workings of the market on the basis that banks' stability is important from a social utility point of view. On the other hand, where safety and prudential safeguards are in fact put in place, these may result in a negative impact on the effective operation of an open market for corporate control for banks and encourage unwarranted state protectionism.

---

59   Ibid., 60, who refers to the issues addressed by Daigre in 'Des offers publiques bancaires. – De quelqes enseignments generaux tires sur l'affaire BNP – Societe generale – Paribas', *La Semaine Juridique Administrations et Collectivites territoriales* No 4 (2000), para. 9, 5.

60   Ibid., 61.

61   The Turner Review, see above n 4, 47.

Regulating the market for corporate control in the banking industry poses an **9.23** extra challenge. The regulatory framework must not only deal with the prioritisation of the common tensions that arise within a takeover context,[62] but also deal with the problems that stem from the opaque nature of banks' financial statements, the informational problems that may arise as a consequence, as well as with the moral hazard problems that may follow if a 'bad deal' takes place. Regulating the relationship between an acquirer and non-shareholders is key in the case of bank acquisitions, as non-shareholders may well be affected by a change in corporate control. This applies especially in the case when the bank which emerges from the acquisition would pose a 'systemic-risk' to the economy were it to fail. Along these lines, public welfare or public interest tests may be brought into play on the sound basis of banks playing a 'systemic role' in a Member State's economy. In order to assess the efficacy of the regulatory framework in regulating such matters, the present section outlines a set of three regulatory instruments. Selected rules of the Qualifying Holdings Directive, the UK City Code on Takeovers and Mergers and the EU Takeover Directive will be referred to.

A. The Qualifying Holdings Directive

Directive 2007/44/EC of the European Parliament and of the Council, hence- **9.24** forth the Qualifying Holdings Directive, amended selected provisions of the Banking Directive,[63] as well as a series of provisions of other financial sector Directives.[64] The Qualifying Holdings Directive regulates in detail the procedural rules and evaluation criteria for the prudential assessment of acquisitions and increase of holdings in the financial sector.[65] The Directive was adopted in 5 September 2007 with a date of implementation for all Member States by 21 March 2009 and sets out a detailed description of the process required for seeking regulatory consent when acquiring a bank, insurer or securities firm.

---

62   For the special agency relationships which may arise when a pubic offer is made by the acquirer to all the shareholders of the target company for their shares, refer to P Davies and K J Hopt, 'Control transactions', in R H Kraakman et al (eds), *The Anatomy of Corporate Law: A Comparative and Functional Approach*, (2nd ed, OUP 2009), 227–8 and 248. As they explain, the transaction may be wealth enhancing for the target shareholders, but threaten the position of the target board or the reverse. A conflict may also arise between the shareholders and the acquirer, also identified as constituting a 'co-ordination problem' between them. The decision to accept or reject the bid is made up by shareholders on an individual basis, and not as a collective decision which binds all shareholders. This means that the acquirer may have an incentive to seek to divide the shareholders as a body. An agency relationship also arises between target shareholders, as there may be a marked divide between shareholders with a long-term investment horizon and shareholders with a short-term investor horizon, so that the former may wish to keep their investment in the target firm, focusing on the corporation's long-term growth, whereas the latter may aim to capitalise on their investment and dispose of their shares once they receive an offer from the bidder.

63   Directive 2006/48/EC of the European Parliament, Banking Directive.

64   Council Directive 92/49/EEC; Directives 2002/83/EC, 2004/39/EC and 2005/68/EC.

65   OJ 2007 L 247/1.

The objectives of the Directive were to: (i) improve the legal certainty, clarity and transparency of the supervisory approval process with regard to acquisitions and increase of shareholdings in the banking, insurance and securities sectors; and (ii) ensure that all proposed acquisitions or disposals of a qualifying holding are treated in the same way throughout the EU and across sectors.[66]

9.25 In 2008 the former three level Committees (CEBS, CESR and CEIOPS) produced non-binding guidelines for the prudential assessment of acquisitions, hereinafter the 3L3 Guidelines, so as to ensure convergent decision-making within the EU.[67] The Guidelines are to be read as background to the Qualifying Holdings Directive[68] and aim to elaborate on the prudential assessment criteria in order to ensure convergent decisional practice within the EU.[69] As clearly outlined, the Guidelines aim to reach a common understanding of the five assessment criteria laid down in the Directive, define appropriate co-operation arrangements ensuring an adequate and timely flow of information between supervisors and establish an exhaustive and harmonised list of information that proposed acquirers should include in their notifications to the competent supervisory authorities.[70]

9.26 The role of the competent authority is to appraise the suitability of the proposed acquirer and the financial soundness of the proposed acquisition, in order to ensure the sound and prudent management of the investment firm in which an acquisition is proposed. The Directive was adopted in order to address the problem that had arisen in the past in relation to other Directives, which afforded wide discretion to Member States in interpreting the regulatory requirements. The concern was that the prescribed regulatory gaps were used to frustrate takeover bids for protectionist reasons. The aim of the Qualifying Holdings Directive is to provide the necessary legal certainty and clarity regarding the assessment process of a proposed bid. In terms of the criteria against which a proposed acquirer is assessed, the Qualifying Holdings Direct- ive has arguably improved the standards and the transparency of the assess- ment.

---

66   See Recitals 2 and 3 of Directive 2007/44/EC of the European Parliament and of the Council.
67   The Committee of European Banking Supervisors (CEBS), the Committee of European Insurance and Occupational Pensions Supervisors (CEIOPS) and the Committee of European Securities Regulators (CESR) joint guidelines for the prudential assessment of acquisitions and increases in holdings in the financial sector as required by Directive 2007/44/EC, CEBS/2008/214, CEIOPS-3L3-19/08, CESR/08-543b Guidelines for the prudential assessment of acquisitions and increases in holdings in the financial sector required by Directive 2007/44/EC, henceforth 3L3 Guidelines.
68   Ibid 4.
69   See Public Consultation on the Application of Directive 2007/44 EC as regards acquisitions and increase of holdings in the financial sector (December 2009), 3, available at: http://ec.europa.eu/internal_market/ consultations/docs/2011/acquisitions/consultation_paper_en.pdf.
70   3L3 Guidelines, see above n 67, 5.

The Directive harmonises the conditions under which the proposed acquirer of **9.27** a holding in a financial institution is required to provide notification of its decision to the competent authority responsible for the prudential supervision of the target financial institution, it outlines a clear and transparent procedure for the prudential assessment of the proposed acquisition by the competent authorities, including setting the maximum period of time for completing the process, it specifies clear criteria of a strictly prudential nature to be applied by the competent authorities in the assessment process, and finally it ensures that the proposed acquirer is informed of the information the acquirer is required to provide to the competent authorities.[71]

According to the Directive an acquirer is required to provide notification of a **9.28** proposed acquisition to the supervisor as soon as he has made the decision to acquire, increase, or reduce a qualifying holding in the target financial institution, as well as when he involuntarily crosses a threshold, or when persons are acting in concert, or in the case of a decrease in an existing shareholding.[72] The Banking Directive defines a qualifying holding as a 'direct or indirect holding in an undertaking which represents 10 per cent or more of the capital or of the voting rights which makes it possible to exercise a significant influence over the management of the undertaking'.[73]

The Directive is a maximum harmonisation Directive in terms of the proced- **9.29** ural rules and assessment criteria, meaning that Member States are not allowed to lay down stricter rules. The Directive does however allow Member States to require notification at a level below the 10 per cent threshold. According to the provisions of the Qualifying Holdings Directive, the competent authorities are called to assess the suitability of the proposed acquirer, as well as the financial soundness of the proposed acquisition against a set of criteria and can only oppose a proposed acquisition if there are grounds for doing so following the criteria set out in the Qualifying Holdings Directive or if the information that the acquirer has provided is incomplete.[74]

The Banking Directive provided a general statement that the competent **9.30** authority could oppose the plan of the proposed acquirer 'if, in view of the need to ensure sound and prudent management of the credit institution', it was not

---

71 3L3 Guidelines, see above n 67, 4.
72 Ibid., 7.
73 Banking Directive, art 4(11).
74 See Banking Directive, art 19a(1), 19a(2), as amended.

'satisfied as to the suitability of the person concerned'. The Qualifying Holdings Directive now provides that the assessment is to be undertaken against an exhaustive list of five specific criteria. Concerning the assessment of the proposed acquirer, the authority will examine two criteria, namely the reputation of the proposed acquirer[75] (specifically whether there are any doubts regarding his integrity and professional competence which may arise from an examination of his past business conduct[76]), and the financial soundness of the acquirer[77] (including his adequacy for carrying on the type of business of the target credit institution). In relation to the acquirer's integrity, it is assumed that the acquirer is of 'good repute' if there is no evidence to the contrary.[78] In relation to his professional competence, the 3L3 Guidelines explain that this covers competence in management and technical competence.[79] Management competence is based on the acquirer's previous experience in acquiring and managing holdings in companies, and should demonstrate due skill, care, diligence, and compliance with the relevant standards.[80] Technical competence may be based on the acquirer's previous experience in operating and managing financial firms as a controlling shareholder or as a person who effectively directs the business of a financial firm, whereby past experience should demonstrate due skill, care, diligence, and compliance with the relevant standards.[81] In relation to the financial soundness of the acquirer the 3L3 Guidelines provide that this criterion can be understood as the capacity of the acquirer to finance the proposed acquisition and to maintain a sound financial structure for the foreseeable future.[82]

9.31 Concerning the assessment of the target institution, the competent authority will examine another two criteria, namely the reputation and experience of the management of the target company as a result of the acquisition[83] and the ability of the target company to continue to comply with its prudential

---

75 Banking Directive, art 19a(1)(a), as amended.
76 See Qualifying Holdings Directive, Recital 8.
77 Banking Directive, art 19a(1)(c), as amended.
78 See 3L3 Guidelines, above n 67, 9.
79 See ibid., 11–12.
80 See ibid., 12.
81 Ibid.
82 See ibid., 17, paras 56 and 57.
83 Banking Directive, art 19a(1)(b), as amended. It is important to note that in relation to the assessment of the reputation and experience of the management of the target company as a result of the acquisition the supervisory authorities often reflect on this using the term 'fit and proper' criteria in the assessment of the suitability of shareholder or qualifying shareholders, meaning that the persons who will effectively direct the financial institution must be of sufficiently good repute and have sufficient experience to perform those duties, which criteria are described as such in the authorisation criteria in art11(1) of the Banking Directive.

requirements.[84] In relation to the latter criterion the provision specifically provides that the assessment will focus on whether the group of which the institution will become a part has a structure that makes it possible to: exercise effective supervision, effectively exchange information between the competent authorities and determine the allocation of responsibilities among the competent authorities.[85] The fifth criterion examined is whether there are any reasonable grounds for suspecting terrorist financing or money laundering in connection with the proposed acquisition or the potential increase in risk of these.[86] Member States must not impose any prior conditions in respect of the level of shareholding that must be acquired nor allow their competent authorities to examine the proposed acquisition in terms of the economic need of the market.[87] As Kerjean explains, the limitations imposed clarify that the authorities are not allowed to interfere in business decisions or strategies and should not attempt to restrict the conditions under which investors decide to acquire shareholdings.[88]

Regarding the information required from the acquirer, the 3L3 Guidelines **9.32** explain that the proportionality principle applies both to the composition of the required information and the assessment procedures. An application of the proportionality principle suggests that the type of information required from the acquirer may be influenced by a variety of factors. The particularities of the acquirer, whether the acquirer is a legal or a natural person, whether the acquirer is a supervised financial institution or other entity and whether or not the acquirer as a financial institution is supervised in the EEA or an equivalent third country are factors that can be taken into account when considering the type of information that should be required.[89] Other variables which may influence the type of information required concern the particularities of the proposed transaction, for example whether it is an intra-group or an 'external' transaction, the degree of involvement of the acquirer in the management of the target financial institution, and the level of the holding to be acquired.[90] In the case of acquisitions by means of a public offer, it may well be the case that the acquirer encounters difficulties in obtaining information which is needed to establish a full business plan. According to the 3L3 Guidelines the acquirer should be prompted to bring these difficulties to the attention of the authority and point out the aspects of its business plan that are likely to be modified in the

---

84 Banking Directive, art 19a(1)(d), as amended.
85 Ibid.
86 Ibid., art 19a(1)(e), as amended.
87 Ibid., art 19a(3), as amended.
88 Kerjean, see above n 33, 58.
89 See 3L3 Guidelines, above n 67, 9.
90 Ibid.

near term.[91] The 3L3 Guidelines also point out that the proportionality principle should be applied so that the acquisition will not be refused on the sole basis of the lack of some required information that can be justified by the nature of the transaction, provided that the partial information appears sufficient to understand the probable outcome of the acquisition for the target financial institution and that the proposed acquirer commits himself to providing the missing information as soon as possible after the closing of the acquisition.[92]

9.33 The Qualifying Holdings Directive has been reviewed by the Commission in co-operation with Member States following Article 6 of the Directive. Following the review, a report was submitted to the European Parliament and the Council, together with appropriate proposals in February 2013.[93] The responses received by the Commission following its public consultation on the application of the Directive indicate that the Directive has overall contributed to the reduction of barriers for acquisitions in the financial sector and that domestic and cross-border transactions are treated equally across the EU.[94] Among other issues, the report discusses the need to take further action to ensure coherent application of the proportionality principle mentioned in the Directive.[95] According to the report, the results of the public consultation provide for some evidence that national supervisory authorities do not sufficiently apply the proportionality principle both in terms of the information required and the assessment procedure.[96] The report also concludes that some assessment criteria laid down in the Qualifying Holdings Directive need to be further clarified, namely that of '*the financial soundness of the proposed acquirer, in particular in relation to the type of business pursued and envisaged in the [financial institution] in which the acquisition is proposed*'.[97] The survey and the public consultation show that documents required by the national supervisory authorities for the assessment differ among Member States and that it is not sufficiently clear whether the solvency of the proposed acquirer needs to be assessed under this criterion.[98] It is also mentioned that there are some

---

91 Ibid.
92 Ibid.
93 COM (2013) 64 final, 'Application of Directive 2007/44/EC amending Council Directive 92/49/EEC and Directives 2002/83/EC, 2004/39/EC, 2005/68/EC and 2006/48/EC as regards procedural rules and evaluation criteria for the prudential assessment of acquisitions and increase of holdings in the financial sector.'
94 Ibid., 4.
95 Ibid., 6.
96 Ibid.
97 See Banking Directive, art 19a(1), as amended. See also ibid., 7.
98 Ibid., 7.

indications that the use of own funds compared to borrowed funds is interpreted inconsistently.[99]

The report concludes that despite the fact that the regime created by the **9.34**
Directive is working satisfactorily overall, there are certain shortcomings in the
Directive that could be addressed so as to better ensure consistent application
throughout the EU and across financial sectors and to provide acquirers with
more legal certainty.[100] In terms of a consistent application of the rules the
report proposes that European Supervisory Authorities (ESAs) attend to the
update and clarification of the 3L3 Guidelines on aspects, such as the application of the proportionality principle and the assessment criteria.[101] Directive
2010/78/EU[102] enables the ESAs to submit regulatory technical standards to
the Commission in order to establish an exhaustive list of information to be
included by proposed acquirers in their notification to acquire qualifying
holdings and to implement technical standards in order to establish common
procedures, forms and templates for the consultation process within the prudential assessment between the relevant competent authorities.[103] In light of
the financial crisis, the report also proposes the incorporation of financial
stability aspects more explicitly in the assessment process, which could be
achieved by introducing a resolvability assessment before the transactions take
place.[104] This criterion however, according to the Report, would need to be
framed in in a way that avoids divergent implementation by competent
authorities.[105]

From a corporate governance perspective, there are additional provisions that **9.35**
could be added so as to better facilitate the authorisation process. At present,
the Directive offers no meaningful guidance on how competent authorities are
supposed to undertake an assessment of financial stability concerns that an
increase in holdings may give rise to. Financial stability risks involved in
mergers and acquisitions in the banking industry have become more apparent
following the financial crisis. The Directive in its present text does not contain
an explicit assessment criterion allowing competent authorities to assess the

---

99   Ibid.
100   Ibid., 9.
101   Ibid., 9.
102   Directive 2010/78/EU of the European Parliament and of the Council of 24 November 2010 amending
      Directives 98/26/EC, 2002/87/EC, 2003/6/EC, 2003/41/EC, 2003/71/EC, 2004/39/EC, 2004/109/EC,
      2005/60/EC, 2006/48/EC, 2006/49/EC and 2009/65/EC in respect of the powers of the European Super-
      visory Authority (European Banking Authority), the European Supervisory Authority (European Insurance
      and Occupational Pensions Authority) and the European Supervisory Authority (European Securities and
      Markets Authority), OJ L 331of 12.12.2010, 120.
103   COM (2013), see above n 93, 9.
104   Ibid.
105   Ibid.

impact of the proposed acquisition on the stability of the financial system.[106] Financial stability is only implicitly addressed in the assessment criteria of the Directive, namely the financial soundness of the proposed acquirer and compliance with prudential requirements.[107] In order for the competent authorities to be enabled to consider the issue of financial stability in a meaningful way, one option would be to explicitly refer to this as an additional criterion added to the authorisation process in the case of emerging entities that are likely to have an impact on the financial stability of the Member State. The creation of potential 'precarious ownership structures' is also a matter which may require that additional or more elaborate criteria are incorporated in the Directive. 'Precarious ownership structures' are deemed as such if the structure in place potentially impedes the proper functioning of the target institution due to a conflict of large shareholders, each of whose shareholdings is large enough to block decisions but insufficient to give control over the institution.[108] An opinion of the European Central Bank dated in 2006 had identified this problem explaining that such an ownership structure could potentially impair the future management of the institution, leading to negative implications for its effective supervision in the long-run.[109] In order to tackle this problem an addition could be made to the legal framework so as to enable supervisory authorities to also consider whether the target institution's corporate governance arrangements are sufficiently robust so as to prevent a potential deadlock in its decision-making processes following the proposed acquisition.[110] Finally, concerning the problems associated with the application of the proportionality principle and the criteria for authorisation, a way forward may be a standardisation of the type of information that the acquirer is required to produce. This allows for only *some* level of flexibility on the competent authority's part concerning the information it requests in order to make its assessment.

B. The UK Takeover Code

9.36 The UK is by comparison to other jurisdictions the most liberal system in regulating takeovers worldwide.[111] The logic underlying the Code is that it is established on a set of general principles which are further elaborated on through specific provisions in the Code's corpus. The rules regulate in significant detail matters concerning the conduct of parties subject to the Code during

---

106 Ibid., 8.
107 Ibid.
108 European Central Bank, Opinion on the prudential assessment of acquisitions and increase of shareholdings in the financial sector, CON/2006/60 (7.2.2007), para 2(6).
109 Ibid.
110 Ibid.
111 J Kay, 'The Kay Review of UK Equity Markets and long-term decision making', Interim Report, (London February 2012), 13.

the offer period and the process that needs to be followed at each stage of the takeover process. A detailed commentary of each of the rules is also set out after each rule, thereby providing clarity on the meaning of those rules.[112] The Panel is given the authority to change the application of these rules on a case-by-case basis only in limited circumstances. The Code's main objective is to regulate the way in which takeovers are conducted and ensure that shareholders are treated fairly and not denied an opportunity to decide on the merits of a potential bid.[113] The most characteristic aspect of the Code is the shareholder primacy norm it endorses, which is to be found in the strict non-frustration principle encompassed in rule 21 of the Code. The rule prohibits target directors from taking any defensive measures against a bid without obtaining prior shareholder approval once a bid has become imminent. The non-frustration rule in conjunction with other rules encompassed in the Code and the broader framework regulating target directors' conduct during a takeover, result in control over UK companies being more contestable compared to other jurisdictions.[114] The non-frustration rule of rule 21 makes it easier for hostile bids to succeed.[115] The Code is not about the economic usefulness of takeovers generally, nor does it allow for the Panel to assess the specific financial or commercial merits of an individual takeover.[116] The openness of the legal framework to takeovers ensures to a large extent that takeovers succeed. This was one of the basic concerns brought forward by the Kraft – Cadbury deal leading to the reform of the UK rules in 2011. Although the Kraft – Cadbury takeover did not involve financial institutions as such, it is worth reflecting on the deal, as it constitutes the key takeover which produced significant changes to the Code. The reforms which the deal prompted are evidence that the operation of the former legal framework was out of step with what a desirable policy should in fact be attempting to bring about, namely facilitating takeovers, but not at the expense of corporations' long-term growth and the interests of the target company,

---

112   D Kershaw 'Web Chapter A: The market for corporate control', in D Kershaw *Company Law in Context: Text and Materials*, (OUP 2010), 40, available at: www.oup.com/uk/orc/bin/9780199215942/resources/chapters/Web_Chapter_A.pdf.

113   General principle 3 of the Code.

114   For an overview of the benefits of the non-frustration principle see D Kershaw, 'The illusion of importance: Reconsidering the UK's takeover defence prohibition', (2007) 56(2) *International and Comparative Law Quarterly* 267, 268–9.

115   For an explanation of the operation of board neutrality within a takeover context within the EU regulatory framework refer to P. Davies, E. Schuster and E. Van de Walle de Ghelcke, 'The Takeover Directive as a Protectionist Tool?' (2010) ECGI – Law Working Paper No. 141/2010; For arguments on the triviality of the rule as such see C Gerner-Beuerle, D Kershaw and M Solinas, 'Is the board neutrality rule trivial? Amnesia about corporate law in European Takeover Regulation', (March 30, 2011) LSE Legal Studies Working Paper No 3/2011, who advocate that it is corporate law rules that do not enable the construction of takeover defences, or undermine the extent to which they can be potently deployed, making the adoption or rejection of the neutrality principle in Member States is of trivial significance.

116   Introduction of the Code.

shareholders and other constituencies. For financial institutions in particular, the implications of the bid on the financial stability of the banking group and the economy merit special attention.

9.37   The reform process of the rules was undertaken by the Takeover Panel Code Committee. The committee found that a variety of factors had in recent times enabled offerors to obtain a tactical advantage over the offeree company.[117] The committee accepted that: (i) it had become too easy for 'hostile' offerors to succeed; and that (ii) the outcome of offers, and particularly hostile offers, may be unduly influenced by the actions of so-called 'short-term' investors.[118] The committee therefore brought forward proposals to 'amend the Code with a view to reducing this tactical advantage and redressing the balance in favour of the offeree company'[119] and concluded that 'a number of changes should be proposed to the Code to improve the offer process and to take more account of the position of persons who are affected by takeovers in addition to offeree company shareholders'.[120]

9.38   The strict non-frustration principle of rule 21 of the Code keeps the board outside the decision-making process on the assumption that there tends to be a strong incentive for the board, including non-executive directors, to look towards their own interests during the takeover process, to maintain their positions in the target company. The non-frustration principle encompassed in rule 21 coupled with the requirement for the board to provide unbinding advice to shareholders on the bid,[121] places significant reliance on the shareholders' decision. The Kraft – Cadbury deal signalled that the share price of the target company should not be used as the sole criterion to evaluate the current and future performance of the target company, considering that not all available information will be encompassed in it. The deal made clear that target directors

---

117   See The Takeover Panel Code Committee, Panel Statement 2010/22, , 'Review of certain aspects of the regulation of takeover bids', 21 October 2010, which constitutes the Code Committee's response to the consultation paper and sets out the Code Committee's conclusions in relation to the principal issues consulted upon, 4–5.

118   Ibid., 3.

119   Ibid.

120   Ibid.

121   See general principle 3 of the Code which imposes a general duty on target directors to act in the interests of the company as a whole. Note that prior to the adoption of the Directive's principles into the Code, the equivalent Takeover Directive's original principle, general principle 9, made clear that priority was to be given to shareholders' interests, with only regard being given to employees' and creditors' interests. It is unclear whether, after the implementation of the Takeover Directive, general principle 3 of the Code imposes a different notion to the interests that directors should serve when providing their opinion of a bid; See Kershaw, above n 111, 46–7, who argues that when interpreting the term it has been rightly observed that the Panel will need to take a purposive approach to ensure compliance with the Directive; see B Sjåfjell, *Towards a Sustainable European Company Law: A Normative Analysis of the Objectives of EU Law, with the Takeover Directive as a Test Case*, (Kluwer Law International 2009), 350, who argues that it should be given an autonomous broader European meaning.

tend to recommend acceptance of a bid that significantly exceeds the company's trading price instead of considering the long-term implications of the takeover bid in their advice.[122]

One of the proposals for reform considered during the reform process of 2010 **9.39** was whether it was necessary to better regulate the advisory role of the target board. The Code Committee specifically considered whether there was a perception under the Code that the board of the target was bound to consider only the offer price in giving its opinion on an offer.[123] The Code was amended and now provides for an additional interpretive text to rule 25. Note 1 on rule 25.2 of the Code stipulates that the target board is not required by the Code to consider the offer price as the determining factor, nor is it precluded by the Code from taking into account any other factors which it considers relevant. In light of the proposed 2011 change, the new interpretation of the section arguably gives target directors greater leeway in referring to the interests of various constituencies in their recommendation of a bid to target shareholders.

In the case of banks and financial institutions, one could argue that directors **9.40** can, in their assessment of the offer, rely on the new provision to recommend rejection of a bid on grounds of financial stability. The information provided would possibly assist the competent authorities during their authorisation process. Regulating in greater detail the content of the opinion of the target board could mitigate the uncertainty that surrounds contested bids in particular, when the bidder is likely to be faced with problems of conducting limited due diligence. Not only will the disclosure of information on the target directors' part prove useful to the competent authorities in their assessment of the bid during the authorisation process but it may also assist shareholders with long-term interests in their decision on the bid, as not all shareholders will prefer a short-term gain without considering the social costs that may arise out of the takeover. Empirical evidence shows that the role of the target board, albeit advisory, remains important in determining takeover outcomes. Evidence shows that the target board's resistance to a bid is 'inversely related to the probability of its success'.[124] Wong and O'Sullivan also show that the main

---

122   T Webb, 'Lord Mandelson calls for overhaul of takeover rules', *The Guardian* (1 March 2010); see also Code Committee of the Takeover Panel, *Response Statement to the Consultation Paper on Review of Certain Aspects of the Regulation of Takeover Bids*, RS 2010/22, 21 October 2010 (First Response Paper) section 2.5., 3, available at: http://www.thetakeoverpanel.org.uk/wp-content/uploads/2009/12/2010-221.pdf.

123   In view of the contradictory authorities of *Heron International Ltd v Lord Grade* [1983] BCLC 244 and *Re a Company* [1986] BCLC 383 it remains unclear whether target directors are under a positive duty to achieve the best price for the company's shareholders.

124   P Holl and D Kyriazis, 'The detriments of outcome in UK take-over bids', (1996) 3(2) *International Journal of Economic Business* 168.

cause of takeover failure is opposition from target management and that, once target management opposes a takeover, the probability of a bid succeeding falls by 50 per cent.[125]

9.41 Another proposal for reform considered during the reform process of 2010 was whether it was necessary to better regulate the standards against which the statements made by the bidder are assessed. The takeover of Cadbury by Kraft was marked by the controversy over Kraft's statements regarding the future of Cadbury's Somerdale factory, which was earmarked by Cadbury for closure. In the aftermath of the deal Kraft revised its initial plans and did not follow up on the undertaking to keep the Somerdale factory open.[126] Kraft argued that the plans to close down the Somerdale plant were so well advanced, that it could not reverse the process in order to abide by its initial plan.[127] In response to Kraft's failure to comply with its undertaking, the Panel issued a statement of public criticism against Kraft finding Kraft in breach of rule 19.1 of the Code.[128] In response to this aspect of the deal, the Code Committee introduced amendments to the Code in order to better address the quality and nature of information transmitted during the process of a bid. In terms of the quality of information provided, rule 19.1 of the Code requires that each document or advertisement published, or statement made, during the course of an offer, to be prepared with the highest standards of care and accuracy and the information given to be adequately and fairly presented. The standard of care for published documents to be observed during the takeover process remains unaltered in the latest version of the Code.[129] The Kraft – Cadbury deal highlighted that there is a legal gap with regard to the enforcement of the bidder's intentions concerning the target's assets and employees after the successful bid is complete in the event that the bidder fails to comply with his initial statement. The Code Committee therefore introduced a new rule imposing adherence to statements for at least a year or other specified period which is provided for by the bidder introduced in

---

125 P Wong and N O'Sullivan, 'The determinants and consequences of abandoned takeovers', (2001) 15(2) *Journal of Economic Surveys* 156, 181.

126 House of Commons, Business, Innovation and Skills Committee, 'Mergers, acquisitions and takeovers: the takeover of Cadbury by Kraft', Ninth Report of Session 2009–10, (The Stationery Office Ltd 30 March 2010) (2010 HC 234), 5.

127 Ibid. 29–30 .

128 The Takeover Panel Code Committee, Panel Statement 2010/14, 'Kraft Foods Inc. Offer for Cadbury plc', 4–5.

129 Note that the rationale encompassed in rule 19.1 was, prior to the adoption of the Directive's principles into the Code, reflected in one of the Code's original general principles, general principle 5. It provided that: 'Any document or advertisement addressed to shareholders containing information or advice from an offeror or the board of an offeree company or their respective advisers must, as is the case with a prospectus, be prepared with the highest standards of care and accuracy.' The principle did not manage to form part of the Code's general principles post the implementation of the Directive in the UK, but is nevertheless reflected in the rules of the Code.

note 3 of rule 19.1 of the Code, unless the bidder can show that there has been a change of circumstances. Following the Pfizer/AstraZeneca deal the Code Committee of the Panel considered a set of new proposals for reform in 2014. In May 2014, in the context of its possible offer for AstraZeneca plc, Pfizer Inc. had stated that, subject to successful completion of its combination with AstraZeneca, it would commit for a minimum of five years to: (a) complete the construction of AstraZeneca's planned research and development hub in Cambridge; (b) base key scientific leadership in the UK; (c) employ a minimum of 20 per cent of the combined group's total research and development workforce in the UK; and (d) retain substantial manufacturing facilities in Macclesfield.[130] The statements were made on a voluntary basis and not as a requirement of the Code. Following the particular aspect of the Pfizer Inc./AstraZeneca plc takeover attempt, consideration was given to regulating in more detail the statements parties to an offer make during the bid process concerning the course of action the parties plan to take after a completed takeover. Specifically, the Code Committee of the Panel issued Public Consultation Document 2014/2 on *Post-Offer Undertakings and Intention Statements*, making proposals to amend the Code in order to make a distinction between actions that parties to an offer *commit* to take and actions that parties to an offer *intend* to take.[131] *Post-offer undertakings* are statements concerning a course of action that a party to an offer *commits* to take, or not take, after the end of the offer period and with which it will be required to comply for the period of time specified in the undertaking, unless a qualification or condition set out in the undertaking applies, whereas *post-offer intention statements* are statements relating to any particular course of action that a party to an offer *intends* to take, or not take, after the end of the offer period, which will be required to be accurate statements of the party's intentions at the time that they are made and based on reasonable grounds.[132] The particular provisions and latest proposals for reform, which would also apply to acquisitions in the banking industry, would better assist parties to an offer in the exchange of more accurate information between authorities, target and bidding firms specifically. Following the Public Consultation Paper and the responses received on the proposed amendments of the particular provisions of the Code, the Code Committee adopted, in most

---

130   Public Consultation Paper 2014/2, above n 25, 1.

131   Ibid., 4, whereby the objectives of the proposed reform are stipulated, namely that: *The objectives of the proposed new framework are to:(a) provide clarity for shareholders and other stakeholders as to the status of statements made by the parties to an offer in relation to action they will, or will not, take following the offer;(b) increase the effectiveness of the enforcement tools available to the Panel when parties to an offer choose to make voluntary commitments; and (c) enable the parties to an offer to make informative statements of intention.*

132   Ibid, 4–5.

cases, the amendments to the Code that were proposed in PCP 2014/2, to take effect on 12 january 1015.[133]

9.42 Another proposal for reform considered during the reform process of 2010 was whether it was necessary to increase or reframe the disclosure requirements contained in the offer document. More information contained in the offer document as to the rationale of the acquisition may assist the supervisory authority in better assessing the motives behind the bid and the bidder's intentions for improving or merging with the business of the target bank. The amendments introduced to the Code post the Kraft–Cadbury deal, namely in rule 24,[134] were made on the basis that any statement of intention by an offeror should be as detailed as is possible in view of the fact that the offeror must have a fundamental business rationale for seeking to acquire the offeree company, which it should disclose as fully as possible.[135] Within this context, the Code Committee clarified that statements of a general nature were unlikely to be acceptable in the context of a recommended offer in view of the fact that the offeror has had an opportunity to undertake full due diligence.[136]

9.43 Concerning acquisitions in the banking sector, an improvement in the quantity, quality and accuracy of information disclosed may better enable the supervisory authority to authorise the approval or rejection of a bid. The issue of disclosure and due diligence processes are especially important for bank acquisitions considering the opaque nature of the financial statements of banks, which creates additional hurdles in overcoming information-related problems that may arise between the bidder and the target boards. Privileged and undisclosed information would hence tend to strengthen the hand of the incumbent board

---

133 See Response Statement 2014/2, The Takeover Panel Code Committee, 'Post Offer Undertakings and Intention Statements' (RS 2014/2, 23 December 2014).

134 The new elements of rule 24.2 are that the rule now attaches more importance to the disclosure of the bidder's intentions with regard to the future business of the offeree company and of an explanation of the long-term commercial justification for the offer. The rule also introduces the requirement that the bidder disclose his intentions with regard to the maintenance of any existing trading facilities for the relevant securities of the offeree company. Another new element of the rule is the concept of the *negative statement*. The bidder is now required to make a statement if he has no intention to make any changes in relation to the matters described under rule 24.2(a)(i)–(iii) or if he considers that its strategic plans for the offeree company will have no repercussions on employment or the location of the offeree company's places of business. The Code Committee has introduced these changes on the basis that the ability of the offeree company board and other interested constituencies to comply with their own obligations, and to provide meaningful information to the offeree company shareholders and employees, depends on the accuracy and adequacy of the information published by the offeror in accordance with its own obligations.

135 Response Statement 2011/1, The Takeover Panel Code Committee 'Review of Certain Aspects of the Regulation of Takeover Bids: Response Statement by the Code Committee of the Panel following the Consultation on PCP 2011/1', (RS 2011/1, 21 July 2011), 80–81.

136 Ibid.

of the target bank compared to the position of the target board of a non-financial corporate.

Another amendment introduced to the Code in 2011 concerned the disclosure **9.44** of more detailed financial information on the financing of the offer in the offer document. According to rule 24.3 of the Code the information on financing must now be disclosed in all offers, and not only in securities exchange offers.[137] The Code Committee was of the view that the Code should require the disclosure of the same financial information regarding the financing of an offer irrespective of the nature of the offer, and that constituencies other than offeree company shareholders have an interest in information regarding the financial position of the offeror and its group.[138] The 'other constituencies' considered in this respect included: (i) the offeree company directors having regard to their obligations under rule 25.1 and duties under CA 2006, section 172; (ii) the employees, customers, creditors and suppliers of both the offeree company and the offeror; and (iii) the shareholders in the offeror.[139] A bank entity emerging from M&A with significantly more debt than equity will be highly leveraged. Disclosure of the financing of the bid, is therefore specifically relevant to bank acquisitions, as debt financing will undoubtedly increase the risks assumed.

C. EU Takeover Directive

Directive 2004/25/EC of the European Parliament and the Council of April **9.45** 21, 2004 on takeover bids, hereinafter the Takeover Directive, was adopted in 2004 after almost 15 years of political struggle. Adopting a standard set of legal rules on corporate restructuring was seen, among other things, as a way of avoiding prudential considerations, which if left unspecified could result in the creation of obstacles to restructuring operations.[140] The Takeover Directive, a minimum harmonisation directive, affords Member States extra flexibility in adopting the board-neutrality rule of article 9 and the breakthrough rule of article 11, which combined aim to make control over companies more contestable.[141] In its default form, the Directive follows the UK Code's shareholder primacy norm.[142] Article 9 of the Directive requires that the board of the

---

137   Ibid., 67.
138   Ibid., 69.
139   Ibid., 18–19.
140   Ibid., 9.
141   See the optionality arrangements provided for in art 12 of the Takeover Directive. Article 12 allows Member States and companies a choice in applying the rules encompassed in arts 9(2), 9(3) and 11 of the Directive. As no agreement could be reached between Member States on the mandatory adoption of the board neutrality and breakthrough rules, the compromise of art 12, suggested by Portugal in late 2003, allowed for the Takeover Directive to finally be adopted. Member States can opt out of transposing the board neutrality or breakthrough rule, or both, but they cannot prevent individual companies from voluntarily opting into the rules.

offeree company obtain the prior authorisation of the general meeting of shareholders called for this purpose before taking any action that could potentially frustrate the bid[143] and also places target directors under a positive duty to formulate and communicate their opinion of a bid to target shareholders.[144] The Takeover Directive however does not expressly stipulate that the board of the offeree company should review and comment on the offer document that the bidder issues, nor does the Directive require that the board of the offeree company obtain advice from an independent financial adviser. The Takeover Directive, similar to the UK Code, encompasses provisions on the disclosure of information in relation to the offer.[145] The minimum information that the offer document should contain is outlined in article 6(3).[146] The offer document should include, among other things, information on the terms of the bid, the identity of the offeror, the consideration offered for each security, all the conditions to which the bid is subject, the time allowed for acceptance of the bid, where the consideration offered by the offeror includes securities of any kind, information concerning those securities and information concerning the financing of the bid, as well as the offeror's intentions with regard to the future business of the offeree company and, insofar as it is affected by the bid, information on issues of employment.

9.46 The Takeover Directive in its default form encompasses baseline provisions endorsing shareholder primacy and obligations for the disclosure of a basic level of information concerning the bid to be disclosed by the bidder. At its core, the concerns addressed with regard to the problematic provisions of the Code can

---

Even if the board neutrality or breakthrough rules are adopted at the national or company level, the Portuguese compromise further introduced a third option, that of reciprocity. The reciprocity rule is laid down in art 12(3) of the Takeover Directive and provides that Member States may exempt companies which have opted into the board neutrality and breakthrough rules from applying the rules if the companies become the subject of an offer launched by an offeror company, or by a company controlled directly or indirectly by the offeror, which does not apply the same rules as they do.

142 Takeover Directive, art 9; See also J Winter, C Schans, G Garrido, K Hopt, J Rickford, G Rossi and J Simon, 'Report of the high level group of company law experts on issues related to takeover bids in the European Union', (2002), also known as the 2002 Winter Report, available at: http://ec.europa.eu/internal_market/company/docs/takeoverbids/2002-01-hlg-report_en.pdf, accessed Sep. 2013, 20–21, who argue in favour of the board neutrality rule on the basis that defence mechanisms are costly and may deny the bidder the opportunity to create wealth by exploiting synergies, as well as on the basis that managers are faced with a conflict of interest if a takeover bid is made in fear of losing their positions. It is concluded that shareholders should be able to decide for themselves and that stakeholders should be protected by rules from other fields of law, i.e. labour or environmental law.

143 See Takeover Directive, art 9(2).

144 Ibid., art 9(5).

145 General principle 3(1)(b), see also ibid., arts 6, 8, 9(5), 14.

146 For the minimum level of information that needs to be provided for in the offer document refer to ibid., art 6(3)(a)–(n).

also be raised regarding the Takeover Directive and even more so, due to the fact that the Directive lacks the detail and accuracy in statement which the Code provides.

5. THE MARKET FOR CORPORATE CONTROL IN THE BANKING SECTOR

A commercial bank can be acquired via a merger with another bank or by the **9.47** bidder acquiring a controlling interest of the target bank's common stock. As an acquisition is a private contract between the acquirer and the individual shareholders, it differs substantially from a merger situation, which is completed via a corporate decision between the management teams of the respective merging firms.[147] A takeover, as opposed to other means of a change of corporate control however, possesses a unique characteristic from a corporate governance perspective.[148] From a theoretical standpoint a takeover is distinct as it can effectively displace poorly performing managers and can effectively facilitate corporate restructuring.[149] The shareholder primacy view of the corporation focuses on the 'agency' relationship[150] as between management and shareholders. In companies with dispersed ownership patterns the costs to monitor the directors are high and the likelihood of effective control over the company through the exercise of control rights at the general meeting is low. Agency costs reflect the costs of 'structuring, monitoring, and bonding a set of contracts among agents with conflicting interests'.[151] Shareholders, who can

---

147　Davies and Hopt, see above n 62, 226.

148　H G Manne, 'Mergers and the market for corporate control' (1965) 73(2) *Journal of Political Economy* 110,118; Also see K Lehn, 'Some observations on Henry Manne's contributions to financial economics', (2000) 50 *Case Western Law Review* 263, 264.

149　For an overview of the function of takeovers and usefulness of takeovers refer to F Easterbrook and D Fischel, *The Economic Structure of Corporate Law* (Harvard University Press 1991), 162–74; R Gilson, 'The political ecology of takeovers: Thoughts on harmonizing the European corporate governance environment', (1992) 61 *Fordham Law Review* 161; K Hopt, 'Obstacles to corporate restructuring: observations from a European and a German perspective', in M Tison et al (eds) *Perspectives in Company Law and Financial Regulation-Essays in Honour of Eddy Wymeersch* (CUP 2009), 373–95.

150　In economics the principal-agent model can be traced to a number of articles, i.e. see E F Fama, 'Agency problems and the theory of the firm', (1980) 88(2) *Journal of Political Economy* 288, E F Fama and M C Jensen, 'Separation of ownership and control', (1983) 26 *Journal of Law and Economics* 301, M Jensen and W Meckling 'Theory of the firm: Managerial behaviour, agency costs, and ownership structure', (1976) 3 *Journal of Financial Economics* 305. Also note that from an economic perspective, besides the agency issues, there exist two co-ordination issues among shareholders in a dispersed ownership environment, namely the free-riding problem and the pressure to tender problem. For the free-rider problem see S Grossman and O Hart, 'Takeover bids, the free-rider problem, and the theory of the corporation', (1980) 11 *The Bell Journal of Economics* 42 and for pressure to tender see L Bebchuck, 'The pressure to tender: An analysis and a proposed remedy', (1987) 12 *Delaware Journal of Corporate Law* 911.

151　Fama and Jensen ibid., 304.

ultimately decide on the merits of a takeover bid, can reduce the high monitoring costs by replacing poorly performing management with another efficient one by selling their shares.[152] The takeover ultimately allows the successful bidder to effectively replace the entire internal system, eliminating the inefficiencies of the target and offering shareholders a higher-valued alternative.[153]

9.48 The operation of the market for corporate control in the banking industry defies some of the general assumptions linked to the market for corporate control in other sectors. Justification of the differential treatment of banks can be founded on a series of grounds. The higher opacity of banks' balance sheets, the potential large-scale loss of human capital of investment bankers, the mandatory 'fit and proper' requirement for large shareholders set out by EU law and EU Member State's protectionist behaviour in relation to banks and financial institutions are all reasons why, according to Mülbert, the market for control in the banking industry functions less well compared to other industries.[154] Hopt raises similar points by identifying that the opaqueness of banking structures and business, as well as the different regulatory environments and national protectionism are a few of the reasons why the market for corporate control operates differently in the banking industry.[155] The most controversial issue concerning banks relates to informational problems. Flannery explains:

> the banks' special regulatory oversight reflects a belief that outside investors find it unusually difficult to identify bank asset values and risk exposures. If banks are unusually 'opaque', their debt and equity prices will not accurately reflect how managerial decisions and external events affect the bank's value and riskiness.[156]

9.49 In the case of banks, an important differentiating factor is that the state plays a crucial role, as it is the residual guarantor and bears the ultimate risks in the case of faliure in the banking industry.[157] As explained by Johnston, in order to ensure the stability of the financial system, the state guarantees bank liabilities through explicit and implicit deposit-guarantee schemes, acts as a lender of last resort for banks and introduces banking regulation to limit risk-taking so as to

---

152 Manne, see above n 148, 113.
153 M Jensen and R Ruback, 'The market for corporate control: The scientific evidence', (1983) 11 *Journal of Financial Economics* 5, 44.
154 P Mülbert, 'Corporate governance of banks', (2009) 10 *European Business Organisation Law Review* 411, 426–7.
155 Hopt, see above n 3, 221.
156 Flannery, see above n 9, 377.
157 A Johnston 'Preventing the next financial crisis? Regulating bankers' pay in Europe', (2014) 14(1) *Journal of Law and Society* 6, 9.

protect the public interest.[158] The special case of banks within an M&A context can be better understood if one reflects on the consequences that may follow from a failed change in the corporate control of a bank. As the FSA Report on the failure of the RBS has clearly identified, banks qualify as a special case when it comes to the consequences that flow from bad decision-making and excessive risk-taking. In the case of non-bank companies the downside of poor decisions falls primarily on capital providers, and in some cases on the workforce, and to a much lesser extent to the wider society.[159] As the core function of banks is to issue short-term liabilities to pay against long-term promises to pay from borrowers, risk-taking is an integral part of banking activities.[160] Johnston explains that increases in risk-taking make banks vulnerable to changes in the economy which affect borrowers' ability to pay, and to changes in financial markets which affect their ability to obtain short-term liquidity to discharge their liabilities.[161] Banks are therefore different because excessive risk-taking by banks through an aggressive acquisition for example, can potentially result in bank failure, taxpayer losses, and wider economic harm, so that bank failure ultimately constitutes a matter of public concern and not just a concern for shareholders.[162] A particular danger underlying the case of bank acquisitions is that following the takeover, risk-averse management may be replaced with risk-taking management, who will simply increase leverage in order to improve return on equity.

9.50 The appropriate balance between state regulation and market forces, through shareholder empowerment, remains open. And the fact that the market has failed to indicate corporate governance inefficiencies in banks does not necessarily, as Flannery contends, suggest that there is a need for a special supervisory treatment of banks.[163] Supervisors who are said to see through the opacity of banks compared to investors, were equally surprised when the subprime crisis emerged and non-financial firms had similarly shown a misrepresentation of their value for protracted periods, e.g. Enron.[164] The due diligence conducted in the case of RBS/ABN AMRO was inadequate to assess risks.[165] Risk-assessment is therefore a key factor, which may perhaps deserve special attention when designing disclosure rules for M&A in the banking sector. Bank opaqueness further reinforces the need for regulatory transparency reforms. The

---

158 Ibid.
159 FSA Report, see above n 42, 8.
160 Johnston, see above n 157, 8.
161 Ibid., 8–9.
162 FSA Report, see above n 42, 9.
163 Flannery, see above n 9, 12/19.
164 Ibid.
165 FSA Report, see above n 42, 8; it must be noted however that no one had detected these risks pre-crisis, apart from some heterodox economists.

Third Pillar of the Basel II Accord acknowledges the need to address the exchange of accurate information on the performance of banks. As Flannery reports:

> Rather than specifying ways in which supervisors hope to rely on market discipline, Pillar III seeks 'to encourage market discipline by developing a set of disclosure requirements which will allow market participants to assess key pieces of information on the scope of application, capital risk exposures, risk assessment processes, and hence the capital adequacy of the institution.' (Basel Committee on Bank Supervision, 2006: 226, emphasis added).[166]

Flannery concludes that investors' information on the governance and performance of financial institutions overlaps substantially with what supervisors know. He argues however that governance guarantees for bank failures may severely inhibit investors' incentives to monitor.[167] It is also noted that investors' influence on bank behaviour may be compromised by 'collective action problems' and that market information can be used to overcome supervisory tendencies towards tolerance of underperformance or failure. His suggestion is that specific market signals are examined and interpreted at regular intervals.[168]

9.51 The financial crisis has undoubtedly had implications on the way in which the market discipline of banks is perceived to function. Flannery explains that the data indicate that market monitoring works relatively well across *financial institutions* at any point in time, but it provides *virtually no advance warning* of a financial crisis.[169] He further explains that market monitoring may have been further threatened by the government guarantees extended during September 2008, as government bailouts limit stakeholders' incentives 'to monitor their banks if the government insures them against default loss'.[170] The introduction of Basel III, a comprehensive set of reform measures designed to improve the regulation, supervision and risk management within the banking sector, was therefore introduced by the Basel Committee on Banking Supervision in late 2009, largely in response to the credit crisis.

9.52 The negative implications that may stem from a bad deal on a variety of stakeholders, as well as bank opaqueness, require that the market for corporate control for banks is regulated differently. The bidding war sparked in hostile takeover situations may also superficially drive the share price of the target

---

166   Flannery, see above n 9, 7/19.
167   Ibid., 13/19.
168   Ibid.
169   Ibid., 12/19.
170   Ibid.

company up, which may in the long-term prove to be detrimental for the entity emerging from the acquisition and subsequently the economy of the state in which the bank fully operates in.[171] It is because of such reasons that Flannery concludes that:

> Perhaps it is appropriate to place little confidence in market (counterparty) discipline. We know very little about the market's ability to discipline financial firms directly because direct influence is difficult to identify for any sort of firm. It has been studied for banks only by Bliss and Flannery (2002), who cannot draw strong conclusions. Nor is this necessarily surprising. Atomistic market agents, such as stock and bond investors, suffer from well-known collective action problems.[172]

Imposing limitations on the shareholder primacy followed in general takeover situations, providing more detailed regulation in relation to disclosure require-ments and providing for a better assessment of the implications of the bid can all be justified due to banks qualifying as a special case. One can therefore make the case that as the operation of the market for corporate control in the banking industry defies some of the general assumptions linked to the market for corporate control in other sectors, banks cannot be completely marketised. Banks have a social utility dimension which cannot be overlooked in the context of regulating M&A activity in this sector.

6. THE MARKET FOR CORPORATE CONTROL IN THE BANK SECTOR ASSESSED

The chapter has so far provided an overview of a series of landmark acquisitions **9.53** of banks and selected provisions of the legal framework governing the market for corporate control in the banking sector in the UK and the EU. A discussion on how the market for corporate control in the banking sector defies some of the general theoretical assumptions helped understand why bank acquisitions qualify as a special case and hence deserve to be regulated differently. In an assessment of how best to regulate the market for corporate control in the banking industry, the role of the individual parties to an offer will be discussed, taking into account that: (a) there is often limited information concerning the bid, which makes an assessment of the value of the target firm and subsequently of the estimated success of the deal difficult; (b) from the bidder's perspective, there exists peculiar dynamics between the management and the board, which

---

171   See for example the evidence of the problems that may potentially stem when bids are conducted in such a manner can be easily drawn from the case study of the RBS acquisition of ABN AMRO, whereby Barclays was the other bidder.

172   Flannery, see above n 9, 12/19.

may affect the decision-making process of launching an acquisition for another financial institution; and (c) the 'systemic role' of banks may well require that either the CEO, the executives or the regulator should reflect on the impact of the transaction on the stability of the financial system.

A. The role of the supervisory authority

9.54 It becomes evident from the overview of the provisions of the Qualifying Holdings Directive that there are two key issues that deserve further attention regarding the role of the supervisory authority. The first is the need to ensure a level playing field among Member States. The conditions upon which intervention is conducted should be regulated and the supervisory authority should limit the application of the 'proportionality principle' in its assessment of a bid. Secondly, the supervisory authority should be required to consider the potential impact that the transaction may have on the stability and confidence of the financial system of the Member State and the EU. Considering that systemic risk concerns are not likely to be assessable by any individual institution, regulatory vetting by the supervisory authority becomes paramount.

9.55 In the acquisition of ABN AMRO by RBS the FSA had not intervened. Since the RBS–ABN AMRO acquisition, however, the FSA has arguably changed its approach to takeovers. A recent example is the FSA's intervention in Prudential's planned acquisition of AIA, the Asian subsidiary of AIG, in early 2010. The attempted acquisition was nearing completion in 2010 when the FSA intervened and prevented it due to concerns about the capital implications for Prudential and the overall major changes in the business that would flow from the acquisition. The FSA ended up fining Prudential a total of £30m for breaching FSA Principles. The fines related specifically to the fact that Prudential had failed to inform the FSA at the appropriate time that it was seeking to acquire AIA in early 2010.[173] At a meeting between the FSA and Prudential executives on 12 February 2010, at which the FSA had requested specific details on Prudential's strategy growth in Asia and its plans for raising debt and equity capital, Prudential had not disclosed its intentions with regard to the transaction. The FSA censured Tidjane Thiam, Prudential's Group CEO in March 2013, for failing to deal with the FSA in an open and co-operative manner, thereby breaching principle 11 of the FSA's Principles for Business. According to the press release, the proposed transaction's size and scale would have transformed the group's financial position and had the potential to impact the

---

173 Financial Conduct Authority, press release, 'FSA fines Prudential £30 million and censures CEO for failing to inform regulator for 2010 acquisition plans', 27 March 2013.

stability of the financial system.[174] The FSA assumed a regulatory responsibility to conduct a thorough scrutiny of the proposed transaction and non-disclosure on Prudential's part compromised the FSA' assessment of the transaction.

The extent to which the supervisory authority is allowed to intervene should be **9.56** well defined and should fall within the limits provided for by the free movement of capital of the Treaty. The free movement of capital[175] is encompassed in Article 56 of the EC Treaty and prohibits all restrictions on the free movement of capital and payments between Member States and between Member States and third countries.[176] The European Court of Justice provides that the free movement of capital includes direct investments in the form of participation in an undertaking through a holding of shares which confers the possibility of effectively participating in its management and control,[177] and portfolio investments which refer to the acquisition of shares in order to make a financial investment without any intention to influence the management and control of the undertaking.[178] Article 58(1)(b) EC addresses prudential measures however and provides that the provisions of Article 56 are without prejudice to the right of Member States to take all requisite measure to prevent infringements of national law and regulations, among others, in the field of prudential supervision of financial institutions. The exact limits are not however defined, which may call for greater clarity to be provided in relation to the criteria and the conditions upon which the supervisory authority can intervene to block an acquisition from going through or in fact prompt Member States to create a prudential authority specifically empowered with the task of assessing prudential concerns that arise in transactions that are of large-scale.

In the UK, following the failure of RBS, a Prudential Regulation Authority[179] **9.57** was established, which focused exclusively on prudential issues rather than

---

174 Ibid.
175 Note that the EC Treaty does not provide for an official definition of the term capital movements, but the term has been settled by the case-law of the ECJ, which has referred to Directive 88/361/EEC and the nomenclature annexed to it, so that 'Capital movement' includes any participation in a company, whether realised through 'direct' or 'portfolio investment'.
176 Commission Staff Working Document 'Special rights in privatized companies in the enlarged Union – A decade full of developments', Brussels, 22 July 2005, 26.
177 Case CC-446/04 *Test Claimants in the FII Group Litigation* [2006] ECR I-11753, paras 179–181; Case C-157/05 Holbock [2007] ECR I-4051, paras 33 and 34; also see J Hansen 'Cross-border restructuring' in U Bernitz and W Ringe (eds) *Company Law and Economic Protectionism New Challenges to European Integration* (OUP 2010), 176.
178 Joined Cases C-282/04 and C-283/04 *Commission v the Netherlands* [2006] ECR I-9141, para 19.
179 The PRA was created by the Financial Services Act 2012 and focuses primarily on the harm that firms can cause to the stability of the UK financial system. In April 2013 the PRA, as part of the Bank of England, became the UK's prudential regulator for banks, building societies, credit unions, insurers and major investment firms.

spanning both prudential and conduct concerns.[180] An improvement to the legal framework would be to introduce more detailed provisions which go beyond the basic considerations of box-ticking and which stipulate the exact limits of intervention and the criteria that the authority should consider therein. The failed bid of Pfizer for AstraZeneca in early 2014 prompted a debate on whether the government should have the legal power to intervene in a takeover and on what grounds. A public interest test for mergers can be found in the UK Enterprise Act which allows for a deal to be stopped if it is deemed to be a threat to national security, media plurality or financial stability. The Qualifying Holdings Directive makes a positive improvement of the provisions of the Banking Directive by providing that Member States must make publically available a list specifying the information that is necessary for carrying out an assessment and which must be provided to the competent authorities at the time of notification.[181] Recital 9 acknowledges that the information should be proportionate and hence different information may be needed by a potential acquirer. An improvement to the Directive, as seen from an internal market perspective, would be to harmonize the type and quality of information that the proposed acquirers are called to provide.[182] The 2011 FSA Report makes clear that the authority aims to change its approach henceforth, demanding that firms prove that they have the capital resources to meet large and uncertain risks.[183] Proposals put forward include making it a formal requirement that banks obtain regulatory approval for major acquisitions, relative to the size of the acquiring bank and requiring that the board of the firm obtains independent advice in respect of major acquisitions by regulated firms.[184]

9.58 The case study of RBS–ABN AMRO showed that the due diligence conducted by RBS in relation to this acquisition was insufficient in scope and depth, and inadequate given the risks involved.[185] However, the poor due diligence conducted by RBS could not form the basis for a successful enforcement action, since it had not been found that the FSA's Rules, or its Principles of Business or Statement of Principles for Approved Persons, were contravened.[186] Should the

---

See Bank of England, 'The Prudential Regulation Authority's approach to banking supervision' (June 2014), available at: http://www.bankofengland.co.uk/publications/Documents/pra approach/bankingappr1406.pdf.

180   FSA Report, see above n 42, 12.
181   Banking Directive, art 19a(4).
182   Kerjean, see above n 33, 69.
183   FSA Report, see above n 42, Executive Summary, 30.
184   Ibid.
185   Ibid., 33.
186   Ibid.

lack of conducting adequate due diligence in the situation of bank acquisitions give rise to liability issues? Should formal governance processes in terms of the relationship between the executive management and the board when a substantial transaction is put forward be introduced? In view of the systemic role that banks play in a Member State's economy should the law provide that a higher standard of due diligence is conducted in the case of bank acquisitions compared to non-banks? From the analysis above, indeed it should be the case that a financial stability test applies relative to the size of the transaction. This test would entail an examination similar to that conducted by the Prudential Regulation Authority in its ordinary capacity, which is not related to M&A activity specifically. A forward-looking approach would assess how the bank emerging from the acquisition would perform not just against current risks, but also against those that could plausibly arise in the future.[187] In assessing the prospective 'safety and soundness' of the banking group emerging from the acquisition, consideration should be given to whether the acquisition may result in the disruption of the continuity of financial services.[188] This is an important aspect to be considered, especially in the case of bank takeovers, as problems in relation to the merging of businesses or the alignment of business cultures following the acquisition often arise, which create a disruption to the continuity of critical economic functions. As identified, a firm can adversely affect the stability of the financial system, not only through the way in which it carries out its business in normal times, but also through failing.[189] Therefore, aside the assessment of the acquisition causing potential problems in the disruption to the continuity of critical economic functions, another aspect of the assessment should relate to avoidance of the risk of contagion following bank failure. The PRA has outlined the variables it takes into account in assessing whether firms have in place adequate measures to safeguard safety and soundness, which relate to management and governance, culture and behaviour, competence and structures set in place by the firm.[190] The PRA attaches particular importance to firms managing risks effectively, because, as explained, it is the crystallisation of risk, or concerns about risks crystallising in the future that causes problems for firms' safety and soundness.[191] Acquisitions launched on limited due diligence and financed heavily by debt, undoubtedly increase the amount of risk that the emerging entity post acquisition will assume. It should therefore be the responsibility of the supervisory authority to impose controls on acquisitions

---

187   Bank of England, see above n 179, 6.
188   Ibid., 8.
189   Ibid., 9.
190   Ibid.
191   Ibid., 22.

which foster uncertain risks that may crystallise in the future and affect the financial stability of the financial system and the economy.

B. The role of the board of the bidding company

9.59 Concerning the role of the board of the bidding company, two distinct issues deserve attention. The first concerns the decision to launch a bid, and the second concerns the information upon which the decision to proceed with a bid is based on, namely the due diligence conducted for the launch of a bid. With regard to the decision-making process, the Walker Review identified that the 'challenge' step in the sequence that should be followed in board discussion on major issues, namely presentation by the executive, a disciplined process of challenge, decision on the policy or strategy to be adopted and then full empowerment of the executive to implement, appears to have been missed in many board discussions of the boards of Banks and other Financial Institutions (BOFIs). Having an environment in which the board effectively challenges the management on major risk and strategic issues before decisions are in fact taken is critical to good decision-making from a corporate governance perspective.[192] The Walker Review highlights that in order for this process to be effectively observed, more emphasis should be given to the way in which the chairman of the board of a major bank conducts his role.[193]

9.60 The role of the CEO and other executives during the decision to launch a bid is key to preventing insufficiently thought-out or risky bids for banks from going through. The decision to launch a bid for a bank should be examined specifically in relation to making judgements about when to rein in the CEO and whether points should be raised by the board or the board risk committees when the price at which the bidder proposes to buy the target is in fact too high. As proposed by the Kay Review, a more effective non-executive director may also work as an effective check.[194] The Kay Review has identified that the problem in decision-making on such transactions is that boards may not always act as an effective restraint on a CEO with excessive self-confidence.[195] The example brought forward by the review is that of RBS, where the company's success with the acquisition of National Westminster Bank, encouraged further acquisitions which proved disastrous.[196] In such situations offeror shareholders tended to approve the transactions and support taking on more risk through an

---

192   D Walker, 'A review of corporate governance in UK banks and other financial industry entities – Final recommendations', 26 November 2009 (The Walker Review), 12.
193   Ibid.
194   The Kay Review, see above n 110, 61, para 8.26.
195   Ibid.
196   Ibid.

acquisition. The Kay Review identifies that the development of stewardship activities may be the most effective mechanism of restraint, in light of the fact that optimism bias remains a norm, with managers believing that their acquisition will succeed despite a large proportion of acquisitions failing.[197] According to the review, there should be no changes in the current regulatory framework of merger control in the UK, but weight should be placed on the role that boards and asset managers play as they constitute a powerful safeguard against excess of ambition or hyperactivity.[198]

Better decision-making on a strategic transaction, where an executive is proposing a significant merger, acquisition or disposal, could potentially by ensured by outlining the full sequence of the decision-making processes that should be followed. As identified in the Walker Review, in situations in which investment banking advice is being provided on the basis of a contingency fee, advisers are only paid the full fee if the transaction is completed. This undoubtedly gives advisers an incentive to be more aggressive in encouraging a bid to go through and to not adequately consider its full implications. It therefore becomes important to reflect on a useful proposal put forward by the FSA which addresses this problem, namely to assess whether and how the board of a firm considering a major acquisition obtains independent advice, and reconsider whether this should be from an adviser whose remuneration is linked to the successful completion of the transaction.[199] **9.61**

It is imperative for the board to be insistent on an appropriate sequence for board-level decision-taking to take place for the launch of an acquisition.[200] An effective decision process, as the Walker Review outlines, involves following a two-stage process. At a *first stage* a strategic decision should be made, based on the most rigorous analysis, drawing on whatever external advice may be relevant and considering whether proceeding with the proposed transaction within set parameters is likely to be in the long-term interest of the company and its shareholders. This should then be followed by a *second stage*, which involves embarking on the execution process through consideration of key investment banking advice and engagement.[201] It is common practice that the CEO will be working on a proposed acquisition, devoting a significant amount of time and effort, before presenting it to the board. It stands to reason that when the **9.62**

---

197 Ibid., 62, para 8.27.
198 Ibid., 62, para 8.28.
199 FSA Report, see above n 42, Executive Summary, December 2011, 31.
200 Walker, see above n 191, 12.
201 Ibid., 102.

proposed acquisition is presented to the board, the CEO will seek to receive the agreement of the board. Therefore the chair of the board should, it could validly be argued, be a different person, so as to be in a position to constructively challenge the proposal and guide the board of directors in their decision. The Walker Review further provides that the execution stage should only be authorised after the board has determined, on the basis of a rigorous due diligence appraisal, that the deal would likely benefit the entity and its share-holders. The board would then outline the appropriate to the circumstances due diligence process and the board risk committee would be in charge of the oversight of the process and report on its findings to the whole board.[202] The Walker Review recommends that the board risk committee should, as a matter of good practice, be envisaged with the role of:

> advising the board to ensure that a due diligence appraisal of the proposition is undertaken, focussing in particular on risk aspects and implications for the risk appetite and tolerance of the entity, drawing on independent external advice where appropriate and available, before the board takes a decision whether to proceed.[203]

The board of the bank recommending the launch of an acquisition should therefore ensure that the decision-making process is conducted in the two-stage process outlined and that the decision is also supported by the board risk committee, which will ensure that the appropriate due diligence has been conducted and that the risks and the likely impact of the transaction on the entity and its shareholders have been fully considered by the board. By placing safeguards within the internal structures of the company it is ensured that the business decision to launch a bid has been the product of good corporate governance decision-making.

9.63 A final note should be made in relation to the due diligence processes observed by the bidder. As regards such procedures, a bidder should by law be required to disclose to the supervisory authorities any difficulties he may encounter in conducting his due diligence. A stricter liability should be imposed on bidding boards that fail to adequately consider the full implications of the bid and that fail to undertake the necessary due diligence. In hostile bids particular informa-tional problems may arise due to the fact that the bidder is likely to have limited information on the target company's business. This comes as a result of the fact that the target company board is under no legal requirement to share company

---

202   Ibid., 102–3.
203   Ibid., Recommendation No. 26, 103.

information, especially in a situation in which it does not recommend the bid to its shareholders. The information about the banks or the financial institution that the bidder plans to acquire will normally be obtained from the target institution's latest published accounts. Information on the company's prospects or the company's hidden liabilities though is unlikely to be publically available. Price sensitive non-public information belongs to the company, is confidential and can only be communicated by the directors if that is in the interests of the company.[204] The price offered for the target of the company, may therefore not be reflective of its true value or reversely the risks involved. Informational problems on the company's valuation unavoidably lead to the undervaluation or overvaluation of the company respectively. The latter may arise especially in the case of a hostile takeover, where different bidders compete for the acquisition of the company so that the bidding wars that follow superficially drive the price of the target company upwards. A classic example of such a situation is the case study of the bid by RBS for ABN AMRO, where Barclays was the other bidder.

C. The role of the target board and target shareholders

The board, shareholders and the supervisory authority all aim to secure that **9.64** decisional power is allocated by law to them. The UK and EU rules are drafted on the assumption that concerning commercial firms shareholders are best placed to decide on the merits of the bid. In theory, allocating decisional powers to shareholders appears like the optimal choice. As Kershaw explains, the provisions of the Code appear to be addressing a type of shareholder who has an interest in acquiring the information offered, and who will also devote time to assess that information, so as to make a decision on the bid.[205] As evidenced by the RBS–ABN AMRO case study however, shareholder choice may come to destroy value in the short-term against the pursuit of real growth. This is due to the fact that in practice certain types of investors will attach minimal value, if any, to the information contained in the offer document or the target board's opinion on a bid.[206] One should specifically question whether shareholders of banking groups are indeed best placed to assess not only prudential issues, but sound acquisitions from a commercial perspective. The Kraft – Cadbury deal has shown that it is not uncommon for so called 'long-term' shareholders to immediately dispose of their shares upon announcement of a potential takeover

---

204 Note that according to *Lynall v IRC* [1971] 3 WLR 759, an estate duty case concerning the valuation of shares on open market principles, the target directors were deemed to be under no obligation to give information to the acquiring company or the target shareholders or to advise the target shareholders on the price offered; also see *Percival v Wright* [1902] 2 Ch 421, in which case the directors were buying shares from shareholders but were held to have no duty to disclose a valuable offer that had been made for the whole undertaking of the company.

205 Kershaw, see above n 112, 72–3.

206 Ibid.

bid to other interested investors, which may in fact have short-term interests, such as hedge funds.[207] When an increase in the target firm's share price is marked upon announcement of a potential takeover bid, certain shareholders will choose to trade their shares at this early point in time, so as to transfer the risk of the bid not being successful to other shareholders willing to assume it.[208] The shareholder primacy norm, depending on the incentives of the shareholder deciding, may in fact adversely affect stakeholders and the wider public.

9.65 Reflecting on the strengths and weaknesses of the UK regulatory framework, the Final Report of the Kay Review, published in July 2012, addresses the role of the target board and the decisional powers of shareholders within the context of a UK takeover bid. With regard to the role of the board, the review specifically considers whether target directors are in fact in a position to legally recommend that a high priced bid be rejected and whether this recommendation matters anyway considering that the bid is likely to be accepted by shareholders.[209] This issue was considered to be clearly dealt with by the duty directors have under CA 2006, section 172, namely to have regard to the long-term success of the company for the benefit of its members as a whole.[210] There are two issues which deserve further consideration in relation to directors' duties within a takeover context in the banking sector. Firstly, in the case of banks specifically, does the particular duty prompt directors to consider wider interests when advising on a bid? Secondly, even if a duty to this effect is adopted, would the decision-makers in the process, i.e. shareholders, reflect on the opinion constructed by directors along these lines in their decision on the bid? In relation to the first matter, it is indeed the case that bank directors' conduct is governed not only by sector-specific legislation, but also by the Companies Act 2006, specifically section 172. The Code itself, as pointed out in its Introduction, does impose obligations and limitations on company directors through its provisions, which may impinge on the duties that the directors of the target and bidding company may normally owe. It is assumed however that section 172 remains relevant within the context of takeovers, as the duty is also in alignment with General Principle 3 of the Code and Rule 25 of the Code. What remains open however is whether within the context of bank acquisitions, other considerations should also be taken into account. In July 2013, the

---

207 A S Kalirai, Partner at Field Fisher Waterhouse, 'Post Cadbury-Kraft takeover changes force advisers to rethink strategies', *Legal Week* (15 September 2011) <http://www.legalweeklaw.com/abstract/sweet-deals-post-cadbury-kraft-takeover-changes-8790.
208 Ibid.
209 The Kay Review, see above n 111, 61.
210 Ibid., para 8.23.

Department for Business Innovation & Skills, considered a range of proposals to enhance the transparency of UK company ownership and increase trust in UK business.[211] One of the proposals considered was whether there was a need to change the duties of directors for the banking sector by amending the statutory duties of directors for large banks, so that they are required to prioritise the 'safety and stability' of the firm first and over the interests of shareholders.[212] The recommendation aimed to ensure that bank directors are clear about their primary responsibility to maintain bank stability.[213] An alteration to directors' duties for directors of large banks along these lines was considered as a way of clearly signalling that the pursuit of shareholder value should not be at the expense of financial stability.[214] The proposed alteration was challenged on the grounds that there are difficulties in enforcing the duty, that the duty does not apply to directors of boards of companies outside the UK and that were the duty to be introduced, shareholders of banks would respond negatively to such an alteration.[215] In April 2014, the Government Response to the Discussion Paper was published, rejecting the proposals to amend director's general statutory duties to introduce a primary duty for bank directors to promote financial stability over the interests of their shareholders.[216] Respondents to the proposal argued that a revised duty would not be effective or appropriate as part of wider reforms to the regulation of the financial sector and that the duty of the Companies Act 2006, which was also applicable to bank directors, already made explicit the need to have regard to the 'long-term' and the need to take into account stakeholders other than shareholders.[217] The House of Commons addressed this very issue by highlighting the necessity of interpreting the duties of directors of banks in the light of the 'safety and soundness' of banks.[218] As explained, the obligations of directors to shareholders in accordance to the provisions of the Companies Act 2006 create a particular tension between the interests of shareholders and preserving the financial safety and soundness of banks. In light of this it is recommended that

---

211 Department for Business, Innovation & Skills, 'Transparency & Trust: Enhancing the Transparency of UK Company Ownership and Increasing Trust in UK Business', Discussion Paper, July 2015.

212 Ibid., 16.

213 Ibid., 59.

214 Ibid., 61.

215 Ibid., 61.

216 Department of Business Innovation & Skills, 'Transparency & Trust: Enhancing the Transparency of UK, Company Ownership and Increasing Trust in UK Business', Government Response, April 2014, 12.

217 Ibid, 61–63.

218 House of Commons, 'Changing Banking for Good', Report of the Parliamentary Commission on Banking Standards, June 2013 (HC 175-II).

the Corporate Governance Code, the PRA Principles for Businesses and the responsibilities of Senior Persons who are directors are all amended to reflect that directors' duties are to be interpreted in light of the fact that the safety and soundness of the bank is of utmost importance.[219] Along these lines and within the context of bank acquisitions, a point can be made that, it is necessary to clarify that the advice that the board of the target company is under the obligation to provide shareholders with, should be drafted with an additional test in mind, namely a 'safety and stability' test. This information may not only be of value to shareholders that are accepting a paper consideration for their shares in the emerging entity, but also relevant for the supervisory authority, which will need additional information to assess the wider social implications of the potential bid in the long-term if the bid goes through. It is indeed the case that a separate duty for bank directors to prioritise 'safety and stability' over the interests of shareholders would have a series of drawbacks in application and enforcement. However, in the case of bank acquisitions, and bearing in mind that bank assets are highly opaque and complex, it is important to prompt target directors to consider these issues in their evaluation of a bid to shareholders. Albeit advisory, the influential role that the target board can be called to play within a takeover context was exemplified in the case of the bid made by US-based pharmaceutical company Pfizer for the UK/Swedish rival Astra Zeneca in January 2014. The takeover gave rise to discussions as to the impact that the deal would have on Britain's life sciences sector and the economy as a whole. In observing its role, the target board of Astra Zeneca refused several Pfizer offers, without obtaining shareholder approval, despite the fact that some shareholders were in favour of the deal going through.

9.66 Regarding the second issue addressed, even if a duty which requires a consideration of the 'safety and stability' were to be adopted, it is indeed questionable whether the decision-makers in the process, i.e. shareholders, would reflect on this kind of information in their decision to accept the bid. The Kay Review addresses the issue of shareholder decision-making as a matter of public policy. In a number of controversial contested bids for commercial companies, the outcome had been settled by arbitrageurs, who had appeared on the share register only with the objective of gambling on the bid going through.[220] The problem, according to the Review, was not the existence of arbitrageurs as such,

---

219   Ibid., 344.
220   Ibid.

but rather that the underlying holders of shares were unwilling to challenge an offer, even if they believed that the higher fundamental value of the share would increase in the long-run.[221] The proposal put forward was developing steward-ship activity by asset managers as an effective check on such actions.[222] From a broader policy perspective, the review argues in favour of a change in the culture observed in trading practices.[223] The concerns and solutions similarly apply to the practices that shareholders in the banking and financial sector follow. And it is due to these concerns, that the decision-making powers within the context of bank acquisitions need to be revisited. It is worth considering the costs associated with the adoption of a shareholder primacy norm in the case of bank acquisitions. Shareholder empowerment should be considered through the dual prism of banks' social utility dimension and of the conflicting objectives that may exist, namely between shareholders' interests and the public interest in financial stability. Do bank shareholders carefully reflect on the long-term sustainable performance of banks when exercising their rights as shareholders? Evidence suggests that bank shareholders prompted banks to assume more risk, which may have negatively affected banks' performance. Erkens et al. provide empirical evidence on how corporate governance influenced the performance of financial firms during the 2007–2008 financial crisis, finding that although all firms were affected by the crisis, firms with higher institutional ownership and more independent boards had worse stock returns than other firms during the crisis.[224] Their findings suggest that this occured because firstly, firms with higher institutional ownership took more risk prior to the crisis, which resulted in larger shareholder losses during the crisis period, and secondly, firms with more independent board members raised more equity capital during the crisis, which led to a wealth transfer from existing shareholders to debtholders.[225] Ferreira et al. also produce evidence which is consistent with the hypothesis that banks in which shareholders were more empowered performed poorly during the crisis.[226] In exploring why this may have been the case, they consider the possibility that governance arrangements influence the extent to which bank

---

221 Ibid.
222 Ibid.
223 Ibid., 62, para 8.27.
224 D. Erkens, M. Hung and P. Matos, 'Corporate Governance in the 2007–2008 financial crisis: Evidence from the financial institutions worldwide', *Journal of Corporate Finance*, 18 (2012) 389–411, 407.
225 Ibid., 407
226 D. Ferreira, D. Kershaw, T. Kirchmaier and E. Schuster, 'Shareholder Empowerment and Bank Bailouts' ECGI – Finance Working Paper No. 345/2013; Asian Finance Association (AsFA) 2013 Conference, May 2013 available at www.ssrn.com/abstract=2170392.

managers give effect to equity's risk preferences following the fact that diversified shareholders may have been incentivised to take greater risks as a result of uncosted implicit and explicit government guarantees.[227] The results of the paper suggest that banks whose managers enjoyed a higher degree of insulation from shareholder pressure were less reliant on state bailouts than banks whose managers were subject to stronger shareholder rights.[228] As the authors explain the evidence of their paper is consistent with the hypothesis that banks in which managers enjoyed a higher degree of insulation from shareholder pressure were more able to survive without government support.[229] As they point out, bank shareholders may have incentives to increase risk-taking beyond the socially optimal level, so that it is possible that in search for higher returns, bank shareholders had incentives to push their banks towards less traditional banking activities.[230] In the case of bank acquisitions, stakeholder interests and bank safety become a priority when measured against an open market for corporate control where shareholders are empowered to decide on the merits of the bid. If less shareholder primacy for takeovers in the banking sector is opted for, then what deserves further consideration, which was addressed in detail above, is to better regulate the supervisory authority's intervention in the process and establish that the public interest features as a variable in the regulation of bank acquisitions.

7. CONCLUSION

9.67 The fact that banks defy some of the general assumptions that define the operation of the market for corporate control in other industries reinforces the case of strengthening the powers of the supervisory authority in charge of the authorisation process and regulating the acquisition process of banks in greater detail. The most important differentiating factor for banks however relates to the consequences that may flow from a failed change in the corporate control of a bank. A bad acquisition can potentially result in bank failure, taxpayer losses and wider economic harm, so that bank failure constitutes a matter of public concern and not just a concern for shareholders. The chapter argues in favour of a reform of the rules that will enable the bidding and target boards, as well as the supervisory authority, to play a decisive role in the assessment of the acquisition, giving less power to shareholders to determine the takeover outcome. Striking the right balance between the actors in a

---

227 Ibid.
228 Ibid.
229 Ibid.
230 Ibid.

position to affect the outcome of a bank acquisition remains a challenge however. At a first stage, reforms should focus on better regulating the role of the State. In the EU the creation of a level playing field between Member States can only be guaranteed if the grounds for a rejection or authorisation of a bid are clear and comprehensive for all the individual supervisory authorities. A set of more detailed criteria on the authorisation process will prompt supervisory authorities to carefully consider the overall risks involved, instead of simply following a box-ticking exercise and placing reliance on the information and reassurances produced by the boards and the market. The application of a financial stability test should also explicitly form part of the authorisation process. More consideration should also be given to the funding of the acquisition at hand, especially when the bid is primarily funded by debt, rather than equity. At a second stage, reforms should focus on better regulating the formal governance processes followed between the executive management and the board of the bidding company for the launch of an acquisition, as well as the governance arrangements followed by the target company considering the offer. In these respective processes, defined standards regarding the level of due diligence that the bidding company is required to undertake will help judge whether the due diligence conducted has been appropriate. In terms of the decision-making powers exercised at the level of the bidding and the target company, the chapter has provided evidence that questions the benefits that the shareholder primacy norm within a bank takeover context offers. Bank shareholders may have incentives to increase risk taking beyond the socially optimal level leading to highly leveraged and risky acquisitions which only equate that banks are assuming more risk. Overall, more controls should be imposed on the market for corporate control in the banking sector in the interests of prudence by introducing amendments to the provisions of the existing regulatory framework that regulates the role of the parties involved and the details of the processes observed.

BIBLIOGRAPHY

Armour, J and W G Ringe, 'European company law 1999–2010: Renaissance and crisis', (December 14, 2010), ECGI – Law Working Paper No. 175/2011, 40, available at: http://ssrn.com/abstract=1691688.

Bank of England, 'The Prudential Regulation Authority's approach to banking supervision', June 2014, available at: http://www.bankofengland.co.uk/publications/Documents/praapproach/bankingappr1406.pdf.

BBC News, 'ABN AMRO "wins Italy bank battle"', 15 September 2005.

Bebchuck, L, 'The pressure to tender: An analysis and a proposed remedy', (1987) 12 *Delaware Journal of Corporate Law* 911.

CEBS/2008/214, CEIOPS-3L3–19/08, CESR/08–543b Guidelines for the prudential assessment of acquisitions and increases in holdings in the financial sector required by Directive 2007/44/EC.

Clarke, B, 'Where was the "Market for Corporate Control" when we needed it?' (17 December 2009). UCD Working Papers in Law, Criminology & Socio-Legal Studies Research Paper No. 23/2009 available at: SSRN: http://ssrn.com/abstract=1524785.

Commission Staff Working Document 'Special rights in privatized companies in the enlarged Union – a decade full of developments', Brussels, 22 July 2005.

Curran, L and F Turitto, 'Antononventa: the challenge of cross-border acquisitions of banks in the EU', (2006) *Journal of International Banking and Financial Law* 79–82.

Davies, P and K Hopt, 'Control transactions', in R H Kraakman et al. (eds), *The Anatomy of Corporate Law: A Comparative and Functional Approach*, (2nd ed, OUP 2009).

de Larosière, J, *Report of the High-Level Group on Financial Supervision in the EU* (2009) (de Larosière Report) available at: http://ec.europa.eu/internal_market/finances/docs/de_larosiere_report_en.pdf.

Department for Business, Innovation and Skills, 'Transparency & Trust: Enhancing the Transparency of UK Company Ownership and Increasing Trust in UK Business', Discussion Paper, July 2015.

Department of Business, Innovation and Skills, 'Transparency & Trust: Enhancing the Transparency of UK Company Ownership and Increasing Trust in UK Business', Government Response, April 2014, 61–63.

Dickson, M, 'Debate rages over stimulus fallout', *Washington Times*, 23 February 2010, at A1 (quoting Ruth Stroppiana, chief international economist for Moody's Economy.com).

Easterbrook, F and D Fischel, *The Economic Structure of Corporate Law* (Harvard University Press 1991).

Enrich, D, G Legorano and M Stevis, 'Europe's banks poised to return to acquisition trail', *Wall Street Journal*, 3 February 2014.

Erkens, D, M Hung and P Matos, 'Corporate Governance in the 2007–2008 financial crisis: Evidence from the financial institutions worldwide', (2012) 18 *Journal of Corporate Finance* 389–411.

European Central Bank, Legal Working Paper Series No 6, June 2008, at 58.

Fama, E F, 'Agency problems and the theory of the firm', (1980) 88(2) *Journal of Political Economy* 288.

Fama, E F and M C Jensen, 'Separation of ownership and control', (1983) 26 *Journal of Law and Economics* 301.

Ferreira, D, T Kershaw, T Kirchmaier and E Schuster, 'Shareholder Empowerment and Bank Bailouts', ECGI – Finance Working Paper No. 345/2013; Asian Finance Association (AsFA) 2013 Conference, May 2013, available at: www.ssrn.com/abstract=2170392.

Financial Conduct Authority, press release, 'FSA fines Prudential £30 million and censures CEO for failing to inform regulator for 2010 acquisition plans', 27 March 2013.

Financial Services Authority Report, 'The failure of the Royal Bank of Scotland', December 2011, Executive Summary, available at: http://www.fsa.gov.uk/static/pubs/other/rbs.pdf.

Flannery, M J, 'Market discipline in bank supervision', in A N Berger, P Molyneux, and J O S Wilson (eds) *The Oxford Handbook of Banking Online* (OUP 2012).

Gerner-Beuerle, C, D Kershaw and M Solinas, 'Is the board neutrality rule trivial? Amnesia about corporate law in European Takeover Regulation', (March 30, 2011) LSE Legal Studies Working Paper No 3/2011.

Gilson, R, 'The political ecology of takeovers: Thoughts on harmonizing the European corporate governance environment', (1992) 61 *Fordham Law Review* 161.

Grossman, S and O Hart, 'Takeover bids, the free-rider problem, and the theory of the corporation', (1980) 11 *The Bell Journal of Economics* 42.

Hansen, J, 'Cross-border restructuring', in U Bernitz and W Ringe (eds) *Company Law and Economic Protectionism New Challenges to European Integration* (OUP 2010).

Holl, P and D Kyriazis, 'The detriments of outcome in UK take-over bids', (1996) 3(2) *International Journal of Economic Business* 168.

Hopt, K, 'Obstacles to corporate restructuring: observations from a European and a German perspective', in M Tison et al. (eds) *Perspectives in Company Law and Financial Regulation-Essays in Honour of Eddy Wymeersch* (CUP 2009).

Hopt, K, 'Corporate governance of banks and other financial institutions after the financial crisis-regulation in the light of empiry and theory', (2013) 13(2) *Journal of Corporate Law Studies* 219.

House of Commons, Business, Innovation and Skills Committee, 'Mergers, acquisitions and takeovers: the takeover of Cadbury by Kraft', Ninth Report of Session 2009–10, (2010 HC 234) London, 30 March 2010.

House of Commons, 'Changing Banking for Good', Report of the Parliamentary Commission on Banking Standards, June 2013 (HC 175-II).

Jensen, M and W Meckling, 'Theory of the firm: Managerial behaviour, agency costs, and ownership structure', (1976) 3 *Journal of Financial Economics* 305.

Jensen, M and R Ruback, 'The market for corporate control: The scientific evidence', (1983) 11 *Journal of Financial Economics* 5.

Johnston, A, 'Preventing the next financial crisis? Regulating bankers' pay in Europe', (2014) 14(1) *Journal of Law and Society* 6.

Kalirai, A S Partner at Field Fisher Waterhouse, 'Post Cadbury-Kraft takeover changes force advisers to rethink strategies', *Legal Week* (15 September 2011), available at: http://www.legalweeklaw.com/abstract/sweet-deals-post-cadbury-kraft-takeover-changes-8790.

Kay, J, 'The Kay Review of UK Equity Markets and long-term decision making', Interim Report, (London: February 2012).

Kerjean, S, 'The legal implications of the prudential supervisory assessment of bank mergers and acquisitions under EU Law', European Central Bank, Legal Working Paper Series No 6/June 2008 at 59, available at: http://ssrn.com/abstract_id=1000853.

Kershaw, D, 'The illusion of importance: Reconsidering the UK's takeover defence prohibition', (2007) 56(2) *International and Comparative Law Quarterly* 267.

Kershaw, D, 'Web Chapter A: The Market for Corporate Control', in D Kershaw *Company Law in Context: Text and Materials*, (OUP 2010) available at: www.oup.com/uk/orc/bin/9780199215942/resources/chapters/Web_Chapter_A.pdf.

Kirkpatrick, G, 'The corporate governance lessons from the financial crisis', 96 *Financial Market Trends* 61 OECD (February 2009), available at: www.oecd.org/dataoecd/32/1/42229620.pdfz.

Lagorce, A, 'ABN AMRO wins Antonventa control', MarketWatch, *The Wall Street Journal*, 15 September 2005.

Lehn, K, 'Some observations on Henry Manne's contributions to financial economics', (2000) 50 *Case Western Law Review* 263.

Manne, H G, 'Mergers and the market for corporate control', (1965) 73(2) *Journal of Political Economy* 110.

Mülbert, P, 'Corporate governance of banks', (2009) 10 *European Business Organisation Law Review* 411.

Partington, R, 'FSA given frosty reception on hostile bank M&A call', *Financial News*, 13 December 2011.

Public Consultation on the Application of Directive 2007/44 EC as regards acquisitions and increase of holdings in the financial sector (December 2009) at 3, available at: http://ec.europa.eu/internal_market/consultations/docs/2011/acquisitions/consultation_paper_en.pdf.

Public Consultation Paper 2014/2, The Takeover Panel Code Committee, 'Post-Offer Undertakings and Intention Statements', (PCP 2014/2, 15 September 2014).

RBS Press Release, 'Royal Bank of Scotland Group PLC-Annual General Meeting/General Meeting', 3 April 2009.

RBS, 'Continuation of minutes of a meeting of the board of directors', 28 March 2007.

'RBS timeline: where it all went wrong', *The Daily Telegraph*, 2 December 2010.

Response Statement 2014/2, The Takeover Panel Code Committee, 'Post Offer Undertakings and Intention Statements' (RS 2014/2, 23 December 2014).

Rigby, E, 'Labour to push for tougher rules on takeovers before election', *The Financial Times*, 27 May 2014.

Sjåfjell, B, *Towards a Sustainable European Company Law: A Normative Analysis of the Objectives of EU Law, with the Takeover Directive as a Test Case* (Kluwer Law International 2009).

Takeover Panel, The, 'The Code on Takeovers and Mergers', (11ed, 20 May 2013).

Takeover Panel Code Committee, The, Panel Statement 2010/14, 'Kraft Foods Inc. Offer for Cadbury plc', 26 May 2010.

Takeover Panel Code Committee, The, *Response Statement to the Consultation Paper on Review of Certain Aspects of the Regulation of Takeover Bids*, RS 2010/22, 21 October 2010 (First Response Paper) section 2.5., 3, available at: http://www.thetakeoverpanel.org.uk/wp-content/uploads/2009/12/2010–221.pdf.

Takeover Panel Code Committee, The, Panel Statement 2010/22, 'Review of certain aspects of the regulation of takeover bids', 21 October 2010.

Takeover Panel Code Committee, The, Response Statement 2011/1, 'Review of Certain Aspects of the Regulation of Takeover Bids: Response Statement by the Code Committee of the Panel following the Consultation on PCP 2011/1', (RS 2011/1, 21 July 2011).

Treanor, J, 'Regulator should have stopped RBS from buying ABN Amro, say MPs', *The Guardian*, 19 October 2012.

Tsagas, G, 'The revision of the EU Takeover Directive in light of the 2011 UK takeover law reform', (2013) 10(1) *International and Comparative Company Law Journal* 21.

Tsoukalis, L, 'The Delphic Oracle on Europe', in L Tsoukalis and J A Emmanouilidis (eds) *The Delphic Oracle in Europe: Is there a Future for the European Union?* (OUP 2011).

Turner Review, The, *A Regulatory Response to the Global Banking Crisis* (FSA, March 2009).

Walker, D, 'A review of corporate governance in UK banks and other financial industry entities –Final recommendations', 26 November 2009 (The Walker Review).

Webb, T, 'Lord Mandelson calls for overhaul of takeover rules', *The Guardian* (1 March 2010).

White, A and M van Gaal, 'ABN AMRO loses court challenge to EU ban on acquisitions', *Bloomberg News*, 8 April 2014.

Winter, J, C Schans, G Garrido, K Hopt, J Rickford, G Rossi and J Simon, 'Report of the high level group of company law experts on issues related to takeover bids in the European Union', Brussels, 10 January 2002 (The Winter Report).

Wong, P and N O'Sullivan, 'The determinants and consequences of abandoned takeovers', (2001) 15(2) *Journal of Economic Surveys* 156.

INDEX